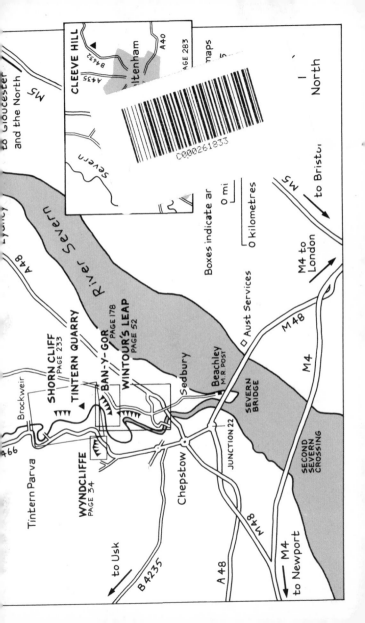

King Kong (HVS) GO Wall, Wintour's Leap
Climber: Chris Craggs   Photo: Craggs col.

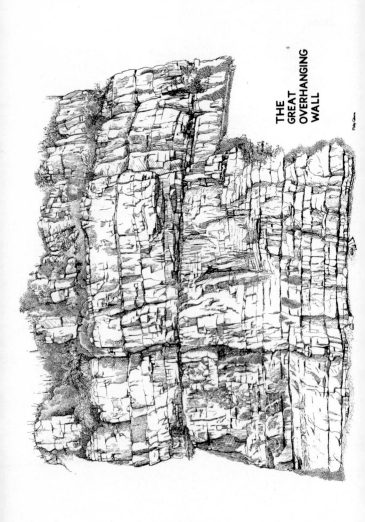

THE
GREAT
OVERHANGING
WALL

Climbers' Club Guides

Edited by John Willson

Wye Valley

by

John Willson   (Introduction; History; Wintour's Leap)

Gordon Jenkin   (Ban-y-gor; Tintern Quarry)

Martyn Cattermole   (Shorn Cliff)

Dave Viggers   (Wyndcliffe)

with contributions from Matt Hammersley, Alan Moore,
James Collier & Roland Helps, and Nigel Coe

Artwork by **Don Sargeant**

with contributions from Philip Gibson, Simon Noyes,
Matt Hammersley, and Alan Moore

Published by the Climbers' Club

Wye Valley – First edition (Cordee 1977)
by John Willson and David Hope

Wye Valley – Second edition (Cordee 1987)
by John Willson, David Hope, Tony Penning, Matt Ward

Wye Valley – Third edition (Climbers' Club 1997)
by John Willson, Gordon Jenkin, Martyn Cattermole, Dave Viggers

© The Climbers' Club 1997

Willson, John   Wye Valley   (Climbers' Club Guides)

British Library Cataloguing in Publication Data

A catalogue record for this book is available from the British Library

796.522

ISBN 0-901-601-60-8

Front cover: Chris Craggs on *Yesterday's Dreams*, North Buttress,
Wintour's Leap (E2)
Photo: Craggs collection

Rear cover: John Shaw on *The Isle of Dogs*, GO Wall, Wintour's Leap (E5)
Photo: John Willson

Frontispiece: The Great Overhanging Wall
Drawing: Phil Gibson

Prepared for printing by The Editor
Produced by The Ernest Press, Glasgow G44 5QD
Distributed by Cordee, 3a de Montfort Street, Leicester LE1 7HD

Contents

LIST OF MAPS AND DIAGRAMS

Climbers' Club Guides

THE CLIMBERS' CLUB
The publisher of this guidebook is the Climbers' Club, which was founded in 1898 from origins in Snowdonia and is now one of the foremost mountaineering clubs in Great Britain. Its objects are to encourage mountaineering and rock-climbing, and to promote the general interest of mountaineers and the mountain environment.

It is a truly national club with widespread membership, and currently owns huts in Cornwall, Pembrokeshire, Derbyshire, and Snowdonia. Besides managing six huts, the Climbers' Club produces an annual Journal and runs a full programme of climbing meets, dinners, and social events. Club members may also use the huts of other clubs through reciprocal arrangements. The Club publishes climbing guidebooks (currently 15 in number) to cover most of Wales and Southern England. The Club is a founder-member of, and is affiliated to, the British Mountaineering Council; it makes annual contributions to the BMC's Access Fund, as well as to volunteer cliff and mountain rescue organizations.

Membership fluctuates around 900, and at present there are no limits on growth. Members of two years' standing may propose a competent candidate for membership and, provided that adequate support is obtained from other members, the Committee may elect him or her to full membership; there is no probationary period.

CLIMBING STYLE
The following policy statement on climbing style was agreed in principle at The Climbers' Club Annual General Meeting on 25th February 1990:

The Climbers' Club supports the tradition of using natural protection and is opposed to actions which are against the best interest of climbers and users of the crags. This applies particularly to irreversible acts which could affect the crags and their environs.

Such acts could include: the placing of bolts on mountain and natural crags; retrospective placing of bolts; chiselling, hammering, or altering the rock appearance or structure; excessive removal of vegetation and interference with trees, flowers, and fauna.

The Climbers' Club policy is that guidebooks are written to reflect the best style matched to the ethos and traditions of British Climbing.

Helyg

GUIDEBOOK DISCLAIMER

This guide attempts to provide a definitive record of all existing climbs and is compiled from information from a variety of sources. The inclusion of any route does not imply that it remains in the condition described. Climbs can change unpredictably: rock can deteriorate and the existence and condition of *in-situ* protection can alter. Please read the note concerning the relationship between gradings and the condition of this equipment. All climbers must rely on their own ability and experience to gauge the difficulty and seriousness of any climb. Climbing is an inherently dangerous activity.

Neither The Climbers' Club nor the authors and editor of this guidebook accept any liability whatsoever for any injury or damage caused to climbers, third parties, or property arising from the use of it. Whilst the content of the guide is believed to be accurate, no responsibility is accepted for any error, omission, or mis-statement. Users must rely on their own judgement and are recommended to insure against injury to person and property and third party risks.

The inclusion in this guidebook of a crag or routes upon it does not mean that any member of the public has a right of access to the crag or the right to climb upon it.

Before climbing on any crag in this guidebook please read the appropriate access and conservation notes, especially the section on trees on page 17.

Editor's Note

When the Climbers' Club agreed to publish this third edition of the *Wye Valley* guide, it was my intention that each cliff should be subjected to a completely fresh appraisal. David Hope and I had looked after Symonds Yat and Wintour's Leap for some twenty years, and we both felt not only that we had done our duty but that a new evaluation was needed, preferably from authors who had been less 'involved' with the cliffs' development over the years and who were perhaps more in tune with modern trends; and Matt Ward, after his pioneering work at Shorn Cliff, had gone underground.

Gordon Jenkin, who offered to provide the Ban-y-gor section, has done sterling work, and must be congratulated for, amongst other things, making the neatest, clearest proof-corrections I could ever expect to see. Unfortunately, little else went quite to plan. However, Dave Viggers filled the Wyndcliffe gap at a late stage and, as he did with *Pembroke*, gave a revitalizing impetus to the whole project when it looked like failing. Martyn Cattermole nobly offered to take a break from his new-routing in Tintern Quarry in order to sort out Shorn Cliff after two earlier prospective authors had backed out, soon having to contend with a remote house-and-work move, and marriage into the bargain. Other small crags and quarries have figured in and out of the reckoning and I am indebted to Matt Hammersley (Shakemantle) and Alan Moore (Plump Hill and Hang Hill) for their topos and text. An especial word of gratitude is due to Brian and Val Collier and Ken and Trish Helps for their kind permission to include the Castle Rock guide prepared by their sons James Collier and Roland Helps before their tragic accident in 1987. The grades and descriptions have been rechecked by Nigel Coe.

Roger Lanchbury has battled determinedly for years with Symonds Yat against business and injury problems, though fortunately local Matt Hammersley has been able to give substantial and invaluable help. In the event, however, it was decided for a number of reasons that this section would be best published separately, and it will follow in handy format during the summer.

And so to Wintour's Leap, still by far the largest and most important cliff in the Wye Valley. A partially revised draft had been produced and circulated by the designated author in 1993. However, when it came to completion time in late 1995 he was not willing to deliver, and at this late stage there seemed no viable alternative to my rewriting and updating my 1987 guide. I am very grateful for the sympathetic encouragement I have had from all concerned in this. Although the interim draft was not without merits and was kindly made available to me, it was not clear how much of it was based on new research; nor was I happy about a mish-mash of styles. I decided therefore to return to source, and the work, warts and all, is my own.

The 1977 and 1987 editions were composite guides, each crag having its own introduction and historical sections. In compiling the *History* this time I set out with three objectives: to integrate the separate crag histories for the first time; to avoid its becoming the usual long list of route-names which largely duplicates the first-ascent list; to be non-controversial, having been involved, at least peripherally, in more than my fair share of guidebook controversies over the last few years. When I circulated the draft, the first two objectives, and the degree of success in fulfilling them, received general approval. However, the third was regarded as at best a 'cop-out' and at worst a 'cover-up'. 'You are guardian of the truth; try harder!' After many weeks of agonizing, I had to recognize the failure of the last guide to address certain issues and the need for this to be rectified here, though I lacked the inspiration to achieve it within the usual context of the *Introduction* and *History*. Thus, a novel section is included before the First Ascent List, written from a personal perspective and attempting to pull together the past, present, and future aspects of ethical and associated issues relevant to the area. This should be seen as a pragmatic solution to an individual problem and not as an attempt to set a new trend.

As Des Hannigan pointedly remarked on more than one occasion when we were working together on his *West Penwith* volumes, 'everyone needs editing, even editors'. I sometimes felt he would have preferred 'especially' to 'even', but the validity of his opinion has become clearer and clearer to me in the years that have followed. I therefore invited my successor-designate as South-West Editor, Nigel Coe, to subject my own sections of this book to his detailed scrutiny and not to hesitate to take revenge for what I put him through with *Swanage and Portland*. However, I was in the happy but unusual position of being able to ignore any criticism I did not like, and therefore any shortcomings are *entirely* down to me.

The editor and authors would like to thank first ascensionists for permission to reproduce their route-descriptions, in particular Gary Gibson and Martin Crocker, both talented and experienced guidebook authors themselves, whose descriptions are of a quality that would grace any guide.

They would like to thank Ken Vickers of *Cordee* for permission to reproduce the magnificent drawings that Phil Gibson made for the 1987 guide and two of the cartoons by Simon Noyes, and those who have submitted photographs for inclusion, especially Chris Craggs, without whose contribution (as so often) the book would be visually much the poorer.

This is also true of Don Sargeant's artwork, the quantity and complexity of which has involved a degree of time and effort that has gone way beyond the call of duty.

Finally, I must thank Nigel Coe and Gordon Jenkin for their unstinting help in the final stages of getting the book together.

Please note: I shall not be around in 2007. JW 1997

Acknowledgements

WINTOUR'S LEAP AND INTRODUCTORY SECTIONS
Work started on the first comprehensive guide to Wintour's Leap in 1975, but the old Gloucestershire Mountaineering Club pamphlets and Jim Perrin's Interim Guide of 1971 provided an essential foundation. Considerable assistance in the checking of routes for the work, which was published in 1977, was given by Tony Pearson and Chris Rumsey. And for both that and the Supplement, which followed in 1981, I was greatly indebted to the late Arnis Strapcans for extensive information and guidance.

For its successor published in 1987, I received much help and advice in the way of information and opinions on gradings and ratings from Richard Harrison, Andy Sharp, John Harwood, and Matt Ward; and especially from Martin Crocker, Gordon Jenkin, and Gary Gibson, who in addition read substantial sections of the manuscript and made much enlightened comment and constructive criticism which has remained useful and relevant still.

Ten years on again, I am grateful to: the many who read and commented upon the *History* section, including the last five mentioned in the above paragraph, Dave Viggers, Frank Cannings, and Ian Parnell; to Ian Parnell and Martin Crocker for various route information, and especially the latter for sorting out the implications of the rockfall on Deceiver Buttress; and to Gordon Jenkin and Martin again for reading the whole script and suggesting numerous modifications.

Finally, on a personal note, I should like to acknowledge my debt to the late 'Joe' Fivelsdal for fostering my love-affair with the cliff in the early days; and to many members of the Rendcomb College Climbing Group for assistance of varying kinds (including the clearing of volumes of rubbish from the cliff!), especially to Richard Hazell, Doré Green, and John Shaw, who all gave substantial help with the climbing and checking of routes for the earlier editions, and whose talents and enthusiasm ensured that my commitment to climbing in general and Wintour's Leap in particular remained inviolate.   JW 1997

WYNDCLIFFE
Every guidewriter relies heavily on previous guides, not so much for what is correct but for what is erroneous, or can be improved upon. I am therefore indebted to Tony Penning for his sterling work in compiling the last script. More recently, John Harwood, Frank Cannings, and Andy Sharp have trawled their diaries to provide missing information, for which I am most grateful.

However, the above is not an attempt to spread the blame. All the routes have been climbed, and reappraised, by myself over the spring and summer of 1996 and, therefore, all the mistakes are mine alone.

May others come to improve upon my work, or at least to provide what the Climbers' Club needs to produce the best possible guides – feedback.   DV 1997

BAN-Y-GOR

The Ban-y-gor script draws heavily upon the excellent groundwork done by the crag's main activists. The bulk of the compilation work was done by Matt Ward and by Gary Gibson: Matt recorded the initial development of the Escarpment (for *BMC New Climbs 1988*) and Gary supplied a full set of descriptions documenting the development of The Main Cliff.

It is every guide-writer's dream to be able to start with a comprehensive draft from day one, so that time is spent only deciphering new additions, writing route preambles, checking detail, and in the more pleasurable business of playing with text on a computer screen. Without the efficient and diligent efforts of both Matt and Gary my time spent producing this section would have been more onerous and certainly a lot less fun.

Particular thanks must go to the ubiquitous Martin Crocker for his extensive appraisal of the routes (especially on The Main Cliff) which was posted in his usual speedy and professional manner. Additional help came from Rob Kingston's *Wye Valley Update* (a collectors item!), as well as comment from Doug Kerr and further notes and proof-reading from Gary Gibson.

Finally thanks to all the following who either sent information or shared their precious climbing time with me checking routes: Frank Cannings, Nigel Coe, Kim Greenald, Chris Jones, Dave Little, Keith Marsden, Chris Shepherd, and Andy Tallant.   GAJ 1997

TINTERN QUARRY

A description of the quarry, along with details of its climbs, was written up in a loose-leaf format by the quarry's principal advocates, Martyn Cattermole and Graham Hughes. Their work provided the basis for the current script.

My thanks go to Martyn for making time for me amidst a busy life in order to get everything finalized for this guide; also to Jim Clayton, Francis Haden, Keith Marsden, and Andy Tallant for some entertaining quarry days (and especially to Francis who knows how to make them go with a bang!).   GAJ 1997

SHORN CLIFF

Matt Ward's excellent original text has been invaluable. I should also like to thank everyone who has contributed to this section and climbed with me at Shorn Cliff, including particularly Graham Hughes, Jeremy Hutchings, Tony Bird, and Peter Millner.   MC 1997

Introduction

The Wye Valley comprised the first designated Area of Outstanding Natural Beauty, and the Forest of Dean, the first National Forest Park. In the final few miles of its journey, the river has carved its devious way through a huge mass of carboniferous limestone to create one of the most spectacular non-glaciated river gorges in the British Isles; and on the western face of the lofty eastern ridge, upon which King Offa built his defences all those centuries ago, man and nature between them have sculpted most of the cliffs described in this book. While the most dramatic views are from and of Wintour's Leap, a spot by a memorial seat high above Shorn Cliff, on the Offa's Dyke footpath a few minutes to the south of The Devil's Pulpit, allows the finest comprehension of the semi-mountainous nature of the surroundings.

Deeper in the Forest, set back from the Wye Valley, are to be found some pockets of 'Pennant' sandstone. Known locally just as 'Forest Stone', it is much sought after for ornamental building work, and a few small worked-out quarries provide a refreshing contrast to the predominating limestone.

The sunny slopes below Wintour's Leap are much brightened by the scented flowers of viburnum, wild lilac, and buddleia in summer, and the brilliant berries of whitebeam and cotoneaster in autumn and winter, but the limestone woodlands as a whole tend to be disappointing, dominated as they are by sycamore, ash, and tatty regenerated elm. The acidic soil overlying the sandstone areas puts on a better show: here, oaks, beeches, and hollies are at their happiest; rowans, brooms, and rhododendrons flourish; even the gorse flowers its heart out non-stop for six months in a fine summer.

They say: "twixt Severn and Wye 't'll ne'er be dry'. In fact, the Lower Wye Valley is very well sheltered by the Welsh hills and the high ground of the Forest, and the weather is often unexpectedly fine. The outlook may be bleak when a moist south-westerly blows up the Bristol Channel, but otherwise there is always a good chance of finding some climbing. In a showery situation especially, when places as near as Lydney and Newport may be heavily affected, the Valley frequently remains dry. It is a four-season area, with winter snow rarely spoiling things, but those who thrive on warmth will find a summer evening most delectable after the generally westerly aspect has fully absorbed the sun's gradually pervading influence.

THE APPROACH

1 From London, the South West, and South Wales: leave the M4 for the M48 and the latter at junction 2 (formerly junction 22 of the M4) immediately west of the Old Severn Bridge. The broad link road leads in less than a mile to a large roundabout (officially 'Highbeech' but popularly known as 'The Lark-field'). If heading for **Wyndcliffe** or the Tintern approach to **Shorn Cliff**, go straight across this and past the Chepstow Racecourse on the A466 road towards Monmouth; **otherwise** turn right onto the A48 Gloucester road and drive past Chepstow and across the new Wye Bridge. Take the first turning left in England (B4228), follow this through Tutshill, turning right at the mini-round-abouts, and reach *The Rising Sun* in Woodcroft in a further mile (four miles in all from the M48).

2 From the Midlands or North: leave or cross the M5 at junction 11. Approach in about 40 minutes via the Gloucester Ring Road and the A48, turning *right* onto the B4228 a mile east of (i.e. before) Chepstow.

PARKING

1 There is space for two or three cars in a square pull-off at the top of the normal **Wintour's Leap** Easy Way Down. This is 600 yards beyond *The Rising Sun*, on the left immediately beyond the last two cottages. On a quiet weekday, it is possible for one or two cars to park in the vicinity of *The Rising Sun*, but this has often caused a variety of problems – please be discreet.

2 Otherwise, for **Wintour's Leap** and **Ban-y-gor** continue along the road, around the right-hand bend, and turn immediately sharp left up a lane signposted Lancaut. At the top of the little hill, beyond the last house, is a large grassy area on the left.

3 For **Shorn Cliff** and **Tintern Quarry** (which paradoxically is approached from Tidenham Chase, not Tintern itself), continue north on the B4228 for another mile, up a long continuous hill.

At the foot of the first slight drop after this there is an unsigned left turn by some stone cottages (and opposite a yard entrance) completely hidden until the very last second. Take this down a swiftly narrowing lane to its end. The track through a green gate on the left descends to Tintern Quarry, while the Forestry track ahead beyond the barrier leads to Shorn Cliff. There is reasonable parking-space here. If the barrier happens to be open, do not be tempted to drive further – it is always relocked and there is no other way out!

> The return exit from this lane is exceptionally dangerous: you cannot see traffic coming from the right, nor it you, until virtually too late. The safest procedure, even if turning right, is to keep close in to the cottages on the left before turning.

4 For **Wyndcliffe**, after passing the racecourse and then the village of St Arvans, the Forestry Commission Tintern/Wyndcliffe car-park on the right is reached. (Do not take the side road on the left after St Arvans signposted 'Wyndcliffe' – this goes over the hill well above the crag.) The main road continues to Tintern where there is plentiful parking in the Abbey car-parks for the western approach to **Shorn Cliff**.

AMENITIES

1 Camping. The best camp-site in the area is at The Beeches (OS Ref 548 006). North again along the B4228 from the Shorn Cliff turning, pass soon Miss Graces's Lane on the left and Tidenham Chase Church, and two turnings on the right. A not-too-obvious private signboard marks the next turning off left into a lane immediately before both sides of the road become forested.

The site is open all year and, being adjacent to Offa's Dyke footpath, caters for walkers and climbers. There are cold-water facilities only and the nearest pub is a long walk, but it is cheap, clean, never crowded, and quite magnificently situated. The site can also be reached on foot from Shorn Cliff and vice versa in about 30 minutes – a pleasant walk with less hill to negotiate than either of the conventional approaches to that cliff!

2   The Rising Sun Inn also welcomes climbers: bar meals and snacks are available at very reasonable prices, but there is no over-night accommodation. The New Route Book is kept behind the bar.

3   Provisions. There are now no shops in Woodcroft, but there is a very well stocked store (with off-licence) in Tutshill (early-closing Wednesday). This is on the right immediately after turning right at the mini-roundabouts. By turning *left* at the mini-roundabouts (or going straight across on the way back) you can find an 'eight-till-late' *Spar* in Sedbury (a little past the Comprehensive School).

4   Doctor. Next door but one to the Tutshill shop is the Doctor's Surgery.

5   Casualty. The nearest (and highly renowned) casualty unit is at Frenchay Hospital, outside Bristol. Reach junction 2 on the M48 via Chepstow. Turn east and cross the Old Severn Bridge. Join the M4, go past the M5 intersection, and take the M32. Leave that at the first exit (almost immediately), from where the hospital is well signposted. There are also casualty units with full facilities at The Royal Gwent Hospital in the centre of Newport, The Bristol Royal Infirmary in the centre of Bristol, and The Gloucester Royal Hospital.

6   Rescue. Cliff rescue is undertaken by the Severn Area Rescue Association, (SARA) with back-up from the Gloucestershire Fire and Rescue Service (Gwent Fire Brigade at Wyndcliffe). Dial 999 and ask for the *Gloucestershire* Police for all cliffs except Wyndcliffe (for which, ask for the *Gwent* Police). **For the full accident procedure, see page 334.** SARA is a volunteer rescue association, formed originally to effect marine rescue in the Severn Estuary above the Newport-to-Portishead line, an area not served by the RNLI. Later, a cliff rescue team was established and the Association's headquarters, now situated at Beachley under the old Severn Bridge, became a designated Mountain Rescue Post in 1982. The Chairman (address on page 333) welcomes contact from anyone interested in its activities.

CLIMBING WALLS
Undercover Rock – Bristol

This indoor climbing wall, situated uniquely in a church, caters for the full range of climbing abilities, with the emphasis on steep routes with relatively large holds. There are bouldering, cafe, and viewing facilities and all the expected distractions of a large city nearby. At the time of writing admission is £4.50 per unlimited session plus £1.00 registration fee for non-members. The wall is open seven days a week 10am to 10pm Monday to Friday, and 10am to 6pm at weekends. There are courses available and some concessions for the unwaged and students. For further details, ring 01179 413489.

To reach the wall, follow the M32 from junction 19 of the M4 to its own junction 3. Continue completely around the roundabout, back onto the slip-road of the M32 (NE) and branch left into Mina Road. Follow this for a quarter of a mile, across a mini-roundabout, until the church can be seen on the right.

The Warehouse – Gloucester

Another indoor climbing wall, this time in an old docks warehouse near the city centre. There are routes for all ability levels and dedicated bouldering areas as well as health-suite/gymnasium facilities. In addition there is a cafe/bar, equipment shop, accomodation, and a full range of courses/classes. Currently, admission prices range up to £4.00 for an adult at peak time, and the wall is open until 10.00pm seven days a week.

To reach the wall from any direction, follow the signs for Gloucester Docks/City Centre, and park in the docks. The wall is 100 yards away in Parliament Street. For further details, phone 01452 302351.

Chapel Rock Gym – Cheltenham

This too combines a leading-wall and bouldering-area with health-suite and gymnasium facilities. Situated in North Place, it has extensive opening hours which vary according to the day of the week. Other attractions are aerobics and yoga classes, videos, and a mirrored wall to admire those rippling muscles. Entry fee up to £3.50. Phone 01242 518075.

FOREST WALKS

For wet days, or for the family, there are numerous trails in the Forest of Dean, while The Wye Valley Walk and Offa's Dyke footpath follow the west and east banks of the river respectively between Chepstow and Monmouth. Good strenuous legwork is to be had in the Shorn Cliff woods area, and routes for all tastes can be constructed from the map on page 233. You can link this with the Wintour's Leap area (map page 52) by walking through the half-mile-long old railway tunnel under Ban-y-gor (torches necessary). Access to the Woodcroft end of the tunnel can be gained from beside the bridge in Netherhope Lane.

GRADINGS

The standard grading system is used; this is now so well established that it requires no explanation. The occasional 'mild' sub-category found in the last book has been eliminated in line with Climbers' Club publications policy. Please **also read** the paragraph on **fixed gear** below.

ROUTE SYMBOLS

[R] shows that the route is subject to a seasonal restriction; please refer to the relevant access notes before attempting to climb it.

† as usual indicates that the route is not known to have had a second ascent in a style comparable with or better than the first.

†† indicates that the route has suffered a substantial rockfall since the last known ascent which will almost certainly have affected the grade and/or description.

‡ indicates that the route or an important part of it has become revegetated,

and that it may thus not be climbable as described without prior top-rope cleaning.

Climbers interested in routes in either of the last two categories are strongly advised to inspect by abseil and carry out any necessary work first.

QUALITY RATINGS

The usual one-to-three star rating-system for route quality has been used. It has been felt that in the last edition, especially at Wintour's Leap, stars were used too freely. Down-rating in this book does not necessarily, therefore, suggest that there has been any change in the quality of a route.

Dave Viggers has suggested the following guidelines, which (with the exception of Cleeve Hill) we have tried to adopt throughout:

★★★ routes should be worthy of national recognition;
★★ routes should be of local importance;
★ routes should be above the average for the crag;
many unstarred routes will still be very well worth climbing.

Bear in mind that the aim of this guide is to enhance your enjoyment, not to provide it – apply your own judgements and feel free to question ours.

FIXED GEAR

Pegs are found at all the cliffs, but in substantial numbers at Wintour's Leap only. Although The Wye is fully tidal well beyond Shorn Cliff, there appears to be no problem with salt corrosion and many of the pegs look as good as the day they were placed. However, as this in some cases was twenty or thirty years ago, looks may be deceptive! In the late 70s and early 80s many of the pegs at Wintour's were cemented in place with epoxy mortar. The purpose of this was to discourage their removal and to obviate the need for people to carry and place their own on lead, which was still the practice then. While the mortar obviously added strength to some placements, to others it did not; and a few, though probably the best available, were marginal anyway. The author is not aware of any accidents due to or exacerbated by fixed-peg failure over the last twenty years; and some spectacular falls have been stopped. Nevertheless, full account must be taken of the potential limitations.

In-situ threads may be ten or more years old or missing altogether. *All* 'tat' should be regarded as suspect and backed up or replaced if at all crucial.

Bolts. Apart from the abseil *Eco-bolts* on GO Wall at Wintour's, which are maintained by the BMC, almost all bolts in the Wye Valley except for some at Ban-y-gor and Tintern Quarry are 8mm; whereas 10mm are currently accepted as the safe standard. The upgrading to 10mm currently in process at Ban-y-gor is not as yet spreading to the other cliffs. Again, there does not appear to have been any 8mm bolt failure in the Wye Valley, and there are no obvious signs of corrosion.

Except where otherwise stated or implied, the grades (and terms in the descriptions like 'well protected') assume that the fixed gear will do what it might **reasonably** have been expected to do **when it was placed**. The authors can, of course, offer no assurance that this will be the case, but there is no other viable basis upon which the guidebook could have been compiled. Climbers must make their own judgements and assess the evidence and risks for themselves.

WYE VALLEY DRILLED GEAR POLICY

At a well-publicized and well-attended BMC SW & S Area meeting on 17th February 1996 at The Warehouse Climbing Centre, Gloucester, the following was agreed by a very substantial majority of those present.

1 No new bolts to be placed at Shorn Cliff, Symonds Yat, Huntsham Crags, or on Fly Wall (Wintour's Leap).

2 New bolts acceptable elsewhere at Wintour's Leap north of the scree slope, provided they do not infringe upon existing routes.

4 Bolts (minimal or sport) acceptable for further development at Ban-y-gor, in the smaller quarries provided this does not conflict with environmental considerations, and in The Woodcroft Quarry (if access permits).

5 No bolts at all to be placed on the Forbidden areas at Wintour's Leap if climbed on with or without the owner's permission, unless and until an access situation has been approved by the BMC and a review of the situation reverses this proposal.

6 Wyndcliffe to be bolt-free.

7 Regearing at Wintour's Leap North Wall to GO Wall: 8mm bolts may be replaced by 10mm bolts or whatever is the recommended standard at the time – this to be the only exception to the like-for-like principle.

ACCESS

On the whole, access problems figure rather less than might be expected. The main one is the proximity of the cliffs to private land, and in some cases their situation within it. For the record, there is no formal permission to climb anywhere in this area. It is merely tolerated, ignored, or not known about. Please read carefully the access sections in the introductions to the individual crags and do everything possible to maintain the currently available facility.

Tthere are very few restrictions due to bird-nesting, but peregrines, goshawks, kestrels, and ravens are found regularly in the Forest of Dean, and there are rumours of red kites too. Please be understanding and co-operative if further seasonal restrictions become necessary, whether legally enforced, agreed with the BMC, or merely a matter of common-sense and voluntary restraint.

TREES

For years we have happily used trees for belaying to and abseiling from; and some worse things have happened, too! Recently, climbers have taken stock of the damage they have been doing to trees elsewhere, and the issue must now be addressed here as well.

There are three ways in which climbers may inadvertently cause this damage:
1 by trampling around the roots (for example when belaying), thus removing top soil and exposing them;
2 by applying force, as when abseiling or falling on a belay, so stressing and possibly loosening and damaging the root-system;
3 by causing friction burns to the bark when retrieving an abseil rope or, quite inexcusably, using the tree as a top-roping anchor without a sling.

Well-established trees will stand a lot of ill-treatment, but if subjected to any of the above practices repeatedly and regularly even they can suffer and eventually die. Remember that trees growing on or very close to the cliff may be existing marginally anyway because of the difficulties they have with moisture and nourishment take-up. It should also be noted that it is an offence in a conservation area to fell, prune, or cause damage to trees without a licence or planning permission.

On the other hand, local factors must be put in perspective.
1 We are not talking here about rare oaks, hollies, or rowans struggling to survive on a barren Welsh mountainside but sycamore, ash, and silver birch, all of which seed themselves with utter abandon in this friendly environment – many are thus technically weeds!
2 To the author's knowledge, the only apparent damage to trees in the area has been caused either by deliberate cutting in the course of route-cleaning, or accidentally in large rockfalls (whether the latter were nature- or man-induced). Even the much-abused silver birches above The Broadwalk and on *Central Rib* (both at Wintour's Leap) appear to thrive on their treatment.

It is worth noting that silver birch develops deep root-systems, while ash prefers to break up the surface material; the former is therefore more reliable and less easily damaged.

At Wintour's, trees are often the only main or running belays. At Shorn Cliff, where there are no viable descent routes, there is no reasonable alternative to abseiling from the trees. Both situations occur to a lesser extent elsewhere, and at all the cliffs trees invariably provide the cliff-top anchors except where bolt belays have been placed.

The current local drilled-gear policy (not to mention lack of will and resources) means that there is no early prospect of universal alternate anchors. A way forward at some time in the future could be to provide a single bolt backed by a sling attached to a tree above; given good choice of placement and correct procedure, this offers maximum safety with minimum environmental impact.

On past evidence and in view of the generally low amount and wide spread of use, it seems unlikely that significant damage will occur provided that climbers exercise restraint and common sense. The authors have no choice but to describe the routes as they are while urging the adoption of these virtues in order to minimize both ecological damage and the risk of curbs on activities.

CONCLUSION

Though one learns never to say that a place is worked out, and an occasional new line will be worthwhile or even a hitherto unavailable quarry may be discovered, the area has been very fully developed. It is not putting it too strongly to say that just too many insignificant lines (not to mention the eliminates and variations upon variants) which very few climbers will want to repeat have been done.

In the growth-friendly environment of the Wye Valley, if routes are to stay in good condition there needs to be a balance between neglect and overuse. In the last two or three years, a number of factors have conspired to promote the rampant revegetation of substantial sections of rock: the violent swings between hot dry spells and long wet and humid ones has been paramount; the smaller number of visiting climbers (due variously to the unavailability of a current guidebook, the reopening of Avon Main Wall, escalating Severn Bridge tolls, enthusiasm for the excellent Undercover Rock and Gloucester Warehouse) has obviously also been relevant.

And so what of the future? It would seem reasonable to remove encroaching ivy, grass, and brambles in order to restore well-established routes to climbability. However, neither wholesale defoliation nor the trundling of huge blocks causing scars to the cliff and havoc on the ground to squeeze in yet another 15 feet of E2 or to recover climbs that no-one ever does can any longer be justifiable, given the AONB–SSSI–Nature Reserve status of most of the rock described in this book.

Please, just come and make the utmost of some highly enjoyable climbing in very special surroundings; don't be tempted to try taking more than is on offer.

Dave Viggers is now the Climbers' Club co-ordinator for guidebook route information in South Wales and South-West England. In the event that anyone manages to find any more *genuine* new routes, please send details to him (address on page 333) and enter them and any other comments or relevant information you may have in the climbers' book kept behind the bar of *The Rising Sun* in Woodcroft.

History

Reams are written about the Wye Valley by ecologists, geologists, and local historians; but for the climbing chronicler the history is relatively recent and lacks mystery and folk-lore. The early first-ascent record contains no names of the great pioneers of the traditional British crags, or of well-known Alpinists. (The 1977 guide added 'or Everest climbers', but no sooner was the page off the presses than Pete Boardman turned up partnering Pat Littlejohn on *The Jackal*). Until 1977, occasional visitors came and went, perhaps doing a route, often leaving it unrecorded or mis-recorded, and few people took the area seriously. It was 'too loose, too vegetated', and after the mini-boom of the late 1960s, confusion about what had been done and where it went was so rife that activity ground to a standstill. Wintour's Leap became contemptuously known as 'The Heap' and, with the exception of Wyndcliffe, which flourished from 1970 onwards as a South-East Wales crag, the other cliffs lay shrouded largely in ivy and ignorance.

The authors of the 1977 guide had planned to include also both Ban-y-gor and Shorn Cliff. However, Frank Cannings, the first activist at the former, considered that the presence of nesting peregrines (then, of course, rarer and less well re-established than now) and the proximity of the cliff-top houses rendered climbing there unsustainable, and was unwilling for his record to be published. A manuscript containing details of early exploration at Shorn Cliff by a small group of South Wales and Bristol climbers mysteriously went missing, and at the same time the Forestry Commission requested a year's moratorium on all climbing at the crag while an ecological survey was made. The satisfactory (for climbers) report came just too late for publication, and the authors later received some unjustified flak for attempting a cover-up!

The 1977 guide, however, started to bring some sort of order to the reigning chaos at Wintour's Leap; and the result of painstaking research and imaginative conjecture was a limited but coherent network of viable routes and, more importantly for some, a clear definition of the large tracts of virgin rock between them. The way was now open for lost time to be made up; and made up with a vengeance it was. After a lead from Pat Littlejohn and the late Arnis Strapcans, Gary Gibson took the crag by the scruff of the neck and dragged it firmly into the 80s. The place was cleaned up and the old nickname was quietly forgotten; Wintour's Leap came of age. A spirited local youngster, Matt Ward, braved the jungles to reopen first Shorn Cliff and later Ban-y-gor, and he under-pinned the development at both before Gibson again took charge of the latter's Main Cliff. Finally, from the mid 80s, Martin Crocker arrived, combining his prodigious ability with his concern for style and quality, to solve some of the Valley's most intractable problems

1958–1965 EARLY DAYS

The first climbing seems to have been in the 1950s when now-unknown members of the Gloucestershire Mountaineering Club established the four easy Wintour's Leap classics: *Original Route, Corner Buttress, Bottle Buttress,* and *Central Rib.* In 1958, a visiting Cambridge University party led by Eric Langmuir (later of *Mountain Leadership* fame) discovered The North Wall and climbed *Left Hand Route, Central Route, Symplex,* (and *Right Hand Route?*).

However, 1961 marked the real beginning when John Grieve from Cirencester found the excellent *Zelda* – his partner's home-made peg, much pulled and fallen on, *still* in place. His explorations continued for five years and a series of remarkably bold leads [excellent training, one imagines, for his later appearances in 'Hamish's Horror Stories' and his eventual succession to MacInnes's hallowed role in the Glencoe MRT] resulted in several undergraded 'VS's, a couple of which, *The Tap* and *Guytha,* have also become standard repertoire.

It was 1965 before anyone else took any interest, but that year produced the two great HVS classics – *King Kong* by Terry Taylor, the first full route on GO Wall, and *The Angel's Eye.* The two Newport climbers responsible for the latter, Terry Broomsgrove and Terry Dove, enthusiastically started work on a complete *Lower Wye Valley* guide to replace the series of Gloucestershire Mountaineering Club pamphlets that had appeared in the late 50s and early 60s, but the pace of development over the next three years outstripped progress, and with their dispersal to other parts the work fell by the wayside. [Which Terry, or Terrys, Terry's Wall is named after, the author has been unable to ascertain!]

1966–1968 DAY OF THE TECHNICIAN

When the Severn Bridge opened in 1966, the quiet, secluded, Wye Valley road suddenly became the route by which climbers from the South-West travelled to North Wales, and the hitherto little-known dramatic limestone crags were fully revealed. More importantly, they were now only half an hour's drive from Bristol and, with completion of large sections of the M4, within easy reach of even London. From the one came Fred Bennett, taking time off from the Avon Gorge, and from the other, though shortly to settle in Bristol, Tony Willmott. A healthy rivalry soon developed and, if Willmott came out on top at Avon, then certainly Bennett took the honours at Wintour's Leap. Climbing variously with his brother Bob, Rob Walker, and chiefly Paul Lennard, he completed four fine routes in The Far South Bay and created his GO Wall masterpieces: *Kaiser Wall, Kangaroo Wall,* and *Technician. Kangaroo Wall* has survived as a free classic – to many, *the* classic, epitomizing all the very best the Wye Valley has to offer. But it was *Technician,* which pegged up the big groove to breach the roofs at their most sensational point, that set the pattern for the time and provoked two major parallel aid routes from Willmott. They each contributed a traverse on GO Wall: this time it was Willmott's high-level *The Burning Giraffe* which was free, while Bennett's *Umbrella Girdle* pegged along under the overhangs. Finally, Bennett forced a way through the huge roofs at the right-hand end of the wall with *Parasol;* but Willmott's matching diagonal (*It's a Beautiful Day*), though first attempted in this period, did not materialize until just before his death in 1972.

These artificial techniques were found useful on the next wall to the south also. Blasting in the Woodcroft Quarry had not long ceased, but it was now possible to walk along the top of Fly Wall (the new top, that is – the ancient top, a large green field at Offa's Dyke path-level, had been removed by the quarrying). The remains of the wall had been largely spared the desecration, and at its far south end it still reached a respectable 200 feet and sported an impressive overhang band. In August 1967, a party of three climbers found their way onto the wall for the first time. The first pitch was led by a 'Miss [G] Pemberton', (the first and only female in the first-ascent list until Gary Gibson brought Hazel into the fray sixteen years later) and the route was called *Firefly*, presumably in her honour [wasn't there a 1930s film of this title about a bold female agent?]. Probably this is also the origin of the wall's name. Anyway, in the next fortnight they also climbed *Dragon Fly*, *Big Fly*, and *Flyover*. [The author has long sought information about this pioneering trio, and diligently searched other guidebooks' first-ascent lists for their names – but can find only one obscure entry for a later superseded aid route.]

However, not all interest centred on pegs and etriers. From North London too came Ben Wintringham to GO Wall for *Surrealist* (its tottering killer-blocks on the first pitch, now long removed, deterring many from continuing up the superb groove and crackline above the Pedestal ledge), and a number of other climbers who helped open up Fly Wall with a dozen also free routes, including the highly and deservedly popular *Freedom*, *Swallow's Nest*, and *The Split*.

For today's climber, that is the extent of permitted territory, but beyond Fly Wall lie the Pen Moel cliffs, the main wall of which is as high as GO Wall, as long as Fly Wall; and its upper tier, at least, is composed of finer rock than either. It is not surprising that this beckoned as well. Bennett, Oliver Hill, and Hugh Banner made successful forays, and Wintringham climbed a route on the vegetated buttress beyond, above an enticing blue pool. Unfortunately, the landowner took the strongest exception to this 'trespassing', and after numerous threats and skirmishes the inevitable had to be accepted. Negotiations were promised but never materialized, and every request since has met with absolute refusal. The only known subsequent activity on this estate was by Strapcans and Chris King in the mid 70s. They managed four routes on the furthest cliff, which they named Amphitheatre Buttress, before being 'moved on'.

1968–1976 NEW CRAGS – FALSE NEW DAWNS

In October 1969 Frank Cannings and Pat Littlejohn climbed *Big Brother* on the front face of The Angel's Tower, the first fully free XS, and for several years the only recorded 5c pitch (which was led by the youthful Littlejohn) at Wintour's Leap. Was this to be the new dawn? Not for Wintour's. A couple of years earlier, when he had re-routed his trips from Bristol to North Wales, Cannings had become aware of the existence of Wyndcliffe across the river, though probably not of the extent and quality of the rock hidden behind the ivy. Now he and Littlejohn turned their attention there. The ivy came off to reveal the classic *Questor* and then *The Don*, *The Firebird*, and *Suncrush*. Cannings frequented the crag for a couple of years with various partners, and several more routes followed. Clive Horsfield and Phil Watkin worked hard at the left-hand end of the crag, between them accounting for the first seven routes in the guidebook. Watkin was the founder-editor of *Rocksport* (the first brave attempt at a British all-rock-climbing magazine) and the early activities were well publicized, not least in an article by Cannings, who also produced an interim guide. The crag buzzed with enthusiasm and activity, and for some while was the most fashionable in the Valley. A group of young climbers from Cheltenham, disgruntled at the lack of interest in harder rock within the Gloucestershire MC, formed their own CMC, and Wyndcliffe became their most regular venue. Chris Milford was the club's leading light, and in 1972 extended the list with the fine *Shaft*, *Klute*, and *Zulu*.

Meanwhile, there was also Ban-y-gor, the most impressive sight of all from the road, though more problematic to reach. However, in April 1970, Cannings and Ian Duckworth, fresh from *Purple Haze* at Wyndcliffe, came and fought their way up *Wait until You See the Whites*. They topped out and ploughed through undergrowth into a garden, startling the woman who lived there, not least with the information that she was perched on the edge of a 250-foot cliff. All was amicable, however, and they were invited in for tea!

Approaching initially by dropping down from Cockshoot Quarry to the old water-pumping station and cutting back up what was then a good track (now all brambles and fallen trees), Cannings, soon to be followed by Horsfield, had reached the Main Cliff and the exit via Ladder Gully and the water-service station (less well-fortified than now!). With various partners, they dug out (usually on lead) and climbed about a dozen routes taking the full height of the crag, which they graded VS and HVS. Quite where these went is a mystery, such has been the ravage of vegetation growth and later systematic cleaning.

After its initial boom, Wyndcliffe suddenly fell quiet for a four-year stretch. But at the end of the long hot summer of 76, when standards soared everywhere, E2 replaced VS as the norm. A few short autumn weeks saw eight more routes added to The Right-Hand Crag, most of which Andy Sharp had something to do with, the harder ones led by him on-sight after the lines had been cleaned for him by Horsfield or John Harwood (an ethic being practised elsewhere in the South-West at the time). Horsfield was involved for the last time, as was Phil Thomas, who had also been making some impressive repeats of the Bennett and Willmott routes at Wintour's, while Harwood was making his first appearance in the Wye Valley first-ascent lists.

Jim Perrin's *Interim Guide to Wintour's Leap*, published by the BMC in 1971, failed to generate any enthusiasm, and in the four years after *Big Brother* only three new routes were recorded. 1974-5 saw the revival of just a flicker of interest with, importantly, first contributions from Tony Penning (*Jos'e and the Fly*), Arnis Strapcans (*Zebrazone* and *Lord of the Flies*), and John Willson (*John's Route* and *The Angel's Girdle*). Next year King made a major breakthrough by free-climbing *The Umbrella Girdle*. But the Wyndcliffe late flourish did not extend across the water: everyone now was sitting tight, waiting just behind the starting-line for the new guide.

1977–1980 DAY OF THE JACKAL

It came in November. The big GO Wall artificial routes were first in the firing line and, though the formidable barrier of overhangs ensured that things rarely went quite according to plan, Wintour's Leap got its first ever series of really fine hard free routes. First on the scene, within days of publication, was Littlejohn to claim *The Jackal* (with Boardman) and *Hyena Cage* (with King), which between them eliminated at a stroke all the aid of Willmott's *The Pulsating Rainbow* and all but the crux roof (which was avoided) of *Technician*, as well as adding in some difficult new pitches. In the New Year, Strapcans and King reduced the aid on *Kaiser Wall* to one point (shortly to be eliminated by the Gibson brothers) and created *Vulture Squadron*, containing what is still for many the most brilliant and adrenalin-pumping section of climbing in the Valley. Later in the year, Strapcans forced a way through the overhangs of the great buttress between *King Kong* and *Kangaroo Wall* (though not quite by the original *Interstellar Overdrive* aid line) to give *Empire State Experience*, and free-climbed the unlikely upper roof of *Parasol* to make *Joe the Lion* (the lower roof remaining inviolate for another thirteen years).

Fly Wall also was screaming for attention, as the photograph in the 77 guide made apparent. One rainy February day, Willson and a young Rendcomb College pupil, Richard Hazell, set about clearing the undergrowth at the bottom of the crag and arrived below the ivy-choked chimney which was quickly cleaned and climbed to become *Flyhole*. Strapcans almost got there first, but was soon back with an enthusiastic Bristol contingent. Through April and May the wall was alive with blaring radios and whistling stones, and there was once again a whiff of competition in the air (not least in the choice of risqué names) as the number of routes promptly doubled.

Over the next year or so, Willson and the 15-year-old Hazell, the latter now doing most of the leading, set systematically about The North Wall, where they were unchallenged, producing the superb *Notung*, and made forays back on Fly Wall for *Split Flies*, which remained the wall's test-piece for a couple of years, and the first free ascent of *Firefly*. Sadly, by the autumn of 1980 Hazell was forced to give up serious climbing because of a bone defect in his right arm, and Strapcans disappeared on Mont Blanc. However, enough had already been done to outdate the guide, and a speedily compiled supplement was published in early 1981.

1980–1984 FLIES ALOFT
Of the Bristol climbers, only Gordon Jenkin remained faithful to Wintour's, making such significant contributions as *Swansong, Entrance Exam*, and *Acid Test*. Adding a first pitch to the latter, he was fixing a belay when a pillar collapsed, knocking him backwards. Nuts ripped, and it was only Willson's sense of self-preservation fleeing the shower of shattered blocks that enabled a low peg to check the fall inches from the ground. Jenkin heroically walked to the top under his own steam, only to have a broken neck diagnosed on reaching hospital. This was so nearly the end of all things for him, yet nine months later he was back with Nipper Harrison to climb *Lurking Fear*.

Meanwhile, Penning achieved the long-awaited upper traverse on Fly Wall, *Fly Major*, and climbed *Jannock* and *Lionheart*, two bold undertakings that showed how much there was still to do on the left half of GO Wall.

Willson brought another Rendcomb boy, Doré Green, along to help tidy up the North Wall with *Exodus* and missing pitches to *Notung* and *Swansong*; this was after Green's début, *Hunky Doré*, had achieved a mention on *Blue Peter*. Local schoolboy Matt Ward hung around the crag looking for partners and made a few inauspicious incursions upon the new-route scene.

But at the beginning of this era a new force had arrived, the one that has largely dominated it since, in the form of Gary Gibson, the now-famous new-route obsession already biting deep. Initial forays in the South Bays from late 1980 opened the account with *Themeninblack* and *Waiting for Themeninblack*, but it was the upwrench of standard with *Vapona* on Fly Wall a year later that pointed to the future. In three days in July 1982, four major routes were climbed in the North Wall Area, of which *Strange Little Girl* became the outstanding hard route of the crag north of GO Wall.

Already, though, he had set about ravaging Fly Wall. Working from dawn to dusk and sometimes beyond, he established more routes there in the month than had been achieved by all contributors together in either of the two previous waves of development, many of them, such as *La Folie, Gendarmerie, Idealist*, and *Flies Aloft*, of a high standard of difficulty and great quality.

Space eventually started to run out, but in early 1983, GO Wall's 'last great problem' – the *Technician* roof – finally yielded to give him *Feline*. A month later Littlejohn returned for *Big Bad Wolf*, thus laying claim to the hardest route in the valley for the third time. Thereafter the pace at Wintour's Leap slackened again as attentions were diverted.

1984–1985 LAUGHING CAVALIERS
A chance meeting in March 1984 at Wintour's Leap changed the course of Wye Valley history. Gibson was secondless for a route he had cleaned in The Far South Bay; Ward was there! Ward obviously made a good effort in getting up *Gospel: According to Themeninblack* because Gibson soon 'adopted' him

and booked him for his annual late-summer Lundy trip. More significantly, Ward, feeling he was not putting his talents to good use at Wintour's, had started searching for pastures new and had recently taken a walk up to Shorn Cliff. Gibson too had been to look but claimed to have been unable to find the cliff!

In early June 1984, however, Ward guided Gibson and his new wife to The Great Central Cave slab; and did those cavaliers laugh when the very first ivy they stripped off revealed an immaculate HVS – and another four neighbour-ing lines scarcely less good! A second visit followed a week later and one more before the Lundy trip. Gibson's work here was done, but the crag provided Ward with the opportunities he had sought. He introduced some of his friends to the crag, notably Rob Kingston, and throughout July, August, and September new routes were being recorded several times a week. In late October, Penning and Harwood made a fleeting raid to 'christen' Hit and Run Buttress.

Next April saw Ward and Kingston back at work at almost the feverish pitch of the previous year, and by mid-summer the word was getting around. Roy Thomas had been one of the crag's explorers in the early seventies and now returned to find it transformed. He was able to identify a few of those old lines but, as at Ban-y-gor, the ravages of time, vegetation, and then recleaning had altered so much beyond all possibilities of recognition. Nevertheless, with Mick Learoyd mostly in the lead, he started reclaiming lost time, and a series of E3 routes appeared (only Gibson's Lundy Calling having reached this standard then). At last, but inevitably, Martin Crocker arrived to provide the daunting test-piece Three Score Years and Ten, which remained the hardest route on the crag until he himself capped it in 1992.

1986 was different. Kingston did a few fillers-in. Ward was hard at work with his guide script. But the circulation of information about what had happened in the last two years enabled many visitors to experience a thrill of delight at this unexpected new crag. The development had taken place with remarkably little incident, the only one of any seriousness being when a block was dislodged and struck Mick Learoyd in the face, resulting in a broken nose and a cut requiring seventeen stitches. He was able to commemorate the event by calling the routes he had just completed The Hit and Nosey Bleeder. A less dire incident had occurred when Kingston disturbed a bees' nest while cleaning on Abbey Buttress; his abseil to escape became fast and hot!

Ward especially, but also Kingston and to a lesser extent some others, had done an excellent job in opening up and developing the crag so thoroughly and improving their own techniques into the bargain. Ward was now climbing regularly elsewhere with both Gibson and Crocker, and was setting his sights higher.

1985–1986 ENDGAME

With what should have been a month before the next guide's going to print, Willson, doing some final GO Wall checking, speculated on the large gaps, and Rendcomb protégé number three, John Shaw, was soon celebrating his sixteenth birthday by climbing *Stairway to Heaven*. Gibson, prompted by criticisms of the pitch below the *Feline* crux as 'scruffy', came back for 'one last look' and replaced the offending section with a better, harder one. But the fire was lit: GO Wall had worked its magic again.

Frenzied visits followed as one route after another was cleaned for when the rain stopped, and there began the most feverish episode of development in the history of the cliff. Partnered mainly by Ward, but otherwise grabbing anyone he could find to hold his ropes, Gibson launched an onslaught so fierce that it achieved in two months what had taken even him two years on Fly Wall. As damp December passed through jaded January to frost-crackling February the rock at last dried out and the huge space between *Kaiser Wall* and *Lurking Fear* was filled. The Interstellar Buttress was sorted out, *Dog Eat Dog* made a superb direct eliminate between *Hyena Cage* and *The Jackal*, and at the right-hand end of the wall *The Isle of Dogs* took a startlingly photogenic path straight through the overhangs above The Pedestal.

Even with all this going on, he still found more space (and time) for another eight routes on Fly Wall. A four-month delay in the completion of the guide was the inevitable result, duly taken advantage of by Shaw, Willson, and Ward to identify the remaining gaps and compete for the last line in the book: at a late stage, Willson's *Endgame* was thwarted by Ward's *Can't Fly Any Higher*.

Throughout this period, Crocker and Sharp had been repeating most of the hard routes but neither had shown much interest in new routes at Wintour's. Crocker had been concentrating his creative activities at Cheddar; but at the very last he stepped in to to grasp the coveted line on the upper, leaning right wall of *King Kong*: *Primeval* shot straight to number one in the graded list.

Having introduced the 6c grade to Wintour's Leap, Crocker added more of the same, and he climbed another three important lines on Fly Wall, the ever-faithful Ward in support. Ward himself was concentrating on producing a series of hard, short, clip-up routes. And just in time for inclusion in the guide, Shaw and Willson climbed *Childhood's End* and *Yesterday's Dreams*, which rapidly became the two most frequented E2s on the crag.

1987 WINTOUR'S LEAP – RETROSPECT AND AFTERMATH

As always, Gibson's rush for new routes had provoked some controversy. The negative aspects which prompted the criticsm have been discussed elsewhere, but none of this could invalidate the *enormous* significance of Gibson's overall contribution, which was very largely responsible for transforming the crag from a backwater into a major climbing-ground of the 80s. His activities at Wintour's Leap were now concluded, but this was by no means the last the

Valley was to see of him.

The long-awaited publication of the guide in early July, together with six months of superb weather punctuated only by the famous October hurricane, brought more visitors to Wintour's Leap than ever before. Ward, now at leisure between college and a job, and Shaw, with Willson in permanent support, embarked upon yet another spree in contemptuous defiance of the latter's concluding comment of the 1987 *History*. The North Buttress was finally filled (to over-flowing) and more test-pices were added at the bottom of Deceiver Buttress; most important, Shaw and Willson climbed *Blitzkrieg* left of Kaiser Wall, the most direct and independent full-length GO Wall new route to be climbed complete in a single day for many a year!

1978–1988 DEEP IN THE FOREST

David Hope had been undertaking a full survey of the many small quarries scattered around the Forest of Dean, most of which were disused and few of which had been credited with any potential for climbing. However, he had found one major exception deep in the Forest, almost completely hidden from view by the trees. He concluded a partial access agreement with the Forestry Commission and the Gloucestershire Wildlife Trust, and with members of the Worcester Mountaineering Club who centred most of their activities upon Symonds Yat, cleaned and climbed nearly twenty routes at Spion Kop (so named after a Boer War battle in 1902 in which the English came off decidedly the worse). In the summer of 1986, he introduced Penning, who had become disillusioned with the way things had gone at Wintour's Leap, to the cliff and the two big lines of *Love Story* and *The Power of Love* appeared on the front face of the striking Central Tower.

As soon as the details appeared in print Ward and Crocker (after a long search to find it) were there, and throughout the autumn months Ward kept returning with various of his regular partners. The number of routes doubled and the permitted parts of the quarry were soon worked out. Ward's E6 *Labour of Love* up the Central Tower face became the route of the quarry, but it was not achieved without a protracted effort. Meanwhile Crocker was able to indulge his penchant for exposed arêtes.

Next spring, Ward, Crocker, Kingston, and Jenkin investigated the other quarries that Hope had listed (plus a couple more) and, one by one, these also yielded many more routes than had been foreseen. Point Quarry was certainly the finest but has unfortunately had to be abandoned to the birds. Shakemantle (Ruspidge Slab Quarry) was perhaps the biggest surprise: a large, open, south-facing area on the very outskirts of this village, itself on the edge of Cinderford. Although much of the rock is a mess, a fine-looking slab offered a dozen interestingly mobile lines.

1988–1996 BACK TO BAN-Y-GOR

By mid-June 1988 all this, bar the last few routes at Point Quarry, was done.

To Ward, still a gentleman of leisure, and Kingston, fully enthused by his activities of the last four years, there was an obvious solution: Ban-y-gor would finally have to be sorted. The Main Cliff and its only known approach appeared a truly daunting prospect, but to their surprise they found a quite straightforward alternative way to the long line of lower and cleaner cliffs over to the right – The Escarpment.

It must have seemed just like the first weeks at Shorn Cliff all over again, though the average grade was several notches up and bolts were 'in'. *East of Sweden* and *Stars and Stripes* by Ward, along with *The Tao* and *Duhka*, by Kingston, immediately confirmed the true potential of the crag as did Ward's ascent of the hard, test-piece arête, *Nelson Mandela*.

Less than a fortnight later Crocker and Jenkin were joining the party. Crocker's first route, *Bad Man from Bodie* was a typically demanding addition (with only a single repeat to date) and pointed the contrast in style between the strict minimalist bolt (and don't forget the *RPs*) ethic and the plentifully-geared routes mainly favoured by Ward. Nevertheless, both styles flourished and, unsurprisingly, the clip-up routes received the repeats.

After the initial foray, attention shifted across to the Overhanging Bays on the Left-Hand Escarpment. Here Ward started vacuuming up the lines, with *Violation of Trust* quickly becoming popular, while Kingston found the best of them here in *Avatamsaka*. Jenkin added lines of his own in the Overhanging Bays as well as sharing leads on *SoFB Country* with Kingston.

Crocker had, on his first visit, sorted out the intimidating roof of *Felt, Batten, and Smile*, (*RPs* required!) and now turned attention to Crawl Buttress, undoubtedly the best feature of The Escarpment, creating an impressive portfolio of hard routes with *Just Too Hot, Too Hot to Touch, Good Jab'*, and (using only two bolts) a dazzling pitch, *Latest Craze*. Seeming as at home in the damp as in the cold, he next moved his abseil rope over from Crawl Buttress to Crawl Wall and set about the awesome roof-stack belonging to *Really Big Sur*, and the serious *Craters of Mono*.

The summer of 1988 will be remembered by those climbing at Ban-y-gor most for its perpetual bad weather. It seemed that at every weekend (and most of the week!) it would rain; and the route names reflected that experience: *Always the Rain, Summertime Blues* and *Mondays Never Rain*. Paradoxically, it was due precisely to these poor conditions that new-routing attention remained focused so intently upon Ban-y-gor as the canopy of trees and general angle of the rock meant that it proved 'climbable' in quite adverse conditions (given enough fortitude and like-minded friends!).

In August, Penning came for a look and with Pete Cresswell, John Harwood, and Roger Lanchbury pushed leftwards to The Ladder Gully Area, the buffer between The Escarpment and the still silent, ignored, virtually unseen Main

Cliff. By early September the fifty-route tally had been passed; two months later the century was only eight short and seemed certain to be reached within days.

For word of the goings-on had reached Gibson, who had recently brought his equipment bang up-to-date with the acquisition of a *Hilti* drill. Gibson, having regarded the Wye Valley as 'put to bed', was heavily involved elsewhere, but had to come and see what the fuss was about. A couple of minor routes were done, but his eye was captured by the Ladder Gully buttress being developed by Penning. On November 8th he returned with his wife Hazel and John Holdcroft. The events of that day are told in his own words.

'We arrived quite early, trooped along the crag and set up base below *Merthyr Bob*. I soloed up *Top Cat* to find a very convenient terrace and began cleaning and drilling: the minor arête right of *Top Cat*, the impressive roofs left of *Amnesty* and for a final reconnaissance a look at the big roof left again'. [On the Main Cliff itself, at last!] 'I abseiled down, hammered in a few pegs and clipped the rope in to pull me in. My final memory is of sorting my *Jumars* out to go back up the rope and have some dinner but what truly happened remains a mystery. We guess that something hit me on the head and cut the rope (glass from the ivy above?) or did the rope just shear? Whichever, my injuries were a fractured skull, jaw, cheek-bone and orbits and the net outcome was a lengthy stay in hospital on a ventilator, a titanium plate in my head and a very distraught wife and friend – thank goodness they were there, I owe them my life.'

In fact, he fell around 80 feet and he owed his life to events and others than just his wife and friend, as he has generously acknowledged elsewhere, not least by raising a substantial donation to the rescue team. Holdcroft climbed the old ladders and raised the alarm while Hazel stayed with him, fearing the worst. When the rescue team arrived she told SARA Chairman, Jim Hewitt, 'I think he's dead.'

Climbing at Ban-y-gor had been in progress less than five months and, although word of it had reached Jim Hewitt on the grapevine and he had done a preliminary reconnaissance, it was brand new rescue territory. Nevertheless there was a good turnout, and Gibson was kept alive and secure. The really fortuitous circumstances were the presence in the area of a *Sea-King* on training and the proximity of a slight clearing in the woods which provides probably the only viable pickup-point in the vicinity of the crag.

Although Gibson writes, 'After recovering very slowly from my injuries…', the first-ascent list reveals he was back at it in exactly three months. Though only a couple more minor routes were done on the day of his return, he and Roy Thomas took the opportunity to push their way on through the jungle below the Main Cliff and comprehend for the first time its staggering potential. A week later he bagged *Gimme Back My Head* and *Sea-King Me*, thus launching the macabre route-name theme of this sector; and in May he finally laid the ghost to rest with *Head Tennis*. This name proved even more appropriate than he could have foreseen. To settle his score with this route, he felt he needed a glued-on hold. Attempting a repeat, Crocker involuntarily cranked it off and embedded it in his own head.

There matters rested for several months, but inevitably the man was back in late autumn, this time with a highly-motivated Doug Kerr and occasionally Roy Thomas, and another fifty climbs were added before the end of 1990, concluded by a ten-route round-up (nine led by GG, the other one seconded) on 13th October. The most significant aspect of this period was Gibson's decision in March of that year to adopt the out-and-out sport-climb principle. To this point, he had employed the minimalist ethic, with many of his routes being very bold affairs; the flash ascent had still been the intent, even if not always realized. Now, lines such as *Aerial Combat*, *Wye Me*, and *96 Tiers* were fully geared, and 'the redpoint' became the goal. Ban-y-gor was to become the sport-climbing venue of the region.

But it turned out that the 'heady' days were over: a prolific August weekend with Jenkin, a gloomy November day with Thomas and Kerr, and Christmas Day, spent playing see-saw with Hazel to overcome *Rudolph's Roof Route*, were all that he managed in 1991, and things slowed further in subsequent years. Occasional visitors added a smattering lines on the escarpment, but no-one other than Gibson and his few allies claimed anything on the Main Cliff. Twice in a decade, Gibson had made a major Wye Valley wall largely his own; with this third he had succeeded in doing the job completely.

1990 UPDATE

Matt Ward, unaccountably, began rapidly to lose interest in the open air and went underground, and he managed too often to distract Jenkin from the real thing as well. Crocker, robbed of Ward's persistence in local jungle-bashing, preferred better things elsewhere and anyway had his milestone *Avon and Cheddar* guide to complete. Thus deserted by many of his friends and partners, Kingston turned to compiling a chronicle of every development in the Valley since the guide. The main new routes of 1987 and 1988 had appeared in BMC *New Climbs* volumes of those years, and Gibson, somewhat miffed at his exclusion from the Escarpment gold-rush, was keeping his Main Cliff activities under wraps; but the *1990 Update* remains an invaluable source of detail, as well as correction and revision of the 1987 guide itself.

1990–1996 MORE QUARRIES

Dismissed generally as 'loose and insignificant', the Wyndcliffe Quarry below and north of the main Wyndcliffe crags, possessed two major virtues: immediate accessibility and seemingly permanent sunshine, which inspired Jenkin and Andy Tallant to make available some short fun routes.

More significantly, Graham Hughes and Martyn Cattermole discovered that even Matt Ward had been blinkered when he had said of Tintern (known locally as Walton-Gooddy) Quarry, '…not of any interest to climbers and should be avoided'. Dormant only, but by no means abandoned, this is not only the largest quarry in the whole of the Wye Valley and Forest of Dean, but contains higher walls than any any of the natural crags. They are, of course, mostly appallingly loose and split by numerous rubble-piled ledges, but here and there are easily accessible sections of cleanable and climbworthy rock. Fewer scruples may be in order about the heavy cleaning and drilling – the routes and their fixed gear may well have been blown up by the time you get there!

A late bonus was received in 1996 with the opening of one of the Bix Slade quarries. Though it is technically available only to booked groups, a discreet and considerate approach is likely to permit recreational climbers to sample half a dozen Crocker sport routes on soft but sunny sandstone.

1991–1992 WINTOUR'S LEAP POSTSCRIPT

Kingston's objective in his *1990 Update* was to ensure not only that every hold that had been used was detailed, but that every hold *had been used*! [His undoubted near-total success in the latter has not always endeared him to the authors of the current guide, and for various but obvious reasons will fail to be fully credited by posterity.] However, GO Wall did still pose three contrasting challenges, which seemed unlikely to be solved by anyone of lesser stature and determination than Crocker.

First, *Big Bad Wolf* had been howling for a repeat for nearly a decade and, although a number of leaders had expressed interest, nobody as sporting as Penning (Littlejohn's original second) could be found to follow its desperate, exposed, and only modestly-protected long traverse. Crocker solved the problem by reversing the pitch (with only minimal assistance from the rope) after climbing it.

In the course of this, he was able to get a perfect view of the crux section of a potential line over the widest part of the lower roofs, below which had hung a white sling from a bolt placed years earlier by Gibson to aid reconnaissance and then abandoned as hopeless. Crocker's main problem was gearing the route without intruding a bolt into the *Big Bad Wolf* crossing; he found a way, though, and *Dinosaur Heaven* was rapidly and fittingly achieved.

Finally, to the one persistent aid section on the crag – the first roof of *Parasol*, long regarded 'impossible' to free. Fred Bennett's extraordinary upside-down metal wedge and a rotted *in-situ* sling were replaced by a single bolt. Crocker launched horizontally past the bolt and clipped the peg on the lip; at that point a whole sheet of the roof exploded. Fortunately, the peg remained secure, while the long-suffering Willson watched the blocks, still shattering in mid-air just above, somehow scatter around him. Crocker's next attempt was success-ful, but his second then, Pete Oxley, did not escape unscathed either.

Balls Out (E2, first ascent) Fly Wall, Wintour's Leap
Climber: Gordon Jenkin   Photo: Frank Cannings

Vampire Strikes Back (E5, first ascent) Fly Wall, Wintour's Climber: Martin Crocker   Photo: John Willson

AND SO TO THE MILLENNIUM
One learns to stop saying that anywhere is fully developed, even when one believes it...

So what has the Wye Valley to offer the 'ordinary' climber? One and two decades ago the future seemed bright and the prospects exciting. Although the area had had a poor reputation, the guides sold well, and people came, and enjoyed it. Now things are less certain. The vegetation is like inflation: just when you think it is beaten, at least under control, it lashes back with a vengeance. Access is always on a knife-edge; many of the 'agreements' we have are ancient, unconfirmed, unratified. The cemented pegs, so widely appreciated for twenty years, must sooner or later reach the end of their usefulness, as must the 8mm bolts littered around enthusiastically in the late 80s.

However, life goes on. Climbers will need to treat the environment sensitively, and sooner or later a proper regearing must be undertaken. Nevertheless, there remains a great wealth of fine climbing at all grades and in all styles to be enjoyed.

But best of all would be a solution of:

THE LAST GREAT PROBLEM
Access to The Forbidden Wall, Wintour's Leap – undoubtedly the finest crag in the Valley.

How about it, BMC?

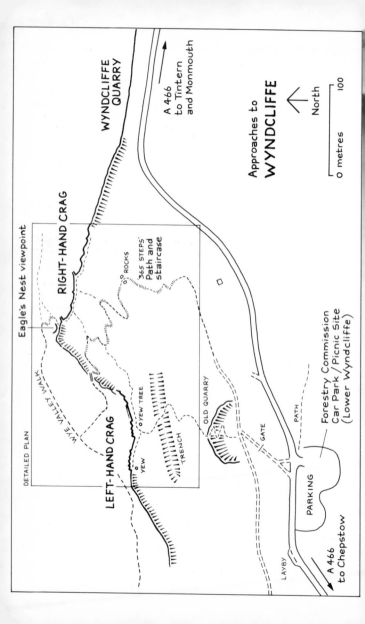

Approaches to **WYNDCLIFFE**

North

0 metres 100

WYNDCLIFFE QUARRY

A 466 to Tintern and Monmouth

RIGHT-HAND CRAG

Eagle's Nest viewpoint

DETAILED PLAN

WYE VALLEY WALK

ROCKS

'365 STEPS' Path and staircase

LEFT-HAND CRAG

YEW

YEW TREE

TRENCH

OLD QUARRY

GATE

PATH

Forestry Commission Car Park / Picnic Site (Lower Wyndcliffe)

PARKING

LAYBY

A 466 to Chepstow

Wyndcliffe

Easily visible from Wintour's Leap, Wyndcliffe (or Wynd Cliffe – the OS cannot make up its mind) comprises the pair of tree-shrouded limestone crags high above the Lancaut meander of the River Wye, and a short distance above the A466 Chepstow to Monmouth road. Such was the area's scenic popularity, the Victorians constructed 'The 365 Steps' woodland path and staircase leading to the Eagle's Nest viewpoint. One of the relics of this, a metal-handrailed staircase between the two crags, now provides a convenient descent route. The crags face generally south-west and thus benefit from the afternoon and evening sun, although the surrounding trees ensure they remain dank for long periods in the winter.

Once extremely popular with climbers, the crags have steadily declined in usage, having gained a reputation for loose, dirty climbing. This is only partially justified as there are some quality routes, often with strong lines, especially for the middle-grade climber. This quality is, however, concentrated in a relatively small number of climbs, which in consequence, have become polished and may well seem a little tough for their grades.

A significant number of routes have been reclaimed by nature and are now virtually unclimbable owing to copious vegetation and dubious rock. Descriptions are, however, included for the historical record and to aid the socially-minded exhumer in his/her quest for their redemption. Such routes are marked with the ‡ symbol and **extreme caution** is advised.

Stars have been re-appraised since the previous guide in an attempt to reflect national trends and so as not to mislead the starstruck.

APPROACH
From the old quarry opposite the carpark (see page 13), both crags can be reached in under ten minutes. Camping is also possible here provided a low profile is kept.

DESCENTS
Descent from both crags is by following small paths through the woods to reach the central steps or, much more conveniently, by abseil from any of the numerous trees. However, please refer to the section on trees in the General Introduction (page 17).

LEFT-HAND CRAG
To reach this cliff, scramble up a steep path through the centre of the old quarry to reach small tracks leading, through woodland, to a large trench. Cross this leftwards to reach the lowest point of the crag.

The crag is divided above its lowest point by a large, bramble ledge-system,

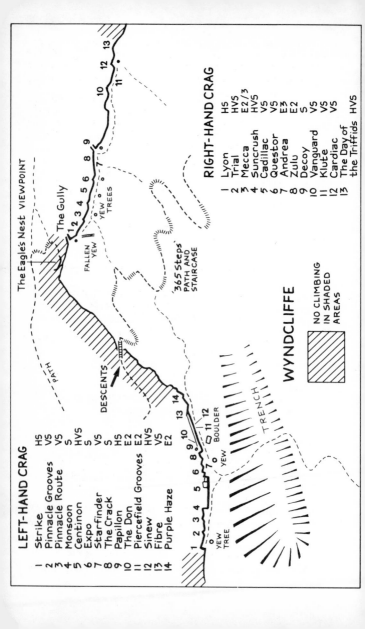

LEFT-HAND CRAG

1 Strike — HS
2 Pinnacle Grooves — VS
3 Pinnacle Route — VS
4 Monsoon — S
5 Centinon — HVS
6 Expo — S
7 Starfinder — VS
8 The Crack — S
9 Papillon — HS
10 The Don — E2
11 Piercefield Grooves — S
12 Sinew — HVS
13 Fibre — VS
14 Purple Haze — E2

RIGHT-HAND CRAG

1 Lyon — HS
2 Trial — HVS
3 Mecca — E2/3
4 Suncrush — HVS
5 Cadillac — VS
6 Questor — VS
7 Andrea — E3
8 Zulu — E2
9 Decoy — S
10 Vanguard — VS
11 Klute — VS
12 Cardiac — VS
13 The Day of the Triffids — HVS

WYNDCLIFFE

The Eagle's Nest VIEWPOINT

The Gully

FALLEN YEW

YEW TREES

'365 Steps'
PATH AND
STAIRCASE

PATH

DESCENTS

BOULDER

YEW

YEW TREE

TRENCH

NO CLIMBING
IN SHADED
AREAS

left of which is a series of corners, grooves, and cracks. To the right are more pronounced grooves, which give substance to the better climbing on this cliff. From the lowest point a path leads up left to another large yew tree just right of vegetation, which is an ideal base for routes on the far left section of the crag.

Climbing is currently restricted to the area between *Strike* on the left and *Green Symphony* on the right. A route has been climbed outside the permitted climbing area and should not be attempted, as this would threaten the access agreement. **Q.E.1.** (120 feet Hard Severe ‡ 9.1.72) takes a groove/chimney line, leading to a flake and poor exit, in two pitches.

★Strike   130 feet   Hard Severe 4b   (3.10.70)
The obvious, right-facing corner to the left of the tree is followed to a ledge on its right. Move back left under, of all things, a peg, to finish up a widening groove.

The next two routes both have loose or vegetated sections requiring care and experience at the grade.

Hostage   130 feet   Very Severe 4c   (3.10.70)
Fifteen feet right of the corner and directly behind the tree is a shattered arête.
Follow the cave to a ledge and continue up a crack to another ledge on the right. Step back left to a steep crack which leads to yet another ledge, and continue carefully rightwards to a blocky finish.

The author offers no apologies for rationalization of the next few routes in order to make the best of the available rock.

Pinnacle Grooves   130 feet   Very Severe 4c   (26.9.70)
Ten feet right of the yew tree is a corner.
Climb the corner awkwardly to a ledge on the right of an overhang; then trend left to gain a ledge and, subsequently, a pinnacle. Climb rightwards up a shattered wall, then left to finish as for *Hostage*.

Pinnacle Route   120 feet   Very Severe 4c   (26.9.70)
Move right from the start of *Pinnacle Grooves* and climb a shallow corner to a rickety pinnacle on the right, above which a flaky groove gains the oak tree (see below). The corner on the left is climbed to a bulge which is crossed, left then right, to finish.

Thirty feet right and downslope of the yew tree is a small clearing below an oak tree on a half-height ledge.

Monsoon   130 feet   Severe 4a   (13.9.70)
Slippery cracks and a dirty finish detract from an otherwise pleasant outing. Cracks on the left lead over small ledges to the oak, from where the crack

on the right gains an earthy corner-system.

The next series of routes may well be the reason for the crag's decline in popularity during the 1980s, being generally dirty and vegetated in their lower sections. Those who persevere, however, will be rewarded by much better climbing towards the top of the cliff on most of them.

Skyjack   130 feet   Hard Very Severe   4c   (13.9.70)
Short of both reliable protection and quality, this route has little to recommend it.
Climb the corner on the right of the clearing, through brambles, to the left end of the bramble ledge that divides the crag. Zigzag scarefully (*sic*) up the wall until level with the oak, and then trend diagonally right across the wall to finish as for *Syrphus*. (Or better yet, don't!)

Thirty feet left of the lowest point of the crag is a dirty crack leading to the bramble ledge.

Syrphus   140 feet   Severe   4a   (19.9.70)
The initially dirty section is hardly worth overcoming.
Follow the crack to an earthy exit onto the ledge. Continue up the crack to a short, wide chimney giving access to the final earthy corners.

Above the lowest point of the cliff, three grooves appear above overgrown ledges.

Centinon   140 feet   Hard Very Severe   4c   (22.3.70)
Fine bridging up the top left-hand groove fails to justify, by a wide margin, the horrors of the first section.
From the lowest point of the crag, gain a flat-topped pinnacle on the left and continue, JCB in hand, up loose, mixed ground to the sanctuary of the upper groove. Finish rightwards.

Expo   140 feet   Severe   4a   (4.4.70)
The central section of vegetated ledges spoils what might clean up to be a worthwhile route.
Step off a flake, just right of *Centinon*, into a steep groove which gains a series of ledges. Above these follow the central groove past a jammed block.
Variation (Very Severe 4c 4.89): a rather pointless exercise as it is no cleaner or better than the original. Climb the groove right of the parent route to gain it and its final groove. Finish rightwards at the top.

Umbo D'Jingo   140 feet   Very Severe   4c   (29.5.72)
Start in a small hollow just right of the blocks at the lowest point of the cliff. Climb the steep groove and crack on the right to the right-hand end of the brambly ledges. Trend right over salad to a crack on the left side of a loose

pinnacle, and from here go back left to reach the right-hand groove. Climb this by its left-hand crackline.

Upslope a pair of short, wide cracks converge at a tree at 20 feet underneath a vegetated ramp which slopes up to the right.

Starfinder 135 feet Very Severe 4c (15.3.70)
Climb shattered grooves left of the tree to reach the ledges, and move up thorny cracks to join *Umbo D'Jingo* at the pinnacle. From its top, move up to a ledge, and then swing left under vegetation to cracks in the right of the final groove.

Press the Panic Button 135 feet E1 5a (12.2.84)
Some good moves up the bulging arête compressed between unpleasant and worrying climbing.
Take the left-hand crack to the tree, and then go easily left to the toe of the ramp. Skirt thorn bushes above and trend left up steep cracks to reach the ledge of *Starfinder*. Gain a ledge on the right; then make steep moves on the left side of the bulge to a ledge. Finish by trending leftwards past suspect projecting blocks.

Mustang 135 feet Hard Very Severe 5a (2.5.70)
Follow the previous route to the first of its steep cracks; then step back right to a ledge under a groove. Sustained moves up this lead to a small ledge, from where easier grooves pass some worrying blocks.

The Crack 135 feet Severe 4a/b
Worthwhile for the upper section.
Climb the right-hand of the cracks to the tree, and then go left and up the ramp to a ledge. The wide crack on the right leads to a ledge, from where a step back left over flakes gains a groove. Finish leftwards.

Twenty feet right of *The Crack*, above a pathside boulder, is a deepening groove leading to a tree at 35 feet.

★Papillon 130 feet Hard Severe 4b (4.72)
At last something with not too much botany on it!
Climb the groove to the tree, and then step left to the left-hand of two cracks. Climb this to a ledge (junction with *The Crack*) and go right to the finishing-groove.

To the right a horizontal ledge runs under a clean expanse of rock to join the rising path at its right-hand end. This wall contains a number of grooves and cracks all of which give sustained climbing for their respective grades. The arêtes in between demand care as the rock is generally not above suspicion. For the first three routes, belay on the left end of the ledge or from the path below.

Sundowner   130 feet   E2   5c   (1.3.70)
The leftmost groove is both poorly protected and insecure, having a
number of suspect holds in run-out situations.
Climb the open groove past a rusting peg to reach, with a sigh, a good
solid jug (hidden peg on the left). Somehow gain the ledge on the left and
continue carefully leftwards to reach an easier finishing-groove.

Mercury   130 feet   E4   6a   (18.9.84)
The vague groove-line between *Sundowner* and *The Don* gives sustained
and serious climbing on fragile and explosive flakes.
From a ledge, gain and climb the steep groove past two pegs to exit
slightly left. From the ledge above, trend up left to finish.

The next route takes the more pronounced central groove.

★The Don   100 feet   E2   5b/c   (1.3.70)
A tough little number. A smattering of loose flakes detracts from what
would otherwise be excellent technical bridging.
From the left end of the ledge, climb up to a small ledge below the groove
proper. Sustained bridging past a peg gains a welcome ledge on the left.
Step back right (exposed) and trend right under vegetation to finish.

Jezebel   125 feet   E3   5b   (7.8.90)
Another bold route on suspect flakes – not a life-enhancing experience
even if side-runners are used!
From 30 feet up *Piercefield Grooves*, step left to the arête between it and
The Don. Climb the wall to a peg and gain a second peg (*RPs*) with
difficulty (beware unfaithful flakes). Continue carefully to a ledge on the
right and finish up a small corner behind a block.

Piercefield Grooves   130 feet   E2   5b   (17.9.76)
Below and right of *The Don* is a shallow, open corner – start on the path
below this.
Gain the corner directly from the path and follow it to its end in overhanging
rock. Move right to a crack (*Sinew*), then up and left to a ledge. Step left to a
groove; then move up and left to another groove. Finish up this.

★Sinew   140 feet   Hard Very Severe   5a   (28.2.70)
Right again is a slanting crack, which steepens before reaching a ledge on
the right.
Follow the crack to the ledge and step back left to a groove. This and its right
wall are climbed to an exit left of an obvious projecting block on the skyline.

Above the right end of the horizontal ledge is a deep hand-crack.

Aerial Combat   130 feet   E3/4   5c   (16.3.77/7.10.79)
Opinions vary from E4 6a and a 'bag' to E3 5c and worthwhile; but be

warned! – the peg is unusable and the bulge is in poor shape.
Follow the hand-crack, and its left-hand offshoot, to a detaching ledge
below a bulging wall. Surmount the bulge to a larger ledge and continue
to the projecting block, before finishing up easier ground as for *Sinew*.

★Fibre 140 feet   Very Severe   4c   (1.3.70)
Steep, satisfying climbing which maintains interest almost to the top.
Follow the hand-crack (or the wall/slab to its right) to a ledge on the right
(belay possible). Another groove leads past a ledge to twin cracks and a
jammed block under overhangs. From atop the groove, go rightwards to a
small tree and continue up the slabby wall above.

Purple Haze   130 feet   E2   5b   (18.4.70)
A technical central section leads to insecure, vegetated climbing above. Start
15 feet right of *Fibre* below a short, wide groove containing a large flake.
Climb the groove and the crack on the right to ledges below the obvious
smooth groove. Climb the groove, with a move up the right arête, to reach
broken cracks, and trend right to finish as for *Green Symphony*. The original
finish was described as stepping right at the first peg to an overhung niche
but this has proved impossible to find.

Green Symphony   140 feet   Hard Severe   4a
Start as for *Purple Haze*.
Climb the groove, and then make a long rising traverse rightwards up
various cracks to reach a groove above a large detached block. Follow this
to a vegetated ledge on the left; then finish up loosening cracks to a tree.
Variation
Brown Coda   Very Severe   4a   ‡
From part way along the traverse of the parent route, take a wall and
crack to gain the vegetated ledge. Earthy, loose, and unpleasant.

Left Wing Girdle   300 feet   Very Severe   † ‡   (30.6.71)
This is not likely to have been climbed recently or, indeed, since the first
ascent, but is described for the record. The first ascensionists' description is
used and no technical grades are available. It may well be that parts are
unclimbable owing to rampant vegetation.
1 50 feet.   Climb *Strike* and belay on a good ledge above the crack.
2 70 feet.   Move right past a large oak tree to belay on *Centinon*.
3 35 feet.   Cross the small amphitheatre, move up 10 feet, and swing
right to belay below the final pitch of *The Crack*.
4 40 feet.   Descend 10 feet to a large ledge; move right (crux) and then
up via a large, loose block (peg runner) to a belay on a small ledge above
The Don/Sinew.
5 45 feet.   Spiral down a loose wall to a belay on *Fibre*.
6 60 feet.   Climb up 5 feet; then make a difficult move right to join *Purple
Haze* just above its crux. Finish up this route.

RIGHT-HAND CRAG

To reach this crag, follow the initially level track rightwards from the small quarry towards the Eagle's Nest viewpoint. This path zigzags through wood-land until the crag can be glimpsed across a scree fan on the right. Ignore this view, unless heading for the *Vanguard* area, and continue up the track, past the next handrailed section, before bearing right to the left-hand section of the crag. It is also possible to gain the Left-Hand Crag by heading down and left from the end of the handrail.

The crag is bounded on its left by a gully called, not surprisingly, *The Gully*, and is divided, roughly in its centre, by the dirty chimney of *Decoy*. Further right, after a vegetated section, is a small flat clearing, beyond which the crag continues down and right to peter out in looser, more vegetated ground. There is currently, and sensibly, no climbing allowed outside of the section delineated by *The Gully* on the left and *The Day of the Triffids* on the right.

The Gully   70 feet   Very Difficult
This can prove a useful descent route. Above and left of a fallen yew tree the steepening gully gives slightly better climbing than appearances suggest. Avoid the last steep step on the right.

Lyon   100 feet   Hard Severe   4b   (17.9.76)
A slight route which is becoming overgrown. Start just right of *The Gully*, above the left end of the fallen yew.
From a small pinnacle go left, then right across a detached block to ledges on the right. Finish to the left of a large flake.

To the right a ledge runs across the wall, terminating under the continuous crackline of *Trial*.

★Trial   75 feet   Hard Very Severe   5a   (5.7.70)
The obvious jamming-crack above the fallen yew pulls no punches – unless you use the crack on the right as well. A slapped wrist, and the removal of a technical grade if you do.

Old Smokey   80 feet   Hard Very Severe   4c   (3.4.84)
Really just a variation on the jamming theme of *Trial*.
Climb the wide groove to the right-hand end of the ledge; then finger-jam up the right-hand crack to join *Trial* after 20 feet. Finish as for that route.

To the right is a descending series of three equally-spaced yew trees standing 10 feet out from the base of the crag.

★Mecca   75 feet   E2/3   5c   (15.9.76)
Steep, fingery crack-climbing relents to a precarious groove.
Climb the groove below the right side of the ledge, just left of the first yew, and continue with difficulty onto a small ledge. Trend leftwards, with

interest, up thin grooves to finish left of a large tree.

★Suncrush 80 feet   Hard Very Severe 5a/b   (28.2.70)
Directly behind the second of the three yews is a groove/crack-system leading to an overhung niche.
From the niche, layback boldly up the flake crack on the left to reach easier cracks leading past a square block to the top.

Elan 80 feet   E2/3 5c   (1976)
A bit of a stopper this, being sustained and awkward.
Start as for *Suncrush* but step right almost immediately to the crack on the right. Follow this to a ledge and continue up the groove above until forced to finish up *Cadillac*.

★Cadillac 100 feet   Very Severe 4c   (14.2.70)
After *Questor*, the most popular route on the crag and, therefore, suffering from wear.
Behind the second yew a crack-system leads past a diagonal flake to an impasse at an overhang. From here, traverse left to a ledge, and then go up and back right to a junction with *Pilgrimage*. Take the groove on the left and finish rightwards.

Pilgrimage 110 feet   E2 5c   (8.9.76)
Unnerving climbing in its lower half leads to better (i.e. easier) climbing above. Start as for *Cadillac*.
Climb across a steep, unprotected wall to a crack on the right or, better yet, reach this point from *Questor* – 5b overall and a grudging star. Move back left to a small jammed flake in the base of a corner and up this, through a cracked bulge, to small ledges. Follow easier cracks in the wall above, the arête on the right, or a combination of the two to finish.

★★Questor 110 feet   Very Severe 4b   (14.2.70)
Undoubtably the crag classic, although now a little polished, and it may seem tough for the inexperienced. [Photo p.65.]
The long groove just right of the third yew runs out a little below the top of the cliff into an easy wall.

Christian 100 feet   E2 5b   (1976)
A contrived line with little to recommend it.
Climb *Questor* for 20 feet until a step right can be made to a small ledge; then cross suspect, shattered rock leftwards to a blind crack. Awkward moves (to avoid *Questor*) up this crack allow the arête on the right to be reached. Trend up and left to finish.

Andrea 100 feet   E3 5b/c   (30.8.70)
Start 15 feet right of *Questor* below a short, shallow groove.
Gain this and then leave it, as the continuation groove is even more loose

and flaky, for a ledge (*Christian*) on the left. Climb up and into the bare groove above, and exit this on the left.

The following four routes have been rationalized a little to improve their independence – they do, however, share a common theme of improving climbing and an intimacy of holds and features.

Phoenix   110 feet   Hard Very Severe   4c   (15.2.70)
Good steep climbing with just enough seriousness and exposure to warrant the grade.
Climb the wall 5 feet right of *Andrea*, past some suspect, flaky rock, to a corner and ledges on the left. Finish steeply up a crack on the right.

★Zulu   100 feet   E2   5b/c   (13.4.72)
The thin crack 5 feet right of *Phoenix* leads to a mantelshelf onto a ledge. Continue up the fine groove left of the flying arête to finish up the groove of *The Firebird*. Deduct an E point for moving left or right at the mantelshelf.

Edge of Insanity   100 feet   E4   5c/6a   (17.4.84)
Bold all the way unless steps are taken, left or right, into adjacent routes for protection, rests, or even escape.
Climb the wall, on suspect holds, between the cracks of *Zulu* and *The Firebird* to a ledge. Climb a very shallow groove and then the flying fin, trying to avoid the routes on either side.

★The Firebird   100 feet   Hard Very Severe   5a   (28.2.70)
Start just left of *Decoy* below a thin crack, behind yet another yew tree. Some suspect flakes on the first wall lead to worthwhile climbing above.
Climb the thin crack to a sloping ledge on the left, and step right to surmount the bulge into the fine groove-system above.

President Raygun   100 feet   E4   5c/6a   (29.10.83)
Improving climbing from a very poor, bold, and insecure start.
Climb the wall just left of *Decoy* to a peg, and then up using suspect rock on the right to a second peg. Move right into *Decoy* and, from the top of its chimney, step back left onto the wall to a third peg. Continue, still with interest, up cracks to finish.
Direct Start (E4/5 † 1991-2): climb the lower wall, without deviating onto the chimney of *Decoy*, utilizing a side runner.

Decoy   100 feet   Severe   4a   ‡   (11.4.70)
Now very overgrown, and therefore questionable at the grade, this is included only for historical completeness. Climb the dirty chimney (peg runner) to exit left.

The crag now falls away under vegetation to re-emerge at a small clearing, under a conspicuous groove-system, and below an overhang at 60 feet. In between are four routes which have all become overgrown and have not been climbed by the author.

Wyvern   100 feet   Very Severe   4b   ‡   (5.5.74)
Forty feet right of *Decoy* is a thin crack.
Climb the thin crack and overhang to an earthy ledge. Continue up the obvious cracks on the right, which trend left to a large pinnacle. Finish via scrappy ledges.

Tizer Grooves   100 feet   Very Severe   4b   ‡   (16.1.76)
Start at the obvious clean-cut groove, about 25 feet right of *Wyvern* and to the left of a yew tree.
Climb the groove to a ledge on the right. Step right and climb to an overhanging crack which leads to the top.

Sting   100 feet   Very Severe   4b   ‡   (1971)
Start at a crack beside a yew tree, 20 feet left of the small clearing.
Climb the wall on the left of the crack and traverse left to a ledge. Climb up to a steep wall and finish by the corner on the right.

Apricot   100 feet   E1   5b   ‡   (9.5.70)
Rumoured to have been climbed within living memory. Start at a broken, diagonal flake in the wall to the left of the clearing.
Climb the flake and then cracks to a groove. Traverse right for a few feet and climb up past a bulge before moving back left into the groove. Climb the groove to exit right.

★Vanguard   80 feet   Very Severe   4c   (18.4.70)
A few steep moves above and below an easier section of suspect rock make this route worthwhile.
Climb the left side of the central groove to easier ground on the left. From the top of a large pinnacle finish steeply up a groove.
Direct Start (E3 6b 1986): rather pointlessly, gain the easier ground directly.

Above the central groove is a (still) collapsing overhang which gave the original finish to *Collapse Point*.

Collapse Point   80 feet   E1   5b   (13.10.81/26.11.95)
Climb the central groove to its end; then trend up and left to a shallow corner. Climb this, and exit leftwards to easier ground.

What's Gone Is Gone   80 feet   E3   5c   (24.1.88)
Deriving in part from the original *Collapse Point*, this route still contains much suspect rock in its upper third.
Climb the groove; then continue directly to the roofs. Long reaches off flaky holds allow the roofs to be passed to a tree which is prising the crag apart. Finish up to the right, or lower off sucking on your heart.

★Shaft   80 feet   E1/2 5b   (13.4.72)
Worthwhile for the steep and pumpy top groove.
Climb the wall 10 feet right of *Collapse Point* to blocks at 30 feet, and
continue in the same line to gain the groove. Climb this to good holds at
its top.

★Klute   80 feet   Very Severe 4c   (10.4.72)
The attractive lower crackline, 15 feet right of the central groove, leads past
two small ledges to the more vegetated, but still worthwhile, upper crack

Blood Bank   80 feet   E3 5c   (1979)
Loose rock, dusty rounded breaks, a vegetated ledge, and a friable upper
wall render this route virtually unjustifiable!
Take an under-protected wander up the buttress to the right of the clearing
to a thorny ledge; then move right to join *Cardiac*. Continue up this for 15
feet and then trend leftwards across the wall to finish – again poorly
protected.

Transfusion   80 feet   E1 5a   (24.1.88)
The hardest part of this route seems to be avoiding adjacent routes. Start
below the left arête of *Cardiac*.
Climb the arête, with a tricky move over the first bulge, to the large ledge
of *Cardiac*. Finish up or reverse back down *Cardiac*.

★Cardiac   90 feet   Very Severe 4b   (31.8.70)
Worth seeking out, although a little polished in places.
The obvious corner/groove, above a tree close to the crag, is climbed via a
large ledge to a continuation groove. Swing left under a tree to finish.

Close to the Edge   120 feet   Very Severe 4b ‡   (3.1.76)
A pointless route, rather fortunately lost to encroaching vegetation.
Climb *Cardiac* for 40 feet; then traverse left for 40 feet to a dead
tree-stump on *Vanguard*. Continue going left and, somehow, find the finish
of *Sting* amongst the undergrowth.

Every Trick in the Book   60 feet   E2 5c   (8.9.87)
Slightly bold wall-climbing leads to dubious flakes. A controversial route
originally employing preplaced gear and a bolt lower-off – both now
stripped.
Climb the wall 10 feet right of *Cardiac* to a short crack. Move right, then
left through the overhang, breathing gently on the large flake, and keep
left under vegetation to finish.

The Day of the Triffids   90 feet   Hard Very Severe 5a ‡   (1979)
Yet another route requiring a chainsaw. Start 15 feet right of *Cardiac* below
a tree embracing a block.
Climb through vegetation to gain the tree and yet more vegetation above.

Violater   150 feet   E2   (26.10.76)
Hardly a full-blooded girdle at all really, with little new climbing; perhaps
worthwhile if you've done everything else.
1 70 feet 5c. As for *Elan*, climb the groove for a few feet before stepping
right to climb the groove and crack above to a ledge. Traverse right
(*Cadillac*), and then move up right to a ledge.
2 80 feet 5a. Traverse right across three groove-systems to reach a fourth
just left of the flying fin of *Edge of Insanity*. Finish up this groove (*Zulu*).

Two routes have been climbed on the cleaned wall to the right, and therefore
lie in the forbidden zone – please do not repeat them or undertake any other
routes in this area as this could threaten the access agreement. **Don't Ask
Me** (90 feet Very Severe 4b † 1986) starts on the left of the wall, trends right
past a tree, and then climbs direct. **I Don't Know** (100 feet E1 5b † 1986)
starts at the bottom of the wall, climbs the leftward-trending crack to move
around the overhang, and continues straight up.

WYNDCLIFFE QUARRY
This is the roadside quarry about 400 yards 'upstream' from the woodland
carpark opposite Wyndcliffe itself. The crag is surprisingly well sheltered and
quickly becomes a sun-trap at the first hint of a blue sky; it is also the first place
in the Wye Valley to dry after rain. An ideal spot, amidst the depression of the
winter months, for convenience climbing and the comfort of good protection.

UPPER LIFT
The main feature of the Quarry is its Upper Lift, which rises gradually in height
from 20 feet up to about 50 feet as the climber traverses the vegetated platform
from right to left. Most of the cliff is in an appalling state, having suffered great
torment at the hands of the quarrymen. The rock does, however, improve
dramatically at its left end, where an attractive orange sheet provides the focus
of interest to date.

Canine Crack   50 feet   E1 5b †   (23.9.90)
This takes the prominent, straight crack in the right side of a projecting
arête at the left extremity of the upper tier. Start at the foot of the crack by
the symbol K9 painted in red.
Follow the crack to a rest where it eases in angle at two-thirds height.
Finish straight up (crux) to where an evil finishing-move gains an armful of
veg and good tree belays above.

Bogger Bob   50 feet   E3 6a/b   (25/30.9.90)
The large orange sheet sports an eye-catching, central crack. Enjoyable
climbing with plentiful protection makes this compulsive viewing. Start 40
feet right of *Canine Crack*.
Climb the crack to a rest at mid height, and continue with increasing
difficulty to the crux: either finish up the crack or (harder) climb the wall
immediately right to gain the *in-situ* abseil station (two pegs).

Hong Kong Garden   60 feet   E4   6b †   (23.11.91)
A right-to-left line across the orange sheet of *Bogger Bob*; thin and
technical towards the end, but safe. High in its grade. Start 9 feet right of
Bogger Bob.
Climb straight over the bulge in line with a thin and then shattered crack to
gain the foot-ledge and twin bolt runners on *Shin Gi Tai*. Move diagonally
leftwards on good holds to the crack of *Bogger Bob*; then tiptoe leftwards
above the lip of the bulge and take the difficult wall via a hairline crack
(bolt runner) to reach a finger-jug (peg runner). A short incipient groove
leads to a single-bolt belay (good *Rock 4* placement available).

Shin Gi Tai   50 feet   E4   6a   (23.9.90)
A sustained, well-protected pitch gives meaty climbing up the bare face
and dog-legged crack immediately right of *Bogger Bob*. Start at the foot of
the small arête 15 feet right of *Bogger Bob*.
Pull up the arête and step left to a sloping foot-ledge at 12 feet. Climb the
wall above past a pair of bolt runners to a small ledge, and reach right to
place good nuts in the crack. Make a hard move up the crack to stand on
the ledge, and then continue more steeply (further good runners) to where
an awkward long reach left attains the *in-situ* abseil station (two pegs
shared with *Bogger Bob*).

LOWER LIFT
The Lower Lift comprises a short, rectangular-shaped wall of steep, partly
calcited rock situated above a large open platform. Although the wall is short
it offers some worthwhile technical climbing. The easiest descent is by abseil
from the bush atop *And the Crowds Went Wild*.

The wall at the left-hand end of the platform sports some curious breccia
formations. At its base lies a distinctive, twisting hand-crack (*Still Stuck on You*).

Empire and Revolution   40 feet   E1   6a/b †   (15.4.93)
This climbs the obvious wall to the left of *Still Stuck on You*.
Gain the first bolt easily; then make hard moves to the second. Finish direct.

Still Stuck on You   40 feet   E2   5a/b   (14.10.90)
Climb the twisting crack to the break. Pull carefully onto the wall above
(bolt runner) and continue on good positive holds to the top, finishing very
slightly right. *Friends*, nut, and sapling belay.

Finishing Touch   40 feet   E1   5c   (6.8.91)
Start 10 feet right of *Still Stuck on You*.
Climb the wall with difficulty to the break. With protection from a bolt
runner (and *in-situ* sling) above, pull onto the upper wall and follow good
spaced holds to the large ledge and *Friend* runners. Step across left and up
to the belay of *Still Stuck on You*.

Sweet FA   40 feet   Hard Very Severe 4c   (14.10.90)
This climbs the heavily calcited line immediately right of *Finishing Touch* to reach the large ledge and *Friend* runners. Traverse left to belay as for *Still Stuck on You*.

The Corrective Party   30 feet   E2 6a   (19.5.91)
Start 10 feet right of *Sweet FA* where the number 14 is painted in red on a flake at head height.
Make some hard and 'naughty' moves up the thin wall to gain the break. A bolt runner protects some easier but still awkward climbing to ledges above. Belay up and right on nuts.

Mr Whippy   30 feet   E3 6a   (6.8.91)
Just to the right of *The Corrective Party* lies the unrelenting and rather sterner *Mr Whippy*.
Climb directly up the wall past a bolt runner, a peg runner, and a further bolt runner to the top. Nut belay.

At the centre of the right-hand part of the wall is a shallow orange-coloured corner at mid height.

Diminishing Returns   30 feet   E3 6a   (19.5.91)
Start 5 feet right of *Mr Whippy* beneath the left edge of the right-facing corner. Take a direct line up the wall past a bolt runner to a peg runner and a good nut placement. Finish diagonally right to gain a ledge. Nut and *Friend* belay up on the left. Scramble up leftwards to exit.

Miss Whiplash   30 feet   E4 6a   (19.5.91)
A steep dynamic pitch up the bare wall immediately right of *Diminishing Returns*. Start 7 feet right of that route.
Climb directly up the wall and move slightly left by the second of two bolt runners to reach bigger holds. Pull over onto the ledge above and belay up to the left using nuts and *Friends*. Scramble up leftwards to exit.

And the Crowds Went Wild   30 feet   E2 5c   (14.10.90)
Varied and attractive climbing on the calcite flows on the right side of the wall. Start 3 feet to the right of *Miss Whiplash*.
Some boulder-problem moves off the ground gain better edges and a small *in-situ* thread runner. Pull up to a good finger-pocket; then step across left to a rest and *Friend* and nut protection. Continue steeply to a peg runner and move up to the ledge above. Bush and nut belay.

Shadows Run Black   30 feet   E2 5c/6a   (19.5.91)
Boulder out the wall just right of *And the Crowds Went Wild* to the good finger-pocket. Bridge easily right to a bolt runner and a comfortable rest; then follow the 'scabby' calcite runnel to the top. Scramble up to exit.

Wintour's Leap

OS Ref 542 961

Wintour's Leap rises from the east bank of the River Wye one to two miles north of Chepstow, where one of the river's final meanders has cut deep into the southern end of the limestone ridge, creating a line of cliffs starkly massive, steep, and overhanging; yet, in perfect contrast, the setting is idyllic. The crags lie within the Lancaut Nature Reserve, which is a Scheduled Site of Scientific Interest; and on the B4228 Chepstow to St Briavels road, which runs along the top of the cliff, is situated the village of Woodcroft, with *The Rising Sun Inn* at its centre.

The river here is tidal, and an offshoot of the Severn Bore is often observed working its way up to spend itself in the incipient ox-bow lake below The North Wall. However, the cliff-base is well above the bank and unaffected by the tides. Much of the face was quarried around the turn of the century during the building of the Avonmouth Docks, but activity has now entirely ceased.

The name derives from the legend that Sir John Wintour, hotly pursued by Parliamentarian soldiers in 1642, 'galloped in desperation over the shelving precipice, escaped unhurt on the ground below, and got away by swimming the river' to the Royalist stronghold at Chepstow Castle. This improbable tale need not be discounted entirely, as quarrying and geological development may have altered structures radically. At least, in 1976, Peter O'Toole staged an impressively successful emulation in a BBC TV film of *Rogue Male*, where the Wye Valley deputized effectively for Bavaria, and more recently a leader took a (real) 200-foot free fall into the branches of a tree at the bottom and climbed down it unhurt. However, deep-water solo enthusiasts are not advised to try either of these variations upon their activity!

A CRAG TOUR

The easiest and most revealing descent on a first visit is by means of a path leading down through the woods from a little beyond the grassy parking-area (see page 13), marked by a yellow arrow. Fork left just past the remains of lime kilns (another yellow arrow) and emerge below the ruined chapel of St James, Lancaut, from where there is a fine panorama of the whole cliff. The path runs leftwards along the river bank, and over or round a mound beneath

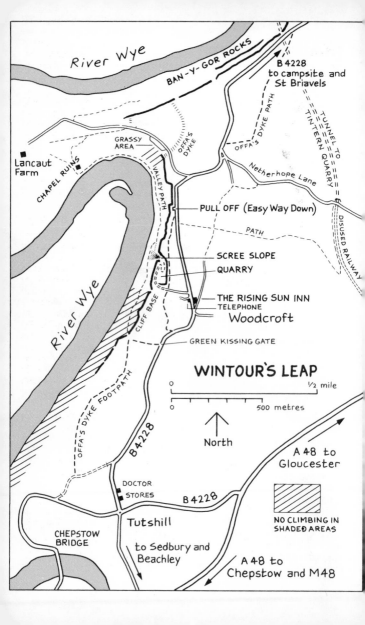

a grotty little quarry. It then enters the woods and rises slightly before falling again abreast of the first major rock-face (not always clearly visible). After passing two block structures on the left, it finally leaves the bank and rises to a wider, level stretch.

The North Wall Area is reached first, and will be the choice of those looking for the warmest, driest, cleanest rock and a good selection of quality routes in the VS - E4 range, mostly of a technical, face-climbing nature. From the top of the above-mentioned rise from the river bank, turn sharp left into denser woods on a side track. Almost immediately in front of you is a low, level earth ridge. The track just left of this leads up left away from it and out into the open, below the three-tiered wall. The North Buttress is behind trees on the left, and The Angel's Tower shores up the right edge, its prominent cave, 'The Angel's Eye', inviting curiosity. Round to the right of its vertical arête, Tower Wall extends into Narcotic Corner, at the junction with the next complex.

The Great Wall, being scrappy, broken, and vegetated, has fewer devotees. A handful of routes work through cleaned (if not clean) corridors, so many parties will find one or more worthwhile at their grade; and in fine spring and early summer months the array and scent of wallflowers, aubretia, and other limestone plants can be positively exotic. The upper half of the left-hand section is known as Compost Wall after its central and original line. Turn off the Valley Path at the top of the short rise, as for The North Wall, but go straight ahead along the crest of the level earth ridge. From just left of its far end, a small path leads up, steeply at first, and then leftwards over rock and grass bands. Below the left margin of Compost Wall is Small Wall, with two quite good little routes and some atrocious ones. Either scramble directly up to it from the clearing right of Narcotic Corner, or turn left off the steep section of the Compost Wall path above the earth ridge and traverse horizontally over the grassy terraces. For the right, and main, half of The Great Wall, go down right off the end of the earth ridge, turn left, and follow a path up rightwards beneath the rock. The highest point is the foot of the normal Easy Way Down.

The Central Bay is the nursery area, laced with Mods and Diffs. In the bottom right-hand corner, below a large ledge on the Easy Way Down known as The Broadwalk, is a 40-foot black wall, often used for abseiling instruction and top-roping (4c-5b). As well as by the Easy Way Down and via the Great Wall, the Central Bay can be reached directly from the Valley Path by taking the steep track up right of the earth ridge, though the start is now somewhat obscured by fallen trees.

The South Bay covers the complete grade spectrum and most of the routes are of a markedly higher quality than those of the Great Wall. Traditionally the preserve of those seeking the classic V Diff and Severe *Central Rib* and *Bottle Buttress* routes, the bay now also offers some sporting VSs, some sport E1s and E2s, and a selection of harder test-pieces. The path under the Central Bay rejoins the Valley Path at the top of the latter's second short rise. The routes left of *Bottle Buttress* start immediately on the left behind the trees. *Bottle Buttress* and *Central Rib* are best reached by a short uphill track from the main path some forty yards further on.

Deceiver Buttress (South Buttress) is 150 feet high and church-door shaped. It separates the South and Far South Bays, and is approached rightwards from the same point. Above its apex the bays merge to form a broad, easy-angled ridge taken by the upper section of *The Beginner's Route*. The central section has some horrendous rock and, although from time to time routes on the flanks and the lower band are done on (appropriately deceptive) 'good' or 'apparently sound' rock, many sooner or later end up on the ground.

The Far South Bay is concave and compact. The range, style, and quality of the climbs are very similar to those of the North Wall, though the aspect is somewhat different. Certainly the excellent *Zelda* at HS should be on everyone's check list, whether it be to lead, second, or solo. A little past the clearing below the South Bay, and thirty yards before the remains of a kissing-gate, the right-of-way branches off right down the bank (yellow arrow again). Exactly opposite this is a small track winding through the woods and up to the foot of the unmistakable corner of *Zelda* in the centre of the bay. Down on the left is a pit where all the routes left of *Zelda* start.

The Great Overhanging Wall, always known as GO Wall, is the cliff's showpiece. It is certainly one of the most impressive pieces of inland rock in southern Britain. The huge central corner-line of *King Kong* is climbed at HVS, and a high-level traverse goes at the same standard. These apart, only the Extreme climber has any place here. There are some hard technical pitches, but it is the overall bulk, the outrageous overhangings, and the wildly sensational exposure that make up the special flavour of the wall. A ridge from the remains of the kissing-gate leads straight to the nerve-centre at the groove of *King Kong*. *Kangaroo Wall* is a few yards to the right, while above and right again the big groove of *The Jackal* leads up to the roofs near their widest point. A number of the routes start from a pedestal half way up the right-hand side of the wall. To reach this, continue along the main path until it runs out onto the scree slope. Climb the slope's left margin, and on the left at the top scramble up 10 feet to a vegetated ledge, which runs leftwards to The Pedestal, overlooking the rest of the wall.

The Woodcroft Quarry above Fly Wall provides a useful means of access and descent, especially for GO Wall and Fly Wall. The aspect is unattractive and much of the rock is of poor quality; yet this has not daunted some of the area's afficionados, and a few lines have been done.

Fly Wall lies beyond the scree slope. Lesser in height than the other areas, it compensates in the variety of climbing it offers. Again there are no easy routes, but a wealth of experience is available at all grades from VS to E5, and the wall is surely the most accessible rock in the Wye Valley. The left-hand end is less than 100 feet high and the climbs are more of an athletic, outcrop type. With rightward progress the top rises, the ground falls away at the base, and the overhangs become bigger and denser. At the top of the scree slope (where you turn left for The Pedestal) turn right up the path through the buddleia, and shortly a small rock arête immediately ahead is encountered: this is the northern end of Fly Wall. Fork right on the downward scree path through the buddleia just below the face. A couple of gaps on the left give access to the first climbs, and then there is another fork. To make a close-up inspection of the rest of the wall, keep left (the right branch goes down to meet the Valley Path). In fact, if only a wide-angled view of the wall is required it is not necessary to climb the scree slope at all. Instead, turn right at the yellow arrow opposite the Far South Bay. This, the true Valley Path, drops down the bank, crosses the foot of the scree slope, and passes below the buddleia mass under Fly Wall.

The end of the buddleia and the return of the deciduous woodland mark the boundary of Fly Wall. South of this point, all the rock, and the woodlands on either side of the path at both top and bottom of the cliffs are privately owned, and all climbing and access (except the path itself) are **strictly forbidden** (please read the note about this on page 56). From here, then, keep to the path, the only public right-of-way, which rises steadily beneath The Forbidden Wall, passes under a wooden foot-bridge, and emerges on the B4228 below the village.

OTHER DESCENTS

1 The normal Easy Way Down on The Central Bay is a convenient descent for all areas except Fly Wall and the right-hand end of GO Wall. From a promontory above and left (facing the river) of the parking pull-off (see page 13), descend over easy ledges keeping generally in to the right (still facing out). Near the bottom is the long flat ledge known as The Broadwalk; from just below and beyond its far end, steps lead down to an apex of paths below the obvious short corner which is the start of the first two Corner Buttress routes. Turn sharp right for The Great Wall. For The North Wall, go straight down towards the river on the steep middle track: just on the right where it levels out is the earth ridge; turn right immediately past the foot of this. The left-hand track from the apex runs back beneath The Central Bay and drops to meet the Valley Path below the South Bay, whence the remaining southerly areas can be reached.

2 The Woodcroft Quarry path is best for Fly Wall and GO Wall especially for routes which start on The Pedestal. The Quarry is reached (on foot – do not attempt to drive up even if the gate is open) by a small gated lane almost opposite *The Rising Sun*, immediately right of Woodcroft Close. At present the Quarry is fenced and gated, but can be entered at a junction of two fences by the north corner of the old building. Follow the path round, and then down, with Fly Wall below on the left. After a Z-bend the path narrows and descends through a little gorge. At the end of the ridge on the left, turn sharp left down a scree track into the buddleia for Fly Wall. For the GO Wall Pedestal, ignore this and keep going straight ahead to the large rotten arête forming the junction between GO Wall and The Woodcroft Quarry. Just beyond the arête, scramble 10 feet up to a vegetated ledge, which runs leftwards to The Pedestal. To reach the foot of the cliffs (other than Fly Wall), descend the right (facing out) margin of the scree slope (this is immediately below the big arête) and turn right into the woods to meet the Valley Path.

3 Another descent, especially good for the south end of Fly Wall, could become increasingly useful if the quarry path were closed or if problems in Woodcroft necessitated parking nearer Tutshill. This is to take the 'Guided Tour' in reverse. Go through a kissing-gate (the lower of two green iron gates marked 'Offa's Dyke') at the bottom of the (road) hill below *The Rising Sun* and follow the path (ignoring the stile into the field on the left) down below The Forbidden Wall.

ACCESS CONSIDERATIONS

1 The quiet little village of Woodcroft is not oriented towards tourism and has no interest in promoting it. Please do everything possible to preserve cordial relations with the local residents. They are generally very friendly and helpful, but there are various ways in which difficulties can result if the due courtesies are not shown. Especially, avoid inconsiderate parking and noisy, indelicate, or unhygienic conduct at the cliff-top, all of which either lies within or is very exposed to private ground and the public gaze.

2 The whole of the climbing area and the woodlands below are situated within the Lancaut Nature Reserve and are an SSSI. Considerable care and restraint are therefore required in treatment of the environment so that the Reserve's Management Committee can maintain their tolerance towards climbing in view of the greater numbers using the cliff. Camping and the lighting of fires within the Reserve are not permitted.

3 Climbing is permitted only from the North Buttress to Fly Wall. Climbing is not allowed on the Far North Wall (the banded overhangs recessed above and left of the North Buttress and not easily seen). The Forbidden Wall lies just south of Fly Wall (the boundary is marked by the change from buddleia to deciduous woodland) and further downstream are some smaller cliffs. Access to all these and to the woodlands above and below them (save the Valley Path itself) is **completely forbidden**. The landowners of these cliffs consider (with some justification) that climbing on their property (especially in view of the extreme proximity of the cliff-tops to the houses) would result in an intolerable violation of their privacy and interests. Further, both areas are sensitive ecologically and valued as undisturbed wildlife habitats by the Nature Reserve Management Committee.

4 The landowner at the top of The North Wall continues generously to permit climbers to exit via his garden (see note in that section); this is not a right-of-way, and the situation could alter if the ownership changed.

5 The owner of GO Wall permits climbing throughout the year but has requested that no exits across his land at the top are made during the months from April to September inclusive. To this end the BMC have installed abseil bolts down three lines from the penultimate belays. The short and generally poor-quality finishes technically remain available during the winter months, but as they will be little used they are likely to become revegetated and the abseil descents will become the norm. The landowner concerned has, however, made it clear that he does not wish this restriction to result in any unreasonable risk to climbers and would regard it as waived in cases of real need. Please do not take advantage of this loophole except in such case.

6 The Woodcroft Quarry has again recently changed hands. It has so far not been possible to ascertain who has bought it, what use is to be made of it, and whether climbing or access will be affected.

PROTECTION

Wintour's has always been something of a law unto itself. In the early days, the only available protection was by pegs and trees. Until the mid 70s, you were advised to carry your own selection of the former with you on routes right down to Very Difficult. The earliest machined nuts (MOACS, *hexes*, straight-sided wedges) were certainly usable in places though they were not ideally suited to the generally poor cracks (the real breakthrough came later with *Rocks*).

The cracks meanwhile were being destroyed both by excessive use of pegs ('if you've got them, you might as well lighten the load by using them') and by repeated insertions and extractions; while those who tried to climb more ethically using the newer nuts where possible were often compromised by finding essential belays missing, and others who liked to prepare their new routes decently found themselves robbed. Such problems were largely solved by the cementing in place of what were considered essential or reasonable pegs. With these, the advent of *Rocks*, *Friends* and *RPs*, and the growth of saplings into sturdy trees, many of the traditional routes became reassuringly protected.

In the 80s, bolts gained increasing acceptance, and many were placed on a rather liberal interpretation of the minimalist principle. There are few out-and-out sport routes, but quite a number which make generous use of fixed gear of one kind or another.

Intelligent assessment of the shorter routes will allow equipment carried to be reduced to the necessary minimum, but on all the longer and traditional routes a good rack should be carried even where a number of fixed pieces are mentioned in the description. *Rocks* are ideal; *Friends* and *RPs* are useful on the E-grade routes; plenty of quickdraws are always needed for fixed gear and wire extensions; and a few longer slings should also be taken for trees and overhangs.

Please refer to the section on **fixed gear** in the general introduction (page 16) and note especially the ways in which it may relate to the grades given.

ROUTE DESCRIPTIONS

The 1987 guide attempted to ensure that *everything* was fully recorded so that posterity could assess what was and was not worthwhile; Rob Kingston took this process to the ultimate in his *1990 Update*. Now that things are clearer (except where obscured by vegetation!) it is time to attempt to judge the wheat from the chaff (as well as being necessary to keep the book to manageable proportions).

To this end, a fair amount of rationalization has taken place. Eliminates and unimportant lines are given outline descriptions only, written up as variations or even dismissed. In the past, unfair advantage has been taken of the numerous friendly opportunities that Wintour's Leap offers for traverses and stepped diagonals. Though a few of the former are of real quality and validity, as on any crag, and climbs like *Animal Magic* and *Rheingold* seemed like a good idea at the time they were done, the proliferation of such routes constitutes a nuisance and a waste of space in the guidebook.

THE NORTH WALL AREA   (Diagram pages 80-81)

The North Wall itself is gently recessed between the North Buttress on the left and the Angel's Tower on the right, and is split by two large horizontal terraces known as the Main Ledge (at 50 feet) and the Great Ledge (120 feet higher). The Lower Tier is smooth and vertical with only one obvious line of weakness, *Symplex*, between its ends. The Middle Tier is slightly more broken and lies back just a little. The Upper Tier has a heavily vegetated band, though this does not materially affect the climbing.

Climbing on The North Buttress is confined to the bottom 140 feet, which is steep and has some weird rock formations (above are vegetated ledges); while The Angel's Tower, also steep, contains some of the hardest routes of this area and is crossed by the most impressive sections of the two upper girdle traverses. Two parallel open corners, *Gryke* and *Left Hand Route*, divide the Buttress from the Wall, the latter being separated from the Tower by the shallow wooded gully taken by *Right Hand Route*. Round the arête to the right, Tower Wall extends from the Tower into Narcotic Corner, where it meets Compost Wall and Small Wall.

In the 1977 and 1987 guides the author followed a deliberate policy of combining pitches on the different tiers to create 'complete' long routes. This resulted in much unnecessary duplication and complicated interweaving. Changing tastes and the nature of subsequent development seem now to require a different approach, and all the pitches that were conceived and climbed as separate routes are described separately: hence the disappearance of *Great North Wall Route* and the restoration of the original pitch names. This makes things easier for those who wish to concentrate on the short, harder pitches of The Lower Tier or the more adventurous but less technical lines on the middle and upper tiers, or to mix and match at will; and it enables the climbs to be ordered more in line with the left-to-right principle. The author has indulged in some minor creative adjustments to the nomenclature to avoid confusion.

There are only a few hard routes in The North Wall Area and no really easy ones, but this section of the cliff will provide many days' absorbing entertainment for the middle-grade climber. Most of the difficulties are of a technical rather than strenuous nature, though the harder pitches are sometimes fingery and the long routes call for both mental and physical stamina. Most of the rock is clean and most is sound. Angled more towards the south-west than the rest of the crag, it gets sun much of the day and, except for some lines on The Lower Tier which suffer seepage, dries quickly after rain; it is certainly the best place to climb in the morning.

The North Buttress delineates the northern extent of permitted climbing. The Far North Wall around to the left, visible from certain viewpoints, is not open to climbing (see page 56).

THE APPROACH

1 Coming from the ruined chapel on the approach from the north (page 51), turn left at the top of the permanent rise from the river bank: the low, level earth ridge is just ahead; take the path immediately to its left, which trends leftwards over, under, and round some fallen trees, past the junction leading to *The Angel's Eye*, to the clearing below the wall.

2 From the foot of the Easy Way Down (page 55), take the middle track, which descends steeply towards the river; where it flattens out, the earth ridge is on the right; go just past the foot of this and turn right up the path beyond.

3 From the scree slope (page 55), follow the almost level path below GO Wall and the South Bays; there is a short drop and another short level section; turn right to the earth ridge 25 yards past a large boulder in the middle of the path (before the next drop, which goes down to the river bank). Take the path just left of the ridge.

LANDMARKS

Along the base of the wall is a long trough. *Gryke* and *Left Hand Route* start just above the left-hand end of this. A third of the way along the trough is the semi-circular overhang of *Tarnhelm*, with the obvious vertical break of *Symplex* just to its right. *Nibelheim* and *Right Hand Route* start in the pit at the right-hand end. *The Angel's Eye* starts in the large square corner in the steep right arête of the Tower. Narcotic Corner, at the far end of Tower Wall, is reached by a short scramble.

WAYS OFF

1 From the top: this lies through a private garden. Although it is not a right-of-way, the owner is helpful and friendly, but he has requested that exit points into his garden be limited to the existing three: at the tops of *Left Hand Route*, *Right Hand Route*, and *Duncan's Dilemma*. It is essential, therefore, that all the climbs should be finished exactly as described and that no new exit points are created. On reaching the garden from *Duncan's Dilemma* or *Right Hand Route*, turn left and go up to the top fence (where *Left Hand Route* finishes); then turn right and go along this fence (which forms the boundary

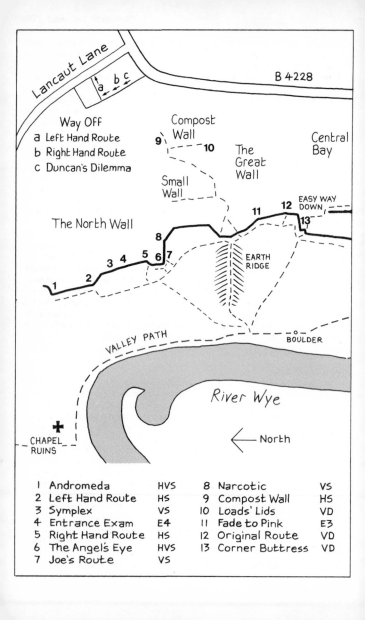

Lancaut Lane

B 4228

a b c

Way Off
a Left Hand Route
b Right Hand Route
c Duncan's Dilemma

Compost Wall

The Great Wall

Central Bay

Small Wall

The North Wall

EASY WAY DOWN

EARTH RIDGE

VALLEY PATH

BOULDER

River Wye

← North

CHAPEL RUINS

1	Andromeda	HVS	8	Narcotic	VS
2	Left Hand Route	HS	9	Compost Wall	HS
3	Symplex	VS	10	Loads' Lids	VD
4	Entrance Exam	E4	11	Fade to Pink	E3
5	Right Hand Route	HS	12	Original Route	VD
6	The Angel's Eye	HVS	13	Corner Buttress	VD
7	Joe's Route	VS			

between two gardens) to exit through the sliding wooden bars into Lancaut Lane. Two discreet signs provided by the BMC point this route. Please do not enter the upper garden.

2　For the North Buttress routes there is an obvious peg and bolt abseil station at the top of *White Feather*, easily reached from the other full-length routes. It is best to keep very slightly right down the line of *Yesterday's Dreams*; this avoids contact with the rock most of the way as well as tangles with the trees.

3　From the Narcotic Corner routes, do **not** climb the short wall above the earth bank, but walk up left (now very overgrown) below it to emerge at the final easy chimney of *Right Hand Route*.

4　From the Great Ledge (where several of the routes do finish and most others can), the most straightforward way to the top is by pitch 4 of *Right Hand Route*. There is also a Moderate scramble, described under The Upper Tier section.

5　Many climbers prefer to abseil from the Great Ledge, but there are no properly constituted abseil stations. As all abseils are down popular routes (also crossed by the traverses), please be **sure** that there are **no climbers below**.

THE NORTH BUTTRESS

No routes were climbed on The North Buttress before 1979, and until mid 1986 there were but three. This may seem strange, as it is easily accessible, the rock is generally good and holds little (by Wye Valley standards) vegetation, it tends to stay dry in rain better than most other sections of the cliff, and the three routes provided worthwhile middle-grade climbing, albeit by somewhat devious lines. The reason lay in the compact nature of the rock, making both nut and conventional peg protection problematic; and the only useful tree is the first *Andromeda* belay. However, once the drill became 'acceptable', pegs and bolts flourished, and within eighteen months almost every hold was booked, sometimes double-booked.

★Andromeda　150 feet　Hard Very Severe　　　　　(11.4.81)
Good strenuous and technical climbing on rock that is better than it looks. Protection, though mostly sound, is rather widely spaced on the first pitch, though two additional pegs have been placed since the first ascent; still high in the grade. Start at cleaned ledges 10 feet right of the awful corner at the extreme left margin of the rock.

1　80 feet　5a.　Pull up carefully on high blocks and swing left onto a small ramp; follow this up left to a ledge almost in the corner. Move up (peg runner with *in-situ* tape), step out right, and climb the short wall on small holds to mantel onto a long narrow foot-ledge (peg runner) with the aid of a crystal pocket. Traverse right awkwardly past an overhang (peg runner, and another on *Turmoil of a White Ocean* low on the right); and then make technical moves up a sandy red scoop (peg runner at top). Traverse right again for 10 feet (hands at peg-level or a little higher) to large holds; then climb down to a small tree belay and nut placements (ignore the bolt below).

2　70 feet　4c.　Climb straight back to and up the groove above (peg runner under its capping roof). Pull out left and move up; then step right and very slightly down across the top of the groove (now possible to clip the peg runner on *Agamemnon* round to the right). Climb up, bearing left to a short deep crack (peg runner just above), and continue up to a sapling below a split nose. Hand-traverse right along an overhung ledge, and move up to a grass ledge with a peg and bolt belay. It may be preferred to use these to protect the second and then go easily right on the ledge to the abseil station.

The next three routes take the somewhat broken rock left of the upper pitch of *Andromeda*; the point of divergence could be reached by a start up the latter or *Turmoil of a White Ocean*, but that used by *Script for a Jester's Tear* is most logical in terms of line and grade; the overall lengths and grades given assume this.

Avant Garde   130 feet   E2   5b   (8.7.90)
Climb to the peg runner at the top of the red scoop, and continue straight up for 10 feet to a small overhang (peg runner above). Move over and up a few feet; then traverse left below some vegetation and go up to a V-groove (peg runner). Climb this and the wall above (two peg runners) to a ledge (peg runner), and finish boldly up the wall on the right-hand side to a thread and peg belay.

The Secret Garden   130 feet   E2   5b †   (8.7.90)
Climb to the peg runner at the top of the red scoop, and continue straight up for 10 feet to a small overhang (peg runner above). Climb the short white wall to a peg runner at its top, and move up to the right of a small triangular overhang (peg runner of *Script for a Jester's Tear* out right). Move up the corner on the left for a few feet, then back right and up the centre of the wall (thread), and over the small roof direct to ledges. Climb the short grey wall above (peg runner) to the peg and bolt belay of *Andromeda* on the right.

Script for a Jester's Tear   130 feet   E2   5b   (21.12.86)
A big, sustained pitch with some committing sections, though escape onto *Andromeda* in the upper half is often too easy. Apart from two or three wires low down and a large *Friend* below the finish, protection is by *in-situ* gear: take lots of quickdraws. Start 10 feet right of *Andromeda*, below a small yellow groove.
Climb straight up on sloping holds to a break and pull round left to climb the small yellow groove. Hand-traverse back right (peg runner of *Turmoil of a White Ocean* on the right) and follow *Andromeda* up the red scoop above (peg runner). Go diagonally right to the edge of the wide break (peg runner) and climb the right arête of the black wall (peg runner out left at top). Continue up trending slightly right (peg runner) until just below the short deep crack of *Andromeda*. Move back left onto the wall and surmount a small overlap using a superb sidecut. Pass the right edge of the

top overhang, clip the peg runner of *Andromeda* on the right, and reach
the sapling below the split overhanging nose. Hand-traverse rightwards
and then go up to the ledge (as for *Andromeda*) and a peg and bolt belay.

Turmoil of a White Ocean   60 feet   E3   6a   (27.11.86)
Only 30 feet of independent climbing: steep and fingery with some long
reaches. Start 10 feet right of *Andromeda* below a small yellow groove.
Climb straight up to a short layaway edge at 20 feet (bolt runner), and
make blind and difficult moves to reach good holds (peg runner in a
crystal crack above). Follow *Andromeda* up the red scoop (peg runner),
traverse right, and step down to the tree and a bolt belay. Abseil off.

★**Sweeter than Sugar**   50 feet   E3   6a   (8.7.86)
A delightful short route, though somewhat compromised by *Agamemnon*;
bold and technical climbing on excellent rock. Start 30 feet right of the
awful corner at the extreme left margin of the rock, and directly below a
borehole in a short rib.
Move up a slight corner and then almost immediately right to climb a faint
rib to a tiny shelf. Climb up past a bolt runner using nice finger-edges and
a pinch out right in order to gain better holds. Easier climbing (possible to
clip the *Agamemnon* peg round to the right) leads to the *Andromeda* tree
and a bolt belay. Abseil off.

★**Agamemnon**   120 feet   E3   6a   (2.12.87)
The most substantial of The North Buttress routes. It is possible to finish at
the tree and bolt at 50 feet, but the easier (E1) climbing above is still well
worthwhile.
From a ledge, climb a short open groove just right of *Sweeter than Sugar*
(peg runner on left) to the roof, and pull up left into a tiny niche (peg
runner). Move up and out right (bolt runner) and climb the wall (*in-situ* wire
and peg runner) to reach an undercut. Pass just right of the bolt and tree,
and climb the bulging rib (peg runner on the right) to a good ledge and
peg runner. Move up left to a higher ledge, and climb straight up through
a small groove (two peg runners) to the ledge. Belay at the abseil station
on the right.

Electra   120 feet   E3   6a   (9.12.87)
Start in the centre of The North Buttress under an overhang capping a
short yellow wall, 5 feet left of the groove of *White Feather*.
From a raised block, climb directly up to a small overlap (peg runner
above) and reach the break just below the roof (bolt runner above). Make
a difficult move over and climb a large scoop to the next roof (bolt above
again). Pull over and then climb rightwards to better holds. Get onto the
overhanging blocks above and move up left to climb a short broad groove
to a ledge and peg runner. Traverse 5 feet right and go through the long
roof at a small gap. Continue directly up the wall (peg runner) and over
the triangular bulge to a sapling; finish just left. The abseil station is above.

The two original routes of the North Buttress, **Alluvium** (14.10.79) and
Antediluvian (9.7.80), have been totally superseded by the more recent
routes. The former climbed the groove of *White Feather*, with the peg for aid,
and took a wandering leftward diagonal line to the top of *Andromeda*. The
latter avoided the roofs of *Achilles* by a very bold (no bolt then) finger-traverse
left; it finished further right in the large loose groove.

★White Feather   120 feet   E3   5c   (4.3.87)

Varied and sustained climbing, but adequately protected and low in the
grade. Start at a thin crack leading to the groove which bounds the left
edge of the sandy wall that extends to the right edge of the buttress.
Climb directly to and up the groove and pull onto a ledge on the left (two
peg runners). From the left end of this ledge, climb steeply up the wall and
cross the rotten band carefully but easily. Continue up a small groove
above to a constricted position under the first roof (peg runner, *in-situ* wire
out right, and good *Rock 6* placement above and left). Pull over onto the
slab and move up boldly to the main roof (peg runner). Go through a
slight weakness, and climb the headwall more easily directly to the abseil
station.

A very tight eliminate, **One Time One Night** (130 feet E2 5c 7.7.90) takes
the double overhangs just to the right of *White Feather*, reached from the first
section of the latter by the groove in the rotten band, and followed by a
rightward finish to the top of *Yesterday's Dreams*. Good climbing nevertheless.

★★Yesterday's Dreams   120 feet   E2   5C   (31.1.87)

This has deservedly become a popular route: a hard, technical crux low
down and a superb roof higher; always well protected (take a full set of
Rocks). [Photos: front cover and opposite.] Start below the centre of the
sandy yellow wall in the lower right section of the buttress.
Move up to the break and climb the centre of the wall (bolt runner) to
reach a narrow ledge just right of the top of the groove of *White Feather*
(peg runner just above). Layback onto the ledge and climb up steeply for
20 feet to stand on a ledge by a second peg runner. Step left and climb the
open groove to the big roof (peg runner below, bolt runner above). Use a
small pocket in the roof and a slot in the lip to gain the first of a series of
jugs which form a ladder up the headwall (*in-situ* thread out right and peg
runner) to a narrow ledge and two bolts which originally formed the belay;
it is now more usual to continue to the abseil station.

Achilles   120 feet   E2   5c   (4.12.87)

A fairly direct and independent line up the right edge of the buttress, but
both rock and climbing quality begin to deteriorate at this point. Start at a
borehole 15 feet left of the groove of *Gryke*.
Climb up rightwards to a platform on the edge and make a thin move to
gain a finger-ledge (bolt runner above). Climb up just left of the lowest roof
to under the triangular overhang, and use the crack on the left to move

Yesterday's Dreams (E2) North Buttress, Wintour's Leap
Climber: Chris Craggs   Photo: Craggs col.

Questor (VS) Right Hand Crag, Wyndcliffe
Climber: Jim Rubery Photo: Chris Craggs

round this onto ledges above (peg runner). Step right and climb the arête onto the overhanging blocks (peg runner). Move up left onto a constricted ledge (bolt runner of *Yesterday's Dreams* out left) and climb directly up the steep wall (*in-situ* thread) until just below grassy ledges. Go diagonally left past the original two-bolt belay of *Yesterday's Dreams* to the abseil station.

THE TRAVERSES

The North Wall Area lends itself to some excellent traversing of greater variety and technical interest than the usual limestone bedding-planes. These routes can, however, cause problems to other climbers on busy days, so try to pick your time.

The Ring 450 feet Hard Very Severe (5.7.82)
A girdle of the complete North Wall Area at a slightly higher level than *The Angel's Girdle*: a more logical line than the latter, but rather less consistent in quality, though still a rewarding outing with an exciting final pitch across the crux of *Acid Test*.
1 130 feet 5a. Climb pitch 1 of *Andromeda*, and continue up its second pitch to belay at the peg above the short deep crack.
2 90 feet 4b. Move 10 feet right on a good ledge, go up to a sapling, traverse right to a large green ledge, and (as for *Gryke*) climb diagonally right across its back wall to a yellow peg runner; traverse right again to the arête (*Suspect Device*) and climb it for a short way to a ledge; then go easily right across *Left Hand Route* and past the flake of *Exodus* to a two-peg belay on *Central Route* under an overhang.
3 100 feet 4b. Move right and step up (peg runner above); then keep going more or less horizontally right to a peg and nut belay in the large gully of *Right Hand Route*.
4 50 feet 4a. Move round the edge and step down onto a slab; hand-traverse right, and then continue more easily rightwards just above the Tower niche and past an *in-situ* thread to an exposed overhung platform on the arête with a peg belay.
5 80 feet 5a/b. Hand-traverse right under the overhangs to ledges and a small tree (semi-resting position at a hole half way and a hidden peg runner slightly right above the overhang); go diagonally right across the little black wall to the top peg runner of *Joe's Route*, step right across the gap, up, and then back left to finish up a break in the wall with a superb little jug at the top. Belay behind the huge boulder on the left; the Great Ledge is just above.

★★★The Angel's Girdle 360 feet Very Severe (15.3.75)
Absorbing and rewarding climbing with good situations all the way: as fine a route of its type and grade as is likely to be found on British limestone. It does not follow a monotonous natural break. Double ropes are essential.
1 80 feet 4b. *Left Hand Route* pitch 1.
2 110 feet 4b. Climb up 10 feet behind the spike (peg runner) and move round the bulge to the right, keeping low, to a peg runner on *Central*

Route. Step up right (second peg runner on the same route) and then traverse right with increasing difficulty to a good white foot-ledge, which ends abruptly at a gap. Reach across to clip a peg runner. Step up on the left and traverse right past the peg (this at chest height) until directly below a sapling. Pull up to it on a superb jug and continue rightwards more easily past a flake and a gap (ignore the *Swansong* belay bolts above) to a large tree belay.

3 40 feet 5a. Descend a few feet to the top of the crack of *Right Hand Route* and traverse right with one very technical move past a peg runner until good holds lead diagonally right to the two-peg belay in the Tower niche.

4 130 feet 4c. Reverse the top of pitch 2 of *The Angel's Eye* as follows: step up and traverse right to the arête past an *in-situ* thread and karabiner (backrope for second); descend for 20 feet until able to move right round to a ledge and two peg runners; then make one step down. Make a difficult move across the gap (hidden peg runner): it is easier to go two moves down the chimney and back up the other side. Continue horizontally until forced up 10 feet at three holes; traverse right again to join *Joe's Route* below the short wall and peg runner; and finish up this: climb the wall to a ledge (peg runner) and the next wall on larger holds left of the little groove to the third peg runner; using holds above the overhang, step right across the gap and mantelshelf up short corners to a peg belay in a small bay just below the Great Ledge.

A fine expedition giving nearly 1,000 feet of VS and HVS climbing can be made as follows. Climb *Andromeda* pitch 1, traverse across The North Buttress (starting with the base of the belay tree at foot-level) to a peg runner on *Yesterday's Dreams*, move round (loose) to the belay on *Gryke*, and climb up and rightwards to the first belay of *Left Hand Route*. Now follow pitches 2, 3, and 4 of *The Angel's Girdle*. Then reverse pitches 5, 4, and 3 of *The Ring* (not appreciably harder in this direction). Go directly to the Great Ledge by pitch 3 of *Tarnhelm*, and finally to the top by *Bacchanalian*.

The next three routes, also, could be linked to make a grand low-level crossing from the extreme left of The North Buttress to the arête of The Angel's Tower, though the link between the last two needs cleaning (not much) and a belay in *Right Hand Route*. Such an outing would have greater appeal if it were more impressively situated. Nevertheless, the climbing is always of sustained technical interest and much of *A Calm Sea*... pitch 1 and of *Cross-Examination* is excellent.

★A Calm Sea and a Prosperous Voyage   160 feet   E3   (4.12.87)

Take a set of wires and a lot of quickdraws.

1 110 feet 6a. Climb *Andromeda* past the first peg runner to reach the ledge (second peg runner), but don't move up onto it. Instead, go rightwards across the buttress, without appreciable deviation up or down, to a small foot-ledge and a two-bolt belay on the far edge (three more peg runners, two bolt runners, and an *in-situ* wire, all on the vertical routes but not in that order). It is possible to descend to the ground to avoid the hanging belay and it is not hard to climb back up.

2 50 feet 5c. Traverse awkwardly into the groove of *Gryke* (peg runner), around the rib of *Punch and Judy* (peg runner), and into *Left Hand Route* (peg runner above). Continue across *Exodus* to the semi-circular block, swing round it to the crack of *Symplex* (peg runner), and climb straight up to The Main Ledge. If continuing along *Cross Examination*, it is again best to descend to the ground to belay.

★**Cross-Examination** 100 feet E3 6a (9.11.86)

Protection is mainly from pegs on other routes, so take plenty of quick-draws. The bolt on *Priory Road* has reduced the commitment somewhat.

Climb *Symplex* until level with the semi-circular block on the left (peg runner). Step right and finger-traverse past a peg runner on *First Degree* to stand on a small ledge on *Entrance Exam*. Move up to clip the peg runner of that route, step back down, and finger-traverse past the bolt of *Priory Road* to the peg runner on *Highway to the Dangerzone*. Move right again to a good rest (on *We've Got the Honeymoon Blues Too* – peg runner above). Descend slightly and continue the traverse (peg runner on *Apology*) until a final thin section leads to a peg runner and a finish up *Swansong Prelude* (peg belay on the Main Ledge). (If continuing along *Event Horizon*, move right from the last peg runner under the overhang of *Nibelheim*, and (pending the appearance of anything better) belay on a tree above in *Right Hand Route*.)

Event Horizon 80 feet E2 5c (11.4.87)

Either, from the preceding route, step right to the edge and traverse above an obvious ledge on the front of the Tower, or reach this ledge directly from below and move up and right (peg runner on *Claire*); then traverse right again, across the corner of *Xenophobia*. Technical moves across the red wall (peg runner) reach *Big Brother* (peg runner above). Continue rightwards (peg runner) past a ledge and peg runner on *Strange Little Girl* to *The Angel's Arête*, and climb this to its two-bolt belay. Absolutely the end of the 'event'! Abseil off.

Verdict (100 feet E2 5c 4.3.87) traverses the upper break of The Lower Tier leftwards from just above the second peg runner on *Swansong Prelude* to a finish up *First Degree*. Strenuous for those too short to reach footholds in the middle break. *Friends* useful, especially a 3.

THE LEFT-HAND SECTOR

The North Wall proper starts where the rock emerges from the trees and begins to look like a full 300-foot cliff. The long parallel open grooves of *Gryke* and *Left Hand Route* are obvious features. These routes start on the platform just above the left end of the long trough below the main part of the wall.

Cantassium (70 feet E1 5c/6a 2.12.87). From the foot of *Gryke*, reach the two-bolt belay on *A Calm Sea and a Prosperous Voyage* and make a technical move up past it. Jump back and lower off, or continue (doing your best to avoid the worst bits of rock) past three peg runners to a ledge and a two-peg belay on the right.

Gryke   130 feet   Hard Very Severe   †† ‡   (12.63)
The left-hand of the two parallel open corners between the North Buttress and the North Wall. Loose and vegetated, and best climbed (if at all) in a dry spell, otherwise the pockets are unpleasant. Nut protection is sparse but the pegs still appear sound. It is possible but rather pointless to continue by a right-trending line to the left-hand end of the Great Ledge (no appreciable difficulties except brambles). Start as for *Left Hand Route*, above the left end of the trough below the wall.
1 60 feet 5a. Climb 15 feet to a small ledge, as for *Left Hand Route*, and straight on up to the disintegrated roof (two peg runners). Move left under the remains of the overhang to gain a foot-ledge and reach good holds above. Pull over and continue more easily, slightly right at first, to a comfortable stance and a two-peg belay at the foot of a groove.
2 70 feet 4c. Climb the groove, using holds on the right wall, past two peg runners to a large ledge on the left. From the centre of its back wall, climb diagonally back right onto the original line (yellow peg runner) and continue up to a higher ledge on the left and tree belays. Abseil from here.

Punch and Judy   180 feet   E2   (7.11.87)
Unlike its immediate neighbours, a really worthwhile route. It takes the steep, slim wall right of the *Gryke* corner. Low in the grade.
1 60 feet 5b. Climb 15 feet to the ledge as for *Gryke* or, more interestingly, by a thin crackline 3 feet to the right. Make steep moves up the short blunt rib (peg runner) and follow a little slab to a platform on the left (old peg runner). Climb directly up juggy rock to a ledge just right of an overhang (peg belay, best augmented by the two-peg belay of *Suspect Device* out right).
2 120 feet 5b. Step up left into the centre of the wall (peg runner above) and climb it past a small overhang to a bulge (peg runner on the left). Pull over on sensational jugs, climb a short groove (peg runner out left), and step back right. Continue straight up (peg runner) and use a flake to gain a ledge. Climb another slight groove on the left, gradually easing, to more ledges and the final moves of pitch 2 of *Left Hand Route*.

Suspect Device   170 feet   Very Severe   (29.6.80)
The arête left of *Left Hand Route*: technically easy for the grade but poorly protected on the second pitch. The middle section is becoming vegetated.
1 70 feet 4b. Follow *Left Hand Route* past the overhang. When a few feet above the level of the Main Ledge (on the right) go diagonally left to ledges and two peg belays in a niche at the foot of the arête.
2 100 feet 4b. Climb the arête by its right wall until a sloping platform is

reached. Move round left to mantel, and fix a thread on the right. Climb the next section by the left wall to ledges. Go diagonally right (across the line of *Left Hand Route*) into the open corner, and follow this direct (a reachy move) to the Great Ledge. Tree belay on the right.

★★**Left Hand Route**   300 feet   Hard Severe   (29.6.58)

Good rock and climbing to the Great Ledge; the third pitch is poor (though easy), but *Bacchanalian* (immediately above the stance on the Great Ledge) provides a good alternative just within the grade. Start above the left end of the trough below the wall, directly below the groove of *Gryke*.

1 80 feet 4b. Climb 15 feet to a small ledge; traverse right to its end, and then go up on polished holds to a peg runner under the overhang. Make a strenuous pull up onto the block on the left, either by direct mantelshelf or (better if you can) by reaching excellent holds on top of the overhang. Bear slightly right above and then go straight up past a borehole to an iron spike and a two-peg belay well above the level of the Main Ledge. (Various direct starts to the pitch are possible, usually a little harder. The overhang can also be taken on its right.)

2 90 feet 4a. Climb the wall behind the spike past a peg runner at 10 feet, and bear left to a niche behind a sapling (peg runner). Move up and mantel onto the left wall, step left, and continue up for 40 feet to a good platform. Go left under the overhang, which is climbed by shuffling your feet leftwards up a small sloping red ledge. There are two small trees above, but a further 20 feet of rope enable a more sound and comfortable tree belay on the Great Ledge on the right to be reached.

3 60 feet. Above the left-hand end of the Great Ledge is a broken, black, crystal corner facing right: climb steps on the left of this to a fallen tree. Continue, bearing left, over easy but vegetated rock to a cluster of trees.

4 70 feet. For access reasons, it is important not to deviate to the left of this line: move up onto an overhanging block and step right to a short wall; climb this and then more easily up an obvious broken line leaning right, or better on walls to its right. Tree belay on the left in the undergrowth.

Misplaced Childhood   50 feet   E3 6a   (19.10.86)

A fine little wall pitch on small but positive holds. Reach the start by climbing pitch 1 of *Left Hand Route* and continuing up its second for 40 feet to the niche behind a sapling (peg belay).

Climb the short corner above to a small tree and move right onto the wall (poor peg runner). Pull up right across the break, and climb directly up the wall, just right of the bolt runner, using a small hidden layaway in the right arête to make the final move (peg runner above). Finish easily to the Great Ledge and a tree belay. A better and purer alternative (E4 6b 1.92) is to climb directly past the bolt without using the right arête.

★**Exodus**   300 feet   E2   (6.7.83)

A nicely sustained and continuous line with good climbing mostly at the lower end of the E2 grade, though the loss of some holds on the first few moves has made these hard. The top pitches are well worth including. Start near the left end of the trough, immediately below a small pointed overhang.

1 50 feet 6a. Climb up with difficulty and get onto the overhang from its right. Continue straight on up (peg runner rather awkward to reach out left) to a bushy ledge, and then easily to the Main Ledge and a peg belay on the right in the back wall.

2 70 feet 5a. As for *Tarnhelm*, climb the narrow cleaned corridor above the belay past a sapling to a large hole at the foot of the bulge. Climb the bulge, slightly right at first, until good handholds are reached: here leave *Tarnhelm* by a short hand-traverse left. Climb the crack in the left side of the bulge to a small slab, and move out left on white rock under a long overhang (poor *Friend*). Climb over the left end of this (hidden *Rock 1*) and then more easily diagonally right to the two-peg belay on *Tarnhelm* and *Central Route* under an overhang.

3 60 feet 5b. Traverse left past one flake crack to a second. Make a strenuous but careful layback up this to reach a superb jug in the wall, and swing right past a peg runner to holds on *Tarnhelm*. Continue directly up past another peg runner and a sapling to finish up a short wall and crack just left of a crystal crack. Tree belay on the Great Ledge.

4 50 feet 5b. Move awkwardly onto the overhung pedestal behind the boulder on the right and climb straight up past a peg runner to stand on a ledge above. Traverse 10 feet right, feet in the lowest fault line, and climb a short scoop to a tree belay.

5 70 feet 5b. Climb over the overhangs (as for *Bacchanalian*) to a narrow grass ledge and a peg runner. Go diagonally left across the slab and then climb directly up the centre of the steepening wall past a second peg runner to the top. Protect the second with a poor runner in the undergrowth and move left to an adequate tree belay. Traverse easily off left to the top of *Left Hand Route*.

Tarnhelm   170 feet   Very Severe   (28.4.79)

Worthwhile for some varied and interesting moves but lacking consistency of quality. Start in the trough, at the obvious break of *Symplex*, and just right of a prominent semi-circular protruding block.

1 50 feet 4c. As for *Symplex*, climb the groove, move 5 feet right, pull up to a small ledge, and clip the peg runner above. Reach out for the block and swing round left in order to mantel onto it (failing the technique to do this neatly, a knee or backside may prove useful). Climb straight up the short wall above to the Main Ledge and a peg belay in the back wall.

2 70 feet 4c. Climb the narrow cleaned corridor above the belay past a sapling to a large hole at the foot of the bulge. Climb the bulge right of centre, pulling over into a small but developing groove, which is followed to a prominent overhang. Turn this on the right and continue, bearing left, to the two-peg belay under an overhang shared with *Central Route* (which comes in from further right).

3 50 feet 4c. Climb directly over the overhangs above the pegs and on

up the steep wall (two peg runners out left) until easier rock leads
diagonally left to a tree belay on the Great Ledge.

THE LOWER TIER

The smooth vertical wall above the long trough provides much of the hardest
climbing in The North Wall Area and it is quite possible to spend a whole
afternoon on its problems without going further than the Main Ledge. There
are adequate belays above all the routes and two bolts just right of centre.
The first route starts just *left* of *Tarnhelm* and was intended as a direct start to
it.

Powers of Persuasion   50 feet   E2   5b   (24.9.83)
Seriously under-protected now that the fault out left has disintegrated. Start
below the semi-circular overhang, and just left of the shallow groove.
Reach (or leap for) a high hold and pull up onto a ledge. Make thin moves
to gain the good left rim of the overhang and mantel onto it. Climb
straight up the short wall above to the Main Ledge and a peg belay in the
back wall.

Symplex   50 feet   Very Severe   4c   (13.7.58)
The upper crack can be greasy when not bone dry. Start just left of centre
of the wall where a ridge leads across the trough to the only obvious line of
weakness in the tier.
Climb the left wall of the shallow starting-groove. Hand-traverse right for 5
feet and pull up onto a small ledge. Reach a high peg runner and climb
the crack to a small tree. Belay on the peg on the left or the leaning tree on
the right at the back of the Main Ledge. (It is also possible to start by
climbing the crack 5 feet to the right directly to the small ledge – slightly
harder, but within the grade.)

First Degree   50 feet   E4   6c   (1.11.86)
A hard but worthwhile eliminate. Start at a small oak tree just right of
Symplex.
Fix a high runner in the tree and then climb desperately up the wall to its
left over a small roof to the break (without assistance from the tree). Step
up right onto the ledge on *Entrance Exam*, move back left onto the smooth
wall (peg runner), and climb straight up with a very long reach, finishing
on large but brittle holds.

★Entrance Exam   60 feet   E4   5b/c   (17.9.83)
Strenuous, sustained, and committing. [Photo p.96.] Start in the centre of
the trough below the wall, 10 feet right of the obvious break of *Symplex*.
Climb a small overhanging groove to a resting-position, and continue
straight up the wall on small holds, with marginal protection until a good
peg runner at 40 feet is reached. Move right and then climb diagonally
back left on improving holds to the Main Ledge and a tree belay (a harder
and more direct finish – avoiding the move right – is possible).

Priory Road   50 feet   E4 6c   (8.7.90)
The blank wall enticed for some time before the solution was found.
Make extremely technical moves up the wall right of *Entrance Exam* past a
muddy slot and a bolt runner to the break (*Friend,* and bolt runner on
Highway to the Dangerzone out right). Continue direct past another bolt
runner to the Main Ledge and a two-bolt belay.

Highway to the Dangerzone   60 feet   E4 6b   (1.11.86)
A fine technical pitch: sustained wall-climbing after a fierce
boulder-problem start (beware the old tree-stump!). Start 20 feet right of
Entrance Exam below a short groove.
Step up and leap for an obvious good hold at the base of the groove. Pull
up into the groove (bolt runner) and stretch for the break. Move left along it
to a slot just above (bolt runner); then climb directly up the wall (peg
runner) on pockets and edges to reach the upper break. Follow *We've Got
the Honeymoon Blues Too* up, left to a slight crack, and up to the ledge.
Peg belay on the right or the bolts on the left.

We've Got the Honeymoon Blues Too   60 feet   E4 6a   (18.3.84)
A good prelude to *Aqualung.* Start 10 feet left of the right-hand end of the
trough.
Climb directly up to a break (*in-situ* thread) and then diagonally left to a
buried peg runner on a faint rib. Climb the rib on a flake and another
buried peg runner just above. Reach another horizontal break and hurry
left to a slight crack for small wires before finishing direct to the Main
Ledge. Peg belay at the start of *Notung* on the right or the bolts on the left.
Variation
Apology   (45 feet E4 6a 2.3.86) is a direct version of the above. From the
thread, go straight on up the wall on calcite pockets and then thin holds (peg
runner) to the upper break. A final hard pull brings the Main Ledge in reach
(peg belay of *Notung* above).

★Swansong Prelude   50 feet   E2 5b   (11.2.84)
A fine sustained little pitch. The two pegs provide the only protection: these
are just adequate but certainly leave the climbing feeling quite bold. Start
in the pit at the right-hand end of the trough.
Climb up 5 feet where the gully meets the wall and reach out left for a
block in the first horizontal break (direct start 5c with dry boots).
Hand-traverse the block to a peg runner and climb directly up the wall past
the second peg runner to a peg belay at the right-hand end of the Main
Ledge. Continuation on page 75.

THE MIDDLE TIER
Here are to be found the main pitches: an excellent selection of middle-grade,
generally just-off vertical, wall climbs. Protection tends to be spaced but
reasonable.

The Main Ledge is most easily attained by climbing the first 50 feet of *Right Hand Route* and traversing left past an isolated tree to a step down. It can be reached, too, from the first pitch of *Left Hand Route* with a traverse right at 50 feet. Obviously, any of the Lower Tier pitches will also get you there. In the centre of the ledge a jutting nose almost bars paasage. Just left of this, close to the rock, is a leaning tree.

Two diagonals on the Middle Tier have been recorded: **The Valley Road** (150 feet Hard Very Severe 5a 24.5.88) goes from the start of *The Tap*, via the two-bolt belay on *Swansong*, to the finish of pitch 3 of *Right-Hand Route*; **Rheingold** (180 feet E1 25.3.86) goes from the *Swansong* belay peg, via the large angle on *Under a Blood Red Sky*, to finish above *Misplaced Childhood*. In fact, numerous exploratory forays of this nature could be made on the wall (provided there are no other climbers about), and adherence to a particular line is somewhat artificial. Neither route has more than an occasional independent move, though both offer the prospect of some exciting swings for the second!

Central Route   140 feet   Very Severe   (13.7.58)
Something of a misnomer as it is well left of centre; and careful route-finding is needed to follow the easiest line. Nevertheless, a pleasantly exposed climb at the lower limit of the grade. Start at the leaning tree.
1 80 feet 4b. From below the left corner of a box recess, climb diagonally left over grassy ledges to a small rib with brambles on its left. Move up to a stalactite thread and climb the rib taking care with the rock (the better holds are on the left). From a peg runner at its top, move right and up a short scoop (second peg runner). A large step up left reaches an easier diagonal line leading leftwards to a stance above one overhang and below another. Two-peg belay.
2 60 feet 4b. Traverse 10 feet right and move up (peg runner). Climb the steep wall above with another high step up left to a platform. A small corner to the right and a high mantelshelf lead to the Great Ledge. Walk left past the boulder to a tree belay. *Bacchanalian* is immediately behind and makes a good finish.

Rheinfahrt   140 feet   Very Severe   4b   (24.2.79)
A clean and reasonable route low in the grade, though in places the rock and protection are less than confidence-boosting. Start at the leaning tree. Climb up into the box recess and move out and across to the left. Traverse back right above (peg runner on *The Tap*) and then move up left to gain the shallow rounded groove-line. Climb this, going straight up past the scoop peg runner of *Central Route*, to a small roof at the break of *The Ring*. Swing right and step up to another peg runner on *The Tap*. Pull up on the left and follow a black overhung ramp to the right into a small bay. Exit to the Great Ledge. Peg belay slightly right in the backwall.

The Tap   130 feet   Very Severe 4c   (4.63)
Traditionally combined with *Symplex* and *Bacchanalian* to create '*Great
North Wall Route*': in good, dry conditions, a fine expedition worth a star.
From the leaning tree, climb up just right of and past the box recess to a
peg runner under a minute overhang. Swing round left before mantelling
onto the ledge and follow a small winding depression past three peg
runners (on the left, right, and left again) to a short steep corner. Climb this
and go straight up through a bay to a peg belay on the Great Ledge.

Under a Blood Red Sky   120 feet   E1 5b   (18.2.84)
A direct but eliminate pitch of no great merit. [Photo p.97.]
Climb up just right of the box recess to a peg runner under a minute
overhang (as for *The Tap*). Climb straight past the peg onto a larger
overhang above. Trend slightly right to peg runner (large angle in a deep
pocket – not easily spotted) at the foot of the bulge. Move up to a short
vertical slot on the right which takes a cluster of wires. Then climb the black
wall by layaways near its left edge (poor handholds and good footholds at
first, then the other way around) past a poor peg runner on the right to a
grassy ledge (use holds on the left to avoid bad rock on the last moves).
Continue direct for 40 feet to a bay: easier but no further protection. Finish
up the right wall of the bay to a peg belay on the Great Ledge: heroics on
the front wall to the right are inadvisable in view of the runout. (See page
77 for top pitches.)

Erda   130 feet   E1 5a   (11.4.80)
Harder and more committing than *The Tap* but equally worthwhile.
Climb up just right of the box recess for 20 feet to a peg runner (as for *The
Tap*). Traverse 10 feet right and go up to another peg runner under a small
overhang; climb boldly up past this until better holds lead to a ledge on
The Angel's Girdle (peg runner across the gap on the right and another,
higher, hidden under the bulge on the left). Climb up on the left with care
and step right into a small groove which splits the prominent bulge (this is
just left of the rounded reddish groove taken by *Notung*). Climb the groove
with difficulty to a narrow ledge (peg runner above) and then more easily
straight up the short wall and over ledges to mantel onto the Great Ledge
(tree belay). (See page 77 for top pitches.)

Lifeblood (50 feet E2 5c 19.5.88) is an eliminate, but with good moves and
mainly *in-situ* protection (three peg runners and one bolt). Start just left of
Notung and climb directly, via a small groove, to a large projecting block.
Mantel onto it and make some tricky moves to a narrow ledge (large angle
of *Under a Blood Red Sky* just left). Continue up any of the neighbouring routes.

★★★**Notung**   130 feet   E1 5a/b   (24.2.79)
Exhilarating wall-climbing: the quality is maintained throughout, and the
line is unusually (for the area) direct and independent. Be prepared for the
'under-protected feeling'. Start at a peg belay in the centre of the

right-hand half of the ledge.

Climb up onto the obvious pointed overhang 10 feet above (peg runner high on the left). Move slightly right, and climb up by two pockets (dubious peg runner). Make hard moves up left to gain an excellent crystal pocket and continue urgently, zigzagging slightly to use the best holds, to a shallow ledgy groove: in balance at last. Climb this delicately (peg runner at top) and exit left onto a white ledge on *The Angel's Girdle*. Step up and traverse right past the peg until directly below a sapling, and pull up to it on a superb jug. Climb the rounded reddish groove above, and layback neatly over its small roof. Clip a peg runner on *Erda* on the left and continue straight up the wall to its right. Climb a small, right-sloping groove and ramp, move up more easily on the left, and mantel onto the Great Ledge. Tree belay. (See page 77 for top pitches.)

★**Aqualung**   130 feet   E3 5c   (3.7.82)

Some good and exacting climbing, sparsely protected and high in the grade. Start at the *Notung* peg belay in the centre of the right-hand half of the ledge.

Climb two short boreholes above and just right of the belay to a thin break. Pull over the bulge on crystalline holds (possible to clip the *Notung* peg runner on the left) and continue direct on spaced holds to an overlap (peg runner, spurious bolt on right which may disappear). Make hard moves over this, slightly left at first, then right, onto a slab. Continue straight up to reach the left edge of the headwall taken by *Swansong*. Climb it (peg runner of *Swansong* tantalizingly out of reach 8 feet right) to easier ground and a tree belay slightly left on the Great Ledge.

★★**Swansong**   130 feet   E3   (26.6.82)

Splendid varied wall climbing: the top half of pitch 2 is immaculate, but serious. Start at the peg belay at the extreme right-hand end of the level part of the ledge.

1 60 feet 5b. Climb straight up just left of a short book groove onto the block at its top. Continue directly up a small black groove and pull over its capping roof into a recess. Climb the right rib for 10 feet and then swing onto the left rib to pull up onto the ledge above. Two-bolt belay just higher.

2 70 feet 5c. Climb up 20 feet (peg runner in the left side of the nose of *The Wrong Tap*), step left, and then climb directly up the steep black wall above, passing just right of a peg runner in its centre, to three cleaned ledges. From the right-hand of these, climb straight up to a tree belay on the Great Ledge. (See page 77 for top pitches.)

★**The Wrong Tap**   130 feet   Very Severe

Good value for the grade and well worth doing. Some of the blocks forming the corner on pitch 2 have fallen, but the difficulty is unaffected. The three pegs of the variation are within reach, which spoils the commitment of the top section somewhat. Start at the extreme right-hand end of the level part of the ledge at the *Swansong* belay peg.

1 60 feet 4b. Step up and climb the short book groove. Follow a slight crack which curves rightwards up to a sapling and mantel onto the ledge on its right. Move slightly right and climb straight up into a spacious bay with two belay pegs.
2 70 feet 5a. Climb up to the horizontal break (peg runner in the left side of the nose above). Surmount the nose rightwards. Move up right to a corner and climb it with care but no great difficulty to easy ledges and then the Great Ledge. Peg belay.
Variation
The Song Remains the Same   E1   (7.6.88)
2a 60 feet 5b. Good moves on excellent rock, but both neighbours are compromised by its proximity and pegs. Continue direct past the first peg runner and up the wall past three more. Minor variants in line and difficulty are possible.

THE UPPER TIER
The Great Ledge is a magnificent feature, extending all the way across The North Wall, turning a right-angle at The Angel's Tower, and continuing part way along the top of Tower Wall. Unfortunately, the rock above does not do it justice, though there are some worthwhile pitches.

The top pitches of *Left Hand Route* go up leftwards off the left-hand end of the ledge. Fifteen feet right is a good tree (at the top of *Central Route*) with the obvious left-facing crystal corner of *Bacchanalian* behind. On the right is a boulder in front of the overhung pedestal from which pitch 4 of *Exodus* starts. Right again is the peg belay of *The Tap*. Fifteen feet further right is the tree belay of *Erda* and *Notung*, at the start of the easy escape route; 25 feet further again is another tree, on *Swansong*. The peg belay of *Nibelheim* is in the backwall just left of where the edge of the upper wall intrudes upon the ledge; and the tree belay of *Right Hand Route, The Angel's Eye*, etc. is above and right of this.

Before climbing the pitches above the Great Ledge or abseiling back down, please read the 'Ways Off' section on page 59.

Bacchanalian   120 feet   Hard Severe   (6.66)
An unlikely-looking but worthy finish for *Central Route* or any of the others hereabouts.
1 40 feet 4a. Climb the crystal corner behind the tree to a ledge on the right at its top. Move as far right as possible and climb the short wall to a tree in the forest.
2 80 feet 4b. Climb the overhanging wall (despite appearance the rock is quite adequate) to a narrow grass ledge with a sapling and a peg runner above. Climb diagonally left across the slab (ignoring the *Exodus* peg runner 10 feet higher), and finish up a short corner to a tree belay. Traverse easily off left to the top of *Left Hand Route*.

Finishing Under a Blood Red Sky 120 feet Hard Very Severe (18.2.84)
1 50 feet 4c. Climb a discontinuous flake crack right of the peg belay to
a narrow ledge. Traverse 8 feet left and go up to a tree belay via concave
pocketed rock.
2 70 feet 4c. Move up through a slight recess on the left to a narrow
grass ledge and a sapling (peg runner of *Bacchanalian* on the left). Climb
the slab directly up to the large tree belay in two short technical sections
with a rest between. It is advisable to remain roped up for the final little rib
and the traverse off left along the ledge above to the top of *Left Hand
Route*.

An unnamed route (110 feet Hard Very Severe 4c 16.7.78) takes the wall just
left of the *Notung* tree belay. Swing left using the large brown pockets above
and climb the discontinuous flake crack (the one started up by the previous
route) to a tree in the forest. Continue over a short messy band and climb the
slabby wall on pockets and some friable holds, aiming directly between the
two trees at the top. Belay on the left-hand one (the upper and larger). A
poorly-protected pitch on some worrying rock. It is advisable to remain roped
up for the final little wall and traverse off left to the top of *Left Hand Route*.

Notung Forged 110 feet E1 (4.12.83)
A direct continuation to *Notung* and worth including.
1 40 feet 5b. Climb the wall behind the tree belay: good technical
moves with no meaningful protection (the crux is at 20 feet). Tree belay
above, below the final wall.
2 70 feet 4c. Move up behind the tree to a large thread and step up into
a hole on its left. Now climb vertical crack-systems up the slab, which
steepens to a wall at half height. A move left is necessary 15 feet below the
top to finish up the right side of a recessed rectangle (tree belay above). It
is advisable to remain roped up for the traverse off left to the top of *Left
Hand Route*.

A less satisfactory variation on the above (110 feet Very Severe 4c 10.12.83)
was climbed as a finish for *Erda*. Start just right on big holds and reach a small
platform, whence two thin moves reach grassy ledges and the tree belay. The
second pitch follows *Notung Forged* to the steepening and then trends left to
finish up the left side of the rectangular recess.

There is an escape route (Moderate) from this point on the Great Ledge.
Scramble diagonally right on large holds to a ledge. From near the right-hand
end of this, trend back left and go up through a gap in the vegetation. A path
with one rock step now goes up right below the headwall to the final easy
chimney of *Right Hand Route*.

Swansong Postlude 120 feet Hard Very Severe (18.2.84)
With the *Exodus* top pitches, the best climbing on the upper tier. Well worth
including in an ascent of the main route or doing on its own.

1 50 feet 5a. Climb the two-tiered boulder-problem wall midway between the two trees; then move left past a boulder to a gap in the vegetation and go up to a tree belay.

2 70 feet 5a. Move up to a large thread, as for *Notung*, and then step right. Climb the technical slab past a minute *in-situ* thread. Above, the wall steepens and then gently overhangs: climb it strenuously on large but not juggy holds directly to the top and a tree belay just left. It is advisable to remain roped up for the traverse off left to the top of *Left Hand Route*.

A very poor finishing pitch for *The Wrong Tap* was made (110 feet E1 5a 25.2.84): loose, dirty, and poorly protected. Climb up over ledges and short walls 10 feet left of the peg belay to a small rotten tree. Climb over the overhang and up the short wall above, and trend up and right easily to the final chimneys of *Right Hand Route*.

The final pitch of *Right Hand Route* is the best part of that route and makes a good, straightforward way to the top.

THE RIGHT-HAND SECTOR
These two routes start in the wooded hollow at the right-hand end of the trough below the wall.

★Nibelheim   300 feet   Very Severe   (3.2.79)
A worthwhile route at this somewhat under-represented grade. The third pitch is excellent value.
1 60 feet 4b. Climb up on the left at the junction between the gully and the wall, going straight over the centre of the larger overhang. Continue to a solitary tree which is just above the level of the Main Ledge on the left.
2 70 feet 4a. Climb up directly behind the tree and step right into a groove. Follow this, turning its overhang on the left; then bear slightly right, taking care with the rock, to a large tree belay on *The Angel's Girdle*.
3 60 feet 4c. Move 5 feet left, go up to a small tree, and climb carefully up to a horizontal break. Follow a short thin crack (some high hidden jugs) and the same line up the superb rough slab above to a long finger-ledge. Steeper, delicate moves lead to a peg runner below a small overhang, which is surmounted with unexpected ease. Continue to the Great Ledge and a peg belay.
4 110 feet 4b. Climb up behind the tree on the right. Climb a short wide crack and pull over the overhang on large but loose holds to a narrow ledge. Go left along this past a tree and climb a small square chimney. Step left at its top and belay at top or bottom of the final easy chimney of *Right Hand Route*. Rather wayward and vegetated: pitch 4 of *Right Hand Route* makes a better finish.

Right Hand Route   280 feet   Hard Severe
The (newish) third pitch makes all the difference! Now a respectable climb instead of merely-useful starting- and finishing-pitches.

1 60 feet. Climb the broken gully-line (detour to the right edge and back at 15 feet) to a tree belay just above the level of the Main Ledge on the left.
2 70 feet 4a. Climb up and emerge from the wood behind two large adjacent trees below an overhanging block. Make an awkward move onto this from the left and climb the crack in the wall in an unexpectedly exposed situation. Continue past a large tree (arrange runner carefully so that at least one rope is above the crux crack for the second) for 15 feet to a peg and nut belay.
3 50 feet 4b. Bridge up for 10 feet and then move left to the remains of a bush at the foot of a groove. Climb the groove to ledges (peg runner) and directly up a short slab (peg runner) to easy ground and the Great Ledge. (The original route moved tamely right at 10 feet onto easy ledges on the edge of the tower.)
4 100 feet 4a. High in the wall and a little left of the belay is a prominent V-cleft in the long overhang. Climb directly up to and through this, and then up the crack above to a ledge. Tree belay at the top or bottom of the final easy chimney. As an alternative to the latter, the red semi-circular chimney just left, climbed facing right with an easy step off right at the top, makes a more entertaining finish at 4b (plus or minus according to your size and shape).

THE ANGEL'S TOWER
This great buttress supports the right edge of the North Wall, and its original and eponymous route, *The Angel's Eye*, starts in the obvious corner at the foot of the arête. Both its faces are vertical, and the climbing, the best of which is excellent, is almost always exposed and exciting.

Claire 180 feet E2 (3.7.82)
A pleasant and amenable climb, marginally the easiest of the trio (with *Big Brother* and *Xenophobia*), though a harder variant on the second pitch is possible. Start near the bottom left corner of the front of the tower, at the foot of a broken rib which bounds the left of a sandy red wall.
1 90 feet 5a. Climb directly up for 30 feet (peg runner under an overhang). Pull over strenuously (good holds high on the right), and continue to a short groove (peg runner). Move up until able to hand-traverse left to a small tree; stand up and step back right. Climb up through a gap and past a hole; then trend right until easy ledges are reached and move right around the rib to a small stance. Peg belay shared with *Big Brother*.
2 40 feet 5c. Climb the rib for 10 feet and clip the peg runner of *Big Brother* on the left. Then traverse delicately right into a small groove (poor peg runner), and climb this, pulling directly over the little capping overhang, to the Tower niche and a two-peg belay. (Alternatively, step right from the belay to a ledge and make some difficult unprotected moves to gain the groove direct – E4.)
3 50 feet 5a. Move up slightly left to a thin crack, and layback onto a narrow ledge. Climb the crack and on up over easy ledges to the Great

Ledge and a tree belay.

Strawberry Dust (240 feet E2 5b 1978) wandered across the front of the Tower but has now been almost completely absorbed by the more direct lines. Follow *Claire* to the tree; then traverse right past the gap to a ledge and peg belay. Continue right in the same line across the Tower to the cave belay of *The Angel's Eye*. Move out left and climb *Strange Little Girl* to a ledge and peg runner; then move right into the groove to rejoin *The Angel's Eye* 10 feet above.

Xenophobia   170 feet   E2 ‡   (18.4.86)
An impressive-looking and sustained direct line (crossing *Claire* at 60 feet), but the rock and climbing prove disappointing, and its neighbours are uncomfortably close. High in the grades, though often escapable. Start immediately right of *Claire*, at the foot of the corner between the sandy red wall and the grey rib on its left. The ivy has regrown here and will need removal before climbing; the red wall just to the right, which has been climbed alternatively, is similarly affected.
1 70 feet 5b. Climb the corner for 30 feet (peg runner of *Claire* on the left). Take the first large bulge direct using good slots on the right. Move up slightly left over the flaky band to a small groove (second peg runner of *Claire*). Make awkward moves up and then right onto a ledge (peg belay just right).
2 100 feet 5c. Pull up to the block and climb up bearing slightly left to a long, narrow ledge below a scarred scoop in a black wall. Climb the left face of the rib on the right for 10 feet to clip the peg runner of *Big Brother*. Either step down slightly and across to the obvious sloping foothold in the scoop, or return to the ledge and climb directly up into the scoop. Make a difficult move to reach good holds above and left, and hurry on up to the short wall crossed by the crux of *The Angel's Girdle* (peg runner). Move right and climb up just right of a tiny groove to reach the finishing-crack of *Claire* or the edge on the left taken by *Big Brother*. Easy ledges then lead to the Great Ledge and a tree belay. The direct version is slightly harder and can be climbed at E4 without preclipping the *Big Brother* peg (RP 4 to start).

★Big Brother   200 feet   E2   (12.10.69)
For many years this was the hardest route on the crag. It later became a trade route giving climbing as safe and enjoyable as any of its standard. Start in the centre of the Tower, 15 feet left of the obvious corner of *The Angel's Eye*.
1 100 feet 5a/b. Climb up and mantelshelf onto a small ledge on the rib on the left (peg runner). Make difficult moves (or a very long stretch) to gain a good hold (peg runner above). Move left and climb a short groove with deep cracks to the overhang. Traverse 10 feet right and climb steeply past a peg runner, keeping right, to a ledge. Move left (peg runner – the belay on *Xenophobia*) and climb onto the block. Continue up, slightly right, then back left, to the foot of the rib (peg belay). It is possible to miss the

TOWER WALL and SMALL WALL

A	The Ring	HVS
B	The Angel's Girdle	VS
1	The Angel's Eye	HVS
2	Acid Test	E3
3	Sold Out	E4
4	Joe's Route	VS
5	Mystic	HVS

6	Psychotic	VS
7	Cryptic	E1
8	Narcotic	VS
9	Duncan's Dilemma	HVS
10	Under a Raging Moon	E2
11	Northerners Can't Climb	E1
X	Permitted exit points	

THE NORTH WALL

1 Andromeda   HVS
2 Yesterday's Dreams E2
3 Gryke   HVS
4 Left Hand Route   HS
5 Bacchanalian   HS
6 Symplex   VS
7 The Tap   VS
8 Entrance Exam   E4

Philip Gibson

9 Notung E1
10 Aqualung E3
11 Swansong E3
12 The Wrong Tap VS
13 Nibelheim VS
14 Right Hand Route HS
15 Big Brother E2
16 Sweetheart Contract E5
17 Strange Little Girl E4
18 The Angel's Eye HVS

Strange Little Girl (E4)
North Wall, Wintour's Leap
Climber: John Shaw
Photo: John Willson

traverse by going straight over the overhang at the top of the groove: bold (E3 5c).
2 40 feet 5c. Climb the rib on small fingery holds (peg runner on left) and move slightly left at the top to gain a good hold. Pull up and then continue more easily up and right to the two-peg belay in the Tower niche. (There is a convenient flake above the difficulties to keep the rope above the second.)
3 60 feet 4b. Climb diagonally left, past the crack of *Claire*, and then climb the arête on good holds until easy ledges lead to a tree belay on the Great Ledge.

Sweetheart Contract   190 feet   E5   (3.10.82)
A fine exposed finish and a hard and serious first pitch, though it is possible to reduce the grade to E3 if a slight detour is made to clip the second peg on *Big Brother*. Start as for *Big Brother*, in the centre of the tower, 15 feet left of the obvious corner of *The Angel's Eye*.
1 70 feet 6a. Climb up and mantel onto a small ledge on the rib on the left (peg runner) as for *Big Brother*. Step right onto the lip of the overhang and move very slightly further right. Then climb straight up the centre of the wall on very small holds to two holes. Continue direct to a stance on a block on the arête. Bolt and peg belay shared with *Strange Little Girl*.
2 70 feet 6a. Climb up just left of the arête as for *Strange Little Girl* (peg runner). Then make hard moves left and up onto a sloping ledge (bolt runner). Step slightly right, and then climb up with a step back left, passing a good layback, to the two-peg belay in the Tower niche (a good vantage point to photo the crux of *Strange Little Girl*).
3 50 feet 4b. *The Angel's Eye* pitch 3.

★★★Strange Little Girl   180 feet   E4   (2.7.82)
A superb direct line up the Tower face; good rock, with the crux in the most exposed position right at the top. The best hard route this side of GO Wall. [Photos opposite.] Start 8 feet left of the obvious corner of *The Angel's Eye*.
1 70 feet 6a. Climb a small slab to the first overhang. Pull over and pass a bolt runner with difficulty to reach a ledge (peg runner). Continue straight up on bubbly rock past a hole, over easier ground, and finally up a small flaky groove to a stance on a block on the arête. Bolt and peg belay.
2 110 feet 6a. Climb up just left of the arête (peg runner) to a good ledge (second peg runner). Climb the fine flake above and continue up to the overhangs (thread *in situ* on *The Angel's Eye* and *Girdle*). Pull straight over the bulge (bolt runner), step right, and climb direct to ledges and then the Great Ledge (tree belay).

The arête itself (comprising some piecemeal rock!) has been subject to piecemeal development. It now needs someone to clean and gear properly a continuous line linking the first and last of these three routes by the middle section of the second. **The Angel's Arête** (60 feet E4 6a 20.2.87) is still a worthwhile pitch; the start is quite serious, though less so if a side-runner is prefixed on *The Angel's Eye*. Start as for that route, reach left to the obvious jug, and make a difficult move to gain poor fingerholds. Climb to the shaly roof and clip a bolt runner using a hold out right. Gain the arête and climb it (*Rock 1* on the left, then peg runner and *in-situ* thread) to the first good ledge and a two-bolt belay. **Towering Angels** (190 feet E2 5b 27.10.81) is a relatively direct line but with some poor rock on both pitches. Climb the first 25 feet of *The Angel's Eye* but then continue straight up the rough crack just left of the main groove to the cave. Climb the groove directly above the cave to rejoin *The Angel's Eye* in 40 feet. A fine finish to this is the contradictively-named **Angelic Inferno** (E4 6c 4.1.92), but a lot of effort is involved in reaching it for its own sake! Continue up the upper groove to the break below the overhangs (peg runner); then pull round the widest part of the roof (bolt runner) and sprint up the upper arête (peg runner).

★The Angel's Eye   210 feet   Hard Very Severe   (9.65)

The large block that used to overhang the niche belay now sits in state by the junction where the little track leading to the foot of the climb leaves the main path. About time! Miraculously, the climber who accompanied it did not go so far and was not seriously hurt. Pitch 3, though a little harder, is now a whole lot less of a worry. One of the earliest harder routes on the cliff, and a classic. Only the start warrants the grade, but this has proved relatively serious: in order to prevent a ground fall from the crux, it is essential to place protection as high as possible under the upper overhang and, needless to say, for the second to pay the utmost attention to the rope here. Thereafter the climbing is more gentle, though still steep and pleasantly exposed. Start in the corner at the foot of the right edge of the Tower, behind a huge fallen block (also once part of the route!).

1 80 feet 5b. Climb up and over the overhangs and continue up the groove for 20 feet to a peg runner. Make an awkward move right onto the arête and climb this, as its angle relents, back left to a two-peg belay in the cave.

2 80 feet 4b. Climb diagonally right around the arête to a chimney. Climb this, mainly by its left wall, to a ledge and two peg runners on the left at the top. Move round left into a groove in the arête, and climb it, very exposed, on big holds to the overhangs. Traverse left past an *in-situ* thread and step down to the two-peg belay in the niche.

3 50 feet 4b. Climb straight up the groove above the belay to easy ground which leads to the Great Ledge. Tree belay above and left.

★Acid Test   160 feet   E3   (1.7.83)

The upper pitch offers bold and strenuous climbing in a fine position. Some dubious rock. Start in the first corner right of *The Angel's Eye*.

1 60 feet 5a. Climb the groove for 20 feet, and then go diagonally left across a short scoured wall (peg runner) to a ledge on the arête. Continue 10 feet to another ledge and a peg belay. (It is possible – at the same grade – to traverse left after 10 feet and climb on up the arête. If the starting-groove is brambled, neither alternative is worth the struggle: reach

the belay by climbing most of pitch 1 of *The Angel's Eye*.)
2 100 feet 5c. Climb awkwardly up above the belay and then up a short loose pillar to a peg runner level with the bottom of *The Angel's Eye* chimney on the right. Continue directly up the rib above, almost on the arête, to a ledge and old peg runner. Climb on up the steep wall (dubious peg runner), using a good flake hold on the right, to a ledge and peg runner on the arête under the overhangs (used to belay on *The Ring*). Hand-traverse 10 feet right (as for *The Ring*) as far as the hole, and then go up over the overhang at its narrowest point (peg runner above and a good hidden wire in a crack well out right). Climb straight up the main crackline to a ledge and a rusting peg belay which should be backed up by small wires. Scrambling leads to the Great Ledge.

TOWER WALL   (Diagram page 80)
The south wall of The Angel's Tower extends rightwards, becoming progessively vegetated from bottom left to top right, into Narcotic Corner.

Three routes seek out some very worthwhile rock to the right of the upper pitch of *Acid Test*, but none has more than 40 feet or so of independent climbing. For **Sold Out** (E4 6a 2.5.86), follow *Acid Test* and/or *The Angel's Eye* to the top of the latter's chimney; step right (peg runner) and trend slightly rightwards up the smooth wall above past an *in-situ* piece of wire[?!] to a small tree; climb the short wall behind this to a break (bolt runner just above), stand up awkwardly, and make a hard move for a good hold above (peg runner) before finishing diagonally rightwards. For **Special Offer** (Very Severe 4c 8.7.83), step up from the *Acid Test* belay and traverse right on large footholds; climb a short broken wall to a shallow open corner, and follow this and the more pronounced groove above to the sapling on *The Ring* (no protection until here); finish as for *The Ring*. **Final Reduction** (E2 5c 3.3.84) crosses *Special Offer* at the top peg of *Joe's Route* and has some good moves if *you* have the strength of character to make them rather than taking the obvious alternatives immediately to hand: follow the first two corners of *Joe Direct* and then continue directly up the bulging buttress (peg runner) to belay at the first of the three pegs of *Joe's Route*; continue to the overhang as for *Joe's Route* (two peg runners), pull over this leftwards to a crack (peg runner – in the same break as the peg on *Sold Out* 4 feet to the left), and go straight to the top. The stance for all three routes is behind the huge boulder a few feet below the Great Ledge

★Joe's Route   160 feet   Very Severe   (11.73)
A rather messy start leads to a fine exposed finish on good clean rock; well protected throughout, and low in the grade. Start in the second corner of Tower Wall right of *The Angel's Eye*.
1 60 feet 4a. Climb the corner to a platform with a thin tree. Move up on the right, and traverse right (some loose holds) to an uncomfortable stance with several trees.
2 100 feet 4c. Step back left onto the rock, and climb up past a large

tree to a rock spike runner on the floor of a small corner. Step up left off the spike and go diagonally left to a short wall split by a thin vertical crack (peg runner). Climb the wall to a ledge (peg runner), step left, and climb the next wall on larger holds left of the little groove to a small overhang (peg runner). Using handholds above the overhang, step right across the gap and mantel up short corners to the right to a peg belay in a small bay just below the Great Ledge.

Variation

Joe Direct (150 feet Very Severe 4c ‡ 18.9.82) is a little harder but of much less quality than the original and becoming revegetated; good moves on the final 20 feet. Follow the first corner of *Joe's Route* to the thin tree on the left, and climb the shorter, steeper corner behind it. Step right to rejoin the main route for 20 feet, climbing straight up just left of the vegetation to the rock spike runner. Bridge up the corner above past a small tree. From a large hole, move up onto a constricted ledge on top of an overhang (peg runner) and climb straight up the wall to the peg belay of the main route.

NARCOTIC CORNER

Facing south and west, and well nourished with earth and moisture from above, this is a haven for vegetation of the most brutal nature. From time to time, enthusiasts have unearthed[!] some sections of climbable, even enjoyable, rock (machetes and ice-axes being the favoured weapons) but, as every gardener knows, the harder you cut back brambles and briars, the faster they regrow. *Psychotic* (pitch 1) and *Cryptic* usually remain viable and perhaps worthwhile propositions.

To reach the climbs, walk rightwards from the foot of *Joe's Route* and make an unpleasant, dirty scramble to an earthy platform 15 feet above ground-level. If proposing to continue to the top, please read the 'Ways Off' notes on pages 59-60; however, the finishing-section really is poor, the earth bank littered with unstable scree, and the exit path very overgrown: where appropriate, abseil descent is preferable.

Frantic   180 feet   Hard Very Severe ‡   (7.6.84)
The start, 20 feet left of *Narcotic* behind two trees, has become revegetated.
1 60 feet 5a. Climb up 15 feet (peg runner) and mantel onto a small ledge. Continue straight up for 30 feet to easier ground and move right to a stance and nut belay on *Mystic*.
2 120 feet 5a. Move back left and climb straight up for 50 feet, crossing a loose break. Move up and slightly right onto a ledge, and then up right onto *Mystic*. Continue as for *Mystic* (peg runner) to the earth ledge; then traverse left onto the broken arête and climb friable holds to a tree belay.

Mystic   180 feet   Hard Very Severe ‡   (5.5.84)
The start, just right of *Frantic*, is similarly affected.
1 60 feet 5a. Climb up and use some dubious small flakes to reach a good hand-ledge on the right (hidden peg runner). Move up past the thorn

bush on top of the bulge to a small hole. Make an awkward move up the left-hand side of the overhang and continue 10 feet to a good stance at the foot of a chimney. Nut belays.
2 120 feet 5a. Climb the chimney for 10 feet, and move up left onto and then up the arête. Step back right into the open corner, climb this, and move up left onto a small ledge to good holds at the base of another corner. Climb the corner and then on up the wall (peg runner) to a large earth ledge. Step right onto the loose finish of *Narcotic*: exit left between two trees and scramble up the earth bank to a tree belay.

Psychotic and *Cryptic* are generally the most amenable routes here, and the first pitches have worthwhile climbing on generally good rock. The upper pitch is worth missing by abseiling from the convenient tree belay.

Psychotic   180 feet   Very Severe   (8.11.78)
A devious but logical line. Start immediately left of the corner.
1 120 feet 4c. Climb over some narrow ledges and then up a small groove-crack just left of the main corner. Step up and follow good holds diagonally left to a bridging-position across the top of a chimney left of a bulging grass ledge. Move up and traverse right along the ledge to a bush. Climb the crack and then move right up a short jagged rib. Ignoring the widening crack above (*Cryptic*), traverse back left to another crack and climb it to the large tree.
2 60 feet 4a. Climb the short steep wall behind the tree, just left of the bore-crack, to a ledge. As for *Narcotic*, continue to the obvious loose exit between two trees and scramble up the earth bank to a good tree belay on the right.
Variation
Analytic (18.5.84): some direct variants to the previous route, slightly harder (though within the same grade), but of lesser quality and little interest. (1) From the starting-ledges the first wall can be taken on the left. (2) It is possible to climb directly onto the bulging grass ledge (poor rock). (3) From the top of the crux crack, pull strenuously up the blank wall.

Cryptic   100 feet   E1 5a   (11.4.80)
A direct line, with a bold sequence of moves to the ledge by the first tree. Those with a good reach may find the climb a grade easier. *RP 4* or *5* and/or *Friend 1½* essential. Start as for Psychotic.
Climb over some narrow ledges and then up the small groove-crack just left of the main corner (as for *Psychotic*). Follow its continuation as a bore-crack and go on in a direct line up the wall. Place protection at the start of the steep section, which must then be climbed decisively on small holds. Do not spoil the continuity by belaying on the first tree (as on *Narcotic*), but move up and mantel onto the large overhang. Then climb the short jagged rib and the widening crack above to the large tree. Abseil off, or follow pitch 2 of *Psychotic* or 3 of *Narcotic*.

Narcotic   170 feet   Very Severe ‡   (3.65)

Pretty terrible! The second pitch provides a brief moment of entertainment but needs to be free from seepage. If brambles bar the first 15 feet or so, start up the little groove on the left taken by *Psychotic*, and traverse back right as soon as possible; otherwise start in the large corner itself.

1 80 feet 4a. Climb the main corner to a narrow ledge and a tree belay.

2 30 feet 5a. Climb the short steeper corner above, with difficulty at the top, to a ledge, and move left to a large tree to belay.

3 60 feet 4a. Climb the bore-crack behind the tree to a ledge. Step left and continue up to the obvious loose exit between two trees. A sling in a high branch will help to prevent the rope from dislodging earth onto the rock below. Scramble up the earth bank to a tree belay on the right.

Quixotic   210 feet   E3 ‡   (6.5.84)

'Straight is the gate &c'. But the weary shall find rest and the faint-hearted protection (or even release) in the *Narcotic* corner on the left. The first ascent made no use of this soft option, and without it the first pitch is E4. Some impressive climbing with intricate route-finding, patches of dubious rock, and yet more vegetation. Start, as for *Duncan's Dilemma*, just right of *Narcotic*.

1 120 feet 5c. Climb the wall 5 feet right of the corner past a rose bush to the second of two peg runners at 30 feet (as for *Duncan's Dilemma*). Step left and go up very slightly rightwards to a shallow niche; and then traverse back left to a peg runner in the centre of the wall. Make a strenuous pull up to the left and further committing moves above to reach good jugs below the horizontal break. Continue up slightly left to a ledge level with the *Narcotic* tree belay; step left and climb the wall to a good crack. Follow this and a right-sloping ramp to join the top of the arête. Move back left across vegetation to a large red ledge and peg belay (shared with *Duncan's Dilemma*).

2 90 feet 4c. As for *Duncan's Dilemma* pitch 3, but continue in the final corner-crack as high as possible before stepping left below the top. Peg and nut belay above in a flat table-top block.

Scarotic (180 feet Hard Very Severe 9.6.84) is a pointless, contrived line covering almost no independent ground: it wanders diagonally across the corner from the start of *Duncan's Dilemma* to the extreme right-hand end of the Great Ledge.

Duncan's Dilemma   210 feet   Hard Very Severe ‡   (19.7.82)

Rather an old-fashioned, mountaineering type of climb, but it could appeal to older *Blue Peter* fans (see First Ascent list). Start just right of *Narcotic*.

1 70 feet 5a. Climb the wall 5 feet right of the corner past a rose bush and two peg runners. Move up and right over a bulge to a thread *in situ*, and climb straight up to a large ledge and peg belay.

2 50 feet 4c. Climb the arête on the left by a series of mantelshelves, and then scramble over vegetated ledges to a large red ledge on the left and a peg belay.

3 90 feet 4b. Move right to another mantelshelf and continue up over more vegetation to a large crack just right of the arête. Start up the crack, and then swing left on a good hold in the wall and finish up the arête to a peg and nut belay in a flat table-top block.

Digitus Extractus (Hard Very Severe 5a 27.10.81) is the black crack and groove in the centre of the wall to the right of the top of the previous climb – harder and looser than it looks, and its is exit off-limits.

THE GREAT WALL
(Crag plan page 60)

The Great Wall is the disappointment of the cliff, especially in view of its substantial surface area and initial impression of steepness. The trouble is that, instead of having just a couple of uniform terraces like The North Wall or the clean-cut horizontal faults of GO and Fly Walls, odd ledges and broken areas holding masses of vegetation alternate with short, steep, blank sections (just the thing for the ivy), and this makes good continuous routes, at any grade, hard to come by. Not all the news is bad, though. *John's Route* and *Original Route* are reasonable climbs in the lower grades and worthy of attention. *Too Clever by Half* is a sporting 'sport' route, and *Fade to Pink* with its new second pitch, though almost wholly on fixed gear, is no mean adventure.

Until 1988, no vehicle over 13 tons could cross the River Wye from the (old) M4 to reach Woodcroft. In that year the Chepstow relief road and new Wye Bridge were opened, and now the 38-tonners thunder up and down all day. Above most of The Great Wall the B4228 is less than two metres from the cliff-top, and when climbing below you can feel the rock shaking: a few bits have fallen off! Though the above-mentioned routes have been strangely immune from the general deterioration and may well remain viable, this instability, the excessive vegetation, and the general lack of quality may mean that the whole wall is best left to revert to nature (or fall down!). All the routes are, however, described in their *current* (1996) state.

THE APPROACH

The Easy Way Down is recommended (page 55). Turn sharp right (facing out) at the bottom, pass below Grey Wall, and go down a steep muddy path. Shortly a branch leads back up right (now facing in) to the start of *Original Route*. A little further down, the path approaches the rock at a short, shallow groove with a steep broken wall on its left: this is the start of *The Willies*. At the bottom of the slope is the cliff end of the earth ridge. To reach Compost Wall, go over its crest and turn immediately right steeply uphill. Soon a small track branches left and traverses horizontally across grass and bramble ledges to the foot of Small Wall. The main path continues up a little and then goes diagonally left over easy rock and grass tiers. The large fallen block looks up at the start of *Compost Wall* on a nettle-strewn platform above (shorts-clad climbers, beware!). To reach the start of *Loads' Lids*, go 40 feet right along a narrow vegetated ledge just below this to a borehole below a small rounded slab.

THE WAY OFF
Finding the way presents no problems: the main routes finish on the road. Take care when emerging: it happens suddenly, the road is narrow with no pavement or verge, and the traffic travels *far* too fast. The way onto and down the Compost Wall path from the top of Small Wall is obvious.

SMALL WALL   (Photo-diagram page 80)
An alternative way of reaching Small Wall is by scrambling directly up a dirty break from below or, reportedly, by climbing **Proper Limestone** (35 feet Very Severe 4b † ‡ 31.3.88) left of the break. However, there is no visible sign of the commodity!

A broad broken rib bisects the wall; the left-hand half has four routes, the right half three. The first two are of modest quality, the remainder terrible. The threads need replacing.

Under a Raging Moon   50 feet   E2   5c   (5.4.86)
Strenuous, but well-protected climbing. Start in the centre of the left half of the wall.
Climb directly up to the bulges (peg runner), and swing wildly through them on enormous jugs (thread runner) to a steep pull onto the upper wall and a good rest. Arrange wires and climb decisively up the headwall with a difficult move to finish. Tree belay on the next ledge above.

Northerners Can't Climb   50 feet   E1   5b   (27.9.81)
Climb the brittle pink wall left of the rib to two dubious threads. Pull strenuously over the overhang: there are good holds but no second chances. Above, there is good protection and delightful jamming in the twin cracks. Good tree belay on the next ledge up.

Tiswas (40 feet Hard Severe 4b 27.9.81) climbs the loose earthy corner formed by the junction of the rib with the left wall. **Amoeba** (40 feet E1 5a 19.6.84) takes the left face of the rib (peg runner) to the break and finishes up *Tiswas*. **Eureka** (40 feet Hard Very Severe 5a 14.6.84) is a one-move problem up the left end of the right-hand half of the wall (peg runner used on the first ascent removed – no other protection). **Meninpunkunderwear** (40 feet Severe 4a 18.4.82): diagonally right across the slab to the obvious weakness; climb this and a short crack to easy ground. **Meiosis** (40 feet E1 5a 19.6.84) climbs the right edge of the wall on loose crystals! Peg runner used on first ascent removed.

COMPOST WALL
Compost Wall occupies the upper left-hand half of the Great Wall and is even more vegetated than the rest, though often very attractively so.

Three 'routes' [?] of absolutely no interest whatever finish in the private part
of the North Wall garden (see page 59), and so are off-limits. **Belvedere
Route** (‡ c.1960) takes the shelfy gully right of *Duncan's Dilemma* (said in the
draft for an early guide to be 'a good outing under snow and ice'[!] – maybe
a one-off in 1963, but certainly never since). **Crumble Corner** (‡ 9.12.79)
and **Galtieri's Gonads** (‡ 20.4.82) find a way up loose rock and dense,
prickly vegetation in and near the corner bounding the left of Compost Wall.
All unmeasurable, ungradable, and probably unclimbable.

Jugged Hare (130 feet E1 5a ‡ 26.6.84) is not a great deal better: less
vegetation, but there are some bad earth ledges, poor rock, and dangerously
unprotected sections. Please use a helmet, if only to keep the earth out of your
hair! Start just right of a borehole at the left end of Compost Wall. Climb up
for 20 feet, go left and up to a tree, continue up left of a triangular overhang
(peg runner), and move left on grassy ledges. Climb the final wall (peg runner)
to the earth bank at the top. Large tree belay on the left over the fence.

Compost Wall　160 feet　Hard Severe ‡　　　　　　　　　　(5.64)
The wall's eponymous route takes the obvious central line. It has been
given a clean periodically but always becomes overgrown again quickly.
Most of the climbing is straightforward, but the top of pitch 1 is unpleasant.
Start in the centre of the nettle platform below the left half of the wall,
about 100 feet above the ground. Thread belay behind the large block
below and right.
1　70 feet　4b. Climb the wall, bearing slightly right to a peg runner with
in-situ tape a few feet below a gouged-out overhanging block. Move up
beside the block, and then go right over vegetation and up at a small
borehole to a good ledge and peg belay under a V-shaped overhang. A
slightly harder (4c) start can be made directly to the peg from the right end
of the platform, overlooking the huge fallen block.
2　50 feet　4a. Climb the rib, keeping generally to the right. From the top
block, move round left to a grass ledge and a peg belay.
3　40 feet. Move up under the overhang and escape to the right. Easier
climbing leads to a gap in the vegetation. Belay on the crash barrier.

Abacus　160 feet　Very Severe　　　　　　　　　　　　　　(19.6.84)
Paradoxically, 'the diagonal' may have greater justification here, as only
intermittent holds will become earthed and the second will be out of the
leader's firing-line! Start at an obvious lone tree midway between *Compost
Wall* and *Gemmell's Groove*.
1　70 feet　4c. Climb up to a flake, and move up and left to beneath the
large square overhang. Go left round this and step back right on top (peg
runner on right). Trend right for 10 feet, and then go left along a good
ledge to the peg belay on *Compost Wall*.
2　90 feet　4c. Move up and left to a difficult move onto a ledge on the
wall (peg runner). Climb the wall slightly rightwards and the slab above to
the left-hand end of a bushy ledge. Continue straight up to a good wire

placement and then traverse left, rising a little, on good holds to the final 10 feet of *Jugged Hare*. Scramble up the earth bank and go over the fence to a large tree belay on the left.

The next three routes were dedicated (without permission) to the original members of the BBC's *Gardeners' Question Time* panel, for reasons which will be apparent. The large tree at the top has now gone, but an adequate one remains.

Gemmell's Groove (150 feet Severe ‡ 3.6.78) climbs the large corner to the right of *Compost Wall* after a start up *Loads' Lids* or a slightly harder, more direct line from the foot of *Abacus*; either way, have a *Kit-Kat* after 40 feet at the tree at the foot of the corner.

Loads' Lids   140 feet   Very Difficult   (14.6.78)
The obvious arête right of *Gemmell's Groove*, giving steep, exposed climbing on large holds. Protection in the middle section is sparse. Start at the right-hand end of a small grassy shelf 40 feet right of the huge fallen block below *Compost Wall*, 100 feet above the ground. Nut belay in a borehole, or an obvious thread a little to the left.
1 110 feet. Climb to a small ledge above the borehole and up the little rounded slab above. Step down left onto sloping rock and traverse a short way left under a small overhang. Climb straight up and then slightly right to the foot of the rib. Make an awkward step right and climb the arête, turning the three obvious overhangs on their right (thread under the third – make sure it is large enough), to easy ledges (and the garden centre!). Two-peg belay above (this is the abseil point on *The Early Morning Traverse*).
2 30 feet. Move across right to a small corner and climb this – easy, but loose at the top. A direct finish from the pegs has been done: 4c or more, loose and unprotected – better not!

Sowerbutts' Sortie (150 feet Severe ‡ 14.6.78) is awful. Follow *Loads' Lids* onto the first overhang on the arête and then take an obvious diagonal rake right to a sitting flake. Move well right, then up, and traverse back left. Climb the short slab to the tree (50m rope necessary).

THE ORIGINAL SECTOR
The remaining routes on the Great Wall are to the right of the prominent central rib and start at ground-level.

Hoof Hearted (260 feet Very Severe ‡ 20.9.81) and **Crazy Horse** (260 feet E1 ‡ 24.7.84) are very poor routes at the left end of the right half of the wall. There is a *lot* of vegetation, and some bad rock low down; though each has a short 'nice' pitch in the middle. The common start 10 feet right of the left margin of rock, leading to a ledge and tree at 30 feet, is completely ivied over, as is the alternative traverse-in from 20 feet up *Black Jack*. *Hoof Hearted* climbed the loose corner on the left and then the groove behind the sycamore on the right. *Crazy Horse* went up more directly, over an overhang and up to the two-bolt belay of *The Bubble Bursts*; from a little right to the sycamore, and to the grass ledge via the crack on the left (you *can* 'abseil off an *in-situ* nut' from here[!]). Both routes (otherwise) then made a way rightwards over assorted rubbish to join *Original Route* to finish.

Half-way up the slope to the right, a very slim clean strip goes straight upwards. This is *Iron Lung*; the first 20 feet originally comprised the start of *Black Jack*. The whole of the wall to the left is now densely ivy-covered, and **The Bubble Bursts** (80 feet E4 6a ‡ (22.4.87) and the first pitch of **Black Jack** (70 feet E3 5c ‡ 13.6.84) are currently unclimbable, though both formerly had some good moves. From 20 feet up the cleaned strip, *The Bubble Bursts* traversed easily 15 feet left, and then made hard and bold moves up leftwards over the bulge (bolt runner); another awkward move attained the ledge (*in-situ* wire to protect second and two-bolt belay on left to abseil). *Black Jack* traversed only 12 feet left to climb a groove onto a slim block (peg runner) and then the borehole above (peg runner) to the ledge (*in-situ* wire on the left, bolt on the right). An optional second pitch (100 feet 4c) took the (still quite clean) wall above over the long overhang to a ledge. A fight rightwards through bushes may get you to the two-bolt belay of *Fade to Pink*.

Iron Lung (55 feet E3 6a †† (22.4.87) climbs the cleaned vertical weakness as for the last two routes (thread runner and peg runner). The loose block above has now (inevitably) gone, which may or may not be of major consequence. Continue straight up with increasing difficulty (poor *in-situ* wire and peg runner) to the ledge and a bolt runner. An optional second pitch, previously climbed as **Galloping Diabonkers** (80 feet 4c 19.6.82), takes the arête above the belay to reach the two-bolt belay of *Fade to Pink*.

★Fade to Pink   140 feet   E3   (20.4.85)
A star for the stonking new second pitch, which gives the best climbing on the wall. The threads on pitch 1 need replacing. Start 10 feet right (upslope) of the cleaned strip of *The Iron Lung*, by the foot of a short vegetated groove.
1 70 feet 5c. Step left onto the wall. Climb to a cleaned ledge, and then more steeply past a peg runner to a ledge. Above is a steeper wall with some excellent pockets (peg runner on the right and two threads on the left). Climb this to small holds in a faint groove left of a rounded bulge. Reach a good hold on the right above the bulge with difficulty and pull over strenuously to easier rock. Go up over ledges to the peg belay of *The Willies*.
2 70 feet 5c. Climb straight up past two peg runners (as for *The Willies*) and then the bulging wall above (bolt runner, then peg runner on the left, thread *in-situ* on the right). Finish slightly rightwards and then traverse back left across the corner to a smaller corner with a two-bolt belay. Abseil off or finish up *Original Route*. (The original second pitch climbed the long corner

– now dirty and vegetated again.)

The Willies   150 feet   E1   (9.62)
Some good climbing on the second pitch rescues this from dismissal, but
the poor rock on the first pitch and the general scarcity of reliable
protection demand caution. Start as for *Fade to Pink*.
1 90 feet 5a. Originally, the vegetated groove and its rounded left edge
were climbed to the long narrow foot-ledge. It is now better to reach this
via *Fade to Pink*. Traverse left along the ledge with rotten handholds, past
the open 'bible' just above. Move up into a depression (peg runner) and
step out right onto the top left edge of the bible. Climb the short groove
above and go up over ledges to a peg belay below the long corner.
2 60 feet 5a/b. Climb the wall past two peg runners on good but
widely-spaced holds, and bear right towards a gash at its top. Below this is
a slab, and a junction with *Original Route*. The correct finish is through the
gash by a strenuous layback up the dubious flake. Alternatively (reducing
the pitch grade to 4c and overall to HVS) follow *Original Route* a few feet
right and up a short crystal corner onto a ledge. Tree and nut belay in a
small groove above the left end of the ledge. Continue to the top by
pitches 3 and 4 of *Original Route* or move carefully down and left to the
two-bolt belay of *Fade to Pink* and abseil to the ground.

Cast A Shadow   135 feet   E2 ‡   (5.4.86)
The first pitch has ivied over. Start 10 feet right of *Fade to Pink* at a slight
nose.
1 75 feet 5b. Climb the nose and then directly up the smooth wall to
reach a small ledge and sapling (the only protection on this pitch). Step left
on foot-ledges and climb up past a pink scar onto the rounded upper slab;
then go up to a good ledge (nut belay with a rope to the peg belay of *The
Willies* on the left).
2 60 feet 4b. Climb pleasantly up the rough black slabs above. At the
second of three short boreholes, step right to a ledge and bear slightly
right to finish up the little right arête of the wall. Tree and nut belay in a
small groove above the left end of the ledge. Continue or abseil as for *The
Willies*.

Original Route   240 feet   Very Difficult
Formerly considered one of the 'classic V Diffs'; it has withstood the
vegetation onslaught remarkably well. Start in a small clearing at the right
end of the wall.
1 60 feet. Climb steeply up an obvious vertical break to a large ledge.
Above, an easier-angled scoop bears left to an iron spike and tree belay
on a small ledge.
2 60 feet. Follow a diagonal line left to a slab left of an eroded groove
containing a sapling. Good holds lead up the slab and back right to a
short crystal corner, which is climbed to a ledge. Small tree belay and nut
placements in a short groove above the left end of the ledge (the cracks

low behind the ledge itself do *not* provide sound placements).
3 70 feet. Climb the groove past the belay, and then the left of two very short corners. Continue over muddy ledges, and mantel left onto a long ledge below the final wall. Tree belay above and beyond the far left end.
4 50 feet. Either, from the belay, climb steeply right and then directly to the top; or, more sportingly, return to the centre of the ledge (old broken peg) and climb the right edge of the wall on small holds just left of a short roofed groove; continue past an overhang and a large tree to the tree belay at the top. A further (4b) alternative is to go right around the overhangs above the right-hand end of the ledge and back leftwards to the large tree. The big corner on the right has also been climbed (4a and loose).

★Too Clever by Half   70 feet   E2   5c   (11.4.87)
This entertaining little pitch has discovered some of best and cleanest rock on The Great Wall. Spaced protection. Start at the first belay (tree and iron spike) of *Original Route*.
Climb the centre of the smooth wall above the belay (bolt runner) to two ledges. From the higher, make difficult moves up a borehole (bolt runner) and climb boldly up the next wall (peg runner with *in-situ* tape) to easier ground and a bolt and peg belay beneath a small roofed corner. Abseil off.

The Rising Sun   220 feet   Very Severe   ‡   (1.7.79)
Pitch 2 is virtually impenetrable.
1 100 feet   4b. Climb pitch 1 of *Original Route*, and then up and right across the wall to a flake crack, which is followed to a narrow ledge and a two-peg and bolt belay.
2 120 feet   4b. Climb the slab to the roof. Move left round this and step back right on top. Climb up 10 feet to a vegetated ledge, and then up on the left towards some trees; finally bear right to a long grass ledge. Step right to join *John's Route* below its crux short wall.

John's Route   200 feet   Hard Severe   (22.9.74)
Good climbing and really deserves a star, but somewhat shaken (if not...) by the traffic passing above. Quite high in the grade. Start as for *Original Route*.
1 90 feet   4b. Climb a vertical break to a ledge as for *Original Route*, and then two short grooves to the right to a large tree level with, and 20 feet to the right of, the *Original Route* belay. Follow small holds diagonally right across the little wall (peg runner). Move up past the peg and continue up on good rock left of the grassy recess to a narrow ledge. Traverse right on this to a flake crack. Nut belays.
2 90 feet   4b. Climb the crack. Continue up right of the first overhang to a poor peg runner below the second. Move right around this with care. A cleaned strip through a vegetated band leads to a short wall climbed by its left edge (good wires on the left) with a difficult move at the top. Climb the little corner on the right to a superb ledge with a seat and a two-peg belay.

3 20 feet. Climb steeply to the top on large holds. No belay: take a stance on the road behind the hedge.

On the Outside, Looking In (90 feet Hard Very Severe 5b 11.4.87) is an eliminate, the main purpose of which is to cross the short, peg-runner wall of *John's Route* in the opposite direction, and the main benefit of which is the thoughtful provision of a bolt from which anyone who has made the mistake of attempting *The Rising Sun* could abseil. After the *Original Route* start, move right to a ledge (peg runner). Pull onto the ramp-line above and continue direct via a blunt rib to the peg runner. Move awkwardly left and take the centre of the slab to reach the two-peg and bolt belay.

The wall lends itself to an indefinite number of utterly useless traverse-lines; two were recorded. **Meninboredom** (c.300 feet c.Severe 11.10.81) starts from the big ledge above Grey Wall (see next section) and crosses the first belays of *John's Route* and *The Rising Sun* before rising slightly to the second of *Original Route*. Drop back down and fight through atrocious vegetation until the final arête is reached. The *pièce de résistance* (and the only conceivable justification for doing the route at all) is a jump into the tree and a climb down it! **Menincontinent** (18.5.82) is merely a harder and lower variant to the section across *Original Route*.

Roger's Route (290 feet c.Very Severe ‡ 5.70) starts up left of *Paul's Wall*, traverses to the first belay of *John's Route*, and climbs 50 feet of the latter before disappearing back into the vegetated gully, which is littered with rubbish tipped from the road and loose chopper blocks. Quite appalling!

THE CENTRAL BAY   (Crag plan page 100)
Going once upon a time by the grand title of 'Main Area' (how things change!), the pleasant little Central Bay offers a variety of scrambling and bouldering, and is ideal for instruction (of the old-fashioned type rather than the modern ten-on-a-top-rope variety), with short pitches separated by spacious horizontal ledges. It is possible to wander almost anywhere, only the north-facing Grey Wall beneath Corner Buttress, the steep Black Wall below the right-hand half of The Broadwalk, and Terry's Wall in the centre at the top offering any resistance.

THE APPROACH
The Easy Way Down (page 55) crosses the bay from top right to bottom left (facing in). Near the bottom is a long flat terrace, The Broadwalk, 15 feet above which are four obvious spaced-out silver birches, referred to in the descriptions numbered from the left. From the far end of The Broadwalk, steps lead down to an apex of paths below the crag. This is the starting-point of Corner Buttress. The path on the right (facing out) passes below Grey Wall before descending to The Great Wall routes; that on the left runs below Black Wall on its way towards The South Bay.

THE WAY OFF
The routes which go to the top finish on a grassy strip between the cliff-top and the road adjacent to the parking pull-off on the right. From the Grey Wall routes, abseil off, reverse the *Corner Buttress* starting-pitch, or reach the large ledge and go round right and scramble back down to The Broadwalk.

GREY WALL
This faces north and receives some shelter from rain. Except for *Paul's Wall*, the rock is clean.

Crystal Tips   50 feet   Hard Very Severe   5b   (12.3.87)
Starting 25 left of the foot of the Easy Way Down, pull onto jugs and stretch for a pocket. Continue on pockets (thread runner) and move left onto a ledge (peg runner out left). Use sloping holds to gain an obvious square foothold, and climb over a bulge to a ledge and a two-bolt belay.

Paul's Wall   75 feet   Hard Very Severe   5a   (8.6.81)
Starting 20 feet left of the foot of the Easy Way Down, climb a vague line of weakness to a small overhang. Using a poor pocket, make a difficult move to reach easier ground. Climb a flake crack to a grass ledge, and then directly up past a rounded overhang. Traverse right to the tree belay of *Grey Wall* and climb the left arête of the corner to the large ledge.

Spinal Tap   70 feet   E4 6a   (5.3.87)
Side-runners in *Grey Wall* reduce the grade to E2; otherwise the crux is excitingly unprotected. Start between *Paul's Wall* and *Grey Wall*.
Climb the pocketed wall directly to a faint borehole arête. Climb the arête with conviction and make a hard move to reach a ledge at the top. Easier ground leads to the tree belay.

Grey Wall   60 feet   Very Severe   5a
An interesting and worthwhile pitch. It is becoming increasingly polished and the central section is not at all easy for the grade.
Starting 10 feet left of the foot of the Easy Way Down, climb pock marks on a short bulging wall to a narrow ledge. The difficult curving crack above leads to another ledge. Bear left up the final wall to a good tree belay.

Espresso Bongo   40 feet   E1 5b   (4.3.87)
A horizontal Rock 3 at 25 feet is the only protection. Start 5 feet left of the foot of Easy Way Down and climb the crystal pillar to a tree belay.

CORNER BUTTRESS
The name refers to the obvious square-cut buttress forming the upper half of the left-hand edge of the bay, rather than the series of short true corners at the foot.

Corner Buttress Route 1   210 feet   Very Difficult
Start just above the foot of the descent from The Broadwalk, by a slim tree in a short corner on the edge of the wall.
1 70 feet. Climb the corner, and two more above bearing left, to a huge ledge and tree.
2 40 feet 4a. Walk right to a crack with a chockstone. Boulder out the overhang to its left, and climb up the next tier by an awkward small groove and ramp to a tree belay. (The difficulties can be easily avoided.)
3 60 feet. Climb the twin cracks behind the tree. Continue up to the foot of the buttress and climb the steep rough crack left of centre to a good platform and tree belay.
4 40 feet. Climb the easy left edge to the top (nut belays).

Corner Buttress Route II   210 feet   Very Difficult
Start as for the preceding route.
1 70 feet. Artificially, climb the first two corners by their right edges to a tree on the right; then climb the tree and/or the wall behind it to a large ledge. Chockstone belay in the crack ahead.
2 30 feet 4a. Climb the crack and then a thinner, quartz-lined one up to the right to a tree belay. (The upper crack can be avoided by walking round to the left.)
3 70 feet. Take the slab right of the tree. Move on up to the steep right edge of the buttress and climb it to a good platform and tree belay. The first move requires a long reach: it is easier to start a few feet right of the arête and traverse back in above.
4 40 feet. Continue easily to the top keeping right (nut belays).

Corner Buttress Route III   270 feet   Moderate
The easiest route on the cliff. Start on the path below the bay, 30 feet south of the foot of the Easy Way Down and the start of the two preceding routes.
1 90 feet. Climb 45 feet to a sapling just below the left end of The Broadwalk. Go diagonally right and then up to the first of the silver birches.
2 40 feet. Climb the short open corner above and left of the tree, and walk left to a crack with a chockstone.
3 40 feet. Climb right of the crack, walk left round the short arête, and scramble up the next tier to a tree belay.
4 60 feet. Move on up and climb the broken left edge of the Buttress on enormous holds to a good platform and tree belay.
5 40 feet. Continue to the top on large holds on the left (nut belays).

The Problems
A series of interesting problems between Corner Buttress and *Direct Route*, separated by easy scrambling. They can be soloed, or bypassed to fix a top-rope.
1 4a. Climb directly over the overhang just left of the start of *Cement Groove;* scramble past the boulder ledge to The Broadwalk.
2 4a. Below and 8 feet left of the second silver birch is a short crack with

Under a Blood Red Sky (E1, first ascent) North Wall, Wintour's Leap
Climber: Doré Green   Photo: Charles Carroll

a hole at 6 feet.

3 4c. Behind the tree and 2 feet left, tiny holds lead to a curving crack and better holds.

4 5a/b. Work left to the large ledge, the lowest below Corner Buttress but above the level of The Broadwalk: the far left edge is a 15-foot vertical arête which offers a variety of options.

5 4b. Diagonally right, climb over the centre of the prominent overhang in the middle of the right-hand face of Corner Buttress.

6 4a. From the tree and platform on the left, finish up the centres of two short walls avoiding holds to left and right.

Cement Groove 250 feet Difficult

Quite good for the grade, though short on protection in the lower half. Start on the path below the bay, below an overhang 60 feet south of the foot of the Easy Way Down.

1 60 feet. Climb up just right of the overhang. After 30 feet, bear left to reach the boulder ledge, and continue straight up to a bush belay on The Broadwalk.

2 50 feet. Above the left end of The Broadwalk, and 20 feet left of the belay, is a short shallow groove which looks as if its back has been plastered with cement. Climb this to a large ledge and a chockstone belay in the crack ahead.

3 80 feet. From the extreme right end of the ledge, step up and climb diagonally right past a borehole into the right-hand of two groove-backed alcoves. Climb out diagonally right onto a ridge and follow this a short way to a solitary sapling level with a large wooded alcove further right. Tree and nut belay.

4 60 feet. Climb up behind the tree, just left of a crack, to grass ledges. Finish up the eroded groove in the rib above which separates Corner Buttress from the gully on its right. Nut belays.

Direct Route 200 feet Difficult

Start 80 feet south of the foot of the Easy Way Down, just right of two trees and just left of the left edge of Black Wall.

1 70 feet. Climb directly up to The Broadwalk (do not bear right up the shallow groove which bounds the edge of Black Wall). Continue to the second (from the left) silver birch, which is multi-trunked.

2 80 feet. Climb up right of the tree, moving back left to be immediately above the belay as soon as possible. Climb the left side of a rounded nose to a terrace, and then the faint groove above. Continue to another ledge. Surmount the nose splitting the recess and then the centre of the long overhang to reach a spacious wooded alcove.

3 50 feet. Scramble up the gully to the left and follow it back right to a short vertical wall to finish. Tree belay a further 20 feet back.

Variation

3a 50 feet Very Difficult. A harder but better alternative (in dry conditions only) is to climb the steep broken wall immediately behind the belays. Then bear left over easier ground to the same final wall.

BLACK WALL

These five routes are quite serious and sustained for their technical difficulty and are often top-roped. Please refer to the section on trees in the General Introduction (page 17).

Pig Iron   50 feet   E2 5b   (18.3.84)

From near the left end of Black Wall, reach the break, move right, and pull up using a good but high hold. Climb up passing two peg runners on the right to finish via the obvious scar. A belay is awkward to arrange.

Black Wall Left   50 feet   Hard Very Severe   5a

An eliminate between *Pig Iron* and *Black Wall*, slightly harder than the latter but better protected. Step right near the top to finish as for *Black Wall*.

Black Wall   50 feet   Hard Very Severe   5a

Steep and sustained with poor protection, but it makes a good strenuous pitch. Start behind a tree 8 feet left of the corner and climb to a gash. Keep this on the right and bear left to a hard finishing move. Easy ground leads to The Broadwalk. Tree belay 15 feet above.

Save Me from Tomorrow   50 feet   E2 5b   (25.2.87)

Plenty of variety for such a short pitch.

Climb directly up the wall immediately left of the right-slanting corner (thread runner) to the bulge and a second thread. Pull over slightly rightwards to easy ground and then The Broadwalk. Tree belay above.

Pavlov's Dog   50 feet   Very Severe   4c ‡   (9.3.85)

A line 30 feet right of Black Wall: always less good than the preceding routes, and now vegetation bars both rock and access.

TERRY'S WALL

The the 30-foot sandy-coloured wall in the central top section of the bay. A narrow grass ledge, with various small trees to belay, runs along its base. This is best reached either by abseil from a tree 20 feet back from the top, or by taking **Centre Route** (100 feet Very Difficult 8.61) up the short corner immediately left of the third silver birch above The Broadwalk and as direct a line as possible on over ledges and short walls.

Terry's Left-Hand Finish   40 feet   Severe   4a   (8.61)

From the tree at the left-hand end of the ledge, climb an obvious broken line to the top.

Terry's Right-Hand Finish   40 feet   Hard Severe   4b   (8.61)

From the tree further right, climb past a small circular hole giving a good thread, and over a shallow overhang. Step left and climb straight to the top.

Terry's Twin   40 feet   Very Severe 4c   (10.5.90)
From a tree at the right-hand end of the ledge, step up left onto the prow 5
feet right of the last route (the thread is just in reach on the left). Climb
straight up the wall via a small niche.

Terry's Gone Crackers   40 feet   Hard Severe 4b   (10.5.90)
Directly from the right-hand tree, climb the obvious crackline past a very
small overhang at 15 feet.

THE RIDGE
High above the right-hand end of The Broadwalk is a blunt, easy-angled ridge
leading past the right edge of Terry's Wall to the top. The routes in this section
start on The Broadwalk and make for the ridge. There are no belays on The
Broadwalk itself, but the ledge is very wide and the 15-foot scramble to the
silver birches is always elementary.

Ridge By-Pass   180 feet   Moderate
Start at the third silver birch.
1 30 feet. *Ridge Route* pitch 1.
2 110 feet. Climb straight over the next tier and then up a short
right-facing corner. Pass just left of the trees, climb a short borehole, and
move up right to a platform with a thread and nut belay.
3 40 feet. Step up and right onto the ridge and continue as for *Ridge Route*,
finishing up the short scoop to an exit right. Tree belay a further 20 feet back.

Ridge Route   160 feet   Moderate
Start at the third silver birch.
1 30 feet. Climb up behind the tree to a ledge and a tree belay on the right.
2 40 feet. Climb a short chimney on the right. Step back left across its top
and climb up, steeply at first, and then easily, to a tree just below the
wooded glade.
3 90 feet. Walk right to the foot of the ridge and climb it to where it fades
into a scoop just below the top. Climb the scoop and exit right. Tree belay
a further 20 feet back.

Wye Knot?   170 feet   Difficult
Start above the right-hand end of the Broadwalk, at the fourth silver birch.
1 50 feet. Zigzag left up a ramp and back right to a large tree on a small
ledge overlooking the start.
2 70 feet. Make a difficult move up the wall behind the tree and climb up
the ridge for 30 feet to a tree belay on a ledge just right of a small fir.
3 50 feet. Climb the broken wall on the right of the ridge directly to the
top (despite appearance, the rock is quite reasonable). Tree belay a further
20 feet back.

There is more broken and vegetated rock to the right, but nothing to make a
route from!

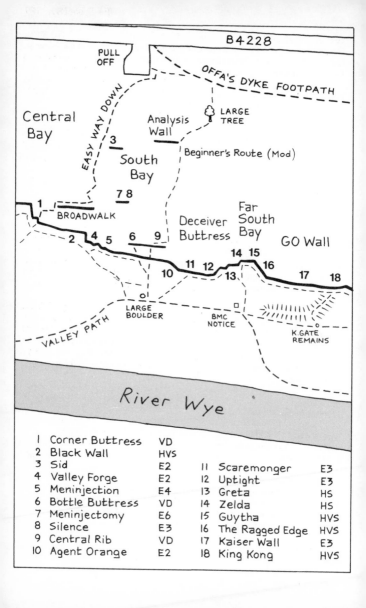

B4228

PULL OFF

OFFA'S DYKE FOOTPATH

EASY WAY DOWN

Central Bay

Analysis Wall

LARGE TREE

Beginner's Route (Mod)

South Bay

3

7 8

Far South Bay

Deceiver Buttress

GO Wall

BROADWALK

1

2 4 5   6   9

11 12   14 15

16

10   13

17   18

LARGE BOULDER

BMC NOTICE

K.GATE REMAINS

VALLEY PATH

River Wye

1	Corner Buttress	VD			
2	Black Wall	HVS			
3	Sid	E2			
4	Valley Forge	E2	11	Scaremonger	E3
5	Meninjection	E4	12	Uptight	E3
6	Bottle Buttress	VD	13	Greta	HS
7	Meninjectomy	E6	14	Zelda	HS
8	Silence	E3	15	Guytha	HVS
9	Central Rib	VD	16	The Ragged Edge	HVS
10	Agent Orange	E2	17	Kaiser Wall	E3
			18	King Kong	HVS

THE SOUTH BAY

'And the lion shall lie down with the lamb'. It is not often that V Diff shares its belays with E6, but this bay is for all sorts. Though it will doubtless continue to be frequented most for its classic easy routes (and where in Britain will you find a better limestone V Diff than *Central Rib III*?), a few of the harder climbs that are easy to reach and follow receive regular attention.

Because of the various route starting-levels (which are not organized in neat tiers as on The North Wall), a strict adherence to the left-to-right principle is problematic, and those who are not familiar with the general topography of the wall may find things confusing. Familiarization by climbing one or two of the full-length routes, and careful reference to the diagram and linking paragraphs will assist clarification.

THE APPROACH

To reach the base, all the ways described in the crag's introduction are convenient, that by the Easy Way Down (page 55) being marginally the quickest. After Black Wall below The Central Bay is passed, there is a short steep drop in the path. At the bottom of this on the left there is a messy area of rubbish and fallen blocks and trees; just above is a groove, the start of *Valley Forge*. Please note: there are **no easy** routes just here. This innocuous-looking groove has often attracted climbers seeking V Diffs, and there have been a number of accidents and even more near misses.

A huge filthy gully, broken by a large roof at 40 feet, separates Forge Buttress from Bottle Buttress. To the right of this is a more open groove with an offset lower section. This is the start of *Meninjection*. Further right still is the 20-foot starting-groove of *Prang*; the groove itself is clean, but above and right the vegetation is growing fast and furiously. Right again is the short easy groove and wall leading to the ledge-system 15 feet above the ground which extends rightwards from the foot of *Bottle Buttress* climb itself to and past the Central Rib.

To reach *Bottle Buttress* and the Central Rib routes directly from the main valley path, take an obvious small path up towards the rock from a large moss-and-ivy-covered block. There is a fork near the top: the left branch goes to *Bottle Buttress* and the right to the Central Rib. Either way, the ledge-system is reached by a simple scramble.

THE WAY OFF

The Forge Buttress and Bottle Buttress routes finish on, or beside the top of, the Easy Way Down. Those to the right emerge directly onto Offa's Dyke footpath: turn left for the parking pull-off at the top of the Easy Way Down, or right and later left for *The Rising Sun Inn*.

FORGE BUTTRESS

The first routes start on a grassy ledge-system high up beneath an overhang

above and **right** of the top of *Valley Forge*. They can be reached by abseil
from a peg and stake belay on a ledge just off the Easy Way Down, 40 feet
below the top: this is the belay at the end of pitch 5 of *The Early Morning
Traverse*; and it is the first ledge (in descent) where you can *walk* round to the
front of the buttress from the Easy Way Down. Alternatively, there are now two
bolts on the next ledge below and just left (facing in) of this. There are also
now two bolts to belay on at the start of the routes.

Sid   40 feet   E2 5b   (27.5.84)
From the centre of the ledge, climb up to a narrow ledge on the left. Move
up to the overhangs (peg runner) and pull over sightly left to slabs. Climb
these with little protection, and taking care with the rock, to a cleaned
ledge on the left. Move up and right to belay at the bolts.

Vicious (60 feet E2 5c 27.5.84) seems now to have been destroyed and
replaced by the next route.

Feline Frolics   40 feet   E3 5c   (10.5.96)
From the right-hand end of the ledge, pull up to a break. Climb up
towards the roof (*Friend 1* placement on left) and, using a large finger-slot
high on the right to gain height, grab the obvious protruding triangular
edge well out left. Pass a bolt runner and dyno for jugs up and left to gain
a ramp-line. Finish easily to the ledge and two bolts.

The next four routes have a common start up the obvious cleaned groove
above the rubbish area at the base of the left-hand end of the bay.

When the Wind Blows   90 feet   E2 5c ‡   (17.10.87)
A good final section; quite sustained but well protected. The pockets below
the crux have sprouted numerous brambles, which would need to be
removed before an attempt.
Climb the groove to the ledge on the left and move up to a higher ledge
(peg runner). Climb up and across left to a small hole at knee-height and
climb a shallow rib (peg runner on the right) to a pocketed break (large
Friend placement). Climb up for 10 feet (bolt runner) and make a thin
traverse right to gain better holds. Layback into a small scoop (junction
with *Valley Forge*) and use an undercut on the left to reach a superb jug
and the top. Two peg belays. Scramble uncomfortably off left or traverse
back right and finish up *Valley Forge*.

★Valley Forge   135 feet   E2 5c   (31.3.85)
A fine route, spoilt only by the aspect. Good rock and protection, and fairly
low in the grade.
Climb the groove to the ledge on the left and move up to a higher ledge
(peg runner). Climb a faint rib (second peg runner), and on up past the
obvious short groove of *Yr Herwehla* out right (large *in-situ* thread, peg
runner above). An awkward move gains a tiny ledge, and a thin diagonal

crack is climbed to better holds which lead to a break. Move 5 feet right to a ledge, and climb slabby black rock and then a short white wall (peg runner) to a large ledge beside the Easy Way Down. Nut belays.

Yr Herwehla   135 feet   E1 5b   (22.6.84)
This climb has improved and is worthwhile; but protection is still sparse unless some of *Valley Forge*'s pegs are clipped, and there is now a naughty bolt on the right below the short upper groove.
Climb the groove and then a slightly overhanging wall above. Step right and climb up past an *in-situ* thread to the bottom of the obvious short overhanging groove. Climb the groove strenuously, and more easily above to a narrow ledge. Join *Valley Forge* up the black slab and white wall (peg runner) to a ledge beside the Easy Way Down. Nut belays.

Fear Is the Key   70 feet   Hard Very Severe 5a   (5.7.90)
Good rock, good value, but somewhat compromised by the next route. Start as for the preceding routes and climb the groove for 20 feet. Move right and climb the centre of the slab until able to move right again to the arête (peg runner missing). Climb the arête to some ledges and then a groove as far as you feel like, and retreat from one of the bolts of the next route. The original abseil point has been removed. It is also possible (E2 5a 5.7.90) to foot-traverse right just above the ground and climb the wall just left of the arête direct.

Therapy   130 feet   E2 5c   (11.5.96)
Start 10 feet right of *Valley Forge* below a bolt runner just right of the arête. Move up on positive holds past the bolt runner to the crackline. Climb the crack and then a pocketed wall to a ledge. Move up (bolt runner), climb up to a small groove (bolt runner), and continue to below a bulge (bolt runner). Technical moves over the bulge (bolt runner) using a pocket on the right lead to jugs. Continue more easily (bolt runner) to a ledge and bolt runner below the top wall. Reach the crystalline crackline (bolt runner) and climb it just past the large roof to a ledge beside the Easy Way Down. Nut belays.

BOTTLE BUTTRESS
Right of the huge dirty, roofed gully, **The Small Time** (40 feet E1 5b 8.10.87) climbs the left arête of the *Meninjection* groove past a peg runner to a bolt belay. It incorporates some of the next route but is the only part of that worth doing.

Death of a Salesman   170 feet   E2   (15.4.81)
An impressive-looking line up the obvious vertical arête, but on dangerous rock, and there is no adequate mid-point belay. Start up the groove as for *Meninjection*, but leave it immediately for the left arête, and continue up to an obvious green bush (90 feet 5b). Continue up the arête, moving right then left to a small finishing-groove. Easy but loose steps lead to the

two-peg belay in a short corner on *Bottle Buttress* (80 feet 4c). Finish by climbing pitch 4 of *Bottle Buttress* or traversing off left a little above onto the Easy Way Down.

Meninjection 270 feet E4 ‡ (6.9.81)

Two well-contrasted pitches, but sustained, with uncomfortably long runouts. The short wall above and right of the starting-groove has ivied over; but there is a recently-cleaned thin crack leading rightwards from the foot of the upper section of the groove which might provide a good alternative (there appears no record of its having been climbed). Start in the offset lower section of the open groove right of the dirty roofed gully.
1 90 feet 5c. Climb the groove a short way and gain the hanging arête on the right. Climb rightwards across the now ivied wall to a large ledge. Trend up and left over ledges for 10 feet to a short crack. Gain the break above and hand-traverse right in it for 10 feet. Lurch up (peg runner) and continue directly up the wall to finish up a short groove. Small tree belay on the right, as for *Bottle Buttress*.
2 60 feet 5c. Climb boldly up the slab into a scoop (peg runner). Reach a thin flake crack above and follow it to good holds and a ledge. Thread and nut belay on the left.
3 120 feet 4c. Climb the easy slab above to the traverse-ramp on *Bottle Buttress*. Step right and climb a short sharp groove. Continue straight up to join *Bottle Buttress Direct* up the left edge of the black headwall. Finish over loose easy ground to a tree belay just below the top.

To the right, the lower wall has become heavily overgrown with brambles and ivy. Two lost routes lie underneath this: **Prang** (4.63) and **Guatemala City** (21.12.84) (both 70 feet Hard Very Severe 5a). They have a common start up a still cleanish groove 30 feet right of *Meninjection* and 15 feet left of the left end of the ledge-system. *Prang* goes directly on up (two peg runners available), with the crux at the top, to reach the small tree belay of *Bottle Buttress*. From the top of the groove, *Guatemala City* moves right on a ledge and takes the weakness in the right-hand side of the wall to the same point.

The next two climbs start at the first belay (a small tree) of *Bottle Buttress*, also used by the three preceding routes. *Meninjectomy* takes the smooth grey pillar to the *left* of the second pitch of *Meninjection*, and *Silence* the black wall/slab to the right of the latter.

Meningectomy 60 feet E6 6a (6.84)

Bold, serious, and uncompromising, despite the bolt, and even with a longish sling pre-attached to it.
From 10 feet left of the belay, climb the blunt rib just right of the green bush with difficulty (bolt runner). Continue direct up the pillar above, less hard but increasingly bold, to further thin moves up left (peg runner). Finish directly and more easily to a good ledge. Either step down on the right to a thread and nut belay, or continue up easy but loose rock for 25 feet to the

two-peg belay in a short corner on *Bottle Buttress*.

Silence   50 feet   E3 6a   (17.10.86)
Precarious climbing on smooth sloping holds: good rock and low in the grade.
Climb up right of the tree belay to some thin breaks (good wires) and move up awkwardly to stand in them. Climb the smooth wall (bolt runner) and then balance up to better holds (peg runner). Finish at the obvious exit to a tree belay just right.

The remaining routes on Bottle Buttress all start left of or behind the green bush in the middle of the ledge-system 15 feet above the ground. Reach this by scrambling leftwards up a short groove and wall 25 feet right of the starting-groove of *Prang* and at the top of the left-hand branch that comes up from the main path.

Bottle Buttress   260 feet   Very Difficult
A rather wayward route, but with some good climbing, not easy for the grade. Care must be taken to protect an inexperienced second on the traverse sections. Start just left of a small green bush in a corner, at the extreme left end of the ledge-system.
1   50 feet.   Make an awkward pull up to the left across the little slab, or climb the corner behind the bush and step left (pointless old peg). Climb through a gap in the overhang and continue, bearing left past a bush on the left, to a short corner with a small tree belay at the top. (This is not the larger tree on the wall to the right which is visible from the start of the climb.)
2   80 feet.   Climb easily diagonally right to a larger ledge and tree (the belay on *Bottle Buttress Direct*). Step up behind the tree and fix a thread. The innocuous-looking slab above is VS; so, from below the thread but above the ledge, traverse 15 feet right, passing a peg runner, and climb a scoop on sloping holds to another ledge. The broken wall a few feet back left leads to a fallen block and two trees.
3   30 feet.   Traverse left onto and along a sloping ramp to a small corner with a two-peg belay. A hidden undercut assists the move past the gap under the overhangs: pay attention to footwork. This is hard for the grade – an easier alternative (especially for the second) is to descend to some grass ledges from just left of the belay and regain the ramp beyond the gap.
4   100 feet.   Step out left of the corner and move up on very small holds. Continue straight up an obvious line, which relents all the while, to reach easy ground beside the Easy Way Down just below the top. Belay on a huge block with the rope, or find various nut placements.

Bottle Out   190 feet   E1   (15.3.86)
Hopelessly eliminate and escapable, but continuously entertaining, and low in the grade. Start 10 feet right of the small green bush of *Bottle*

Buttress, immediately below a tree.
1 100 feet 5b. Use a good pocket to pull up left past the tree. Continue straight up for 15 feet passing a peg runner on *Bottle Buttress Direct* to stand on a small ledge. Step out right on a narrow foot-ledge above the overhang and below some sandy pockets. Climb the blunt arête (two peg runners shared with *Last of the Wine*) until a hard move attains a superb white jug. Trend left over easier rock to a short overhanging arête above a ledge. Climb this (peg runner on right, thread on the left) just on its right to a hard pull over the top. A short easy tier leads to the fallen block and two trees on *Bottle Buttress*.
2 90 feet 4c. Step off the block onto the wall and climb straight up to a grassy band. Move slightly right for the next short tier, and back to an obvious short crack at ground-level. Climb a slight vertical break a few feet left of the edge of the wall (peg runner difficult to reach out right) and step right near the top to good holds on the edge. Large platform and peg belay above. Scramble to the top with care.

Bottle Buttress Direct   220 feet   Very Severe   (c. 1966)
A rather artificial line, its name being justified only in relation to the ordinary route, which meanders even more. However, each pitch is low in its technical grade and the route is worth doing for a variety of interesting and strenuous moves. Start on a small block ledge just above the main ledge-system, 15 feet right of the small green bush at the foot of *Bottle Buttress* ordinary route.
1 70 feet 4c. Climb a short corner-crack to a small roof at 20 feet. Move left and pull up with difficulty and taking care with the rock (peg runner) onto a ledge in a shallow corner. Climb the corner until level with a prominent tree on the left (no further). Foot-traverse the break to the tree, and climb the vague riblet, bearing slightly right, to a large ledge and tree.
2 40 feet 4c. Climb straight up behind the tree past a thread to a ledge, and continue easily to the fallen block and two trees.
3 110 feet 4c. Left of the belays and right of the semi-circular overhang is a short steep crack. Climb this and the tapering slab above. Traverse diagonally left on rough ground below a steep black wall to a dirty crack at its far end, which is used to gain better holds on the right on the wall. Loose but easy ground leads to a small tree just below the top (whence there is an easy traverse left onto the Easy Way Down).

Gotta Lotta Bottle (240 feet Very Severe 4c 2.10.83) is an eliminate, similar in standard to the above, but less worthwhile. Follow *Bottle Buttress Direct* until level with the traverse to the tree. Make two moves further up the corner and step out right onto good holds. Continue straight up, passing just right of the ledge and on past the peg runner of *Bottle Buttress* to the fallen block and two trees (110 feet 4c). Move up right to the flake crack, climb the thin slab on its left, and avoid the black wall by a thin crack on the right. Trend left up easier rock to a platform and peg belay (100 feet 4c). Climb the yellow arête taking care with the rock (30 feet).

Last of the Wine   80 feet   E3 6a   (1.10.87)
Fine steep climbing on good rock; unfortunately, the crux is avoidable on
the left, and taking advantage reduces the standard by a full grade. Start
on the small raised block ledge, as for *Bottle Buttress Direct*.
Climb directly up the wall just right of the small corner (bolt runner) to a
wide break. Continue straight up (peg runner) and make a hard move just
right of the arête onto a ledge (second peg runner). Climb diagonally right
with some delicate moves to reach a flake and a peg runner at the junction
with *Meningitis* and *Broken Bottle*. Stand up to reach a good hold on the
left, and then go diagonally right to the two-bolt belay of *Childhood's End*.
Abseil off.

Meningitis   220 feet   E4   (29.3.81)
A serious first pitch with minimal protection – this does not pass within
reach of the two pegs of *Bottle Out* and *Last of the Wine* over to the left.
Start just left of the large green bush in the centre of the ledge-system.
1 110 feet 5c. Climb directly up the wall left of *Broken Bottle* to a shaly
break. Move slightly left and then up via an undercut to a small ledge.
Continue direct up the slab, still technical, to a peg runner on *Broken
Bottle*. As for the latter, move left and then go up, and left and up again to
the fallen block and two trees.
2 110 feet 4c. Traverse left under the overhang as for *Bottle Buttress*, and
then pull up beside it and step back right on top. Continue up over rough
ground slightly leftwards to join the final crack of *Bottle Buttress Direct*.
Loose but easy ground leads to a small tree a little below the top.

Broken Bottle   220 feet   E1   (c.1967/1978)
Beginning life as an inauspicious aid pitch, this flowered into a good,
enjoyable free climb, lowish in the grade. Start behind the large green
bush in the centre of the ledge-system, below a shallow groove which
indents the upper of two small overhangs.
1 120 feet 5b. Pull up onto a good ledge on the left and continue
straight up to the first overhang (peg runner). Move right and pull over
using superb hidden layaway holds high out right. Step back left into the
groove-line, and continue up this past a peg runner under the second
overhang to a sapling. Above, traverse more easily left past a third peg
runner (junction with the two preceding routes) until the holds run out.
Make one more technical move up into a dark scoop, and then go easily
left and up to the fallen block and two trees on *Bottle Buttress*.
2 100 feet 4c. Go diagonally right to a good flake crack. Climb it and
move up and left to a short crack at ground-level below the right edge of
the black headwall. As for *Bottle Out*, climb a slight vertical break just left
of the edge (peg runner difficult to reach out right) and step right near the
top to good holds on the edge. Large platform and peg belay above.
Scramble to the top with care.

CENTRAL RIB SECTOR
This includes the rib itself and the broken wall on its left. The routes start on the more spacious right-hand half of the ledge-system 15 feet above the ground, between the central green bush on the left and the obvious foot of the rib on the right.

★★**Childhood's End**   70 feet   E2 5c   (21.12.86)
A entertaining and justly popular pitch containing three contrasted elements: a wall, a roof, and an (*ersatz*) crack. Start just right of the central bush on the ledge-system, below a hairline vertical crack.
Reach the crack (peg runner) and climb directly up the wall on sandy pockets. Pull up just right into the break (peg runner) and move up to the roof (peg runner). Swagger over and climb more easily (sapling on left) directly to the prominent borehole (bolt runner). Reach a finger-ledge just above the bolt (with considerable difficulty if you are short) and lunge for jugs at the top of the borehole. Two-bolt belay. Abseil off.

Fifteen feet left of the foot of the rib there is a short left-facing corner with a large tree and some smaller ones near the bottom. *Age of Enlightenment* takes a direct clean line up the wall behind the tree; *Barber's Stool* and *Camp Freddie's Boil* take more vegetated rock to the **left and right** respectively.

Barber's Stool (85 feet Hard Very Severe 4c ‡ 10.12.80) starts just left of the large tree and climbs the wall past a peg runner to a bush at 25 feet. Grassy steps diagonally left, and then a small recessed slab diagonally right lead to the left section of the overhang. A precarious tape on this is the only protection above the bush. The overhang and the short wall above are taken directly to an isolated large silver birch midway between Bottle Buttress and Central Rib. A poor continuation pitch was made but is now very brambled.
Camp Freddie's Boil (90 feet Very Severe 4c ‡ 7.1.81) is broken and scrappy. From the large tree, climb grooves rightwards past a sapling to a sapling and bush, and then a short wall with a long reach for a hold to pull up onto a little slab. Move up and right onto a grass ledge and climb directly up to a green bush and a tree belay, just left of the *Central Rib* corner.

★**Age of Enlightenment**   80 feet   E1 5b   (28.1.87)
A route of sustained technical interest at the upper end of this grade. Mostly peg protection, but small wires are useful around the crux.
Climb up directly behind (but without assistance from) the large tree past a peg runner to a ledge on the right of a bush. Continue up the wall (two peg runners) and pull up left on two obvious holds onto a short slab leading to the main, right-hand section of the overhang. Climb over this rightwards and up to a ledge (peg runner). Easier moves lead to a final overhang (peg runner); finish through the gap. Peg belay above and a tree out right. The first belay of *Central Rib I* is further right. Abseil off or climb *Clutching at Straws*.

Clutching at Straws   40 feet   E2   5c   (5.87)
This entertaining but stranded little pitch starts at the first belay of *Central Rib I*, or makes a worthy extension to *Age of Enlightenment*.
Climb the flowstone wall left of the corner on pockets and tiny edges (peg runner, and two threads which need replacing). Peg belay on the ledge at the top.

★★**Central Rib Route I**   220 feet   Severe
The best route of its grade on the cliff, with a classic second pitch and a testing finish. Start on the ledge-system.
1 80 feet. Climb the centre of the wall left of the rib, behind the vegetation, past a little overhang, and then bear right to a small ledge beside the rib (peg runner). As for *Central Rib III*, climb the groove, moving up left where it steepens to gain good ledges. Climb straight up to the large tree at the foot of the long corner.
2 40 feet 4a. Climb the corner past the horizontal tree to a ledge and peg belay at its top.
3 50 feet. Move up to the ledge above and walk left, past a thorn bush, and just round the edge. Climb diagonally back right to the rib. Pull up leftwards beside a small nose and go on up to an assortment of tree belays.
4 50 feet 4a. Scramble up to the next ledge behind the trees and move left to the centre of the final steep wall. Climb up on small but positive holds passing just right of a small ledge at half height, which can be used or avoided. This pitch proves less fearsome than it threatens, but an easier alternative can be found in the bore-crack on the left. Various fence or vegetation belays: check for soundness.

★**Central Rib Route II**   210 feet   Very Severe   (1973)
The large stances and the proximity of easier routes seem to detract from the seriousness; in fact, the committing top section of the first pitch and the steep little finishing-wall put this quite high in the grade. Start at the foot of the short corner formed by the rib and its left wall.
1 80 feet 4c. Bridge up the corner. Move out right onto the rib, which is climbed directly, easily to start. There is a peg runner at the start of the steep section: take this near the left edge at first, and then move up right to get both hands on an obvious block. Climb up to a large crystal hole in the loose band, step right of it, and make a final awkward move up to a good platform. Peg belay low in the rib behind (look for it: it *is* there).
2 70 feet 4b. Climb the left arête to a large platform (peg runner used as belay on the other routes). Hand-traverse left across the top of the long corner and move on round into a shorter corner. Climb this and then the steep fault on the left in the centre of the wall above. Tree belay just below the forest.
3 60 feet 5a. Move up left of the trees and over an overhang onto the long ledge below the final steep wall. From the right-hand end of the ledge, climb up on small holds to a gash at the top. Various belays behind,

but check for soundness.

★★★Central Rib Route III   220 feet   Very Difficult
A classic: a perfect introduction to rock-climbing on a fine day. And as the
belays are shared with *Central Rib I*, slightly harder, but equally good,
variants can be introduced at will. [Photo p.129.] Start at the foot of the rib,
the second belaying anywhere comfortable to the left.
1 80 feet. Climb the crest of the rib for 40 feet to a small ledge on the left
(peg runner). Climb the groove – useful right holds out on the rib – until
able to reach the first of two good sharp ledges on the left. Bear slightly left
over these and go straight up to a large tree belay at the foot of the long
corner. This section is polished and quite hard for the grade; harder still if
at all damp.
2 50 feet. Go diagonally right to a platform on the rib (peg runner if you
look hard) and climb the rib steeply, slightly right at first, then left, to
another platform. Peg belay.
3 40 feet. Climb straight on up to an awkward move through a gap
between a nose on the left and an overhang on the right. Numerous tree
belays in the forest.
4 50 feet. Scramble diagonally right over vegetation to a small buttress of
clean rock in a nice position. Follow a diagonal crack rightwards across its
face and mantel onto the top. Various vegetation belays: check for
soundness.

THE RIGHT-HAND SECTOR
Not far right of the rib, Deceiver Buttress extrudes from the bay. Near the
bottom, this leaves a limited area of broken rock, which widens out progressively towards the top. *The Beginner's Route* curves round rightwards above
the edge of Deceiver Buttress and is described first as it gives access to the
routes taking the upper walls. Most of these are of little importance. The harder
ones offer the prospect of good climbing, but they have not received many
ascents and tend to get dirty.

The Beginner's Route   260 feet   Moderate
A safe introductory route but, alas, not in the class of *Easy Route* at Avon.
Numerous variations are possible and the pitches can be split or
rearranged at will; there are plenty of sound tree belays above half height.
From the bottom of the Central Rib, the route aims for the prominent tree
just below the right-hand skyline. Start, as for the Central Rib routes, by
scrambling to a large platform below and left of the rib, 15 feet above the
ground.
1 110 feet. Traverse right over vegetated ledges past the foot of the rib.
Climb a vague area of broken rock to a ledge and tree belay, taking a line
to taste – generally easier towards the right.
2 120 feet. Climb to the next tree and up a short open corner behind it.
Now take a diagonal line to the large tree on the right skyline 30 feet
below the top. The final 20 feet to the tree are steep and sometimes

muddy, but holds are enormous. Belay on a branch.
3 30 feet. Step right and climb broken rock with care to the top. Block belay, or tree belay a further 25 feet back.

Right of the upper half of Central Rib is a large vertical black wall. The base of this can be reached easily from *The Beginner's Route*, by a dirty traverse from the first belay of one of the Central Rib routes, or by abseiling from the top of *Central Rib III*, identifiable as the left-hand (facing out) of two fenced gaps a little south of the top of the Easy Way Down. The latter involves some bush-bashing about 20 feet down, but leaving the rope in place can save you having to do this on the way up or, in some cases, belaying and abseiling from a single 8mm bolt.

Rape of the Fair Country (120 feet Very Severe 4c ‡ 19.7.81) takes the unpleasantly vegetated groove between the rib and the wall to beneath a prominent overhang after 50 feet. Move slightly right to pull over, but avoid dangerous rock on the right by making the effort to reach the next holds above. Continue over dubious rock and some vegetated ledges to the finishing-crack of *Central Rib III*.

All Wound Up 80 feet E4 6c †   (29.5.86)
A direct line up the smooth left-hand section of the black wall. A very difficult problem.
Climb the rib as for *Analysis* to good runners in horizontal breaks at half height. Climb straight up the increasingly smooth, steep, and difficult wall (two bolt runners) until a good sidehold slightly left enables a long reach to be made to the horizontal break (two in-situ threads). Continue directly up the short groove to ledges and a tree belay. The finish of *Central Rib III* is directly above.

Analysis 100 feet E5 6b   (18.3.84)
The centre of the wall also gives some fiercely technical climbing which now proves quite serious. A preplaced rope to belay is advised. Start below and right of the first belay of *Central Rib II* at a small slim tree.
Climb the blunt rib which leads up to the left side of the wall and into a black scoop. Cross diagonally right to a good ledge and go up 10 feet (two peg runners). Make hard moves diagonally right to a break (two in-situ threads), and another to reach good holds which attain a single-bolt belay.

Mind over Matter 65 feet E4 6b   (25.4.86)
Just a little less fierce than the two preceding routes. A preplaced rope to belay is advised. Start at a tree below the right end of the wall.
Climb up left of the tree to a cleaned ledge. Continue up past a bolt runner with difficulty to gain better holds and then the wide break (thread in situ, and the *Analysis* threads out left). Stand awkwardly in the break and then shuffle leftwards along it a few feet. Climb up boldly and then bear left on

good holds to the single-bolt belay on *Analysis*.

Two routes take the left and right sides respectively of the blunt nose bounding the right end of the wall. These have now been cleaned up and some pegs and threads fixed. The pegs at half and three-quarters height can be clipped from either route – there is still some loose rock in the obvious band between them; this apart the climbs are now a reasonable proposition and quite worthwhile. **The One that Nearly Got Away** (90 feet E2 5b 15.4.82). **Hic, Hoc, Altera et** (80 feet E1 5a 18.5.81).

Right of the nose, an open dirty groove is topped by a curving flake crack. If **This** (80 feet Hard Very Severe 4c) were clean and sound it would give a classic layback; but it isn't and it doesn't.

Something Else   100 feet   Very Severe 4c   (15.11.78)
Climb pitch 1 of *That*; then go diagonally left to a sapling and diagonally back right past another to the little groove. Start on the right, and then follow the groove to the top. Tree belay.

That   100 feet   Severe   (1.67)
Earthy. Start half way up *The Beginner's Route*, 6 feet right of the groove of *This*, beneath a small overhang on the left edge of the buttress.
1 40 feet 4a. Climb straight up to a platform, and belay on the higher of two trees: steep and somewhat blind, but good holds always materialize.
2 60 feet 4a. Move up over earth and grass ledges a few feet right to a shallow red chimney, which is climbed to a finish out right. Tree belay.

Never Never Land   90 feet   E2   (26.11.86)
Start just right of *That*, at two faint pink streaks.
1 40 feet 5b. Use layaways on the left to reach a good hold. Pull up on it and continue easily to the ledge and large tree belay of *That*. A contrived boulder-problem start.
2 50 feet 5c. Climb the short wall behind the tree (peg runner) and cross two narrow grass ledges. Climb the slim wall of good rock above (peg runner), finishing slightly right.

The Other   120 feet   Very Severe 4b   (8.78)
Start at an overhung corner 20 feet right of *That*.
Climb the corner, step left onto the buttress, and trend up left to the tree of *That*. Go up right as for *That*, but keep traversing right on poor rock, past a large gash, to finish up a small crack at the far right end of the wall.

The next two routes, though slight, are quite reasonable and are easily reached by scrambling (carefully) down the top pitch of *The Beginner's Route*.

Frustration   50 feet   E2 5c   (3.12.86)
The best of the E2s hereabouts. Start below a prominent roof, just below

and left of the very large tree 30 feet below the top of *The Beginner's Route*.
Pull over the point of the overhang and move up left over juggy breaks
(peg runner in the highest one). Climb directly up the centre of the short
wall of good rock (peg runner) to the obvious tree belay at the top.

Brief Encounter 50 feet E2 5c   (3.12.86)
Start as for *Frustration*.
Pull over the centre of the right-hand half of the roof and go straight up
over juggy breaks. Climb the short wall of good rock until a small gash is
at foot-level (peg runner). Make an awkward step left and climb directly to
the top (bush and peg belay).

The last route is just right of the apex of Deceiver Buttress and should
theoretically be described under The Far South Bay. However, its approach
and nature make it more convenient to include it here. Reach large grassy
ledges by scrambling up or down *The Beginner's Route* and moving round
right (facing in) from about 15 feet below the large tree.

Wicked 40 feet E5 6c †   (27.4.86)
A short but disproportionately desperate pitch which takes the smooth dark
wall above Deceiver Buttress, right of the top half of *The Beginner's Route*.
From the right hand-end of the highest ledge, climb the wall (bolt runner)
to undercuts below a small roof. Follow the obvious thin crackline (peg
runner) up and across left until a good hold in the crack enables the top to
be reached. Tree belay 20 feet higher.

DECEIVER BUTTRESS   (Crag plan page 100)
This is by far the most treacherous section of rock at Wintour's Leap. Nor does
it do its dirty work by halves: when rocks fall here, *big* rocks fall… Even so,
the activists have persevered and there are still some climbs standing (but
strictly without warranty).

APPROACH
From the large block where the path up to the Central Rib leaves the main
path, cut diagonally rightwards to the boulder-strewn foot of the buttress, or
find a more direct way through the trees from anywhere a little further south,
but not beyond the BMC GO Wall notice. The large corner of *An Android's
Dream* near the left of the buttress and the wide, overhung, orange recess of
Agent Orange 20 feet to its right are easily identified; so is *Uptight*, a smaller
corner with a well-defined crack topped by two iron spikes, near the right end.

WAYS OFF
There are fixed belays, from which one can abseil, on or available to all the
routes of less than 100 feet. The remainder go to the top of the buttress (which
is some 70 feet below the top of the cliff). From there, traverse easily off left
onto *The Beginner's Route* and scramble up or back down.

John Bennett   50 feet   E1 5b   (16.10.85)
The smaller and left-hand of the two grooves at the left end of the buttress.
Somewhat loose and dirty.
Reach and climb the groove to gain the crackline on the right. Climb the
crack, and pass the overhang, using small layaways on the left (peg runner
on the right), to reach a ledge and tree; continue just right on brittle rock to
another ledge and two small trees. Bolt and nut belay 15 feet above and
right.

The large corner just to the right *was* **Gordon Bennett** (26.8.85), climbed
direct to an exit right. In 1987 it suddenly became much larger and its new
entrails were distinctly unenticing. The next route offered a more sensible
alternative.

An Android's Dream   60 feet   E3 5c   (8.4.90)
Climb the initial corner and move up and right (peg runner) to the right
arête. Make some hard moves to reach good holds and finish direct to the
bolt and nut belay.

It's Your Life...   70 feet   E5 6a   (26.8.85)
A fine pitch with a weird start and a very bold piece of climbing above:
there is no protection to prevent a ground fall from the upper crux.
Pull up to the jutting roof immediately right of the corner of *An Android's
Dream* (somewhat abused *in-situ* wire) and struggle over into the small
leaning corner above, which leads more easily to a break and poor peg
runner. Climb straight up the wall on excellent rock until a final long reach
gains a narrow ledge. Continue directly up (peg runner) to a clean ledge
and the bolt and nut belay.

Do What You Want   60 feet   E4 6b †   (8.2.92)
The excellent arête right of *It's Your Life...* Start as for that route. Caution:
the first bolt is araldited-in only.
Pull up the short groove and make an entertaining mantelshelf onto the
ledge on the right. Climb the white wall to the roof (bolt runner). Reach a
large jug in a slight groove in the arête (bolt runner) and surmount the roof
with a struggle. Climb the arête delicately with a bold move to reach good
holds on *Agent Orange*, and follow its groove (peg runner) to the bolt and
nut belay.

Agent Orange   85 feet   E2 5c   (5.10.85)
A good, enjoyable pitch with a short, well-protected, but perplexing crux.
Start below the obvious pedestal-crack in the wide orange recess.
Pull steeply up to a ledge at 10 feet and climb the crack to a ledge at the
base of the left corner of the recess. Climb the corner to the roof (peg
runner), cross the left wall with difficulty to reach a good hold on the arête,
and pull up onto a resting-ledge above (protection out right). Climb a
shallow groove on good holds (peg runner) and finish left on a cleaned

ledge. Bolt and nut belay.

9½ Lives   70 feet   E5 6b †   (8.2.92)
The centre of the orange wall and double overhang in the recess
containing *Agent Orange*. Not high in the grade, but bold and deceptive.
Start, as for *Sleight of Hand*, 10 feet right of the left corner of the recess.
Pull up to the ledge at 10 feet, step left, and climb the flake crack formed
by the right-hand side of the pedestal to the ledge at its top. Go straight up
a shallow orange groove and pull over a small overhang on the right to
reach the double roof (peg runner). Reach a pinch on the lip and heave
over direct on jugs. Climb more easily to a short steep wall (peg runner,
Rock 8 on the left). Go straight up this with a very difficult move to reach
pockets (*Rock 9*); then traverse easily leftwards to exit as for *Agent Orange*
to the bolt and nut belay.

Sleight of Hand   60 feet   E1 5b   (3.7.86)
The crack is a little sandy, and a couple of obvious loose blocks should be
avoided; quite enjoyable climbing, though. Start 10 feet right of *Agent
Orange*.
Pull up to the ledge at 10 feet to gain a finger-crack, and follow it
awkwardly past an overlap to the larger overhangs (peg runner out left –
hard to clip). Pull straight over into a shallow groove on excellent holds and
follow it to a two-bolt belay. Abseil off.

Prestidigitator   170 feet   E2   (10.7.90)
A rather wayward eliminate, avoiding the worst rock of the next route and
with somewhat more secure protection, but still a challenging lead.
1 80 feet   5b. Follow *Sleight of Hand* to the overhangs (level with the peg
runner out left), and then swing right and move up to the cave of *The
Adulterer* (two peg runners). Pull over the roof on the right and move
across rightwards to the two-bolt belay of *Scaremonger*.
2 90 feet   5a. Move up rightwards and then back left above the belay
(peg runner above). Climb up and then diagonally left past a shale break.
Make awkward moves past a peg runner to better holds in the long groove
of *The Adulterer*. Climb the groove easily for 10 feet and then move out
right onto the face. Go up past a peg runner to a small ledge. Clip the old
peg runner of *The Deceiver* out right and climb the wall to the left past a
final peg runner to a ledge and a small tree belay.

The Adulterer   150 feet   E3 5b   (21.10.78)
Much suspect rock and some poor pegs (old aid relics); though improved
a little in both respects by the preparation of the previous route.
Climb the right of two short grooves 15 feet left of *The Deceiver* to a small
ledge and peg runner. Climb straight up above to a small cave and two
peg runners. Move right to pull over the overhang and back left to a short
bottomless groove. Climb this and the long easier groove above to a ledge
and a small tree belay. A more worthwhile finish is that of *Prestidigitator*.

★Scaremonger   80 feet   E3   6a   (2.10.86)
A fine eliminate with some exciting moves over the roof, though the hard moves are always well protected. Start 5 feet left of the semi-circular overhang of *The Deceiver*, at an excavated ledge.
Gain a standing-position on an obvious wedge-shaped block. Lean right (bolt runner) and make an awkward entry into a shallow scooped groove. Go up the groove and balance up onto some small ledges beneath a smooth, slabby wall. Climb delicately up the wall (bolt runner) to a good peg runner below a tiny corner. Feel for a minute finger-edge over the roof, move up for a jug, and pull on up to move left on good holds. Continue to a break (peg runner) and make a final difficult move to gain a two-bolt belay. Abseil off.

To the right, a long strip of the bottom of the buttress has fallen out and the starts of the next four routes have been affected to a greater or lesser extent.

No attempt at assessing the grade of **The Deceiver** (200 feet †† 13.7.67) is offered. It was originally given HVS, and by the time of the last guide E3 was suggested. The first pitch may still be climbable if anyone can be bothered to reclean it. Start left of centre of the buttress, below a semi-circular overhang which tops a very short rib, flanked on either side by an equally short groove. Escape right and climb an ivy crack past a peg runner. Step right below a small overhang and climb a short corner (peg runner) to the two-peg, two-bolt belay of *Turn a Blind Eye* (60 feet 5a). The next section is horrendous: move awkwardly up to the ledge and step right (two old pegs). Move up over a small loose overhang, and climb a shallow groove to a traverse left. Climb diagonally left past the end of the long overhang and up a short final wall (peg runner); then scramble to a tree belay (140 feet 5b).

Turn a Blind Eye (60 feet †† 24.9.86) appears sadly to have beeen rendered defunct by the rockfall. Formerly E3 6b and worth a star, it climbed fairly directly from an excavated ledge 15 feet right of *The Deceiver* to the double-peg-and-bolt belay. The initial overhang is now twice the size and a low peg runner disappeared with the remnants. Above the overhang, the rock and the two bolt runners are still intact.

Rather less affected is **Easier Said than Done** (60 feet E3 6b †† 1.10.87), which starts from the same point as *Turn a Blind Eye*. Initial rock which contained a crystal pocket and a peg runner is now missing, but some care and removal of debris may enable the break below the roof to be gained slightly to the right. If so, thereafter all should well: climb the wall above using the obvious blunt flake (two bolt runners), pull over an overhang on a large hold (bolt runner), and continue for a few feet before moving left to the double-peg-and-bolt belay of *Turn a Blind Eye*.

The Paladin (60 feet E3 6a †† 9.9.84) too has lost its bottom. The obvious two-tiered groove in the centre of the buttress was originally gained from almost directly below. It could now be reached from a start up *Better Late than Never* and a traverse left above the latter's first bolt runner. The groove is then climbed past three peg runners to the belay ledge. Two poor belay pegs – it may be safer to use the belay of *Turn a Blind Eye* 10 feet left at foot-level. A second pitch (5c † 2.10.83) goes slightly rightwards up to a tree and over the right-hand end of the long roof; it is very loose and dirty with little reliable protection – definitely best ignored.

The next climb starts from the ledge at 60 feet. If possible, reach the double-bolt-and-peg belay by one of the foregoing routes. Otherwise it will be necessary to abseil in, which requires care and some topographical knowledge.

★In the Hands of the Deceiver 100 feet E4 6b † (26.1.92)
A good line aiming for the central weakness in the dominating roof. The rock is reasonable, in contrast to that on the flanks, and the route is quite well protected.
Mantel onto the ledge above the belay. Step right (two old peg runners), and climb a slim groove on jugs to reach a good ledge. Go straight up the cleaned wall until a long reach past a peg runner gains a large flake hold below the roof. Undercut leftwards (*Friend* placements), and make sensational moves through the roof (peg runner, then bolt runner) to reach jugs above. Climb the groove in the headwall (peg runner) to finish direct. Tree belay on the left.

The remaining routes start back on the ground and are (so far!) unaffected by the rockfalls.

★Better Late than Never 65 feet E4 6b (23.10.87)
From an excavated ledge below and right of the groove of *The Paladin*, make a series of hard pulls to get onto the wall (bolt runner). Reach the wide break (peg runner missing, but a sling on the next bolt compensates), from where fingery moves lead up the white wall to the roof (two bolt runners). Swing onto the protruding block and climb the thin crack (*Friend* 1 placement) to ledges (peg runner). Go diagonally right to the bolt and peg belay of *Stay Mellow*.

★Stay Mellow 65 feet E3 5c (5.8.86)
The steep and strenuous start contrasts nicely with a delicate and technical slab above. *Friend* 2½ useful for the groove.
Step up onto ledges 5 feet left of the groove-crack of *Uptight*, and climb up into a steep constricted groove. Continue to the roof using an undercut spike, swing out left and pull up on good holds. Climb past a bolt runner to a hard move, and then more easily to a bolt and peg belay.

Uptight 60 feet E3 5c (29.6.80)
The start is becoming vegetated. Climb the obvious groove-crack past

three peg runners to two stakes.

The start of **Out-a-Sight** (60 feet E4 6b ‡ 26.8.85) is now unfortunately doubly so owing to the ivy. If uncovered, it offers some good and well-protected technical moves worth a star. Climb the V-groove right of *Uptight* to a break (peg runner and *in-situ* wire). Move left and then up onto the rib (bolt runner), which is climbed to a two-bolt belay.

THE FAR SOUTH BAY
(Diagram page 128)

More consistent quality returns again in The Far South Bay, which for its relatively small size holds a surprising number of genuinely independent routes. There are no large ledges, and you can find yourself quite suddenly in situations of unexpected exposure. As with The North Wall, most of the climbs fall into the VS to E2 range, and the climbing tends to be more technical than strenuous. Much of the rock is clean and excellent, with good friction; protection varies from abundant to rather sparse. As the rock catches less sun, however, the drying process is slower. As mentioned elsewhere, the bay's original (and easiest) route, *Zelda*, remains its jewel and is not to be missed.

THE APPROACH

Again, the Easy Way Down (page 55) is marginally quickest. Pass below Black Wall, go out onto the Valley Path, and continue south along it past the South Bay and Deceiver Buttress. By the BMC GO Wall access notice, immediately opposite where the marked path (yellow arrow) turns down sharp right, a small track turns left into the trees over a small bank. If approached from the scree slope, this is 30 yards north of the kissing-gate remains. Keep right and go up a steep bank and subsiding path to a good earth platform in the centre of the bay. This is the start of *Guytha*, with the obvious corner of *Zelda* on the left. *Greta* starts in the pit down on the left. *Cheetah* starts below a vertical break 15 feet right of *Guytha*, half-way down a short slope.

THE WAY OFF

The last two routes go to the top and finish in the woods above GO Wall and are subject to the summer restriction (refer to the GO Wall section for details, page 128). The others finish 60 feet below the top where the bay degenerates into heavily vegetated ledges. From *Zelda* and the routes to its left, scramble diagonally left up the easiest line to the top of *The Beginner's Route*. From the others, it is best to go horizontally left first to where the ledges are cleaner and then scramble diagonally.

The first two routes traverse, respectively, left to the Great Ledge on The North Wall, and right across the Bay onto GO Wall, from the communal stance 120 feet above the ground. This is best and normally reached by the first pitch of *Zelda*, but the starting-pitch(es) of any of the routes between it and *Arabesque*, except *Themeninblack*, can be used.

The Early Morning Traverse   1500 feet   Very Severe   (8.66)

More of an outing than a climb, demanding resourcefulness in
route-finding on vegetated ledges rather than rock-climbing technique.
Little of the route is above Severe standard and much is below, and any of
the sections can be taken separately, as escape is simple from almost all
the belays. Only for people who like this sort of thing. The route is also
possible in the reverse direction. Double ropes are needed for the abseil of
pitch 11.

1 120 feet 4b. *Zelda* pitch 1.

2 120 feet. Traverse left past vegetation to a tree, and follow a diagonal
line onto a huge platform. From its upper level, go round the edge and
descend 5 feet by an iron spike to a tree belay.

3 80 feet. Walk left and descend 15 feet. Climb back up in the earthy
shallow corner beside the Central Rib. From a platform (peg belay of
Central Rib II) step down left to a large tree belay below the corner of
Central Rib I.

4 60 feet. Go horizontally left past another large tree to the fallen block
and two trees at the top of pitch 2 of *Bottle Buttress*.

5 120 feet. Follow pitch 3 of *Bottle Buttress* along the sloping ramp to a
small corner and two peg runners. Step out left and climb up for 30 feet
until able to traverse left round the edge to a large platform beside the
Easy Way Down. Peg belay and a large stake.

6 100 feet. Go horizontally left over grass and rubble, and then
diagonally up to a bush belay on the side of The Ridge.

7 120 feet. Continue diagonally to the grass ledge at the base of Terry's
Wall. Go along it and pass just above the alcove on *Direct Route* to reach
the platform and tree belay on the Corner Buttress below the short top
pitch of its routes.

8 90 feet. Descend the easy left edge of the buttress and cross a bay in
the broadest part of the vegetated gully. Continue, ascending slightly, to a
suitable tree belay.

9 120 feet 4a. Continue the gently rising line over bad rock to the
cleaned strip of *John's Route*. Step up and follow an obvious, but narrow
and mainly grass, ledge horizontally all the way to the large ledge below
the top pitch of *Original Route*. Tree belay above and beyond the far left
end.

10 70 feet. Walk left behind the trees and move up 5 feet (loose and
earthy). Traverse horizontally and cross a small corner to a two-peg belay
on the edge of *Loads' Lids*.

11 120 feet. Abseil down the left of the rib to the foot of the rock.

12 80 feet. Walk left along the base of Compost Wall (this, of course, a
long way above the ground) and scramble up and round to a block belay
in a cave.

13 110 feet. Traverse left, easily at first across a wide grassy gully, gaining
a little height. Cross Narcotic Corner onto the opposite wall (more
exposed), and climb down a short borehole on the left to a large tree on
Narcotic.

14 90 feet 4a. Climb back up the wall just left of the borehole and move left onto the edge. Step down to a tiny platform and hand-traverse round and along to easy ground just above the Great Ledge. Continue round the edge to a tree belay.

15 100 feet 4a. Pitch 4 of *Right Hand Route* leads to the top.

★Real to Reel 130 feet E2 5b (22.10.86)

A fine girdle of the bay. Further pitches were climbed in a stepped diagonal line to reach *Big Dong*, but are best left for personal rediscovery. Apart from the tree after 10 feet, protection is entirely on the fixed pegs. Start at the communal belay at the top of the first pitch of *Zelda*.

Step down and go right for 10 feet to stand by the small tree. Traverse right along the twin thin breaks with increasingly technical moves across *Themeninblack* (peg runner) and *Hunky Doré* (peg runner) to a good resting-position in the gully of *Guytha*. Keep going right (peg runner on *Cheetah*) to the overhang of *The Ragged Edge* and move down slightly to clip the peg runner underneath it. Step right (peg runner on *Never Say Die*) and then make a hard move up to the right (peg runner above). From just below this peg, traverse across the corner of *Jannock* onto a small, exposed stance on an overhanging prow. Bolt and peg belay. Prepare carefully and make an airy abseil to the ground.

"Yeeaaghhh!" (40 feet E2 6b 9.11.86) is a short but extremely difficult problem up the smooth corner to the right of the obvious beak of rock dividing the Far South Bay from Deceiver Buttress. Move up from broken ledges and climb the corner (bolt runner) to a naturally-cemented block at its top. Swing out left along the break and pull up onto a small ledge on top of the rib. Reach right to a two-bolt belay.

At the left end of the pit are two square-cut grooves. **Anticipation** (50 feet E2 5b 15.5.86) takes the left-hand one. Some difficult unprotected moves to start. Once a good ledge is reached, bear right more easily to the niche and peg belay of *Greta*.

Arabesque 190 feet Hard Very Severe (19.10.80)

A variant of *Greta*: two short problems. Start in the right-hand of the two corners.

1 40 feet 5a. Climb the corner to the ledge. Follow *Greta* up the corner above (peg runner) to the niche (peg and nut belay).

2 40 feet 5a. Bridge up, but where *Greta* goes out right, move slightly left and pull up to a ledge. Make a knee-scratching move over the centre of the overhang above, and move up and right to a peg belay in a borehole.

3 110 feet 4a. Step right into the depression on pitch 2 of *Greta* and follow this climb to the top.

Themeninblack; the Soundtrack 160 feet E4 † (12.6.82)
A direct line between *Greta* and *Senta*: not technically desperate, but with
minimal protection and the prospect of huge falls resulting from a mistake.
Care is needed with some of the holds on the middle section of the first
pitch. Some homework is advisable before an attempt. Start in the pit, at a
faint groove in the centre of the slab.
1 110 feet 5c. Climb the groove to the ledge and traverse left to the
corner. Climb up to the overhang and go over its right edge. Climb a
scoop, using holds on the right, to just below a small roof. Move
awkwardly out right and go up to a ledge. Continue straight up via a thin
crack to a peg runner at a vague traverse line (*Senta*). Move left and go up
to the communal stance and two belay pegs.
2 50 feet 5c. Climb the arête above the belay, starting just left, to a small
ledge; continue more easily up the edge to a larger ledge and a crack for
nut belays.

★Greta 210 feet Hard Severe (3.65)
A pleasant and worthwhile route. Start in the pit, at the right-hand end of
the slab.
1 60 feet 4b. Climb the slab leftwards to a narrow ledge. Traverse to its
far left end and climb the corner past a peg runner (some awkward
sloping holds) to a niche. Peg and nut belay.
2 70 feet 4b. Make your second small and bridge out over the niche to
an old peg runner just below some bushes. Climb diagonally right to a
small ledge (peg runner above). Climb up past the peg until level with
some loose flakes on the right. Move left on or above grass ledges into the
centre of the depression (the *Arabesque* belay peg is reachable further left
but causes complications with the rope). Climb up with hidden jugs and
then bear more easily rightwards to a small platform and the two-peg
belay shared with *Zelda*.
3 80 feet 4a. Move left past a bramble to a short wall and climb this
behind a sapling in its centre to a sloping grass platform. Climb a pillar on
the right past a smaller grass ledge to a hidden peg runner at its top, and
make an awkward step right round the bulge. Climb up 10 feet to a ledge,
and then scramble on up to the first convenient tree.

Senta 170 feet Hard Very Severe ‡ (1.7.77)
The obvious groove between *Greta* and *Zelda*: some good climbing, but
the rock is of lesser quality than that of its neighbours and the central
section urgently needs recleaning.
1 40 feet 4b. Climb the slab, as for *Greta*, bearing left to a narrow
ledge. Step left and go straight up to a stance extending rightwards under
an overhang. Peg belay.
2 80 feet 4c. Move up and out right of the overhang, up a little, and then
back left to the foot of the long groove. Climb the groove past a peg
runner and exit left at the top. Traverse 15 feet left, passing a poor peg
runner, and go up on sloping holds to the shared stance with a two-peg

belay.
3 50 feet 5a. Step up and move right, as for *Zelda*. Climb straight up past the peg runner to rejoin *Zelda* at the sentry-box (peg runner). Follow *Zelda* over the little roof and up the corner above to a large platform and a tree belay.

★Themeninblack   195 feet   E2   (17.8.80)
Fine climbing, but with sparse protection on the first two pitches. Start as for *Greta*.
1 100 feet 5a. Climb straight up for 10 feet and then step right to a ledge below a groove in the arête left of *Zelda*. Climb the groove to a small ledge on the left and continue up to an awkward move right below a bush, which leads out onto *Zelda* above its crux. Continue more easily for 20 feet and then climb diagonally right to a peg and nut belay in a borehole above a narrow ledge, 10 feet left of the larger stance on *Guytha*.
2 60 feet 5b. Traverse left to a small shallow groove. From good footholds below the little rib on the left, make difficult moves up and slightly right to a ledge (peg runner). More bold moves lead up and right to a small overhang; step left and go up to the alcove on *Puma*. Sapling and nut belays.
3 35 feet 5a. Climb the leftward finishing-crack of *Cobra*.

★★★Zelda   180 feet   Hard Severe   (5.61)
A classic of its grade with bold and exposed moves on fine rock: not to be missed. Protection on the first pitch is plentiful; on the second it is sound but spaced enough to enhance the feeling of commitment. Start on the earth platform above and right of the pit, at the foot of the obvious right-facing corner in the centre of the bay.
1 120 feet 4b. Climb the corner for 30 feet to stand in a break (peg runner out left); then traverse left to the arête and make a hard pull up using a hidden jug. Continue up more easily for 20 feet, and then follow an obvious line steeply leftwards to a small tree. Stand by the tree, traverse easily 10 feet left, and go up to a small stance on the edge with two peg belays shared with *Greta*.
2 60 feet 4b. Step up and traverse horizontally right (peg runner above). Make committing moves right again onto and round to the right face of the nose, where excellent holds materialize. Climb up slightly leftwards (peg runner) to reach a narrow ledge, and hand-traverse left on this a short way before stepping up to a sentry-box (peg runner). Bridge over its little roof and climb the corner above to a large platform and a tree belay.

Sweetest Victory   80 feet   E2 5c   (11.12.87)
A good direct pitch up the headwall between *Zelda* and *Themeninblack*. Unfortunately, someone has tried to 'clean off' the shattered-looking rock near the start.
From the tree near the top of the first pitch of *Zelda* (90 feet 4b), move up right to reach the thin breaks (peg runner) and climb the wall past a bolt

runner to a rounded ledge. Continue more easily and climb the borehole directly. Exit right, and mantelshelf awkwardly onto a constricted ledge (*in-situ* wire out right). Climb the centre of the final wall (peg runner) to the finishing jugs of *Themeninblack*. Tree belays on the left.

Hunky Doré 170 feet E1 (12.3.83)

Eliminate, but it makes a fine direct line, and the independent sections are genuinely good.

1 80 feet 4c. Climb the corner of *Zelda*, but instead of leaving it at 30 feet, continue to a tree at its top. Move up and then go diagonally right to the stance with two peg belays on *Guytha*.

2 90 feet 5a. Move up on the left as for *Guytha*, but then step left into the small groove above the hanging flake. Climb it past a peg runner to the break. Step left and go up a few feet (as for *Puma*) to a sapling. Pull up right onto a small ledge at the foot of a groove and crack bounding the left of the black wall. Climb the crack, rejoining *Puma* at a small ledge on the left and peg runner. As for *Puma*, traverse right onto the rib and climb it to the top. Easy ledges lead to a large platform and good nut belays in a long slab crack.

★Waiting for Themeninblack 150 feet E3 (12.10.80)

A fine middle pitch on excellent rock. Protection is sparse throughout. Start as for *Guytha*.

1 60 feet 5a. Step up left to a shelf and then climb on up the wall with little protection to a good hold at the foot of a small vegetated groove. Follow the left rib of the groove and then move up left to a narrow ledge. Peg and nut belay in the borehole as for *Themeninblack*.

2 60 feet 5c. Climb the borehole above the belay with difficulty to a constricted ledge (peg runner on left). It is possible to escape up left on *Themeninblack*; instead continue boldly up the wall very slightly right to join *Puma* at the easy break. Follow *Puma* up broken blocks to a tree and nut belay.

3 30 feet 5c. Move up and right to a small ledge and peg runner as for *Puma*. Then climb the wall above by a faint groove. Go up to a large platform and nut belays in a long slab crack.

★Guytha 160 feet Hard Very Severe (8.66)

A straightforward line on good rock. Low in the grade, which is warranted only by the exciting start and entertaining finish. Start at the highest point in the centre of the bay, 10 feet right of the obvious corner of *Zelda*.

1 60 feet 5a. Step up left onto a small shelf and make a finger-traverse right to a good hold (peg runner up right). Climb urgently up the wrinkled band to reach large holds and pull up left. Continue more easily up the gully, passing a peg runner under a small overhang, to a good platform and two peg belays.

2 100 feet 5a. Move up from the left of the ledge, best avoiding the hanging flake, and trend back right. Climb the gully all the way to a grassy

bay at the top (peg runner to protect the final awkward move). Go up left onto a large platform. Good nut belays in a long slab crack.
Variations
Cobra   Hard Very Severe   5a   (c.1967)
Very enjoyable climbing, typical of the grade, though its only independent section has been gobbled up by *Themeninblack*. This, the finishing-crack, is strenuous and well protected, in contrast to the finish of *Puma*.
2a   110 feet   5a.   Follow *Puma* to the alcove; then climb the gently overhanging crack, which curves up left to a platform and a tree belay.
★★**Puma**   Hard Very Severe   (c.1967)
Though like *Cobra* this has also suffered from the cannibalism, it is too good at its grade to be relegated: a superb, but serious and mind-blowing finish.
2b   120 feet   4c.   Follow *Guytha* to an easy horizontal break. Traverse left along this for 15 feet and climb broken blocks to an alcove with a sapling. Step up and right to a tiny platform and dubious peg runner. Traverse right onto the rib and climb it to a superb finishing-hold. Easy ledges lead to the large platform.
Gospel: According to Themeninblack   E4   (18.3.84)
An elegant pitch up the slender pillar between *Puma* and *Guytha*. Very good rock.
2c   100 feet   6a.   Follow *Guytha* to the large break. Step left and climb a faint groove to an overhang. Go over it and then straight up the wall (peg runner) via a tiny groove to a shattered niche (peg runner). Stand up in this and finish direct. Go up left to the large platform.
★**Llama**   Hard Very Severe   (7.2.81)
Now on the other side of *Guytha*; another section of absorbing technical climbing on superb rock. High in the grade.
2d   110 feet   5a/b.   Move up from the left of the ledge and trend back right. It is also possible to climb up from the right of the belay ledge (5b). At the first break, step right and climb up to a small overhang midway between trees on *Guytha* and *Cheetah* (protection from the former). Pass the left edge of the overhang and make thin moves up right (peg runner) to the foot of a prominent groove (the left of two). Climb the groove to a hawthorn, move left, and go up to belay on two trees on a dirty ledge. It is advisable to remain roped for the traverse off this ledge to reach easier ground over to the left.

Note that the remaining routes are subject to the GO Wall summer restriction: from April to September inclusive, please abseil from the two-bolt station at the top of *Cheetah* pitch 2 (which is also easily reached from *Never Say Die*). There is no official provision for abseiling off *The Ragged Edge* (along with *Jannock* and *Blitzkrieg*); a 50m abseil from the third stance is possible – various *in-situ* items.

★★**Cheetah**   270 feet   Very Severe   (24.10.79)
A magnificent middle pitch up the impressive walls between *Guytha* and

The Ragged Edge, which when viewed from neighbouring climbs look most unlikely to accommodate a route of this grade. Start as for *The Ragged Edge*, half-way down the short slope right of *Guytha*, below a vertical break.

1 80 feet 5a. Make a hard mantel onto a small sloping shelf, and climb the brittle crack (peg runner on right) to some easy steps and a small ledge (so far as for *The Ragged Edge*). Climb slightly left up some rounded bands (little protection) and then move right behind the bushes to a small stance and two peg belays shared with *The Ragged Edge*.

2 110 feet 4c. Climb directly up to a small hand-ledge at the foot of a borehole and swing left (peg runner). Climb a shallow groove to a good tree and step right just above. Continue up the wall, keeping right at first, then trending left past a peg runner, and climb the right-hand of two short grooves to a small hawthorn. Move right into the centre of the wall and make two large pulls to a ledge. Two pegs and the abseil bolts under a low overhang.

3 80 feet. Surmount the overhang and go up to a tree. Keep left up the short wall behind the tree, step right on the ledge above, and climb a crack to a large alcove. The final cracked wall (some loose holds) leads to a large tree belay at the top.

Variation

★**Let Us Prey** E1 (27.4.86)

A more direct version of the second pitch and scarcely less fine, though sparsely protected in its upper half. Poor and eliminate first and last pitches were added, which seem no longer worth recording.

2a 100 feet 5a. Climb up above the belay to the foot of a borehole, as for *Cheetah*. Then climb the borehole and pass just right of the tree. Continue very slightly rightwards with no further protection for 30 feet until a thin horizontal break taking wires is reached. Twenty feet higher is another break (*Friend* 1½). Mantel onto the triangular ledge on the left to rejoin *Cheetah*, and finish on large spaced holds to ledges and the pegs and bolts under a low overhang.

The Ragged Edge 270 feet Hard Very Severe (c.1967)

The route's former main attraction, a huge perched flake at half height, lies on the ground below; all of it, that is, bar a wafer thin slice – the bit that matters. Amazingly, the climbing is barely affected, but the crucial move requires a little more delicacy. Start half-way down the short slope right of *Guytha*, below a vertical break.

1 80 feet 5a. Make a hard mantel onto a small sloping shelf and climb the brittle crack (peg runner on right) to some easy steps and a small ledge (as for *Cheetah*). Step right and climb the corner past a tree to a small stance and two peg belays beside some bushes.

2 50 feet 5a. Climb up to the overhang on the right (peg runner) and over it. Continue up past a small tree to a larger one at the foot of a corner (belay shared with *Jannock* and *Never Say Die*).

3 40 feet 5a. Move up and traverse right to the right-hand crack in the flake. Climb the crack with care and layback delicately onto the minute remains of the ledge. Continue directly up the next short tier (near the left edge) to a large platform. Peg and nut belay (in the corner on the right). The abseil is from here (50m ropes).

4 100 feet 4a. Climb the rib on excellent holds. Go up over grass between trees; then move left and mantel into the alcove to finish as for *Cheetah*.

THE GREAT OVERHANGING WALL (Photo-diagrams pages 144-145)

Whether your viewpoint is at the bottom or either side, or even Wyndcliffe over a mile away across the river, your first impression of GO Wall is of the vastness of its total bulk and especially of its central band of overhangs. Yet even this impression prepares you inadequately for the actual experience: perched on the lip of the main overhangs you can sense an exposure of Dolomitic proportions. Architecturally, GO Wall is a masterpiece, flawed only by its top wooded terrace.

Apart from the overhangs, the most striking feature is the huge continuous groove-line of the classic *King Kong* in the centre, and for all but the most ambitious it provides the ideal introduction. The very first moves give an idea of the scale of things, and as the first pitch progresses the size of the overhangs over to the right becomes apparent. Each of the big retaining walls of the upper section gives a superb pitch, and soon, as these are viewed close up, a taste of the exposure is experienced.

The large vertical wall left of *King Kong*, extending to *The Ragged Edge* at the boundary of the Far South Bay, is broken by only sporadic and relatively small overhangs. It takes its name from its original, and for many years only, route – *Kaiser Wall*.

Thirty feet right of *King Kong* is another, less continuous, but also classic groove-line – *Kangaroo Wall*, and sandwiched between them is a slim, but bulging buttress containing *Big Dong* and *Howling at the Moon*. Thirty feet right again a thin crack leads to the big groove below the overhangs. *The Jackal* climbs it and goes through at a shallower point on the left, while *Feline* takes the weakness through the roof just right. The lower pitches of the routes to the right avoid the overhangs by curving rightwards to the half-height pedestal. The original and still most popular of these is *Surrealist*, which starts near the right-hand end of the wall, where the ground begins to rise.

Its numerous horizontal breaks in exposed positions have made GO Wall enticing traverse territory. *The Umbrella Girdle*, naturally, takes shelter underneath the roof-system at half height. *The Burning Giraffe* follows the very obvious wide break 60 feet above, splitting the headwall. Twenty-five feet below it, a thinner break gives *Zebra Crossing* and 25 feet lower again, running along the lip of the overhangs is the sensational middle pitch of *Vulture Squadron*.

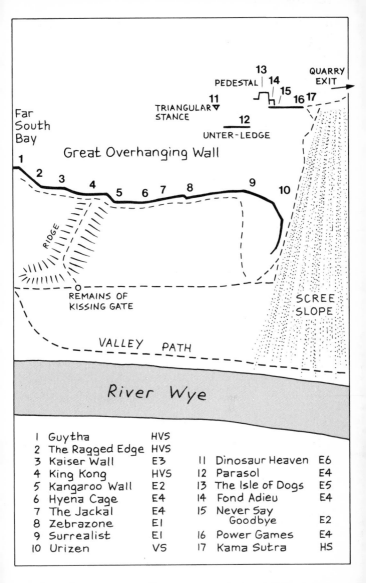

QUARRY
EXIT

13
PEDESTAL | 14
15
16 17

TRIANGULAR ▽
STANCE
11

12
UNTER-LEDGE

Far
South
Bay

Great Overhanging Wall

1
2
3
4
5 6 7 8
9
10

RIDGE

o
REMAINS OF
KISSING GATE

SCREE
SLOPE

VALLEY   PATH

River Wye

1	Guytha	HVS		
2	The Ragged Edge	HVS		
3	Kaiser Wall	E3	11	Dinosaur Heaven	E6
4	King Kong	HVS	12	Parasol	E4
5	Kangaroo Wall	E2	13	The Isle of Dogs	E5
6	Hyena Cage	E4	14	Fond Adieu	E4
7	The Jackal	E4	15	Never Say Goodbye	E2
8	Zebrazone	E1		
9	Surrealist	E1	16	Power Games	E4
10	Urizen	VS	17	Kama Sutra	HS

The Pedestal is the starting-point for *The Umbrella Girdle*, *Big Bad Wolf*, and *The Isle of Dogs*, and it gives access to the *unter*-ledge on the left. More routes start from the grass terrace below and right of The Pedestal: *Fond Adieu* and *Never Say Goodbye* take the first recess, and the upper pitch of *Surrealist* is in the corner to the right. *Power Games* surmounts the dividing bulge, and the easy chimney of *Kama Sutra* 10 feet beyond the right-hand end of the terrace provides the start for *The Burning Giraffe*.

GO Wall is no place for the timid or fumbling. Route-finding is generally straightforward, but the climbs can be unexpectedly time-consuming, and retreat is often problematic; so it is best to allow a generous margin of daylight, equipment, and competence. Most of the rock is solid, but the problems of cleaning in this situation have meant that there are still a few loose blocks; and the left-hand end is marred by a thirty-foot soft band half-way up the lower wall. These caveats apart, GO Wall is an ideal crag for those who revel in big exposed routes.

THE APPROACH
1 By the Easy Way Down (page 55) or the long approach from the north. Walk south along the Valley Path and turn left at the remains of a kissing-gate, now partially buried by fallen trees. An almost level ridge leads between two large bowls directly up to *King Kong*.
2 Descend the right margin of the scree slope (page 55) and turn in to the Valley Path. Turn immediately right again into the pit: a small track leads towards *Surrealist* and then goes sharp left to *Kangaroo Wall*.
3 To reach The Pedestal, follow the Woodcroft Quarry descent only as far as the top of the scree slope. Above this is the big rotten arête dividing GO Wall from the Quarry. Just left of it, scramble up 10 feet to a grassy terrace which leads leftwards to The Pedestal.

WAY OFF AND DESCENTS
The full-length routes all finish in privately-owned woods or grassland between the cliff-top and the Offa's Dyke footpath. For many years this land was unused, and the owner permitted climbers to cross it. The owner is now making family use of what is in fact part of his garden, and has asked that climbers **do not** do this during the summer months from April to September inclusive. The BMC has concluded an agreement to this effect and under its auspices *Eco-bolt* abseil stations have been established on three routes, which provide descents for most of the routes from penultimate belays. Double ropes are essential.

The first of these is at the penultimate belay of *Cheetah* and caters also for *Never Say Die* and *Let Us Prey*. Keep left down the line of the latter and, if using 45m ropes, swing left near the bottom to land on the highest ground.

From *The Ragged Edge*, *Jannock*, and *Blitzkrieg*, abseil from the platform at the top of pitch 3 (pitch 2 of *Jannock*) – no bolts but an assortment of fixed

THE FAR SOUTH BAY

1	Greta	HS
2	Themeninblack	E2
3	Zelda	HS
4	Puma	HVS
5	Gospel: According to Themeninblack	E4
6	Guytha	HVS
7	Llama	HVS
8	Cheetah	VS
9	The Ragged Edge	HVS

Philip Gibson

Central Rib III (V Diff) South Bay, Wintour's Leap
Climbers: Jim Rubery and Sherri Davy   Photo, Chris Craggs

gear.

For the several routes which converge upon the boulders at the top of pitch 3 of *Kaiser Wall*, either go right along the terrace with care to the *King Kong* station, or abseil from threads formed by the boulders to the two-peg belay of *Lionheart* and thence to the ground – it is advisable to carry some tat for the purpose.

It is possible, and generally easy, to traverse the top terrace to the *King Kong* station from all the routes between *Kaiser Wall* and *Feline*. The bolts are round left of a small vegetated edge from the normal stance. The first abseil goes to the mid-height terrace and another station here is again just left of the big corner to take you to the ground.

A number of routes in The Pedestal area finish at the four-peg belay on *The Burning Giraffe*. You can abseil from here, keeping right to land directly back on The Pedestal.

Most of the remainder converge upon the *Surrealist* belay. There is one station here, and another just below the terrace best for *Surrealist* itself; a single abseil from either will land you on The Pedestal terrace.

For the record and for winter use, the routes are described in full with their original finishes, but these top pitches are already revegetating heavily, and without regular ascents most will probably become impassable. However, it is likely that those of *Cheetah*, *King Kong*, and *Surrealist* will remain viable (though the latter may be brambly).

The BMC undertakes a periodic inspection of the five *Eco-bolt* stations and makes every effort to ensure that these are safe and reliable. The absolute reliability of fixed abseil stations cannot, however, be guaranteed, and climbers should always make their own safety checks before using them. The other suggested abseil points are not subject to any inspection or maintenance and may at any time be in an unsafe condition. Climbers must make their own judgements about procedures and precautions. Some of the abseils are moderately serious and require precise landings; and, as they are all down the lines of popular routes, great care must be taken to avoid tangling with or dislodging debris onto other climbers.

The landowner wishes it to be understood that he would not want the restriction to inflict unreasonable risk upon anyone, and in a case of genuine need he would regard it as waived. However, please do not take advantage of this loophole *except* in such a case.

KAISER WALL
★Never Say Die   260 feet   E2   (8.5.86)
Fine varied climbing at the junction between the Far South Bay and GO

Wall: better and harder than *The Ragged Edge*, better and less serious than *Jannock*. After the delicate first 15 feet protection is always adequate, and on the crux it is excellent. The finishing pitch is of lesser quality and it is preferable to abseil from the *Eco-bolt* station or, in winter only, hop up the top pitch of *Cheetah*. Start 10 feet right of *The Ragged Edge*, behind a tree at the left end of GO Wall.

1 90 feet 5b. Climb the wall behind the tree on very small holds, past a low break, to a small circular flake in the next break (first protection). Continue straight up on more positive holds, slots, and pockets (passing two peg runners) to a good ledge on the arête. From a higher ledge, sling a large tree on the left; then move out and up right (peg runner low on the right) and climb directly up to a ledge. Two-peg belay on the left.

2 50 feet 5b. From the small cleaned pedestal, climb the crackline to a ledge (peg runner), and continue up the crack above (peg runner) to a tree at the top of the short wall. Pull up leftwards and move up easily over loose ground to a tree belay at the foot of a corner (shared with *Jannock* and *The Ragged Edge*).

3 50 feet 5c. Move up and left over ledges to below the obvious crack in the bulge (peg runner). Climb the crack, and then go up left over more ledges to a bolt belay beside a borehole. The abseil station is on the left, under an overhang.

4 70 feet 5a. Climb directly to and up the overhanging wall above – some dubious rock but there are sufficient usable holds. Step right to a tree and go up grass to a short wall. Climb the right end of the wall and finish easily rightwards to a horizontal tree root.

Variation

1a Never Say Never Again 5c (3.6.88) *Just to the right of Never Say Die*, a line of pegs leading past the large red hollow provides an alternative first pitch to the former, slightly harder technically but with more protection.

A stepped diagonal, **Flanders Field** (400 feet E4 8.11.87), starts up *Never Say Die* and finishes in *Stairway to Heaven*. A demanding outing.

★Eva Brawn 70 feet E5 6c   (28.4.87)
Very technical climbing up the blank lower wall left of *Kaiser Wall*. Start 15 feet left of that route, as for *Jannock's* direct start. The elder tree may be getting in the way.
Climb to the wide horizontal break and mantelshelf rightwards. Climb the slightly rounded wall with difficulty (two bolt runners, one peg) to the red band and reach a cramped rest under the roof (two peg runners). Reach over blindly to jugs in the break above (bolt runner with old bootlace). Haul up slightly rightwards on sandy pockets to a ledge (thread runner). Bolt and peg belay just above.

Jannock 280 feet E4   (23.2.82)
A serious first pitch, requiring care with the rock much of the way, though

quite well protected: challenging but not in the class of *Lionheart*.
Unaffected by the rockfall.

1 140 feet 5c. Climb *Kaiser Wall* to its first peg runner. Climb up 10 feet
(second peg runner), traverse horizontally left for 10 feet (third peg runner),
and move up left (fourth peg runner). Make a difficult move round the left
end of the long overhang to good holds, step right above, and follow a
broken crack bearing left up to the foot of a long corner. Climb the corner
– some hard moves and poor rock, but well protected. Exit right at the cap
into the bushes, traverse left round the edge, and go up to a tree belay on
The Ragged Edge.

2 40 feet 5b. Start up the corner, as for *The Ragged Edge*; then continue
straight up to exit right at the large platform. Peg and nut belays on the
right. Abseil from here (50m ropes).

3 100 feet 4b. *The Ragged Edge* pitch 4.

Variation

1a 6b. A direct start on better rock than much of the route. From 15 feet
left of *Kaiser Wall*, by a coppicing elder, gain and climb a faint leftward
ramp (two peg runners). Climb diagonally right on the red band to join the
ordinary route at the end of its 10-foot traverse (and third peg runner).

★Blitzkrieg   300 feet   E4   (18.9.87)

A fine direct and largely independent line. There is no outstandingly good
climbing, but the general quality does not diminish with the difficulty as one
gets higher. The third pitch has been altered by the rockfall and needs
some cleaning up, but the grade is unchanged.

1 70 feet 6a. Climb *Kaiser Wall* to its first peg runner and go on up 10
feet to the next peg runner of *Jannock*. Move 5 feet left and climb a hairline
crack to the break. Continue up to the roof 5 feet left of the red gash (peg
runner below, bolt runner above). Make a long and blind reach for pockets
above and pull over slightly leftwards; then trend more easily leftwards to
the bolt and peg belay of *Eva Brawn*.

2 70 feet 6a. Go straight up 10 feet (bong runner) and climb the red
wall with care to a small ledge. Move up and right across the white slab
(bolt runner) to a good undercut hold. Climb up and slightly rightwards
again to gain a small break and move back left (peg runner). (This section
was originally climbed direct, using a now rotted-away sapling root as a
handhold.) Climb the finger-crack above (peg runner) and reach the huge
boulder belay on the terrace.

3 60 feet 5a. Stand on the boulder and pull over the roof on excellent
holds. Climb straight up the obvious line to a good platform. Peg and nut
belay shared with *The Ragged Edge*. Abseil from here (50m ropes).

4 100 feet 4c. Climb the wall on the right on good rock without
protection until a peg runner at 40 feet. Take care with the holds above
and reach the top terrace. Pull up left onto the rib and climb just left of the
arête before moving out onto the knife-edge to finish.

★Lionheart   300 feet   E5   (11.9.84)
A magnificent finish to the first pitch. Serious, with long runouts and some dubious rock in the middle section of the first pitch.
1 140 feet 6a. Follow *Kaiser Wall* to its bolt runner and then on over its first small overhang to a peg runner below the higher overhang. Now step left and pull over leftwards to move up on the left of a rose bush (peg runner). Continue directly up to the base of a shallow groove of perfect grey rock (two peg runners). Climb the groove (another peg runner after 20 feet) to the terrace. Two peg belays.
2 100 feet 5c. Climb the thin crack in the left of the overhang above the belay to a jug under the roof, swing right, and pull (or roll) up to a ledge. Climb straight up the wall (detour at a tree for protection after 30 feet – little else) to a huge boulder at the top. Move right and go up through vegetation to the boulders and threads of *Kaiser Wall*.
3 60 feet 5b. Move 15 feet diagonally left to a shallow niche just left of the earthy groove (*in-situ* wire). Climb the obvious crackline above over two overhangs (two peg runners) and step left onto the arête at the top.

★★Kaiser Wall   300 feet   E3   (c.1967/1.78/5.3.78)
Absorbing technical wall climbing, steep and sustained. The rock is less than perfect in places, and some of the *in-situ* gear is ancient (aid relics) but there is plenty of it. Classic, almost hallowed, status. Start 30 feet from the left end of GO Wall at a small vertical break.
1 90 feet 5c. Climb the break and a thin vertical crack above (peg runner). Ignore the peg 10 feet above (*Jannock*); instead, move 5 feet right (peg runner out right) and go up to a small overhang (bolt runner). Go over it and move up left to a higher overhang (peg runner). Pull over this onto its right lip, and climb the wall above more easily, trending right and passing three peg runners, to the large tree – the last 10 feet are loose but not hard.
2 50 feet 5a. Climb a broken crack on the right, step right, and follow a small groove to the terrace. Thread belays *in situ*. Alternatively (6a), climb directly above the tree (bolt runner, then peg runner) to a flaky crack, which leads to ledges just below the terrace. The belay is 15 feet right.
3 110 feet 5c. Climb the shallow overhanging groove above (peg runner, then bolt runner). Traverse left in the break and move up to the obvious groove. Climb the groove (peg runner to start and another shortly on the left) to a grassy break. Continue straight up the wall (peg runner), mostly easier but take care with the rock. Go up through vegetation to large boulders and good thread belays on the top terrace.
4 50 feet 4c. Walk 10 feet right and climb a clean white groove above the centre of the overhung ledges to a tree at its termination. Finish easily on the left.
Variation
Der Fuhrer   E3   (26.9.87)
Some worthwhile alternatives.
1a 140 feet 5c. Follow *Kaiser Wall* almost to its tree belay, and then go

diagonally left up good large flakes to a narrow ledge (peg runner). Using a flake on the right, climb the white streak in the wall above to reach a thin break under a shallow overhang (peg runner). Pull over onto another narrow ledge and continue directly up, passing a bolt runner, to the main terrrace. Two-peg belay as for *Lionheart*.

3a 100 feet 5c. Reach the centre of the ledge 20 feet above the terrace by the start of *Lionheart* pitch 2 or *Kaiser Wall* pitch 3. Peg and bolt runners or belay. Then climb directly up the centre of the wall between the two (peg runner at 20 feet). Reach a superb hold above and stand up on it. Continue on sloping holds of excellent rough rock to a break (peg runner). Easier but looser climbing leads soon to the *Kaiser Wall* exit.

Doctor Hay Fever (110 feet E2 5b 16.6.89) traverses from just above the slots 40 feet up *Kaiser Wall* to the two-bolt belay of *The Lurking Smear*. Various peg runners and a thread.

★Mein Kampf   290 feet   E5   (25.1.86)
A fine line, unfortunately flawed by the 30-foot loose band at the top of the first pitch. Elsewhere the rock is very good, protection reassuring, and the climbing of sustained quality and difficulty. Start 10 feet right of *Kaiser Wall*, at an obvious thin vertical crack.
1 85 feet   6b.   Climb the crack to a break (peg runner above) and traverse 8 feet right. Make an awkward stand up (bolt runner) and climb the smooth wall above to a good slot (peg runner). Move up right on the red band (peg runner and two threads, one *in situ*). Use a large hole on the right to reach the break and a poor hold above. Lurch left to a good hold and stretch for a slot (bong runner). Stand on the ledge above and traverse to its left end; then bear slightly right to the large tree as for *Kaiser Wall*, passing the final two peg runners.
2 155 feet   6b.   Move left and up into a fine, shallow grey groove. Climb this (peg runner soon) with some bold moves to reach the terrace. Step right and haul strenuously over the roof (wire *in situ*) through a boxed groove to a good ledge. Traverse right and move up a small groove to a bulge (above the belay of *Kaiser Wall*). Pull over (wire *in situ*) and step right again. Climb the headwall to the obvious gash in the ledge above and continue up until a little below the vegetation. Then bear left to the *Kaiser Wall* exit and go up through the bushes to large boulders and good thread belays.
3 50 feet   6b.   Move up left onto a ledge, and climb the depression above (peg runner) to a small ledge on the left arête. Finish up the steep but straightforward wall above.

★★Heil Hitler!   290 feet   E5   (15.12.85)
Another hard, exciting, and direct line up the cliff, with two absorbing and contrasted crux pitches, though again the upper section of the first pitch reduces the merit. Start at an obvious groove 20 feet left of *King Kong*.
1 140 feet   6b.   Climb the groove to its top, above which a baffling move

gains a bolt runner. Make some more difficult moves to reach a slot (bong runner) and continue more easily up the red band (peg runner). Traverse 10 feet right and go up over a bulge onto a ledge with a nick. Climb straight up over good ledges to a short wall (stake well out right on *Lurking Fear* if required). Climb the wall (peg runner on left at first) and then bear left over more easy ground to the terrace. Thread belays *in situ* as for *Kaiser Wall*.

2 110 feet 6a. Just right of the small groove of *Kaiser Wall* is a pocketed crack: climb this with difficulty to the break (thread *in situ*). Climb straight up the leaning wall (wire and then thread, both *in situ*) to a ledge in the main break, and then more easily up the flake crack of *Lurking Fear* to the upper terrace. Scramble up the bank to the overhung rock ledges. Peg belay at the right-hand end of these.

3 40 feet 5a. Pull up onto the slim bulging wall between two small white grooves and climb it to the top.

★The Lurking Smear 60 feet E4 6b (1.2.86)

An excellent problem, which deserves more attention.

Climb the groove of *Heil Hitler!* to the break, and traverse right to below an inverted ramp (bolt runner). Technical moves onto and up this lead to a final unnerving pull out (bolt runner). Move up (peg runner to protect the second) and then right to a two-ancient-bolt belay.

★The Lurking Sear 60 feet E6 6c (10.7.87)

A desperate problem, still waiting to be on-sighted. The gear is well tested – and well stressed! Start just left of *King Kong* at a block that is steadily floating away from the cliff. At present, this assists the first moves, but eventually...

Smear up the slab to the break. Reach round the roof (bolt runner) for a jug and power up (in-situ bootlace thread runner) to another good hold. Climb the shallow groove to the capping bulge (bolt runner) and then go left to holds in a calcite vein. Make a final long reach to good holds and pull up (peg runner) to the two-ancient-bolt belay of *The Lurking Smear*.

KING KONG SECTOR
Lurking Fear 300 feet E4 (4.7.84)

Aptly named for the second pitch, which takes the large bulge left of *King Kong*.

1 140 feet 5b. Follow *King Kong* over its first overhang and up the groove above to the capping roof. Now move round left and step onto a narrow ledge. Go up 10 feet to two ancient bolt runners (belay of *The Lurking Smear*). Climb 10 feet diagonally left and move up and back right to a quarry stake at the foot of a slim corner. Climb the corner to good ledges, traverse right, and go up to the old tree. Belay on the abseil bolts.

2 130 feet 6a. Climb a small groove just left behind the tree (poor peg runner) and then move left to the roof (peg runner with long sling). Pull over slightly left (another peg runner above) and follow a quartz crack on the left to a bulge. Continue up past a small rock spike to the large break, step left, and climb the flake crack (joined here by *Heil Hitler!*) to the upper terrace. Scramble up the bank to the overhung ledges. Peg belay at the right-hand end of these.

3 30 feet 4c. From just right of the ledges, climb either the two-tiered groove or the left-slanting crack and wall 3 feet to its right.

★★**Stairway To Heaven**   300 feet   E2   (20.11.85)

An impressive second pitch up the left-retaining wall of *King Kong*. Most of the rock is very good and protection is ample all the way. Once *King Kong* is left the route's independence is maintained.

1 140 feet 5b. Follow *King Kong* for 50 feet to the start of the easy section (peg runner on left where the groove deepens). Traverse 10 feet left and climb up, bearing slightly left to a short steep wall (peg runner). Make a couple of moves up the wall to reach some spiky jugs and continue to a small overhang (peg runner). Traverse right to an obvious foothold and mantel onto a ledge. Climb the crack above, taking care with the left underprop, directly to the old tree. Nut belays in the big corner.

2 130 feet 5c. Pull over the bulge 10 feet left of the main corner and work diagonally left to a short corner formed by the overhang of *Lurking Fear*; then climb cracks above to the main break. Pull over the overhang and climb directly up the wall (thread *in situ* fairly soon, then peg runner) on small pockets with some good vertical slots on the left for layaways and protection. Reach a thin break a few feet below the top (peg runner just above) and finger traverse right to the *King Kong* exit. Go up to the first tree and then left straight up the bank to a small clean wall with a large tree just left (hiding a dirty corner behind). The abseil bolts are just to the right.

3 30 feet 4c. Climb the wall (easier with a long reach) and the left-slanting groove above to a tree belay at the top.

★★★**King Kong**   300 feet   Hard Very Severe   (6.65)

A superb and classic climb of its grade: this tremendous natural feature is visible for miles, and very strikingly from Wyndcliffe across the river. Excellently protected on all the harder sections. Despite the route's original grade of only VS, the first brutal overhang not infrequently leaves seasoned HVS leaders grounded. Plenty of time should be allowed as the climbing is sustained, and rope weight and drag can gnaw deeply into stamina, especially on the first pitch. [Photos: reverse frontispiece.] Start, unmistakably, at the huge continuous groove-line just left of centre of the wall, under a large overhang.

1 140 feet 5b. Climb up to and over the overhang on its left: a determined and dynamic approach is called for. (The overhang can be avoided by a diagonal line from a start 10 feet right: less strenuous, but technical, polished, and difficult to protect – 5a.) Climb the groove above, facing right, to the roof. Feel for good holds to pull out right and move up to a cave. Step back left and climb the long groove (peg runner on the left where it deepens, and another on the right after the easier section where it narrows and steepens again). At this point, traverse right across a short wall at half height to the arête, and bear left up a short slab (peg runner). Step left and climb the twin cracks (generally starting in the right and moving to the left but various combinations are possible) to the terrace. Nut belays in the corner.

2 130 feet 5a. Climb the long crackline just left of the corner. Move left under the large roof and pull over (peg runner). Easier bridging leads to the upper terrace. Scramble up the earth bank to thread belays below a short wall and chimney-corner. The abseil station is 10 feet to the left round a vegetated rib.

3 30 feet 4a. Climb the corner and then the left wall to the top. Tree belay.

★★★**Vulture Squadron**   380 feet   E3   (1.78)

A magnificent excursion through some of GO Wall's finest scenery. Sustained and exposed, serious for leader and second, it follows the lip of the overhangs to a fine thin crack up the centre of the headwall.

1 140 feet 5b. *King Kong* pitch 1.

2 50 feet 5b. Climb 10 feet to the first break and traverse out right onto the prow; stand to clip a peg runner above. Move back down and hand-traverse right to a nut belay in the chimney of *Kangaroo Wall*.

3 50 feet 5b. Continue rightwards by exposed hand-traversing and fist-jamming to a dramatic hanging belay at a pocketed crack (nut and several pegs).

4 90 feet 5c. Climb strenuously up the wall on finger-pockets to gain a thin crack in a hanging column, which leads to a rest in the break of *The Burning Giraffe* (fix good protection here – there is little of any use above). Climb into the scoop above and move out left and steeply up the wall to pull over the final overhang to the terrace. Go up through vegetation to a good tree belay. The finishing groove of *The Jackal* is above; the abseil station is reached by a walk and scramble left and up to the *King Kong* thread belay before moving 10 feet left round the vegetated rib.

5 50 feet 5a. *The Jackal* pitch 4.

★★**Primeval**   310 feet   E6   (6.4.86)

An outstanding, ferocious pitch taking a direct, natural line up the centre of the leaning right wall of *King Kong*.

1 140 feet 5b. *King Kong* pitch 1.

2 70 feet 6c. Climb a short wide crack just right of the corner to the first break. Climb straight up the wall and small blind groove (two peg runners) and then move rapidly right (*in-situ* thread) to a good resting-place on the arête of *Big Dong*. Go back left immediately and climb a line of finger-pockets (peg runner) in the smooth white wall to gain a good jug in a slim, shallow groove (*in-situ* nut on the right). Continue directly by means of a totally desperate layback and wild dyno to a jug out right which enables the break at the top of the wall to be grasped (peg runner). Pull up right to a grassy ledge. Peg and nut belay on *Big Dong*.

3 100 feet 5a. *Big Dong* pitches 3 and 4. The abseil station is encountered between the two.

Big Dong   300 feet   E3   (21.2.82)
Fine positions on the second pitch, though there is some poor rock. The
first pitch is often escapable after the first chimney. A good continuous line
nevertheless, it follows the right arête of *King Kong* throughout. Start 10
feet right of *King Kong*, below a small overhanging chimney
1 130 feet 5b. Climb the chimney increasingly awkwardly until able to
pull over left on good holds and reach a small cave (now partially fallen
away). Move up left into a higher cave (peg runner). Pull up and slightly left
again out of this and move round left above to a rest and protection in
King Kong. Step back round the arête and climb straight up for 40 feet
(passing a peg runner just right) and step left to a ledge, above which the
arête becomes a square edge (peg runner high on the left). Swing right on
a good hold and heave up on successive jugs to a short spiky slab –
junction with *King Kong* (peg runner just above). Step left and climb the
final right-hand crack of *King Kong* to the terrace. Nut belays in the corner.
2 70 feet 5c. Climb the corner for 10 feet and traverse right in the first
break out onto the prow as for *Vulture Squadron*. Stand up (peg runner),
move up left, and climb the bulging arête to a small ledge. Swing up and
right to reach a break. Climb the rounded groove for a few feet and then
move back left and climb the arête on good holds to a grassy ledge. Peg
and nut belay.
3 70 feet 5a. Climb a thin crack in the arête above, move right (peg
runner), and pull over the bulge to the upper terrace. Go up the bank to
thread belays below the final corner of *King Kong*.
4 30 feet 4b. Move left (abseil bolts now to hand) and climb a small
groove in the arête to a break; continue in the same line to the top.

INTERSTELLAR BUTTRESS
Development of the slim but overhanging buttress between *Big Dong* and
Kangaroo Wall has got itself into an awful tangle. It was first climbed with an
artificial second pitch by **Interstellar Overdrive** (A2 1.68) and later free
by a varied line, **Empire State Experience** (E3 1.6.78), still an exciting
adventure for the E3 leader by following *Vulture Squadron* onto the prow. The
best sections of these were then incorporated into *Howling at the Moon*, which
must now be considered the definitive line. Later still, two eliminates were
added, **King Louie** (E2 4.9.90) and **Wild Cat** (E3 13.9.87), which meander
between and beyond the others (and account for pegs which may be found
but are not mentioned elsewhere). Numerous such variations are often
possible and do not seem to justify description.

★Howling at the Moon   290 feet   E5   (29.12.85)
Audacious and spectacular climbing on the second pitch: a sustained,
direct line on clean rock, with *in-situ* gear where it is most needed. Start 20
feet right of *King Kong*, immediately above where the ground slopes down
to the start of *Kangaroo Wall*.

1 120 feet 6a. Climb behind a tall tree to a pedestal, and straight on up (peg runner) to a choked crack. Move up the short flake on the right (two old peg runners) and continue to the shale break. Traverse 10 feet right and follow a small groove and wall to the crack of *Kangaroo Wall*, which is climbed to the stance with high and low peg belays.

2 70 feet 6a. Climb the wall above the left of the stance to a peg runner under the first overhangs. Climb the small groove through them to the break of *Vulture Squadron* and a rest on the right. Pull straight out over the roofs via a tiny groove (two peg runners and *in-situ* thread) to a good hold on the lip (*in-situ* wire). An awkward move gains the large corner which soon leads to a stance on *The Burning Giraffe*. Tree and peg belay.

3 60 feet 5a. Step left of the tree and climb the wall passing an *in situ* thread to a cleared exit. Scramble up the bank to a tree belay below the final *King Kong* corner. (Abseil station up and left.)

4 40 feet 6a. Transfer right round the arête to below the left corner of the white wall. An awkward move just left of the corner gains the left wall and the first of two *in-situ* threads. Step left to the second and climb the wall to a small exposed finishing arête.

★★★**Kangaroo Wall**   300 feet   E2   (5.66)
Only the second route to be climbed on GO Wall, and the first 'XS' at Wintour's Leap. Despite the use of some aid on both the first two pitches and a fixed rope to surmount ivy at the top of the third, a magnificent achievement, and still, now purged of its aid and ivy, a magnificent and classic climb. [Photo p.144.] Start in the centre of the wall, 30 feet right of *King Kong*, at an obvious roofed corner.

1 120 feet 5c. Climb the groove (peg runner near the top) and move out right (peg runner) and up with difficulty. Continue straight up more easily and move left to a prominent flake crack which leads to a good stance and peg belays at both foot- and chest- level.

2 80 feet 5c. Climb slightly rightwards (peg runner and jammed hex) to the overhang (very ancient peg runner, much used in the past for resting, aiding, and falling on). Pull over to a small *in-situ* thread, and then move right on better holds (peg runner of *Crocodile Tears*) to a large chimney. Climb this to the cave stance and nut belays. (Or you can pull over to the right directly to the upper peg as for *Crocodile Tears*.)

3 60 feet 5a. Chimney up and move out right onto the face in a superbly exposed position. Climb the wall (peg runner) to a gap in the vegetation and go on up and slightly left to a peg belay below the white wall.

4 40 feet 5a. Climb the clean wall above near the groove on the left. Below the upper overhang, step right and layback to the top. Alternatively (5c), climb the right-hand crack all the way.

Two more eliminates based on *Kangaroo Wall* have been recorded. At best there is room for one, and **Cat Gut** (E3 15.5.83) has been merged with *Crocodile Tears*.

Crocodile Tears   300 feet   E4   (29.12.85)
Start 10 feet right of *Kangaroo Wall*, below a thin vertical crack.
1 100 feet 6a. From a small shelf at 6 feet (peg runner above), make a
sequence of hard moves up left onto a ledge. Climb the faint groove
above (peg runner) to a small overhang (peg runner) and swing right onto
another ledge. Continue straight up over easier, ledgy rock to a small
stance 10 feet right of the base of the *Kangaroo Wall* crack. Peg and nut
belay.
2 90 feet 6a. Climb the orange wall above (two bolt runners) to a
junction with *Kangaroo Wall*; follow this to the bulge (jammed hex and old
peg runner) and pull round further to the right (peg runner). Reach the
break of *Vulture Squadron*, climb a small pink groove left of the big
chimney, and break out left onto the lip of the overhangs. Climb up and
slightly left to the tree and peg belay (on *The Burning Giraffe*) of *Howling at
the Moon*.
3 70 feet 4c. Climb the wall on the right, just right of a prominent scar, to
the upper terrace (thread *in situ* out left below the top). Go up the bank to
thread belays below the final corner of *King Kong*.
4 40 feet 4c. Climb the right wall of the chimney to where it closes up;
hand-traverse right to the arête and climb it to the top.

THE CENTRAL OVERHANGS
Animal Magic (450 feet E3 2.3.86) was the first, and begetter of the
subsequent rash of stepped diagonals. It started by the first pitch of *Kangaroo
Wall* and finished by the last of *Surrealist*.

The Pulsating Rainbow (A3 15.12.68) and **Technician** (A2 8.66), two
artificial originals, provided the inspiration for the four following superlative
free climbs.

★★Hyena Cage   300 feet   E4   (29.11.77)
A superbly sustained and exposed route, giving good technical and
strenuous climbing. The first pitch is poorly protected, and hard if not bone
dry (a brushing from time to time helps matters). Above, protection is
generally good. 50m rope necessary on the second pitch to reach a
satisfactory belay. Start 15 feet right of *Kangaroo Wall* at a shallow groove.
1 100 feet 5b. Climb the groove and steep walls above to a good ledge
and multiple-peg belay below the streaked walls.
2 160 feet 6a. Climb the wall by discontinuous cracks to reach a good
slot on *The Umbrella Girdle* line. Climb the crack above to the first break
(*Vulture Squadron*). Hand-traverse right for 10 feet to a groove (above
where *The Jackal* breaks through) and climb it with difficulty (peg runner in
the right wall) to the next break. Traverse this 10 feet left and make steep
moves over a small roof to enter a bottomless groove. Climb the groove
past a small ledge on *The Burning Giraffe* and on up to the *Kangaroo Wall*
exit. Go rightwards up the bank to nut belays below a wide crack in a
groove.

3 40 feet 4b. Climb the crack and struggle past the tree to the top.

★★Dog Eat Dog   290 feet   E4   (8.2.86)
A fantastic and lonely lead starting up the arête between *The Jackal* and
Hyena Cage below the roofs; above, it links sections of those routes with
the missing pieces to create the ultimate *diretissima*. 50m rope required.
1 90 feet 4c. *The Jackal* pitch 1. There is a rather brittle and dirty
alternative 3 feet to the left if required (5b).
2 160 feet 6a. Move up left onto the obvious arête. Climb straight up the
arête (two bolt runners) to a foot-ledge below the roofs (peg runner). Climb
through the bulge above (peg runner) as for *The Jackal* into the obvious
groove and follow the groove to its top as for *Hyena Cage*. Pull just right
over the large bulge into a thin crack (wire and thread *in situ*). Reach a
ledge on *The Burning Giraffe*, and climb the bulging finishing-groove of
The Jackal directly above to the terrace. Go straight up the bank to nut
belay below the final wall.
3 40 feet 4b. *Hyena Cage* pitch 3.

★★★The Jackal   310 feet   E4   (25.11.77)
A majestic climb, the first of the big free routes on this section of the wall,
and now a classic. There has been a rockfall at the crossing of *The
Umbrella Girdle* and some debris remains – the grade should be
unaffected. Protection is quite plentiful but the pegs are ancient. Start 30
feet right of the groove of *Kangaroo Wall*, at a long thin crack which runs
up to the big groove.
1 90 feet 4c. Climb the crack to a small overhang (peg runner). Step
right and go up ledges (peg runner and some vegetation) to a stance and
peg and nut belay at the foot of the big groove.
2 100 feet 6a. Climb the groove past a small overhang and a quarry
stake, and then strenuously up the crack to *The Umbrella Girdle* line (peg
runner). Move left and down across a slab to a good foothold (peg
runner). Move up and pull over the bulge (peg runner) to reach the break
of *Vulture Squadron*. Traverse 10 feet right in this and then climb direct to a
good stance in a groove. Peg and nut belay.
3 70 feet 5c. Climb the groove to the wide break of *The Burning Giraffe*
and move left to beneath a shallow bulging groove. Start this with difficulty
and climb direct to the upper terrace. Scramble up and right to a tree belay.
4 50 feet 5a. Climb a clean-cut groove to its roof, pull out right, and
continue to the top.

★★Feline   300 feet   E5   (19.3.83)
A direct assault on the great barrier of overhangs gives a sensational and
gymnastic (though excellently-protected) crux to an exceptionally sustained
and cumulatively demanding climb. Start 10 feet right of the thin crack of
The Jackal.
1 90 feet 5b. Gain the obvious scoop and make a couple of moves up
it; then leave it for the left arête. Climb the rib for 15 feet and move back

right (peg runner). Pull over the overlap (thread *in situ*) and continue direct for a few feet until it is possible to move diagonally left into the main corner. Climb the corner (peg runner and vegetation) to the stance and peg and nut belay.

2 60 feet 5c. Move out right to a borehole and climb the wall (bolt runner) passing a good nut-slot. Thin moves up and right lead to a three-bolt (two very ancient) belay below the roofs.

3 40 feet 6b. Move up left to the roof and climb through the box-shaped gap by a series of heel-hooks and one finger pulls (assortment of *in-situ* protection). Reach the break above (*Vulture Squadron*) and belay on nuts and *Friends*.

4 70 feet 6a. Climb a faint rib to an undercut flake. Move right round this and up to the break of *Zebra Crossing*. Pull over the overhang and climb a thin crack to *The Burning Giraffe*. Pull over the next roof (thread *in situ*) and climb directly up the bold wall to the upper terrace. Tree belay.

5 40 feet 6a. Almost directly above, and just left of the clean-cut groove of *The Jackal*, is an overhanging corner: climb it to the top.

SURREALIST SECTOR

The remaining routes starting from the base of the wall all avoid the main overhangs. Three trend right to The Pedestal and continue to the right again. The others finish at The Pedestal or stop somewhere short of it. The lower sections of the first two were knotted together – the stitches have here been unpicked.

In Quarantine 270 feet E3   (14.5.83)

A long, wandering route. Some poor rock and sparsely-protected sections. Paradoxically, the first pitch provides probably the most interesting way to the first stance of *The Jackal*.

1 100 feet 5c. Climb the scoop of *Feline* for 20 feet; then step right and climb the continuation groove (peg runner). Continue up and slightly right to an open corner (peg runner, junction with *Endangered Species*), and then go diagonally left (peg runner) until able to traverse left into *The Jackal's* corner. Climb this (peg runner and vegetation) to the stance and peg and nut belay.

2 60 feet 4c. Move out right round the arête and go right quite low down. Then go diagonally right past a nut-slot and a peg runner to the triangular stance on *The Umbrella Girdle* (bolt and peg belay).

3 40 feet 5a. Climb up to just right of the large bush and then traverse right to The Pedestal (peg and nut belay).

4 70 feet 5b. Climb the crack above to the break and continue up the small groove in the arête left of the main corner (peg runner) to a roof. Step left and go up to another roof. Step left again onto the lip and climb the large flake to the multiple-peg belay on *The Burning Giraffe*. Abseil off here or continue as for *Zebrazone*.

Endangered Species   130 feet   E3   5c   (28.9.86)
Check the bolt first: its 8mm is the only protection in the top half of the
climb. Start up the scoop of *Feline*.
After 12 feet, move right to a ledge (peg runner low on the right). Climb
the groove just left (peg runner), and then go diagonally left (peg runner in
corner of *In Quarantine*. From the top of the corner, move up and right to
gain another corner leading up to the overhangs. Follow this until forced
right a couple of moves (peg runner). Go up to the shale break, traverse
right (peg runner), and make a long reach directly above to gain better
holds. Continue up easier ground, and then pass a bolt runner with
difficulty to gain a small ledge. Continue direct up the wall above until able
to move right to the triangular stance (bolt and peg belay). Abseil off.

Natural Selection   140 feet   E4   5c   (23.9.86)
Hops around selecting from its neighbours in turn. Quite serious even so.
Climb the *Zebrazone* groove for 20 feet and hand-traverse left to the ledge
and low peg runner of *Endangered Species*. Climb its groove just left (two
peg runners) and then move up and right over a small overlap. Trend up
right (peg runner) to a shale break (peg runner) and move up slightly left to
another break. Continue, trending right on good holds, to a junction with
Zebrazone but, instead of moving right onto its belay ledge, climb a
shallow groove (peg runner) and move up left on better holds to the
ramp-line of pitch 2 of *In Quarantine*. Follow this rightwards to the
triangular stance and bolt and peg belay. Abseil off.

Zebrazone   290 feet   E1   (9.7.74)
A parallel line to *In Quarantine*, but of no greater quality. It needs
recleaning (again!). Start 25 feet right of *The Jackal*, at a groove which
runs up to a buddleia growing out of its cap.
1 120 feet 5b. Climb the groove and move left and up onto a higher
overhang. Climb up rightwards for 25 feet to easier ground (peg runner)
and then straight up to the left end of the *unter*-ledge. Peg and nut belay.
2 40 feet 4c. Climb diagonally right across the wall to The Pedestal. Peg
and nut belay.
3 70 feet 5b. Climb the crack to the break, step right, and climb the
main corner (peg runner in the left wall near the top) to the multiple-peg
belay just left on *The Burning Giraffe*. Best to abseil from here.
4 60 feet 4c. Climb the corner above, and go up right through appalling
vegetation to the abseil station below the final wall of *Surrealist*.
Variation
1a I Used to Be a Werewolf... 5b (30.4.87). A cleaner and more
technically interesting lower section, starting 5 feet to the right, climbs a
crack and slab past two additional peg runners to reach the easier section
at its peg runner.

Chase Darkness Away   120 feet   E1 5b   (19.6.85)

A parallel, but better, line to the first pitch of *Zebrazone*. High in the grade. Start 30 feet left of *Surrealist*, and 15 feet right of *Zebrazone*, under a large pointed roof.

Climb to the roof and step right to a ledge. Move up onto the polished tapering slab and reach a handhold in the corner under the roof. Pull over on better holds on the right and follow a right-slanting groove and ramp to gain a small ledge. Climb up (peg runner on the right) to an overhang, step right, and go up to good ledges. Climb rightwards up some thin flakes and then up the left edge of a black slab to an overhang (peg runner). Move a good 5 feet left to avoid bad rock and climb up to the *unter*-ledge. Peg and nut belay. Abseil off, or follow *Zebrazone* to The Pedestal.

The next two routes take problematic lines up the steep and relatively unbroken wall to the right. They share a start 20 feet left of the wide groove of *Surrealist*, and below and right of the overhang of *Chase Darkness Away*.

Tony   70 feet   E3 6b †   (29.12.91)

Pull up a narrow groove, step left to a cracked groove, and climb up to ledges beneath the smooth wall (*Friend* ½ and good wire). Climb up immediately left of the bolt runner above with difficulty, and continue on good holds to a small roof (peg runner). Pull straight over on good holds and reach a small ledge. Wire belays above on *Chase Darkness Away* – continue up that route or *Surrealist* to the right.

John   70 feet   E3 6b †   (29.12.91)

Follow *Tony* to the base of the smooth wall, but traverse easily rightwards for 10 feet to a good ledge below a short angular groove (*Friend 1* and good wire). Climb the groove and on up the wall above with a hard move past the bolt runner, and reach a ledge above on *Surrealist*. Trend leftwards up flakes to the wire belay of *Tony*.

★Surrealist   320 feet   E1   (6.68)

A classic third pitch makes this a highly recommendable route despite the lesser quality and discontinuity of the lower pitches. Start near the right-hand end of the wall just before the floor rises, below a wide but shallow groove-crack system with a flake resting in the bottom pointing the way.

1 120 feet 5a. Move up left, and climb over the flake and up the crack to mantel leftwards onto a ledge. From the left end of the ledge, climb up left over some blocks, and then back right to a shallow open groove. Climb the groove to its end at a small roof and traverse 10 feet right (peg runner). Climb the wall above (some holds need care) to the *unter*-ledge. Peg and nut belay in the right-hand corner.

2 30 feet 4b. Climb the groove just left of the corner (two peg runners) and traverse right to The Pedestal. Peg and nut belay.

3 130 feet 5b. Traverse right along the red band to the far corner of the large recess (or climb directly up to it from the terrace below). Pull into the groove and climb it to its termination at *The Burning Giraffe* (peg runner out left). Move right and climb a fine crack (difficult and overhanging to start) until able to step left to a small ledge just below the upper terrace. The lower abseil station is here. Alternatively, go on up, and then leftwards through vegetation to the upper station below the final short wall.
4 40 feet 4b. Climb the wall, starting on the left and finishing out right.

LowGO (280 feet E3 1.8.90) traverses the horizontal break at 40-50 feet from the *Fugazi* belay to the bolt runner on *Kaiser Wall* (the last 60 feet being *Doctor Hay Fever* in reverse). From here it follows *Lionheart* to the rose bush and then goes left and up to the bolt and peg belay of *Eva Brawn*. Take intermediate belays in *The Jackal* and *Big Dong*. It eats gear all the way, especially quickdraws and *Friends*.

The next three routes, though short, are easily accessible and good value.

Fugazi 50 feet E1 5c   (15.10.86)
A neat, well-protected problem. Starting as for *Surrealist*, climb the slim corner above, just right of the main groove, to a small roof (peg runner). Pull over leftwards to reach a good ledge. Avoid going into the *Surrealist* groove as long as possible, but eventually pull over its overhang onto the ledge. Use cleaned holds on the right to reach a fixed peg.

Beside Myself 50 feet E2 5c   (27.8.86)
A rather more meaty pitch than the preceding; a technical grade less for those with a long reach, but still quite a serious E2. Start 10 feet right of Surrealist.
Climb a short slab and then flake cracks to a tiny overlap (poor *in-situ* nut). Pull steeply round (peg runner) until a long move gains a good ledge. Pull up to more ledges and a two-bolt belay. Abseil off.

Incubus 60 feet E1 5b   (21.12.86)
Less good than the other two; 20 feet right of *Surrealist* an obvious short groove runs up to a roof. Get onto the ledge at its base (preferably while no-one is looking). Climb the groove and pull right round the roof (peg runner). A couple of delicate moves up the slab brings good ledges within reach. Continue straight up these and the large flakes above just right of a crack. Step left to a tree and bolt belay. Abseil off.

Come and Get It 45 feet E1 5c   (19.3.87)
Problematic and much harder without a long reach. Start 10 feet left of *Urizen*, at the right-hand end of the wall.
Step up onto ledges. Climb up (peg runner) and make a hard stretch for a tiny shelf on the right. Ignore holds on the right and make a hard crank on small face holds to grasp a higher shelf. Continue on ledges to reach a

Kangaroo Wall (E2) GO Wall, Wintour's Leap
Climber: Chris Craggs   Photo: Craggs col.

GO WALL from the north-west

1	Lionheart	E5
2	Kaiser Wall	E3
3	Mein Kampf	E5
4	Heil Hitler!	E5
5	Lurking Fear	E4
6	Stairway to Heaven	E2
7	King Kong	HVS
8	Vulture Squadron	E3
9	Big Dong	E3
10	Howling at the Moon	E5
11	Kangaroo Wall	E2

**GO WALL from
the south-west**

12	Hyena Cage	E4
13	Dog Eat Dog	E4
14	The Jackal	E4
15	Feline	E5
16	Big Bad Wolf	E6
17	Parasol	E5
18	Zebrazone	E2
19	Fond Adieu	E4
20	Never Say Goodbye	E2
21	Surrealist	E1
22	Captain Beaky	E2
23	Kama Sutra	HS
A	The Burning Giraffe	HVS
B	Zebra Crossing	E3

The Burning Giraffe (HVS) GO Wall, Wintour's Leap
Climber: David Moore   Photo: Alan Moore

tree belay.

Urizen (90 feet Very Severe 4b c.1966) and **Aharia** (40 feet Very Severe 4c c.1966) are the two obvious grooves in the large right-curving corner of the wall. Poor, and often dirty, though recently cleaned a little. Abseil from the first convenient tree in each case. The crack just right of the second has also been climbed.

THE PEDESTAL SECTOR
The remaining routes on the wall are reached from the top of the scree slope. Take the path to its end, whence a scramble up 10 feet reaches the terrace. The Pedestal is above its far end, and the *unter*-ledge is gained by abseiling or climbing down the (slightly loose) corner the other side (25 feet 4a). The 'triangular stance' is 15 feet back up from *its* far end. Belays on the terrace are difficult except in the crack at the left-hand end, but there is a good peg on The Pedestal and one at each end of the *unter*-ledge; all three can be backed up with with nuts.

Enter the Dragon   80 feet   E4   6b   (2.3.86)
A traverse of the central section of the lower wall, giving a few fierce but well-protected moves.
Reach the triangular stance and its bolt belay (by pitch 1 of The Umbrella Girdle). Traverse down and left for 20 feet (bolt runner on Feline). Make a step down, and then go left into the big groove of The Jackal. Cross the left wall (bolt runner) to the arête of Dog Eat Dog (bolt runner), and continue at the same level across Hyena Cage into a shallow corner. Cross the orange wall (bolt runner on Crocodile Tears) to the stance on Kangaroo Wall (high and low peg belays). Abseil off.

★The Umbrella Girdle   160 feet   E2   (10.67/14.7.76)
Though lacking the positions of the higher traverses, the second pitch gives good technical climbing. Provided it is free from seepage, it can normally be climbed in all weathers. The route originally continued along the belay terrace from King Kong to Blitzkrieg and then diagonally across the right-hand half of The Far South Bay to finish in the groove of Llama, but (especially with abseil bolts to hand) no-one ever does this now. Start on The Pedestal.
1 60 feet 4a. Descend the corner to the *unter*-ledge (peg runner). From the far end (peg runner), climb back up a borehole to the triangular stance (bolt belay).
2 100 feet 5b. Move leftwards up to the roof and traverse left (three bolt runners together at foot-level and then peg runner). Swing down on a good hold and finger-traverse strenuously round a bulge to the top of the crack on The Jackal (peg runner). (Still some rockfall debris here.) Move down left across a slab to a good foothold (peg runner) and then back up left across Kangaroo Wall (jammed hex above and peg runner). Keep left close under the roofs (one more peg runner on Howling at the Moon) to

reach the *King Kong* stance and abseil station.

★★★**Dinosaur Heaven** 70 feet E6 6b F7c †   (27.10.91)

Innovative and sensational roof-climbing through the main barrier of overhangs between *Feline* and *Parasol*; the best route of its type in the Wye Valley. The first two bolts are 10mm. Start from the triangular stance (though the second will find it more comfortable to belay at the left end of the *unter*-ledge).

Climb straight up to the roof via a thin flake crack (peg runner). Extend for a monster jug over the first roof (bolt runner) before a brisk layback (*in-situ* wire and thread) leads to the overhung ledge on *Big Bad Wolf* (*Rock 2/3*). Powerful moves rightwards around the second roof (bolt runner, then peg runner) gain a superb pocket over the lip. Make one thin move (bolt runner) and then with jugs in hand (peg runner) pull over onto the small ledge on *Zebra Crossing*. Peg, thread, and nut belays. Abseil back to the stance.

The next section *was* terribly complex: three old aid routes, bit-and-piece freeing, numerous variants, and a rockfall. It is now immeasurably simpler! And that is how it will be kept here – please refer to the first-ascent list for a full chronological analysis. Suffice it to say:

Joe the Lion (10.6.78) free-climbed the upper roof of *Parasol*, a fine achievement at the time, but now overtaken; and its upper pitches are no longer viable. There is too little left of **It's a Beautiful Day** (2.72), aid or free, above or below the roof, to justify description. **Lioness** (5c 26.1.86) and **Slinkin' Leopard** (5c 18.1.86) are pitches trending left across the headwall from above the upper lip of *Parasol* to the most impenetrably vegetated section of the terrace below the old tennis-court; compulsory early retirement seems inevitable.

★**Parasol** 90 feet E4 6b †   (9.67/14.12.91)

Completely free at last! Some spectacular manoeuvres over the first roof. Start at the peg and nut belay at the right-hand end of the *unter*-ledge. Climb the *Surrealist* groove left of the corner to the two peg runners; then traverse left and step up to a monster undercut at the break (peg runner). Stretch past a bolt runner to the lip of the roof (peg runner) and 'chin-it' round to the resting-shelf on *Big Bad Wolf*. Move up by the little nose (peg runner), make awkward moves out to the lip (peg runner), and pull round with difficulty (another peg runner above and right). Climb up the headwall for 10 feet to the break of *Zebra Crossing* (two old peg runners) and traverse right to a large crack (old peg runner), which leads easily to *The Burning Giraffe*. Move round right to the multiple-peg belay and abseil off.

★**Monosculpture**   90 feet   E5 6c †   (5&9.11.91)

The roofs between *Parasol* and *The Isle of Dogs* provide two boulder-problems in space.

As for *Parasol*, climb the *Surrealist* groove to the two peg runners; then continue straight up to a broken niche below the first roof. Enter the groove piercing the roofs (bolt runner) and follow it directly (peg runner) to the traverse band on *Big Bad Wolf* (peg runner on the left). An angular black rib points the way: pull through the next roof with great difficulty (10mm bolt runner and *in-situ* wire above) and gain the foot of the easy finishing-crack of *Parasol*. Follow this; then move right to the multiple-peg belay.

★★**Big Bad Wolf**   90 feet   E6 6b   (24.5.83)

A sensational and serious route venturing into a remote position: a strong-nerved leader and a reckless second are essential. The route originally continued directly to the top of the cliff (5b, with belays on *The Burning Giraffe* and the top terrace) instead of moving right to the belay described. The terrace vegetation barring progress to the top tier or leftwards to reach the *King Kong* abseil point renders this inadvisable – it stands as a brilliant pitch on its own. Start on The Pedestal.

Climb the crack to the break and traverse left (various old peg runners) to the little nose – unique resting-shelf below. Swing down left (peg runner) and continue the traverse (peg runner) to an overhung ledge (peg runner above). Pull into the overhanging groove and climb it with difficulty (peg runner difficult to reach out right above its roof). Step right, follow some pockets to reach the break of *Zebra Crossing*, and swing right to a small ledge. Peg, thread, and nut belays (as on *Dinosaur Heaven*). Abseil off to land on the *unter*-ledge.

★★**The Isle of Dogs**   70 feet   E5 6b   (11.1.86)

A wild pitch gaining a sensationally exposed position in a very short distance: excellent value. Strenuous, but with good *in-situ* protection.

From a start on The Pedestal, swing up left onto the wall (bolt runner – this can be clipped first from the crack above the belay), make a hard move up, and reach the break. Enter the hanging niche above (bolt runner) and exit left onto the small arête (peg runner and wire *in situ*). A blind move over the bulge leads to good holds (nut *in situ*) and easier climbing up the large flake goes directly to the multiple-peg belay. Abseil off.

★**Fond Adieu**   80 feet   E4 6b   (18.1.86)

A strenuous but well-protected crux.

From an intermediate shelf on the right-hand side of The Pedestal, climb the groove over a bulge to a ledge. Continue up the V-groove (peg runner and *in-situ* thread) to the large roof and battle round it (nut *in situ*) to good holds above. Climb a thin crack on the right to the peg and bolt belay of *Never Say Goodbye*. Abseil off.

★★Never Say Goodbye   85 feet   E2 5c   (23.1.83)
Pleasantly sustained and enjoyable climbing.
From the left-hand end of the terrace, climb a crack leftwards to the first
overhang. Pull straight over this to a huge jug and a break. Continue over
a bulge up a thin disjointed crackline with a couple of awkward moves to
the next break. Step up again (peg runner) and make some committing
moves to *The Burning Giraffe* break (peg runner). Lurch straight over the
overhang above on big holds into the fine groove. Climb this to the top
and move left to a peg and bolt belay. Abseil off.

The prominent groove-line to the right of this route and to the left of the large
bulging nose is the third pitch of *Surrealist*.

Liquid Leather   90 feet   E3 5c   (15.2.83)
…Fluid rock!
Climb the third pitch of *Surrealist* to the first break, and traverse out right
onto the ledge above the overhangs. Climb the very dubious flake crack to
the next break (peg runner and thread *in situ*). Continue up to *The Burning
Giraffe* and take a nut belay below the overhanging crack. Traverse 15 feet
right to the peg belay on *Kama Sutra* and abseil off.

The large bulge on the right is so fully equipped with *in-situ* gear that it is best
to sort out what belongs to what before tackling the next four routes.

★Surreal Thing   80 feet   E5 6b   (4.1.86)
A gymnastic and mean route, linking a series of hard problems up the left
side of the bulging walls right of the third pitch of *Surrealist*. Good rests
abound but the hard sections are strenuous enough to warrant respect.
The threads need replacing.
From the centre of the terrace, climb a faint black groove, just left of a
small rib, to near the left end of the roofs. Pull desperately round (peg
runner) into an awkward hanging corner (*in-situ* wire), and struggle
strenuously to gain the ledge above. Move up right onto a higher ledge
and climb a series of pockets (two *in-situ* threads) to a bulge (third thread).
Lunge round the bulge (*in-situ* wire) to good jugs, and then move up right
onto another ledge. A problem move over the next bulge (*in-situ* thread
again) leads past a wobbling block to the lower *Surrealist* abseil bolts.

Hell: Just for Leather   35 feet   E4 6c   (11.1.86/22.7.86)
A fine little roof-problem; but the former injunction to 'reverse back down
and jump onto the bolt to lower off' sounds, ten years on, rather blasé.
Ponder first!
From just right of the rib under the overhangs, climb to the roof (peg
runner). Lurch right to a layaway and jump for a sloping edge above the
roof (bolt runner). Somehow reach the break above and then…

★Power Games 80 feet E4 6b (2.3.84)

A biceps-pumping challenge through the roofs.

Climb the wall to the right end of the roof (peg runner). Move left (peg runner in roof) and fight through (*in-situ* thread on left) to a final hard move to stand up. Move to the right-hand end of the ledge (*in-situ* thread on right), and climb the wall to the *Zebra Crossing* break. Step left and climb a pocketed crack to a nut belay on *The Burning Giraffe*. Traverse 15 feet right the *Kama Sutra* peg belay and abseil off.

The following routes (other than the two traverses) have been rationalized.

One Cockatoo 160 feet E3 (21.12.85)

Start under the right-hand end of the overhangs, as for *Power Games*.
1 100 feet 6a. Move up to a ledge and pull round the right end of the roof to a calcite crack. Climb this using holds on the right (peg runner, then thread *in situ*). Continue straight up and climb a blunt arête using a flake to reach *The Burning Giraffe*. Climb the shallow groove above to the upper terrace. Tree belay (from where you can wander left and up to the *Surrealist* abseil station).
2 60 feet 5c. Scramble up left to a ledge and climb a flake (*in-situ* thread) to an overhang. Move awkwardly left and go more easily (passing a second *in-situ* thread) to the top.

★Zebra Crossing 340 feet E3 (9.5.82)

Good climbing and situations. It is nowhere desperate, but requires sustained concentration. Protection is adequate: take a full rack including *Friends*.
1 80 feet 5c. Follow *Captain Beaky* to the 'good hold below a groove'. Traverse left in the break (peg runner on the crest, small thread *in situ* just above) to reach the groove of *Surrealist*, and arrange nut belays.
2 70 feet 5b. Cross the wall and the corner, and move out onto the arête. Continue left, passing three old peg runners, across a slab to a blunt rib with a small exposed foot-ledge. Peg, thread, and nut belays (as for *Dinosaur Heaven*).
3 90 feet 5b. Continue straight left, gradually easing a little, to reach the chimney of *Kangaroo Wall* and climb this to the cave and nut belays.
4 100 feet 5a. *Kangaroo Wall* pitches 3 and 4.

★Captain Beaky 120 feet E2 (13.1.80)

A popular route of its grade. Start at the right-hand end of the terrace, as for *The Perfumed Garden*.
1 80 feet 5c. Climb to and over the overhang to a ledge. Hand-traverse left with the overhang at chest-level and pull up on a hidden hold (before reaching the *Power Games* thread). Climb the wall to a good hold below a groove at the break of *Zebra Crossing*, and climb straight up the groove to take a nut belay on *The Burning Giraffe* below the overhanging crack.
2 40 feet 5b. Climb the crack and go up the ivy bank to a good tree

belay. Wander up and left to the *Surrealist* abseil station.

The Perfumed Garden   85 feet   Hard Very Severe 5a   (7.7.79)
From the right-hand end of the terrace, climb up to and over the overhang
to a ledge. Then climb the long corner all the way to the break of *The
Burning Giraffe*, and move right to the peg belay of *Kama Sutra*. Abseil off.

★The Burning Giraffe   380 feet   Hard Very Severe   (4.6.67)
A pronounced break crosses the wall from end to end. The second pitch
gives good climbing, but the long pitch, though very finely situated, tends
to become a little monotonous. An extension across to *King Kong* has
been made at the same grade. Take plenty of large nuts and (if available
but not essential) *Friends*. [Photo p.145.]
1 70 feet 4a. *Kama Sutra* pitch 1.
2 70 feet 5a. Traverse easily left to the large rib and go round it with
increasing difficulty to a small ledge and peg runner just left of the
Surrealist groove. Hand-traverse strenuously left and cross the corner to
pull up onto a ledge and the multiple-peg belay.
3 140 feet 4c. Continue straight left along the fault to the cave on
Kangaroo Wall by a mixture of hand-traversing and knee shuffling. Nut
belays.
4 100 feet 5a. *Kangaroo Wall* pitches 3 and 4.

Kama Sutra   180 feet   Hard Severe 4a   (12.66)
The only 'easy' route on GO Wall, and giving little feel of its atmosphere.
The route's main function is to provide access for *The Burning Giraffe*.
However, as the first pitch often stays dry for half an hour or so after the
onset of rain it can provide brief entertainment when all other climbs of this
standard are sodden. Start below the obvious chimney, just left of the huge
arête above the top of the scree slope, and right of the terrace.
Climb the chimney (peg runner 15 feet below the top), to finish just left on a
good ledge at the the wide break of *The Burning Giraffe*. Peg and nut belay.
Abseil off. Various loose and dirty continuations above have been made.

Two awful routes, **Blossom and Blood** (E2 16.4.84) and **Clank Honk
Tweet** (Hard Very Severe 30.9.79), have been recorded on the huge arête.
Both encounter dangerous rock (if it's still there) and dense, prickly vegetation
(which certainly is!).

THE WOODCROFT QUARRY

This somewhat unattractive feature gives very convenient access to Fly Wall and The Pedestal Sector of GO Wall, as well as providing a good descent to the Valley path along the whole cliff-base. Climbing in the Quarry has been less appealing. The ownership seems to change regularly (usually around the times the guides are published!) and successive owners have been unhappy about the use of the Quarry itself, while prepared to turn a blind eye to activity on Fly Wall, which is part of the same property. The Quarry has again just been sold, but it is not known to whom, or to what use it will be put. If the new owners will tolerate climbing, doubtless those still desperate for virgin rock will attempt to develop it in a more user-friendly fashion. Watch this space!

Access from the top of the central section is problematic: climbing over the fence is not acceptable. It is possible to traverse left from the left-hand half of the backwall onto the land at the top of GO Wall, where the routes on the north (left-hand) wall end anyway, but that is subject to the restriction and so is permitted **only** in the winter months (see page 128). For worthwhile development in most of the Quarry, it would be necessary for proper abseil stations to be fixed.

There are large areas of unpredictable and dirty rock though, undoubtedly, determined preparation would enable a number of reasonable routes to be climbed. Those that are known to have been done already are printed below for (with one exception) the first time. In addition, there are some fixed single-piece belays at around 30 feet in the south bay of the Quarry, and there is evidence of recent cleaning elsewhere.

The descriptions are those of the first ascensionists, and the routes have not been checked or, in several cases, even identified. It is likely that the passage of time, the force of gravity, and the goings-on during the filming of an episode of *Casualty* in 1991 will have combined to change things. Except from the first route, all peg runners used are believed to have been subsequently removed. Before attempting any of these climbs, you are **strongly** recommended to make a careful abseil inspection, determine the correct line of the route, and carry out any cleaning and gearing that may be needed.

A Nightmare of Brown Sugar   130 feet   E5   5c   †   (25.4.89)

A very serious pitch involving unrelentingly bad rock to approach some spectacular and enjoyable moves over the roofs of the headwall. An abseil rope was used on the first ascent to protect the gully approach. Start on the platform below the red rock pillar right of the large arête overlooking the scree slope descent path.

Scramble/grovel up the gully until it is possible to transfer onto the red pillar (the transition from sandy gully to 'rock' is barely perceptible!). Continue up with heart in mouth (poor peg runner) to the first roof (poor peg runner). In desperation, launch up and over the roof on good holds to a welcome rest in a groove (better peg runner above). Swing up and over the second overhang to search for good holds and so reach the top.

The last section of the above may actually be the next route.

Gorilla Thriller   40 feet   E1   5b   †   (c.1983)
The clean white buttress above the red wall.

Nice and Sleazy   130 feet   E1   †   (29.9.79)
Probably the most reasonable proposition in the Quarry. [Photo p.192.]
Start right at the bottom, in the open corner where the left-hand sidewall
meets the backwall.
1 40 feet 4c. Climb the corner to a small tree belay on the left.
2 90 feet 5a/b. Continue up the corner, traverse right from a grass
ledge, and climb a blunt arête to a niche. Climb above this to a ledge, and
move right and back left to finish.

The next four routes were described as starting 'from a tree on a platform
below the smooth wall right of *Nice and Sleazy*.'

Ideas for Walls   75 feet   E2   5b   †   (c.1983)
Climb the sandy wall over to the left to a peg runner; then move right to
join *Toad in the Hole*.

Are We Not Men?   90 feet   Hard Very Severe   5a   †   (c.1983)
Start as for *Ideas for Walls*, and climb the flake on the right; then go left
and up to a bush (peg runner). Move right and go up to an overhang.
Finish up the rib and slab to the left.

Toad in the Hole   70 feet   Hard Very Severe   5a/b   †   (c.1983)
Traverse left into a chimney, and climb it to where it fades. Move back up
and right to below an overhang, and finish up a crack.

Safety Dance   50 feet   E3   6a   †   (c.1983)
Traverse left and climb a blank scooped groove (two peg runners).

Men without Hats   75 feet   Very Severe   4c   †   (c.1983)
Start at the left end of the terrace.
Trend right to a wobbly corner behind a bush. Move up and step left to
layback a flake crack.

Industrial Disease   60 feet   Hard Very Severe   5a   †   (c.1983)
Climb cracks in the obvious red wall between two loose corners to a
second terrace.

FLY WALL   (Photo-diagrams pages 160-161)
South of the scree slope and below the path descending from the Woodcroft
Quarry is Fly Wall. Straight and unrecessed, vertical apart from the terrace
which splits it at half height from end to end, its base guarded by a huge mass
of tangled wild buddleia falling to the river, and only the sky above, it looks
from the foot of the scree slope strangely like 'The Lost World'. The left-hand
half gives short, dynamic routes, mostly between VS and E2. Further right the
bottom of the cliff falls away as the top rises to give longer and sometimes
more serious routes.

One or two of the oldest local residents can remember when Fly Wall could
boast the full 300 feet of its neighbours, and a green meadow sloped gently
back from its summit. Being longer and less wooded than the other areas, it
must have been the most impressive feature of Wintour's Leap. Alas, it was
never climbed, and no-one has any photos. Alone, it escaped the pick and
shovel of the past, but 20th century technology intervened to remove its top
half, together with the meadow, in gouging out the monstrous Woodcroft
Quarry. Not all is lost, however, for the remaining rock has survived largely
unharmed: natural cracks and surface features are intact, undisfigured by
unnatural boreholes and rusty stakes; thus a greater variety of climbing
techniques is brought into play.

The quality of both the rock and the climbing varies, but much of it is good,
and the best is very good. Most of the vegetation was removed, though some
has returned; and some of the exits onto the terrace and a few of the finishes
in the central area are earthy: care is needed on these. In general the upper
wall is superior to the lower, and several of the climbs are equally well started
on the terrace; however, it is best to get the feel of the wall with a few complete
routes first. If abseiling in, take the greatest care that no-one is below as the
rope almost invariably dislodges stones at the top.

In the VS–HVS band, *Freedom, Swallow's Nest, The Split,* and *Dragonfly* offer
classic crack-climbing of a type little found elsewhere on the cliff at this
standard, though they are becoming very polished, and one or two bits have
dropped off. At E1–E2, *Bulging Flies, Split Flies,* and *Firefly* provide excellent
strenuous jamming and laybacking. Of the hardest routes, *La Folie, Gendarmerie, Idealist,* and *Flies Aloft* combine excellent wall-climbing with wild
roof finishes.

THE APPROACH
1 Through the Woodcroft Quarry: this is described on page 55.
2 A little further, but very straightforward, and probably the best anyway for
the southmost routes is the last option mentioned on that page: walk down
the road below *The Rising Sun* and go through a green kissing-gate (this is
the lower of two iron gates marked 'Offa's Dyke'). Follow the obvious path
(ignore yellow arrows off to the left) under a wooden footbridge and down
past The Forbidden Wall. Where the deciduous woodland gives way to the

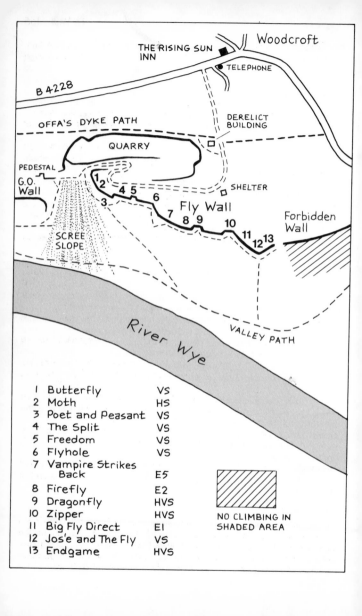

1	Butterfly	VS
2	Moth	HS
3	Poet and Peasant	VS
4	The Split	VS
5	Freedom	VS
6	Flyhole	VS
7	Vampire Strikes Back	E5
8	Firefly	E2
9	Dragonfly	HVS
10	Zipper	HVS
11	Big Fly Direct	E1
12	Jos'e and The Fly	VS
13	Endgame	HVS

NO CLIMBING IN SHADED AREA

buddleia, turn right and go up to the rock. To reach the north end of the wall, it is probably best now to follow the path under the cliff; although this is rough in places, the alternatives are worse.

LANDMARKS
From the path under the cliff, starting at the left (north) end of the wall:

1 The first gap on the left gives access to the left-facing corner of *Butterfly*.

2 The second gap leads to the groove of *Moth*, with the cracked corner of *Flies Rise* on its right.

3 Next the path forks: the right branch goes down to the Valley Path but gets very overgrown; the left branch rises to an earthy platform below a small, ribbed section taken by *The Split*.

4 Another short rise leads to the square-cut tower of *Freedom*, bounded on the left by the groove of *Phoenix* and on the right by the corner of *Swallow's Nest*. The base of the cliff is at its highest at this point.

5 At the end of a level section below a short wall (*Flew* and *Flyte*) is the long, two-tier chimney-line of *Flyhole*. Just right again, the first pitch of *Bulging Flies* takes a shallow, right-facing corner, with *Vapona* and *Flyover* almost on its doorstep.

6 The base of the cliff now falls away sharply; the path moves away from the rock below *Flyhole* and curls round to return just below *Vampire Strikes Back*.

7 Ten feet below this point is a larger than usual and somewhat gnarled buddleia: this is the start of *Flypast* and *La Folie*. A further 8 feet right is a similar but now collapsed buddleia at the foot of *Firefly* and *Wurlitzer*.

8 To the right there is a short rise to a mound from which the long groove of *Dragonfly* runs right up the cliff.

9 Across a short dip is another mound: *Zipper*, which has suffered a severe rockfall, takes the less clear-cut groove-line above.

10 Again the ground falls away steeply. Direct access to the prominent slab is barred by a long roof just above the ground. At its far end, half-way down the slope, a tiny foot-ledge leads into a niche, which is the start of *Big Fly*.

11 The bottom of the slope, the lowest point of the wall, is marked by an up-turned boulder standing in a corner at the start of *Jos'e and the Fly*: this is the point reached from Approach 2.

12 To the right the wall is broken and vegetated, but almost at the top of the slope is a faint clean rib, vertical to start, but lying back a little above: this is *Endgame*.

13 The far right-hand corner, *Can't Fly Any Higher*, marks the boundary of Fly Wall and of permitted climbing. All the rock to the right of this is part of the Forbidden Area (see page 56).

THE WAY OFF
All the routes finish on the quarry path. Go up and out through the gap in the fence left of the ruined building onto Offa's Dyke footpath. Turn left for the parking pull-off, or right then immediately left for The Rising Sun. If the quarry exit should be closed, it will be necessary to descend to the Valley Path, either by the scree slope or by the path below Fly Wall, and return by one of the

other approaches.

THE TRAVERSES
Fly Wall waited a long time for a traverse, but then two came in a rush. The first two can be linked to give a superb high-level girdle of the whole wall.

★Fly Major   340 feet   E3   (28.6.81)
An exhilarating traverse of the upper break, with gradually increasing exposure. For both leader and second, strenuous and committing, though the top is within easy reach much of the time. The crux is the section from *Flyover* to *Flypast*: the rest is easier.
1 45 feet 4a. *Moth* pitch 1 (page 158).
2 65 feet 5b. Continue up the groove of *Moth* to the overhang, and hand-traverse a flake under it strenuously. Continue with difficulty (peg runner) across the wall of *Time Flies*, and then move more easily round from the little corner of *Flies Rise*. Step down onto a large loose flake and down again to a small tree belay on *Poet* (wires up left).
3 65 feet 5b. Follow *Peasant* back onto the flake and across to the larger, turf-covered flake of *Chameleon*. From its far end, step down and traverse, as for *Bzzz Splat* (old peg runner). Continue horizontally across the wall of *Fly or Die* and the groove of *Swatter* to the wide crack of *The Split*. Stand up on the ledges and traverse on good holds at this slightly higher level to a stance and nut belays in a short wide groove, the finishing-groove of *African Killer Bee*.
4 45 feet 5b. Traverse right into the groove of *Phoenix*, and step down and across *Dazed and Confused* to a good foot-ledge on the edge of the wall. Make trying moves (and worrying for the second) down and right into the dièdre of *Freedom* under the roof (peg runner), and then swing round right into *Swallow's Nest*. Cross the wall at this level and move round into the chimney of *Flyhole* to stand on its bridge. Good large nut belay behind a tongue of rock 5 feet above.
5 120 feet 5c. Step round the edge and continue the traverse, sometimes strenuous, along the break above the left wall of *Flyover* to the 'upside-down thing' and peg runner in the corner under the big roof. Continue along the break, small spaced holds at first, gradually improving, until the bottom of the original easy finishing-corner of *Wurlitzer* is reached. Cross *Firefly*, still with hands in the break, and then stand up on a block on *Lord of the Flies*. Peg runner above. As for that route, climb the incipient crack to easy ground and a large block belay at the top.

★★Fly Major General   230 feet   E4 †   (10.9.86)
The natural extension to *Fly Major*, from *Lord of the Flies* to (effectively) the end of the wall. Harder and more strenuous throughout, especially on pitch 2. Superb climbing on the middle pitches. Start on a small ledge 10 feet below the top of the steep section of *Lord of the Flies* (page 167), at the point where *Fly Major* meets it. Belay on its top peg runner with a rope also to that of *Firefly* out left.

1 50 feet 5c. Swing down right and hand-traverse the break around the arête, past *Gendarmerie*, until a step up a groove gains foot-ledges on a blunt rib (above the hard section of *May Fly*). Place some wires, move back down, and hand-traverse the obvious break to the pedestal in the *Dragonfly* corner. *Friend* and nut belays.

2 60 feet 6a. Clip the peg runner on *Flight of the Phoenix* (back-rope for the second) and move across to its sharp rib. Move down right and across (crux) to gain an obvious projecting hold on *Blue Max*. Swing down right to jugs and hand-traverse right to pockets on *Flight Barrier* (peg runner). Move up right with difficulty (peg runner) to good footholds (peg runner on *Flying Fortress*) and then right again to the groove of *Jet Stream*. Climb its crux and then hand-traverse the break to belay on the pedestal in the corner of *Zipper* (peg and wires).

3 70 feet 5c. Make a hard move right to a projecting handhold on *Whip Lash* and then move more easily into *Big Fly*. Hand-traverse the break across the *Idealist* wall (peg runner and thread *in situ*) to its end at the wide crack of *Jos'e and the Fly*, in which climb to the terrace and the yew belay on the right.

4 50 feet 5c. The top pitch of *The Height Below* makes the most novel conclusion as it goes back in the reverse direction! For alternative ways off, see page 175.

Spirit of St Louis   310 feet   E1   (30.6.81)
A girdle of the lower wall, less good than upper routes in terms of climbing as well as position. Some cleaning urgently needed. Start as for *Bulging Flies* (page 164).

1 40 feet 5a. Follow a sightly-rising rightward line across vegetated ledges to some small thorns below a thin tapering groove on *Flypast*. Climb this to a peg belay at its top.

2 90 feet 5b. Climb back down to the break and traverse it under a long overhang (high peg runner in a groove through this on *Firefly* and another shortly on *Lord of the Flies* at the end of the overhang). Continue awkwardly below more overhangs to the prominent corner of *Dragonfly*. Move up right to a small ledge and a good nut belay.

3 70 feet 5b. Traverse across at this level past a peg runner and round an edge to a peg runner and sapling on a little ledge on *Zipper*. Step down and hand-traverse strenuously under the overhangs (peg runner above in a leaning corner) to a short shallow groove. Pull up and right past a peg runner to the stance of *Big Fly*. Two peg belays.

4 50 feet 4c. Traverse right to a large thread on *Jos'e and the Fly* and climb its chimney above to the terrace.

5 60 feet 4b. *Jos'e and the Fly* pitch 3. Refer to that route (page 175) for alternative exits.

BUTTERFLY SECTOR
The routes are all reached by short scrambles from the path before it forks, or from the left fork half-way back up the slope. The earth ledge at the base

of the rock has eroded badly, which makes starting and belaying awkward for some of the routes.

Gadfly (80 feet Very Severe 4c 10.2.80) takes either of the two loose cracks near the extreme left edge of the wall, and then the groove in the left edge above to a messy finish.

★Papillon   85 feet   E2   (14.3.83)
A nicely exposed, 'monkey-up-a-stick' finish. Start as for *Butterfly*, a few yards down the path below the first (left-facing) corner.
1 45 feet 4c. Climb the wall 5 feet left of the corner via a faint groove: rather artificial, but more interesting than the easy corner. Thread belay below the crack.
2 40 feet 5b. Mount the tall block on the left. Step left and climb the arête direct. A crack in the second quarter gives the only protection until a wire out right for the final reachy move. Belay on dubious stakes or a good boulder a further 30 feet back.

★Butterfly   85 feet   Very Severe
Start a few yards down the path below the first (left-facing) corner.
1 45 feet. Climb the corner to the terrace. Thread belay below a crack.
2 40 feet 4c. Mount the tall block on the left and use the crack to move up right to gain some good holds. Now climb the excellent upper crack to the top. Belay on dubious stakes or a good boulder a further 30 feet back.

Moth   85 feet   Hard Severe
A pleasant route, one of the easiest on the wall. Start below a short wide groove, a little right of *Butterfly*, and above the path before it forks. The upper pitch runs up by the left-hand side of the large roof.
1 45 feet 4a. Climb the groove to the terrace. Peg belay at the foot of the upper groove.
2 40 feet 4a. Climb the upper groove to the top. Belay on dubious stakes or a good boulder a further 30 feet back.

The Bionic Walnut   90 feet   E4   (17.5.83)
A savage pull in a good situation.
1 45 feet 4a. *Moth* pitch 1.
2 45 feet 6b. Climb a small groove just right of *Moth* to the roof. Swing right and surmount the overhang to a good hold. Another difficult move to a tiny thread (*in situ*) leads to better holds and the top.

Time Flies   100 feet   E2   (13.6.82)
A committing second pitch.
1 50 feet 4b. *Flies Rise* pitch 1.
2 50 feet 5b. Pull up left to a small ledge. Climb the wall on the left on small holds (some awkward-to-place wires half-way). Traverse right in the break to the pointed block, pull over, and go more easily to the top.

Flies Rise   100 feet   Hard Very Severe   (21.6.78)

This was an entertaining VS until someone cleaned off the heap of earth from the ledge above the belay, which you could stand on to reach the first holds. Now a very awkward move. Start below a wide crack in a shallow left-facing corner right of *Moth*.

1 50 feet 4b. Climb the crack; exit right and go up the earth bank and then left to two peg belays.

2 50 feet 5b. Climb the short wall on the left and step right to a small square corner (peg runner above). Somehow reach high handholds, and then a thin layback leads to a protruding block and the overhang, which is turned on the right. Move back left and finish up a short scoop to good block belays.

Poet and Peasant   90/100 feet   Very Severe   (15.11.78&23.10.67)

Start at a large right-facing corner, reached by doubling back from the left branch of the path half-way up the slope.

1 90 feet 4c. This is considerably the better of the two alternatives. Climb the corner, and continue up onto a block on the left of a tree. Swing left on a good low hold and climb, trending slightly left, to the top. Good block belay.

1a 100 feet 4c. Climb the corner, and continue to the tree. Mantel onto a loose, standing flake on the right, and hand-traverse right to the turf ledge on top of the large *Chameleon* flake. From its far end, climb to the top on awkward polished holds. Good block belay.

Exit and Chameleon   90 feet   Very Severe ‡   (3.2.68&21.5.78)

Start just right of the large corner of *Poet and Peasant*.

1 90 feet 4b. Of little interest or quality. Climb a shallow groove a short way and move left onto the rib. Above, earth and brambled slopes lead into a steep corner. Climb the corner and mantel onto the loose, standing flake. Move up over a shallow overhang and finish up a smooth scoop. Good block belay.

1a 90 feet 4c. A much better alternative, though not free from the rampant vegetation here. Climb the shallow groove a short way, move left onto the rib, and go up to the tangled ledge on the right of the corner, beneath a huge hanging flake. Climb the short wall to the flake with care, and then up round the left side to a ledge on top. Step up left to finish up the smooth scoop.

Bzzz Splat   100 feet   Hard Very Severe 5a   (24.5.78)

Start 10 feet right of the large corner of *Poet and Peasant*.

Climb the wall on the right: steep juggy moves to start with some brambles and loose holds. From the terrace, climb the flake crack in the open groove above to a small roof. Traverse right past an old peg runner and a shallow groove to a short deep crack, which leads to a ledge and the top.

SPLIT WALL
The path arrives upon a level earthy shelf below a small ribbed section. The latter is taken by the first pitch of *The Split*, which is used by most of the other routes as well. Various 'alternative starts' have been made up the wall to the left, but holds seem to come and go by the day.

Fly or Die   90 feet   E3   (21.5.78/13.2.83)
1 40 feet 5a. *The Split* pitch 1.
2 50 feet 5c. Move left and mantel onto a ledge (as for *Swatter*). Climb the light-coloured groove above with difficulty. Use pockets on the right to move up and climb broken cracks to the top. Good block belays.

★Swatter   100 feet   Hard Very Severe   (22.4.78)
Good sustained climbing.
1 40 feet 5a. *The Split* pitch 1.
2 60 feet 5a. Move left and mantel onto a ledge. Traverse right along the wall above the overhang to gain a shallow groove, which is climbed to the top and good block belays.

Fly Logic   85 feet   E3   (3.7.82)
A good test-piece.
1 40 feet 5a. *The Split* pitch 1.
2 45 feet 6a. Pull up direct past the belay and go up to the first break on little pockets. Step right and enter the minute groove above. Climb the groove and the vague arête above to easier ground near the top.

★The Split   90 feet   Very Severe   (12.67)
Two fine, well-contrasted pitches. One of the earliest routes on the wall and now something of a classic. The first pitch is very polished. Start on the earth platform at the top of the first short rise after the path fork, by a large fallen block.
1 40 feet 5a. Move up to a small thread. Continue up the wall (holds on the little left rib) to a horizontal crack and peg runner. Make awkward moves right and up, and then go up the earth bank to a thread belay.
2 50 feet 4b. Move right and climb the two-tiered crack to the top by your favourite technique. Good block belay.

★Split Flies   90 feet   E2   (16.6.79)
Excellent strenuous climbing.
1 40 feet 5a. *The Split* pitch 1. (An alternative start is a small corner to the right: one 5c move off the ground leads to good holds and a finish to right or left.) Walk right past the upper crack of *The Split* to the peg belay of *Ecliptic*.
2 45 feet 5c. Climb the wall left of the belay using a crack on the left. Make difficult moves round the overhang (peg runner) and follow the crack, gradually easing, to good finishing holds. A resting-ledge on the left just above the main difficulties can be welcomed or disdained. Good block

FLY WALL from the north-west

1	Papillon	E2
2	Butterfly	VS
3	Moth	HS
4	Flies Rise	HVS

5	Chameleon	VS
6	Swatter	HVS
7	The Split	VS
8	Split Flies	E2

9	Phoenix	HS
10	Freedom	VS
11	Swallow's Nest	VS
12	Flyte	HVS

13	Flyhole	VS
19	Firefly	E2
27	Big Fly Direct	E1
B	Fly Major General	E4

FLY WALL from the south-west

A	Fly Major	E3
10	Freedom	VS
14	Balls Out	E2
15	Bulging Flies	E2
16	Flyover	E3

17	Flypast	E3
18	La Folie	E4
20	Wurlitzer	E1
21	Lord of the Flies	E2
22	Gendarmerie	E3

23	Dragonfly	HVS
24	Flight Barrier	E5
25	Jet Stream	E3
26	Zipper	HVS
28	Little Fly	E1

29	Idealist	E5
30	Flies Aloft	E4
31	Jos'e and the Fly	VS

belays.

Ecliptic   100 feet   E1   ‡   (22.9.68)
Bold climbing on clean but unstable rock above the terrace. The first pitch
is vegetated: use the first pitch of *The Split* until it has been cleaned. Start
(anyway) as for *The Split*.
1 50 feet 4c. Go diagonally right over easy ledges above the brambles
to a square-cut groove, and climb it to the terrace (peg belay).
2 50 feet 5b. Move up on the right under a smaller overhang right of the
main roof and pull over to a small ledge (peg runner). Step left across a
gap and climb a good crack. Some committing and reachy moves above
lead to easier ground and good block belays at the top.
Variation
2a Mutchos Butchos 50 feet E2 5b (19.4.83). From the belay, climb
the short wall under the largest part of the overhang. Use a pocket in the
roof to reach good holds well above and right. Pull up and then, ideally,
climb the tottery pillar, avoiding the *Ecliptic* crack which is 3 feet right as
long as possible. However, life may be felt to be worth more than this.

★Mosquito Bite   110 feet   E1   (4.7.82)
A delightful little route on good rock. Start as for *The Split*.
1 50 feet 4c. Go diagonally right over easy ledges above the brambles
to the square-cut groove of *Ecliptic*. Climb the groove for 10 feet, and then
move right and climb a good crack to the terrace. Peg belay.
2 60 feet 5b. Walk right round the edge and climb a short wall to a
break. Move up and slightly right and then step left to a thread *in situ*.
Climb directly to the top, steeply but on good holds. Belay across the path.

FREEDOM SECTOR
The path rises again to a smaller earth platform below the obvious square
tower. The base of the wall is at its highest here. The first routes start in the
open groove to the left of the tower.

Three additional 'routes' have been recorded in this sector, for which there
cannot possibly be any room.

African Killer Bee   100 feet   Very Severe   4c   (17.5.78)
A pleasant route of its grade. Start as for *Phoenix*.
Climb the groove direct to the terrace. Step left, climb up for 10 feet, and
traverse 10 feet left to a niche. Step back out right and climb up to a wide
groove which leads to the top. Belay across the path.

Pigs Might (90 feet E1 5b 1.3.83) is a tight eliminate climbing the right arête
of *African Killer Bee* above the terrace.

Phoenix   90 feet   Hard Severe   4b   (3.10.67)
A straightforward route, fairly low in the grade. Start in the groove left of

the tower.
Step up in the groove and swing right onto the rib. Climb the rib to the terrace, rejoin the groove, and climb it to the top. Belay over the path.

Dazed and Confused   100 feet   Hard Very Severe 5a   (23.4.78)
A good line up the left wall of the tower. Follow *Freedom* straight up for 15 feet, passing a large thread, and take a whitish groove slanting slightly left to the terrace. Move 10 feet left and climb straight up past a large hole. Follow a crack with good holds at first but gradually closing up. A final awkward move leads to easy ground and the top. Belay across the path.

★A Fly in the Eye?   90 feet   E3 5c   (23.1.83)
Steep and direct with nice exposure. Take *Dazed and Confused* to the terrace. Climb the arête above, past an *in-situ* thread, to a hole giving a good undercut. Climb the left wall on small holds, trending back right until able to reach the overhanging ledge. Swing right and pull up left onto it using a good sidecut. A good layaway edge on the right leads to the top. Belay across the path.

★★Freedom   100 feet   Very Severe   (12.12.67)
A Fly Wall classic: good rock, superb situation, excellent climbing. Quite stiff for the grade. Start at the foot of the tower, at the top of the second rise from the path fork: the highest point of the bottom of the wall.
1 40 feet 4b. Climb straight up for 15 feet, passing a large thread. A faint groove-line slightly right leads to the terrace and a good nut belay.
2 60 feet 4c. Climb the crack in the dièdre above to the roof (peg runner). Hand-traverse boldly right into the corner of *Swallow's Nest* at its crux and climb this to the top. Belay across the path.
Variation
2a 50 feet HVS 5b (12.3.83). A direct finish from the peg: continue bridging up to gain a standing-position on the ledge on the right (don't belly-flop onto it); place wires above and make a difficult layaway on the arête to reach good holds and the top.

★Swallow's Nest   90 feet   Very Severe   (3.12.67)
More classic climbing on fine rock. Low in the grade except for the tricky move near the top. Start in the corner bounding the right of the *Freedom* tower.
1 40 feet 4b. Climb the groove, keeping left, to the terrace. Peg and nut belay.
2 50 feet 4b. Take the overhang direct and climb the corner to the top. Be prepared for an awkward move on a sloping hold just where the obvious traverse-line from *Freedom* comes in. Belay across the path.
Variation
2a Flyaway 60 feet HVS 5a (11.2.81). From the overhang above the stance, step right and climb a finger-crack to a break. Traverse right and climb the short rib bounding the left of the top groove of *Flew*.

FLYTE WALL
Right of the tower is a rectangular wall while the path along the base remains more-or-less level. The first three routes start together at its centre.

Flew 110 feet E2 5b   (22.4.78)
Good dynamic climbing, but it will be under protected for some tastes; and some of the rock is not above suspicion. Start as for *Flyte*.
Bear slightly left up a faint corner-line to the terrace (peg runner, or belay, in the corner on the left – 4c so far). Climb up a short wall above the first pitch to reach the overhung ledge and hand-traverse right until able to stand up on it (protection in the groove of *Flyte*). Move up and swing left to the foot of a shallow groove which is climbed to the top. Belay over the path.

Flyte 100 feet Hard Very Severe   (10.9.67)
Good varied climbing. The first pitch is quite intricate and poorly protected, and should not be under-estimated. Start 10 feet right of *Swallow's Nest*, in the centre of the wall.
1 40 feet 4c. Move up and step right above the brambles; then climb straight up the wall via short broken grooves. Twice all seems lost, but each time there are good layaways to be reached for on the right. Large thread belay.
2 60 feet 5a. Climb straight up to a small ledge. Make two hard pulls into the groove above and climb it to the top. Belay across the path.

Fly Havoc 100 feet E3   (18.1.86)
Fingery climbing with good protection. Start as for *Flyte*.
1 40 feet 4c. Move up and step right above the brambles. Then climb diagonally right to the arête overlooking the chimney of *Flyhole* and follow it to the terrace. Peg belay.
2 60 feet 6a. Pull over the bulge of *Flyhole* on the left, and climb the leaning column on an assortment of small pockets and up-turned flakes to a cleaned ledge. Finish up the sharp arête and belay across the path.

Flyhole 100 feet Very Severe   (18.2.78)
Entertaining and unusual, though well-protected, moves on the lower half of the second pitch. The crucial hold in the hole tends to earth up which makes the move a lot harder. The lower chimney has some ivy, but it is not intrusive at present. Start at the obvious chimney-line 20 feet right of *Swallow's Nest* above a little cave.
1 40 feet 4a. Climb the chimney and exit left onto the terrace. Peg belay on the right.
2 60 feet 5a. Pull over the bulge on the left and move up slightly right (peg runner). Climb up to the hole and mantel onto the bridge. Easy climbing up the chimney above leads to another exit left. Belay across the path.

★Balls Out   110 feet   E2 (21.5.78)

[Photo p.32.] Short but sensational: a must for those with the...
1 40 feet 4a. *Flyhole* pitch 1.
2 70 feet 5b. Just right of the belay is a shallow right-facing corner:
make a thin move up in this to reach good holds. Pull up left onto the lip of
an overhang and climb straight up with little good protection to a break.
Step left to a ledge almost on the arête and finish diagonally right. Belay
across the path.

FIREFLY SECTOR

From the *Flyhole* chimney, the cliff base makes a long and steady drop to a
level section, whence *Firefly* starts. At the same time, the top of the cliff continues
to rise and so the routes quickly become longer. The overhangs become larger
and more persistent, and the outcrop-like atmosphere changes to that of a
more serious wall. The path leaves the cliff-base for a short while and the first
few routes are a little awkward to reach.

★★Child's Play   100 feet   E5 (19.3.83)

An excellent pitch with sustained climbing and sparse protection.
1 40 feet 5a. *Bulging Flies* pitch 1.
2 60 feet 6a. Climb the wall on the left past a break to the first roof (peg
runner). Pull over leftwards on good holds and then climb up and right
round the next roof. Now traverse back left along the upper break and
climb up to a niche with a thread *in situ* below the final roof. Make an
awkward move out of the niche and climb directly to the top. Block belay.

★★Bulging Flies   100 feet   E2 (22.4.78)

A fine upper pitch on good, well-protected rock. Excellent jamming in the
overhanging cracks. Start 10 feet right of the chimney of *Flyhole* at an
open, right-facing corner above where the ground has started to slope
away.
1 40 feet 5a. Climb the corner-cracks, and move left at the top to avoid
the overhanging vegetation. Peg belay on the terrace.
2 60 feet 5c. Climb decisively up the wall to a break. Use a high pocket
to attain jams in the overhanging crack and climb this to a thread *in situ* in
a horizontal slot. Move up left strenuously on pockets to reach the good
finishing-crack above. Block belay.

★Vapona   120 feet   E5 (13.9.81)

Two well-contrasted pitches: the first, technical with poor protection; the
second, a real fly-killer, strenuous but with good protection. Start as for
Flyover.
1 50 feet 5b. Climb the black slabby wall to some rounded ledges.
Above is a small delicate arête: using a tiny groove on the left or some
holds on the right reach some good holds and move up and right to the
terrace. Peg belay of *Bulging Flies* on the left.
2 70 feet 6a. In the double overhangs just right is a sharp V-groove.

Climb the wall to this and pull straight over the roofs to a good hold above the lip of the second. Move 5 feet right with difficulty to a good pocket below a brown scar (peg runner). Climb the rib above with more hard moves to reach a break, swing left, and finish up a short square corner. Block belay. (It is possible to make a very long pull more directly right over the first roof to the pocket at 6b.)

★**Flyover**   140 feet   E3   (2.9.67/5.79)

A good clean second pitch up the big corner and round the large roof to the left: sustained climbing with a hard move past the peg and a committing finish. Start 10 feet right of the open, right-facing corner of *Bulging Flies*.

1 60 feet 5b. Climb the small groove for 10 feet and step right to a ledge. Climb the long, irregular, pocketed crack to the terrace. Nut belay below the corner and peg belay 10 feet right.

2 80 feet 6a. Reach the base of the corner and climb it past a peg runner to a monstrous metal object in the roof and a peg runner. Traverse left in the break and climb the wall (thread runner) past the left edge of the roof to the top. Block belay.

Variation

2a Fly the Flag 70 feet E4 6a (25.1.86). Reach the base of the corner and clip the peg runner above; then move left and climb the wall past a slot. Make a long reach for the break, stand in it, and cross right above the roof into a groove (thread *in situ*). Climb easily to the top. The only belay is in the pit beyond the path.

★**Vampire Strikes Back**   140 feet   E5   (12.4.86)

An intensely sustained and technical pitch on the right wall of *Flyover*. [Photo p.33.] Start half way down the slope, between *Flyover* and *Flypast*, and behind a tree just left of where the path returns to the rock.

1 70 feet 5b. Climb direct up cleaned ledges for 25 feet to a ledge below an undercut slab. Pull directly onto the slab left of a nose and climb to the terrace.

2 70 feet 6b. Reach the base of the corner and clip the peg runner above. Move right onto the smooth wall (bolt runner) and climb straight up (peg runner) to jugs in the break. Pull steeply into the shallow groove above (thread *in situ*) and climb it, soon easing, to the top.

★**Flypast**   160 feet   E3   (20.10.74/6.80)

The star is for a fine second pitch up to and over the centre of the overhangs: the last artificial pitch on Fly Wall to be climbed free. The first pitch needs an urgent clean. Start at the left of the two large gnarled buddleia 8 feet apart situated to the left of the bottom of the slope.

1 80 feet 5a. Climb directly up a thin vertical joint to a holly and continue slightly left to a higher bush. Climb a tapering groove to a peg runner near the top, and traverse left into a corner which leads to the terrace. Peg belay.

2 80 feet 6a. Climb up above the belay a few feet to the first overhang.

2 80 feet 6a. Climb up above the belay a few feet to the first overhang. Move slightly left and make a difficult move over into the long groove with a good hold in the crack above. Climb the groove for 10 feet, and then move across left into a parallel groove and get established on a sloping hold (bolt runner). Using a hold in the break and the thin crack in the roof above, make more difficult moves to reach excellent holds above and right. More good holds lead to easy but loose ground and a finish between the large blocks. It is possible to belay precariously on the left one, but better to fix a runner and walk up the path to the thread of *Firefly*.

The next three routes are the finest in this sector, and among the finest on Fly Wall. Unfortunately, they were criss-crossed by two later eliminates, **Queen Bee** (E5 9.2.86) and **Strangled Fly** (E3 12.3.83), which are best left stung and strangled, and which account for a bolt and other bits of noose not mentioned elsewhere.

★★★La Folie   180 feet   E4   (12.6.82)
Immaculate technical climbing on the upper pitch. After the start, the first is unaffected by the vegetation on *Flypast*. Start as for *Flypast*.
1 90 feet 5a. Climb the slabs slightly rightwards past some grass to a hawthorn in a small left-facing corner formed by the left end of the long overhang. Climb the wall above to an obvious jug and then work up left in thin cracks to a short corner leading to the terrace. Belay with a *Friend* 2½ in the break and a rope out to the *Flypast* peg belay on the left.
2 90 feet 6a. Pull over the bulge and up to a break. Gain a standing-position on a protruding triangular hold on the right and go up to a thread *in situ* just above. Traverse 5 feet left into a shallow pinkish groove and climb this to the upper break. Move right and up into another obvious corner which leads to the top. Thread belay under the large block of *Firefly* up the path.

★★★Firefly   190 feet   E2   (17.8.67/9.6.79)
The original route of the wall and, now purged of its aid, one of its very best. A superb upper pitch of its grade through the shallow overhangs on the left face of the great prow; sustained, but without extreme technical difficulty, and well protected. [Photo p.193.] Start at the right (but now collapsed) of the two large gnarled buddleia 8 feet apart situated to the left of the bottom of the slope.
1 100 feet 4c. Climb the small depression keeping left of the jagged up-turned flake, and then trend slightly right to an obvious groove breaking through the centre of the overhangs. Climb the groove (peg runner) and wall above until a short traverse right leads to the centre of three short grooves. This goes up to the terrace. Peg belay in the corner.
2 90 feet 5c. Climb the corner and pull up to the right. Climb the leftward-curving crackline past two peg runners to reach the upper break. Move slightly right and over a small roof (good peg runner above). Make a difficult move up left and mantel onto a narrow ledge. Finish up the short clean crack splitting the final bulge. Thread belay under the large block on

the path.

★★Wurlitzer   190 feet   E1   (23.4.78)

Fine continuously steep climbing. High in the E1 grade, though the single
5c move is well protected. Start as for *Firefly*. (Note that these two route
cross at the belay.)

1 100 feet 4c. Move up and right to the overhung platform right of the
jagged up-turned flake. Climb the short wall (peg runner) and continue
slightly right. Go over the centre of the main overhang by reaching for
excellent holds and continue straight up via an overlapping flake to the
centre of three short grooves (where *Firefly* joins). This leads to the terrace.
Peg belay in the corner.

2 90 feet 5c. Move up, traverse 10 feet left, and pull up onto a small
ledge on the left (peg runner). Make a technical short traverse right and
reach for the first of three magnificent jugs which lead up and left to the
break. Continue up the fine pocketed headwall (peg runner) until a long
reach gains a narrow ledge. Mantel onto it and move right to the final
crack of *Firefly* which is followed to the top. Thread belay under the large
block.

★I Fly   160 feet   E4 †   (18.5.86)

Exciting climbing through the big roof between *Firefly* and *Lord of the Flies*.
Start 10 feet left of the latter.

1 80 feet 5c. From some ledges, move boldly up a short wall to the
ledge on *Lord of the Flies*. Climb past a gash and up to a prominent
overhang (peg runner) taking care with the rock. Pull over to flat holds and
make an awkward move to stand up. Climb the white wall and move right
to belay on *Friends* and wires in the break 15 feet below the roof.

2 80 feet 6b. Climb a short corner to a ledge below the roof. Pull over
via a short groove (peg runner) and climb the thin crack above to the
traverse ledge of *Lord of the Flies*. Climb the smooth wall above (bolt
runner) and pull over the double roof using a hanging flake to enter the
short hanging groove. Move up to join *Firefly* (peg runner) and follow it up
left to a narrow ledge and up the final short crack.

Lord of the Flies   190 feet   E2   (10.10.75)

The first route of its grade on Fly Wall. It has lasted well but there must be
some doubt about whether the pillars on pitch 2 can defy gravity for ever.
Impressive situation, and worth a star if you are not worried on this score.
Start at a large two-trunked tree close to the rock half-way up the slope,
and immediately below the point of the great prow high above.

1 100 feet 5a. Climb a line of holds slightly leftwards with care to a large
ledge. Go left along this and climb an obvious line straight up via a flake
and peg runner into a shallow groove-line which leads to the terrace: a
short detour left 10 feet below the terrace is advisable to avoid an
awkward pull onto grass and earth. Peg belay in a corner as for *Firefly*.

2 90 feet 5b. Climb the corner to the first overhang. Hand-traverse or undercut 15 feet right along the break and stand up on a small ledge on the point of the prow. Gain high holds on the right and move left into and up the bottomless groove to a ledge on the left at the top (peg runner above). Climb the incipient crack just right to a loose bay and, and go up to blocks on the path.

★★Gendarmerie   180 feet   E3   (12.9.82)

One of the better lower pitches on the wall leads to a sensational upper that weaves through the overhangs on the right face of the great prow. The finishing holds tend to earth over: it is advisable to brush these first (fix a short abseil rope on the biggest block complex half way up the quarry path and descend over easy-angled earth keeping well right and above the tree until the obvious relevant holds are reached). Start as for *Lord of the Flies*.

1   100 feet   5c. Climb directly up the shallow groove past a sapling to its termination (peg runner). Move up and traverse 5 feet left; then climb the wall to a long reach for a good ledge and go up rightwards over ledges beneath the prow to the terrace and the large thread belay of *Dragonfly*.

2   80 feet   5c. Step up and move left to the arête below the overhang (peg runner in the roof). Pull straight over and step right (peg runner). Climb a shallow groove just right of the arête to the break, step right, and enter a vicious groove beside the large triangular overhang. At the next roof, move left and climb the short final corner. Go left up the earth bank to block belays at the top.

A more direct but inferior version of the above is **The Sweeney** (160 feet E4 6a † 9.2.86). Starting the same, it continues directly to a stance on a ledge below the roofs, with a rope to the *Dragonfly* thread. It goes through a niche in the roofs to cross *Gendarmerie*, and then climbs the arête and a bulge above before traversing right to the exit. Another case closed?

DRAGONFLY SECTOR

The full-length but slightly offset open groove-line of *Dragonfly* is an obvious feature. It starts from a mound right of the low point beneath the great prow.

May Fly?   180 feet   E3   (28.2.83)

A rather disjointed and contrived line but with a nice crux, quite hard for its grade. The lower pitch is very dirty. The upper pitch is right of the next route. Start 10 feet right of the large tree of *Lord of the Flies*, on a large block.

1   90 feet   5c. Climb up 15 feet (peg runner) and on up the shallow groove to a large scar. Then continue past this in the same line to layback past a large block wedged in the groove. Finish directly up to the thread belay of *Dragonfly* on the terrace.

2   90 feet   6a. Walk right and climb to the top of the short pillar in the groove as for *Dragonfly*. Step down left and climb the black wall (wire *in situ*) to a break. Step left and mantelshelf; then climb a thin crack to loose and easy ground leading to the top.

Stone Spider Reaction 180 feet E3 †† (22.4.78)

Nerve-racking climbing on dubious and poorly-protected flakes on the right-hand face of the great prow. Surprisingly, it is the start that has fallen away leaving an extra overhang and a lot of drooping vegetation. Start as for *Dragonfly*.

1 100 feet 5b. Move up and left round the overhangs. Move back right and climb the groove above to exit right onto the arête by a block overhang, and go up to the terrace. Thread belay on the left as for *Dragonfly*.

2 80 feet 5b. Climb the wall right of the belay and just left of the *Dragonfly* groove to a large triangular flake. Move left and use a hanging flake to enter a groove. Climb this boldly and finish out left above the triangular overhang. Easy but loose ground leads to the top.
Variation

2a E5 6b † (1988). Climb the corner by the belay and then rightwards through the roof to a dynamic move for a flake, above which the parent route is joined. Two *RP* 3s protect the crux on the lip.

Dragonfly 180 feet Hard Very Severe (19.8.67)

A classic line though some of the rock is suspect (take special care at the exit onto the terrace). Nicely sustained but fairly low in the grade. The rockfall has taken part of the initial overhang and its peg runner; but alternative holds and gear are available. Start on the first of two mounds right of the low point.

1 100 feet 5a. Reach a small overhang and climb the long corner-line above to an exit left onto the terrace. Walk left to a large thread belay in a small trough.

2 80 feet 5a. Go back right and climb up the left side of a slim pillar. Follow the layback crack above to loose but easy ground which leads to the top. Small thread under the block on the left but safer to take a rope up to the iron stake above the path.

The Flight of the Phoenix 160 feet E5 (12.1.86)

A tough climb on mainly good rock.

1 90 feet 6a. Climb the corner of *Dragonfly* to a good ledge on the right at half height, and go on up the wall past a bolt runner to reach good holds which lead to the terrace. Bolt belay just right.

2 70 feet 6b. Climb up slightly left of the belay (*in-situ* wire) and swing way up right to holds in the break. Move back left with difficulty to huge pockets (peg runner) and make thin moves up and left to a sharp edge. Harder moves above (peg runner) lead to a good hold and a finishing-crack. A testing pitch, high in the technical grade.

The lower wall between *Dragonfly* and *Zipper* is dirty and vegetated and the next four routes are best started on the terrace, which can be reached by abseil from the iron stake above the path. The routes are described in full for the record but it is not advisable to attempt the lower pitches without prior cleaning.

Blue Max   170 feet   E4   (1.3.83)
Serious and worrying climbing up a heavily cleaned and scarred line, still
with some dubious rock. Start 15 feet right of *Dragonfly* behind a scarred
tree.
1 90 feet 5c. Pick the easiest and cleanest line up a vague groove and
some dirty rock to a break (peg runner). Continue straight up the technical
wall to the terrace, better but with poor protection. Bolt belay of *The Flight
of the Phoenix*.
2 80 feet 6a. Climb straight up (peg runner) over the left edge of the
overhangs onto a small ledge. Finish up the fluted pillar to the upper
terrace and easy twin cracks above.

Flight Barrier   190 feet   E5   (12.3.83)
An intimidating second pitch through the upper barrier of overhangs. Start
as for *Blue Max*.
1 100 feet 6a. Follow *Blue Max* to the break at half height (peg runner).
Traverse 10 feet right and move up (peg runner). Climb a thin crack to a
large block, step left, and go up to the terrace (*Friend* belays).
2 70 feet 6b. In the centre of the wall is a short right-facing corner. Climb
this and over the bulge in a minute V-groove to three holes. Climb up to
the roof (peg runner); move up, and then up left and over (jammed wire).
Climb the groove above to the upper terrace. Tree belay.
3 20 feet 5b. Climb a ridiculously loose crack behind the tree.
Alternatively, go off easily via the twin cracks of *Blue Max* on the left.

Flying Fortress   160 feet   E4   (16.6.84)
A fine but mean second pitch. Start just left of *Zipper* behind a tree.
1 80 feet 5a. Climb the leaning wall behind the tree and then follow the
groove to a peg runner and sapling on a small ledge on *Zipper*. Move up
left on poor rock and climb the shallow corner to the terrace (*Friend* belays).
2 60 feet 6a/b. Climb directly up the steep right wall of the short
roof-capped corner, and pull into the groove above. Swing out left on
good holds, move left again to an undercut flake, and then back up right
to a peg runner below a short groove in the roofs. Climb straight up the
groove to the terrace. Tree belay.
3 20 feet 5b. Climb the loose crack of *Flight Barrier* (or go easily off right
to the final corner of *Zipper*).
Variation
2a 60 feet 6b. The undercut flake is reached via a small arête, the blue
groove, a bolt runner, an extra peg runner, and a hold of dubious
provenance.

★Jet Stream   80 feet   E3 5c   (22.5.82)
The original first pitch (5b) started up what is now *Big Fly Direct* and curved
across the wall to the *Zipper* stance, but has been consumed piecemeal by
more direct lines. The second is well worth doing on its own.
Traverse left from the belay and climb diagonally into the obvious curving

groove (above the start of the last route's second pitch). Climb the right wall of the groove to a small corner. Finish directly up the bigger corner above, as for *Zipper*.

Overcooked Fly (25.1.86) pretended that *Jet Stream* and *Zipper* did not exist. Its ashes may safely be scattered amongst the buddleia.

Zipper   160 feet   Hard Very Severe   ††   (14.10.79)
Varied and absorbing climbing. A rockfall has wiped out the first 25-foot section but this should be viable at the grade with further recleaning. Above, there are several committing moves on rock that still needs care: worthwhile, but a more serious undertaking than *Dragonfly*. Start on the next mound right of *Dragonfly*, at the top of the long final downslope on the right.
1   90 feet   5a.   Climb up the scarred lower wall to a sapling and peg runner. Stand on the peg ledge to make delicate moves across right and then up left into the bottomless groove, which is climbed to the terrace. Go right and then up the earth bank to a peg belay below a shallow groove.
2   70 feet   4c.   Surmount the fragile cello-case-shaped pillar (peg runner above at a horizontal crack), and continue straight up to easy ledges and the large corner on the left. Boulder-thread belay; but it is safer to take a rope up to the iron stake above the path.

BIG FLY WALL
Below *Zipper* the path falls away sharply to the right and the wall reaches its greatest height with a band of big roofs right at the top. The three routes that start on the terrace can be gained either by climbing *Little Fly* or by abseil from the tree behind the red-brick shelter above the corner of the path.

★Whip Lash   190 feet   E4   (12.6.82)
A good sustained route on fine rock; a fierce section over the roof above the top belay of *Big Fly*. Start 10 feet downslope right of *Zipper* where the long overhang runs into the ground.
1   120 feet   5b.   Climb a short square pillar to the first break and move right and up to a small overhang (peg runner). Traverse right in a thin break and make an awkward pull onto a ledge (peg runner). Move up right and then climb a left-slanting crack (peg runner) to the roof. Make difficult moves right to a superb hidden incut (wire *in situ* below) and pull up. Climb straight up for 15 feet (peg runner) and then diagonally left to reach a good finishing-jug. Go up the earth bank to the peg belay on *Zipper* below a shallow groove.
2   40 feet   5c.   Climb the arête on the right, using the odd pocket and a thin crack, past a good hold to the upper terrace and two peg belays of *Big Fly* in a corner under the roof.
3   30 feet   6b.   Climb the corner and make an exhausting but exhilarating pull round the roof to a good hold at the lip (peg runner). Pull over strenuously and finish up the groove. Various block belays, but check for

stability.

Little Fly   130 feet   E1 5b   (19.3.86)
One of the best pitches on the lower wall. Start as for *Big Fly Direct* and
traverse into the niche. Climb up on its left to a ledge and then diagonally
left to the break. Traverse left in this (peg runner above) almost to the end
of the slab and climb up to a small overhang (*Whip Lash* peg, not clipped).
Traverse 10 feet back right in a thin break (peg runner directly above the
first) and stand on the ledge. Climb diagonally right to good pockets below
the overhangs. Move right and go up to reach holds above the lip. Step
back left to go over at two slots, and climb directly up cracks past a peg
runner to the terrace. Find the best tree (or the peg on the right) to abseil
off, or continue up *Big Fly Direct* or one of the harder pitches to the right.

★Big Fly Direct   190 feet   E1   (26.2.86)
An excellent direct line on good rock, with no let-up in the interest. Start
half-way down the long slope.
1 120 feet 5a. Traverse right along a narrow foot-ledge under the end of
the overhang to a niche. Climb up on its left to a wide but shallow pillar.
Climb this, pull up right (peg runner), and continue straight up passing
another peg runner to a small ledge a little below the main overhangs. Go
through at their shallowest point by a small open groove (peg runner) and
pull up right towards the *Big Fly* stance (its upper left peg belay can be
used for protection). Climb on up the wall using the crack behind the huge
pillar (peg runner out left, awkward to reach), move left, and go over a
small overhang to exit left onto the terrace. Go up to a good nut belay on
the green ledge above at the foot of the fine leftward-leaning corner.
2 40 feet 5a. Climb the corner (peg runner after 10 feet) to the upper
terrace and two peg belays in a corner on the left under the overhangs.
3 30 feet 5a. Walk left along the ledge, but instead of going up into the
easy corner climb directly up the wall on its right with a peg runner to start.
Belay on the iron stake above the path.

The original **Big Fly** (220 feet Hard Very Severe 20.8.67) was a wandering
route with some unstable rock. Its justification was the crux corner pitch
incorporated into *Big Fly Direct*. From the same start, it climbed up past a tree
on the right and then diagonally right for 25 feet before moving back left to
a two-peg belay on a balcony on top of some overhangs. Thence to the
terrace; the fine corner; and a walk left to the easy finishing-corner.

★★Idealist   70 feet   E5 6a   (13.2.83)
The large bare wall right of the *Big Fly* corner gives an unnerving lead to
an exciting finish through the overhangs above. The crux bulge (above the
upper terrace) is unprotectable except by preplacing a longish sling on the
peg of *Flies Aloft* to the right. Start on the mid-height terrace by a peg
belay just right of the raised ledge.
Climb a faint groove above, keeping left of the decorated shallow groove

of *Arms Like a Fly*. Some committing moves lead up to and past two peg runners in successive breaks to the upper terrace. Move right and pull onto a blunt bulging rib using poor pockets. Move up and pull up left past a small overhang into the hanging groove, which leads with good holds directly to a tree belay.

Tight between *Idealist* and *Flies Aloft* there is a shallow groove-line with a somewhat incongruous trail of brightly-coloured *in-situ* gear. **Arms Like a Fly** (80 feet E5 6b 19.1.86) climbs the groove and continues straight up the wall to make a long reach for holds just below the upper terrace. Above, it crosses left of *Idealist* to go up a faint groove to the roof and pull round it rightwards to rejoin the latter's finishing-groove.

★★Flies Aloft   80 feet   E4   (13.6.82)
The most sensational route on Fly Wall: two fine, contrasted pitches on quality limestone; the first, a steep and satisfying wall, leads to a wild finale through the huge canopy roofs. Start on the terrace as for *Idealist*.
1 50 feet 6a. Climb the shallow groove for 10 feet to a break. Hand-traverse right until above a tree, stand in the break, and pull up (peg runner). A hard sequence of moves on a layaway and two pockets leads to another break. Swing up and left to a shallow groove which leads to the upper terrace. Walk right to the yew belay on *Jos'e and the Fly*.
2 30 feet 6a/b. Go 10 feet back left and climb a thin crack (peg runner out left and another above) desperately to the roof and round it to the top. Tree belay a further 10 feet above.

At the foot of the long downslope and round to the right of a pillar there is a large up-turned block sitting in a corner. The left face of the pillar has an obvious ledge at 20 feet.

Jos'e and the Fly   210 feet   Very Severe   (21.4.74)
The route improves as it goes. The final pitch is hard for the grade – an alternative way off is to step across the top of the chimney on the right and go round to the right and up an earth bank. Start by the up-turned block.
1 60 feet 4a. Mount the block, and climb the left-bearing groove to a small tree belay.
2 60 feet 4c. Climb straight up for 25 feet to an ivy root. Move left to a large thread and climb the chimney above to the terrace and a tree belay.
3 60 feet 4b. In the wall on the left are three parallel vertical cracks. Climb the left (and largest) of these all the way to the upper terrace. Yew tree belay on the right.
4 30 feet 5a. Climb the wall above past the gnarled tree. Tree belay above.
Variations
1a That Nice Route 70 feet E1 5b (17.10.93). Climb the left face of the pillar past the obvious ledge at 20 feet. Two bolt runners and one peg runner.

3a Surprise, Surprise 50 feet HVS 5b (10.6.86). Climb the centre of the three cracks and then the left-facing corner above. At its close, swing out right onto the arête and go up to the yew tree.

The Height Below 110 feet E3   (7.6.81)
The impressive finish is a great way to sample this exciting rock at a couple of grades lower than the routes it crosses. Start on the terrace, at the second belay of *Jos'e and the Fly*.
1 60 feet 5b. Climb the right-hand crack and move up right onto a protruding ledge. Climb the obvious V-corner above, and make steep moves left out of it to finish directly to the yew tree.
2 50 feet 5c. Climb up to fix a runner on the gnarled tree, step back down, and traverse horizontally left below the *Flies Aloft* roofs (peg runner). Move up left to a small overhang, and pull diagonally left into the hanging groove of *Idealist* to finish.

THE END WALL
The cliff-base now slopes steeply back up to a corner at the very end of the wall. This section is considerably more sparsely populated than the rest of the cliff, unsurprisingly in view of the relationship between effort and reward involved in cleaning.

Death on a Dinner-Plate 180 feet E3   (6.5.85)
Possibly just that. An impressive-looking line but there are some dubious flakes and a lot of revegetation. Start 15 feet right of the up-turned block.
1 120 feet 5c. Climb the wall to the second of two ledges (peg runner between). Move right to a thin quartz column (peg runner above) and climb it with difficulty direct or just right to reach a good hold. Traverse back left and make an awkward stoop to clip a low peg runner. Climb straight up (peg runner) to a blunt black nose, and then up to a larger, white one. Climb a short slab to a large pocket (peg runner out right), and then straight up a scoop to the large tree belay.
2 60 feet 4c. Climb a small groove in the right wall of the chimney for 20 feet and traverse right with a sapling at foot-level to a crack. Climb this with an awkward exit onto blocks on the upper terrace (tree belay). Walk round right and scramble up the earth bank.

End of the Affair 170 feet E1   (21.11.87)
The obvious way to explore this remote area. Well-protected, but it badly needs recleaning. Start 30 feet upslope right of the upturned block at a faint groove.
1 120 feet 5a. Climb the groove (two peg runners) and swing out left at its top to reach a ledge (peg runner). Move up and slightly left to another ledge; then pull up (peg runner on the right) to reach a sapling beneath a small overhang. Surmount the overhang from the left, step right (peg runner), and continue up into the obvious corner above. Tree belay.
2 50 feet 5b. A few feet right of the chimney is a shallow curving groove.

Climb this strenuously, and pull right at the top using a hidden jug. Step back left to a good foothold and finish easily to a tree belay. Walk round right and scramble up the earth bank.

Endgame   170 feet   Hard Very Severe   (1.3.86)
Quite a worthwhile little route, which should not be neglected because of its remoteness. The top of the first pitch needs regular clearance of dead leaves, and the second has also greened up a bit. Start 40 feet right of the up-turned block and 10 feet left of the top of the slope, at a faint black, but red-spotted rib.
1 100 feet 5a. From small ledges just right, move up and left over the overhang to a thread *in situ* in a bored hole in the arête. Climb straight up the crest of the rib (peg runner on the right) to a ledge and good tree on the right. After another short steep section the angle eases and the rib broadens. Continue directly up the crest to a large tree belay at the top. Then transfer 20 feet diagonally left to the right-hand of two firs near the right end of a grey wall.
2 70 feet 5a/b. Pull up steeply behind the left fir and step left to a foothold. Fix plenty of protection here in the abundant slots because it's quite a way, with some tricky moves, before there is any more. Don't lurch for the ledge above – it's rounded. Work up high to reach a small hidden hold on the left above the little earthy ramp, and then move up to mantel. Step right and climb a short flake to good holds and then easy ground. Belay on the first suitable tree. Scramble straight up the earth bank above.

Can't Fly Any Higher   75 feet   E2 5c   (27.8.86)
Good climbing up the wall right of *Endgame*. Well supplied with *in-situ* gear but there is not much else. High in the grade. Start at the top of the slope at the end of the wall.
Climb the small corner to a steepening (peg runner out left) and move up into a faint groove (bolt runner). Reach good holds in the break above (sling on tree root). Step right and climb pocketed rock for 10 feet (*Friend* 3) and then go leftwards and boldly over a tiny overlap to a good rest (peg runner). Traverse 10 feet right (nut *in situ*). Make a final steep pull above it to a jug and pull up to a tiny ledge. The final bubbly wall leads past an *in-situ* thread to a tree (sling and *in-situ* karabiner). Abseil off.

This is the limit of the permitted climbing area. Climbing is not allowed on any of the rock to the south of this point.

THE TERRACE

CONTINUATION WALL | WYE SECTOR | ACCURACY SECTO

Ban-y-gor

OS Ref 544 969

INTRODUCTION

Upstream from the majestic display of Wintour's Leap are a collection of cliffs facing north-west and known as Ban-y-gor. The Main Cliff of Ban-y-gor is the compelling piece of rock architecture that catches your attention as you look across the river from just north of Wyndcliffe. A large towering crag, some 200 feet high and split by a narrow terrace, The Main Cliff has features that are similar to those of The Forbidden Wall at Wintour's Leap.

Unseen to the idle viewer is a further section of crag on the downstream side of The Main Cliff – a long escarpment carefully secreted amidst the trees and foliage. Divided into two sections by a broad gully (Glass Gully), it is imaginatively named The Left-Hand Escarpment and (you've guessed it) The Right-Hand Escarpment.

Ownership of the Ban-y-gor rocks and woods has recently passed to the Gloucestershire Wildlife Trust and the area is likely soon to be incorporated into the Lancaut Nature Reserve (which already includes most of Wintour's Leap); and it is covered by the same SSSI. No official permission to climb has been sought or given, and to date (thanks to a subdued profile by the activists) no access problems have occurred.

The second vital consideration when climbing at Ban-y-gor is the proximity of the houses to the top of the crag; indeed those above the Upper Tier of The Main Cliff have gardens which extend to the very edge of the cliff. As a result, development of The Main Cliff has been voluntarily restricted to its lower tiers to avoid any unnecessary confrontation or risk to access. Please maintain this restraint.

THE TERRACE

CEMETERY SECTOR   APEDEX SECTOR   HEAD SECTOR

Currently it is possible to enjoy the delights of quiet, un-crowded climbing, and all of it away from the public gaze. Respecting the situation outlined above and sticking to the standard approach described below will help to keep it that way.

But what of the climbing? Well the geologists amongst you will undoubtedly recognize this as Drybrook limestone, while everyone else will think of it as being typical of the Wye Valley (i.e., steep, fun, some bits of veg about the place, and plenty of trees to trip over/abseil from). The rock is generally pretty good and there are lots of quality routes to get stuck into (or stuck on!).

Climbs on The Escarpment are short, steep, and athletic, as well as being mostly well protected (*Friends* are especially useful). All of the routes have either a chained abseil station or substantial trees at their tops for the usual abseil descent. Despite its low stature, The Escarpment, with its wide variety of climbing styles and grades, currently receives the most traffic, and it is no surprise that the sport and semi-sport climbs have proved to be the most popular.

The Main Cliff is definitely the bigger brother. A much more meaty proposition than The Escarpment, it offers a liberal selection of routes both traditional and sport in style but with the emphasis mostly on the upper grades. The impressive bulges and roofs on its right side, offering as they do clean and well-bolted lines, will probably prove the greatest attraction. Descents from The Main Cliff are usually by abseil from chained bolt belays.

The majority of the climbs at Ban-y-gor were developed within a fairly short time-frame: 1988 to 1991. Despite exposure in Gary Gibson's *BMC New Climbs*, as well as in free handouts to all interested parties, Ban-y-gor has remained little known and as such has not received many visitors. Fortunately,

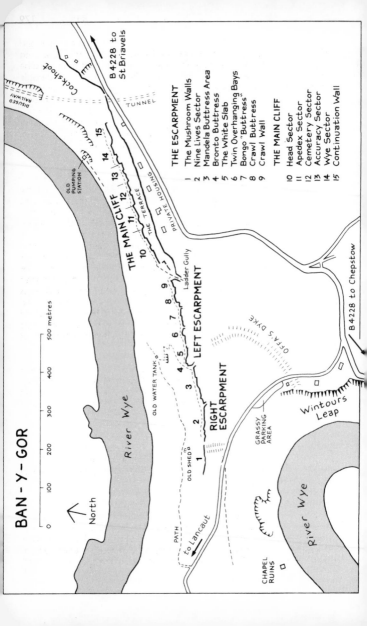

even with infrequent traffic, the escarpment climbs have remained clean and in good condition. Despite some heroic gardening, cleaning, and equipping operations (that man Gibson again!) parts of The Main Cliff have become re-infected with the Wye Valley vegetation. At the time of writing, considerable effort is being made to reclean the better routes, along with a campaign of re-equipping or retro-bolting as appropriate. Consequently, some of the route descriptions in this guide will become out-dated as work progresses. (So don't forget to put some extra quick-draws on your harness!) It is hoped that greater activity generated by Ban-y-gor's full exposure in this guide will help maintain the crag in good order and justify the endeavour (and vision) of its original developers.

APPROACH
Park at the grassy areas above Wintour's Leap North Wall (see page 13). Walk on down Lancaut Lane through a wooded area until just before where the road swings to the left and emerges into open fields. On the right is a track – follow this for about 200 yards until you reach a derelict shed next to an abandoned tractor and small water-tank. Carry on down the track for a further 250 yards until you bump into another small water-tank. Four yards back from this second water-tank start your progress up the hillside by stepping across a couple of rock slabs, ducking under a fallen tree, and traversing left under a small outcrop. A poor path heads steeply up slope, first to the right then slightly back left, to bring you, fully warmed-up, to the base of Bronto Buttress at the extreme right-hand end of The Left-Hand Escarpment (routes described right to left). The attractive-looking rock over to your right is the *Stars and Stripes* wall at the beginning of The Right-Hand Escarpment (routes described left to right). The walk-in to this point should take your stretcher-team about 20 minutes at most.

Various other approaches from below or from the north are possible at certain times of the year, but are at best extremely unpleasant and time-consuming. One day a path-system might link Lancaut, via all the cliffs, to the tunnel exit near Tintern Quarry. Until then, the standard approach described is the only viable option.

A QUICK CRAG TOUR
The approach up the slope has brought you to the side of a broad gully that separates the two halves of the escarpment. This is known as Glass Gully; fall over and you might find out why. All the routes are described as you would approach them from this point.

The Left-Hand Escarpment provides an easy stroll past a lichenous slab and a couple of steep bays until its best feature, Crawl Buttress, necessitates an easy traverse above a bit of a drop (known as Lucky Wall). A short distance beyond, The Escarpment ends at a pair of ladders in The Ladder Gully Area. Two well-separated and indistinct tiers continue the climbing interest until they merge into the bulk of The Main Cliff – just look up: if it's big and if it's steep, then you know where you are. When it is time to pack up, return via the same route to Glass Gully. The Right-Hand Escarpment is also an easy walk, its far end deteriorating into a small scruffy outcrop before making a brief comeback with The Mushroom Walls.

EMERGENCY EXITS

After a day on the crag when you have had enough (or it has started to rain again), exit by following the approach path in reverse.

In case it should be necessary to summon help quickly in an emergency, it is useful to understand that alternative exit routes do exist at each end of the crag. Both routes encroach upon private land and should therefore not be used otherwise.

In Ladder Gully it is possible to ascend the old ladders (take care) to reach the cliff-top. If it is not possible to use a telephone in one of the houses, then exit onto the B4228 via a private fenced paddock and the well-secured water service-station. **Use in dire emergencies only.**

A less drastic option is Glass Gully. This leads easily up to a pleasant flat path along the top of The Right-Hand Escarpment to where it meets the top of the (also easy) Developer's Gully at the corner of a fenced field. Follow the fence clockwise around the field to a stile, and then cross the field to a barred gate at the road opposite the parking-area.

THE RIGHT-HAND ESCARPMENT

The routes are described from **left to right**.

MANDELA BUTTRESS AREA
About 40 feet in from Glass Gully is a tall, straight yew tree that almost touches the crag. The first route starts here.

That Historic Reach   40 feet   Very Severe   4b †   (10.8.91)
Climb the yew tree to a wooden thread at 12 feet; then step leftwards onto the crag and pull steeply up to the break. Climb the groove above and abseil from a tree on the right. (A direct start has been climbed at 6a.)

★Dry Day   40 feet   E3   6a   (23.10.88)
Some lovely technical climbing. Start immediately right of the yew tree. Climb the short wall (just left of *Lotus Wing*) past a bolt runner and a peg runner on the right. From a good ledge at the break, make the crux moves (bolt runner) to enter a short, awkward groove, whence better holds lead right to an abseil station.

★★Lotus Wing   40 feet   E2   5c   (23.10.88)
A choice pitch; perhaps the best of its grade on The Escarpment. Quite potent. Start 8 feet right of the yew at a groove-system breaking through

two horizontal roofs.
Climb the groove with interest to the first roof (peg runner on the left) and
pull over on a finger-crack in a (solid) block to a constricted rest. Swing out
over the second (crux) roof (*in-situ* thread) to good holds, and finish up the
groove to an abseil station.

★Flat Baps   45 feet   E6 6b F7b †   (11.8.91)
A stern, power-problem assaulting the centre of the bare wall. Sadly
contrived owing to its proximity to *Bad Man from Bodie*. Low in its grade.
Start as for *Lotus Wing*.
Climb up right to a peg runner, surmount the roof, and climb direct past
two bolt runners to a peg runner in the break. Finish up and left to the
abseil station on *Lotus Wing*.

★Bad Man from Bodie   40 feet   E5 6a   (2.7.88)
Some difficult, serious, and exciting climbing with a limited supply of
protection. Start 12 feet right of *Lotus Wing*.
From a hand-ledge at 7 feet, move left and up to the roof. With protection
from a peg in the faint groove up right, pull decisively over the roof and
continue quickly to the break (*Friend* 2½). Finish up a small groove on jugs.

★★Stars and Stripes   45 feet   E3 6a   (2.7.88)
An excellent pitch, technical and dynamic, that overcomes the wider section
of roof just right of *Bad Man from Bodie*.
A hard start leads up the wall to a wobbly peg runner under the roof.
Positive holds (bolt runner) continue the momentum over the roof and up
(past an *in-situ* wire) to a rest on the right at the break. Climb straight up
the wall above via a thin groove (peg runner) to a tree.

★Ninety-Nine Rabid Feminists   45 feet   E3 6a   (20.8.88)
Another salubrious pitch. Start immediately right of where the cliff turns the
corner into a small bay.
Climb up to the roof (bolt runner) and pull through to gain a rest at the
break. Traverse left for 10 feet, and then ascend the grey wall (using a
layaway to start), passing a peg and a bolt runner to a cleaned exit.

Join the Union, Jack   35 feet   E2 5c   (16.7.95)
Climb the short wall and overlap right of *Ninety-Nine Rabid Feminists* (two
bolt runners) to a ledge. Continue more easily up the wall above to an
abseil station.

An unfriendly-looking roof is bounded on its right by an equally unfriendly-
looking chimney. These features are the *Roof of Gore* and *The Chimney
Crusade* respectively. Neither route is popular or likely to be so.

Roof of Gore   35 feet   E2 5c †   (23.8.88)
An unappetizing problem that is apparently 'easier than it looks'.

Move up to the roof on disposable holds, ease around the lip (crucial *Rock 5*), and pull up to a sapling in the break. Continue up the wall above to a shared chained abseil station.

The Chimney Crusade   40 feet   Hard Very Severe   4c †   (16.7.95)
The obvious loose chimney. Hard Very Loose may be more appropriate.

Spunk Trumpets   40 feet   E3   6a   F6c   (16.7.95)
A good pitch which is fast becoming popular. Start a few feet to the right of the obvious loose chimney.
Climb the short wall and overlap (bolt runner) to a ledge. Continue straight up the middle of the vague white tower past two bolt runners to a tree belay.

Sperm Wales   40 feet   E3   5c   (14.8.88)
This takes the unusual, hump-backed overhang on the right of *The Chimney Crusade*. Start as for *Spunk Trumpets*.
Climb boldly rightwards to flake holds under the roof, whence an awkward swimming manœuvre should gain a standing-position above. Step left and finish up an easier groove.

★★Nelson Mandela   40 feet   E5   6b   F7a   (25.6.88)
A hard yet popular test-piece. Ample protection makes it an attractive proposition. Start below the bulging and rounded arête. Low in the grade.
Swing up left on jugs to a peg runner, step up into the orange niche, and continue with difficulty past a bolt runner and a peg runner to reach the break (peg runner). Make a long strenuous pull (two peg runners) to good holds and the top just above. Tree belay.

★East of Sweden   45 feet   E3   6a   F6c   (21.6.88)
A good, absorbing pitch with a fingery crux. Start 5 feet to the right of the arête of *Nelson Mandela*.
Climb to a thin break, step left (peg runner), and move up to the main break (peg runner). Swing left to the peg runner on *Nelson Mandela* and begin a tricky sequence up the steep, shallow groove (bolt runner) to get to a good hold. Either escape left to easier ground, or better (but harder) continue straight up past another bolt runner and finish direct over the capping bulge to a tree.

★Blabba Mouth   45 feet   E4   6b   (10.8.91)
A direct eliminate line offering some intricate technicalities. Start as for *East of Sweden*.
Climb straight up on good, hidden holds (but no gear) to reach the break and a peg runner on the left. Continue directly up passing an *in-situ* thread and bolt runner and make some perplexing moves (crucial *Rock 2*) up the slight rib. Finish up leftwards to the tree atop *East of Sweden*.

Duhkha   40 feet   E3   6a   (25.6.88)
Some interesting and tricky climbing. Start on the left of the block-filled groove.
Climb easily to the break, and continue straight up past two peg runners to good holds in a tiny corner and an *in-situ* wire. Finish direct.

Crack around the World   100 feet   E1   (30.10.88)
Quite an absorbing traverse, and strenuous on the crux. Start a few feet to the right of *Duhkha* beneath the block-filled groove.
1   60 feet   5a.   Move up to the break and follow it leftwards (peg runners) all the way along to a restricted stance and peg belay on *Ninety-Nine Rabid Feminists*.
2   40 feet   5b.   Traverse with some rapidity across under the overhangs (peg runner) into *Lotus Wing* (*in-situ* thread runner). Step left onto *Dry Day* (bolt runner) and exit into the adjacent yew tree. Abseil from a convenient branch.

To the right of the block-filled groove is a smooth, slippery wall sporting a shallow groove (*Slug Control*) and a blank corner formed by a small but noticeable arête.

It's a Fluke   30 feet   E4   6b †   (18.9.94)
A fairly desperate eliminate through the bulge that forms the right edge of the block-filled groove. Step right at the top to the abseil station atop *Slug Control*.

Slug Control   30 feet   E2   6a   F6b+   (4.9.88)
Some awkward and quite difficult moves.
Climb the shallow groove past a bolt runner and a peg runner to reach an abseil station.

The Disillusioned Bronto Machine   30 feet   E3   6a   F6c   (24.6.88)
Hard climbing up the smooth, red wall immediately left of the blank corner.
Climb the wall past two bolt runners and finish leftwards to a shared abseil station.

Doyouthinkhesawus   30 feet   E2   6a   F6b+   (16.7.95)
The blank corner provides a safe but very technical exercise. Three bolt runners. Tree belay.

Trans-African Drum Battle   30 feet   E3   6b   F6c+   (14.8.88)
The prominent, projecting arête entices – perhaps?
Move up to the arête and climb it direct (enigmatic) past a bolt and peg runner.

★**Squelch**   30 feet   Hard Severe   4b   (4.9.88)
A clean and enjoyable pitch taking the fine little corner just right of the

projecting arête. Start from the left.

Mondays Never Rain   30 feet   E2 5c   (14.8.88)
Start at a tree 15 feet to the right of *Squelch*.
Climb up to a slight overhang (*in-situ* thread runner) and pull through this
onto a slab. Finish up a thin crack.

NINE LIVES SECTOR
The Escarpment is now broken by the easy but quite loose 'Point Five Gully'.
The first feature to the right of this gully is a smooth wall. The first route climbs
the left arête: **Totally Manning** (40 feet Hard Very Severe 5a 1996).

The Chubby Brown Syndrome 40 feet Hard Very Severe 5a (30.10.88)
Climb the shallow groove in the left side of the smooth wall.

The Unpure   40 feet   E4 6b   F7a+ †   23.10.88)
A testing eliminate. Start immediately right of *The Chubby Brown Syndrome*.
Climb the centre of the lower part of the wall to an *in-situ* thread runner,
and then move right (bolt runner above) to gain the arête. Adhere strictly to
the left-hand side of the arête, passing a second bolt runner, to reach the
top.

Self-Preservation   40 feet   Very Severe 4c   (2.7.88)
This takes the first groove-line to the right of Point Five Gully. Climb this
groove and exit right at the top.

Self-Destruction   40 feet   E4 6a †   (2.7.88)
An aptly-named (and awkward to protect) pitch up the wall right of
Self-Preservation.
Climb straight up over a bulge to gain a break; then surmount the next
bulge (*in-situ* thread runner) to reach some poor holds. Finish leftwards.

Nine Lives Gone   40 feet   E1 5a   (18.9.88)
This tackles the steep, hanging flake/groove 20 feet to the right of
Self-Preservation.

Discharge   40 feet   E3 6a   (16.7.95)
A powerful crux bulge.
Climb the overlapped wall 5 feet right of *Nine Lives Gone* (bolt runner) to
gain the dusty break (small *Friend*). Step right awkwardly and climb the
tricky slim groove, and step right again at the top. Pull over past a sapling,
and belay on a good tree further back.

★**Gonna Write a Classic**   40 feet   Hard Very Severe 5b   (14.8.88)
Possibly the best route of its grade on The Escarpment. Start 10 feet to the
right of *Nine Lives Gone* and climb directly up the crack to a tree.

The most noticeable feature hereabouts is a steep and smooth corner.

Private Life   40 feet   E3 6a   (23.8.88)
Quite taxing and insecure near the top.
Climb the steep and smooth corner past a peg runner to an exit left.

Viva Ramirez   40 feet   E3 6a   (23.8.88)
Climb the wall immediately right of *Private Life* by means of a thin crack.

Twenty feet to the right of the steep, smooth corner of *Private Life* is a narrow system of grooves giving three routes.

Gordon   40 feet   Hard Very Severe   5a   (17.8.88)
Dark glasses required.
Climb the subsidiary groove on the left of the main groove to reach the half-height break. Step left and climb (very carefully) up a precarious flake to the top.

Matt   40 feet   Hard Very Severe   5a   (17.8.88)
Follow Gordon to the half-height break and climb the left-hand of the two main groove-lines.

Peter   40 feet   Very Severe   4c   (17.8.88)
The least unappealing of this suspect trio. Climb the right-hand, continuous groove.

Twenty-five feet further along lie three clean, solid, 40-foot grooves. **Citadel** takes the left-hand groove, **Dinosaur** the middle, and **Mammoth** the right-hand. The first two are Hard Very Severe 5a; the last Very Severe 4c. (All 13.9.88).

Around the corner from *Mammoth* is a tall clump of yew trees with a right-angled corner behind.

Jah Wobble   25 feet   E3 5c †   (3.8.96)
A short but poky little number up the bare wall behind the yew trees. Start at the base of the corner.
Climb up the white stain to reach *RP* placements in a hairline crack; then swing steeply left to better wires and an awkward finishing mantel. Tree belay.

Ivy Sep'   20 feet   Severe †   (3.8.96)
Climb the little right-angled corner, taking care with the holds at the top.

THE MUSHROOM WALLS
The Escarpment now diminishes in stature where it is broken by the easy Developers' Gully. A bit vegetated and with a forgotten air, The Mushroom

Walls comprise the final part of the cliff. They do, however, have some worthy offerings on mostly solid, well-protected rock.

Mycology   30 feet   Very Severe   4b   (7.11.88)
Start 40 yards to the right of Developers' Gully at a shallow, cleaned groove. Climb the groove on excellent holds to a solid finish.

Fly Agaric   35 feet   E3   5c   †   (7.11.88)
Start to the left of *Mushroom Boys*.
Climb onto a pedestal and go up the wall to reach a thin crack on the right edge of the overlap. Go for the top.

Mushroom Boys   30 feet   Hard Very Severe   5a   (18.9.88)
This climbs the well-cleaned groove-line 20 feet right of *Mycology*, identifiable by a V-shaped scoop at the half-height break.

Laccaria Laccata   30 feet   E2   5c   †   (28.6.91)
Climb the steep wall immediately right of *Mushroom Boys* to the overhang. Move up and right (peg runner) and gain the open-book corner with difficulty. Mantel onto the ledge and finish direct up two short walls.

Phallus Impudicus   30 feet   Severe   4b   †   (28.6.91)
Start 10 feet to the right of *Mushroom Boys*, directly below a tree situated half-way up the cliff.
Boulder out the initial steep wall and follow an easy groove to the tree. Climb either of the two corners above to the top.

Twenty-five feet to the right of *Mushroom Boys* is an unmistakable, elevated prow of rock.

We Are the Champignons   30 feet   Hard Very Severe   5a   †   (28.6.91)
Start underneath the prow, just left of the pedestal crack.
Climb the wall, with aid from the short wide crack, to the overhang (peg runner). Surmount the overhang to gain the large ledge, and edge right on top of the flake. Climb direct up the wall on the left side of the prow.

★A Little Stiff'ner   30 feet   E2   5b   (23.10.88)
A good little pitch swinging merrily up the very edge of the jutting prow. Move up onto a block on the right side of the prow and gain a break above. Go left (peg runner) and climb airily up the front of the prow. Take some *Friends*!

On the right-hand side of the prow is a large tree projecting from above the break. The next route is adjacent to this.

Shaggy Ink Cap   30 feet   Difficult   (30.10.88)
Climb the dirty, open corner at the right-hand end of the escarpment.

Morel   30 feet   Severe   (30.10.88)
Climb the wall and wide crack 6 feet right of *Shaggy Ink Cap*.

THE LEFT-HAND ESCARPMENT
The routes are described from **right to left**, the direction of approach.

BRONTO BUTTRESS
This is the squat buttress at the head of the approach path. Its main features
are two disjointed corners on the right (*The Tao*), a large tree growing from
the break at the foot of the buttress, and a large corner just left again containing
the off-width crack of *Darkside*.

★The Tao   45 feet   E2 5c   (5.7.88)
Start at the foot of the short, smooth corner on the right-hand side of the
buttress. Enjoyable technical climbing.
Climb the corner past two peg runners (crux) and exit left onto the wall.
Move up to a ledge and horizontal break (large *Friend* runner) and
continue to the foot of the top corner. This proves surprisingly stubborn.

★One Step Ahead of the Blues   45 feet   E3 6a   (10.8.91)
A technical eliminate best subdued by the forceful approach. Start as for
The Tao.
Pull steeply up the left side of the small arête to gain better holds above a
bolt runner; then continue more easily to meet the left end of the ledge
below the top corner of *The Tao*. Swing out leftwards onto the projecting
arête and climb this dynamically past a second bolt runner to finish.

Breaking for Spares   40 feet   Hard Very Severe 5a   (20.7.88)
The initial dismal struggle onto the tree is compensated for by a much
better finish.
Gain the tree that projects from the crag as best you can and then climb
the wall above to a break. Step up left onto the arête, gain a ledge above,
and move out right to a concealed hold on the crest of the arête. Finish up
this.

Darkside   45 feet   Very Severe 4c   (30.10.88)
The prominent corner with the wide off-width crack proves more
engrossing than appearances might suggest. Good value.
Climb the corner until just below the top, and then traverse left on
foot-ledges to where it is possible to reach over for a root hold at the base
of a large tree.

Summertime Blues   45 feet   E3 5c †   (9.7.88)
Start as for *Darkside*. Low in its grade.
Pull up just left of the corner and move on up leftwards onto the wall.
Continue to a small ledge on the left side of this wall (*Friend 4*); then ease
carefully up to better holds and a finish on the left.

Always the Rain   45 feet   E3 6a   (20.7.88)
A flawed product but interesting nonetheless. Start 15 feet to the left of
Darkside.
Gain a slight groove from the left and follow it for 15 feet to a 'blocked'
overlap. Move up rightwards to a ledge, traverse across to the left, and
(with a small stump as a foothold) pull steeply up the rounded arête (peg
runner). Move right (peg runner) and then go straight up (crux) passing an
in-situ thread runner to reach the top.

Indian Summer (45 feet Very Severe 4c † 9.10.94) follows the start of
Always the Rain before moving left behind bushes and climbing a groove/cor-
ner to a ledge. Walk off to the right.

THE WHITE SLAB
One of the few slabby pieces of rock at Ban-y-gor, The White Slab derives its
name from its mantle of lichen. Climbing interest hereabouts is short-lived. At
the foot of the slab sits a large flake block marking the start of *Tinaderm.*

Kawrona   35 feet   Very Severe 5a   (26.11.89)
Better than it looks. Start a few feet right of *Tinaderm*. Small wires needed.
Climb up to the right-hand end of the flake block and then follow the
continuous hairline crack directly above to reach a ledge and saplings.
Abseil off, or traverse over to the left and go on up to belay on a huge tree.
Note: variants have been climbed either side of the hairline crack; the
right-hand variant (following the 'layback crack') ends in a difficult move.

Tinaderm   60 feet   E1 5b   (20.8.88)
Essentially just a couple of thin moves which small wires (just about)
protect. At the centre of the slab is a large flake block.
Step off the flake and climb the slab just right of a thin crack to reach a
sapling. Continue diagonally left to the huge tree.

Ought'n Be   50 feet   Hard Very Severe 5a   (26.11.89)
The best of the trio; 'some nice moves but on the wrong route'. Start 10
feet to the left of *Tinaderm*. High in its grade.
Climb the slab direct, using the thin cracks, past two ancient peg runners to
a ledge and saplings. Continue easily to the huge tree.

There's a Lot of It About   30 feet   Hard Severe 5a   (30.10.88)
An oddball pitch offering an appropriate challenge for the faint of heart.
Follow the two short, disjointed corners in the left-hand side of The White
Slab.

TWIN OVERHANGING BAYS
These are easily identified as such. The right-hand bay is characterized by a
gloomy atmosphere, the rock being shaded and coated with a veneer of white
lichen which tends to remain dank in other than settled, dry weather. Its most

obvious features, running right to left, are: first, a chimney of sorts with a projecting tree (*Ugooloo*); then an unpleasant fissure gully; a prominent curving corner (*Les Miserables*); and finally the jutting roof of *Felt, Batten, and Smile*. Further along, the larger and more open left-hand bay has as its most striking line the mid-height break travelled by the girdle *High and Dry*.

Avidya   40 feet   E3 5c   (20.7.88)
This tackles the centre of the roof at the right-hand end of the right-hand bay. A good pitch worth doing. Start 15 feet right of *Ugooloo*.
Pull steeply up (peg runner) and mantelshelf onto the ledge in the groove on the left. Step up to the main break (*Friend 4*) and reach for holds and a peg runner over the roof. Gain the hanging slab above and finish up easier ground.

Ugooloo   35 feet   Very Severe 4c   (16.7.88)
A feature with little redeeming merit.
Bridge up the open groove to reach the projecting tree at 25 feet. Continue for a few more feet and abseil from a good tree on the left.

Who Is This Man Dukakis?   40 feet   E2 5c   (16.7.88)
A reasonable route, varied and well protected. Start 10 feet left of *Ugooloo* and immediately right of the fissure gully.
Gain a smooth little groove (bolt runner) and continue to a ledge at the level of the main break. Step right and follow the steep crack on positive holds to a convenient tree at the top.

Josie Swoonpence   35 feet   Very Severe 4c   (17.9.88)
Pleasing climbing up the capped corner on the right side of the prominent roof.
Climb the corner to a *Friend 1* placement just above the break. Move back down and stride right (below the break) to where a high step gains the rib that forms the left side of the fissure gully. Follow this and finish leftwards to a tree belay. (A poor direct start has been climbed at 5b.)

★Les Miserables   35 feet   Hard Very Severe 5a   (10.5.92)
Quite good; the action is centred on a few steep, awkward, but amply-protected moves. Start up *Josie Swoonpence* but follow the corner as it curves out leftwards to gain an abseil station.

Gordonzola   35 feet   E3 6a F6b+   (10.5.92)
'Just a few quick pulls.' Start 4 feet left of *Josie Swoonpence*.
Climb the short wall (bolt runner), pass through the large roof (peg runner), and gain a ledge and small tree. Continue straight up to an abseil station.

Felt, Batten, and Smile   40 feet   E4 6b   (2.7.88)
The roof – what you see is what you get! Start beneath its widest point.

Climb easily to the roof, and cross it with difficulty to the crux at the lip. If you are able, gain the ledge and small tree above. Continue up rightwards to an abseil station.

Around the to the left from the big roof is a large, squat pedestal.

Alienation   30 feet   E3   6a/b   (16.7.88)
The innocuous-looking slab to the right of the pedestal block proves irritatingly troublesome. Small wires required.
Take the obvious crack to reach the break and attack the bulge dynamically, precariously, or uselessly according to taste and ability (peg runner). Incut holds above form a path to the top. Abseil from the tree.

Block and Crackle   30 feet   Hard Severe   4a/b   (15.8.94)
Start at the base of the large, squat pedestal.
Climb the right-hand side of the pedestal to its top, and follow a crack for 10 feet until a step right on superb jugs permits an easy exit (as for *Alienation*) to a tree belay.

Herbsman Hustling   30 feet   E2   5b   (15.8.94)
Start on the left side of the pedestal at a tree-stump at the bottom of an obvious chimney.
Move up to and follow the crack above with mounting interest to a bulge. Surmount this with difficulty and finish at a tree.

★Victimization   35 feet   E2   5c   (16.7.88)
A tricky pitch with an unexpected finish that rejects a growing number of aspirants. High in its grade.
Start 6 feet to the left of the pedestal beneath a white scoop. Take a direct line up the lower wall past a peg runner and enter the scoop (bolt runner) to stand on a biscuit foothold immediately above the break. Climb through the small bulge above (sapling runner) and step up to gain an abseil station.

High and Dry   120 feet   E1   (20.7.88)
The girdle traverse of the main break of the second bay gives an excellent outing. Bring along a set of large *Friends*, some old clothes, and a sense of humour.
1 50 feet 4c. Follow *Victimization* to the break (peg runner) and pull up left onto the lie-down ledge on *Avatamsaka*. Continue along the break past two *in-situ* thread runners to the ledge on *Up a Gum Tree*, and belay here with wires and a high bolt.
2 55 feet 5b. Step left (low bolt runner) and crawl along the narrow overhung break (*in-situ* thread runner) until a swing down gains a good foothold and peg runner. Hand-traverse strenuously left into *Violation of Trust* and take a breather (thread runner high up). Carry on past a niche (*in-situ* thread runner) and then to a peg runner beneath the groove of *So*

Gross. Step up onto a grassy ledge and belay to a bolt and old peg.
3 15 feet 5a. Move left and climb the finishing-crack of *Crocker's Ash* to an abseil station.

Polarization   35 feet   Hard Very Severe 5c   (27.6.92)
An eliminate with one very hard move.
Climb the uninviting crack (of sorts) just left of *Victimization* to a 'lie-down' ledge (large *Friends*). Pull directly through the overhang/bulge above (bolt runner) and follow a pleasant groove to an abseil station around to the right.

★Avatamsaka   40 feet   E2 5b   (26.6.88)
A deservedly popular pitch that breaches an unlikely overhang on good holds. Start beneath a short, slanting V-groove 12 feet left of *Victimization*. Climb a depression and step left to the base of the V-groove (peg runner). Enter this with difficulty and gain the lie-down ledge above (large *Friends*). Reach up left to a hidden peg and then swing left on jugs to a second peg runner. Have a dangle, pull over the lip, and continue more easily to a useful tree at the top. Abseil from the 'ringed' tree.

★★His Master's Voice   35 feet   E4 6b F7a   (2.9.90)
An improbable yet choice eliminate that deserves popularity.
Starting 6 feet left of *Avatamsaka*, climb direct past a lone bolt runner to reach the break and two large *in-situ* threads. Pull straight over the roof with ease and follow *Avatamsaka* (peg runner) up the wall above to the tree at the top. Abseil from the 'ringed' tree.

★Habit of a Lifetime   35 feet   E3 6a F6c   (9.7.88)
Some powerful climbing with a thuggish crux.
Follow a faint diagonal line of holds running up the bulging wall 15 feet left of *Avatamsaka*. At the overhang (peg runner) make a very strenuous reach leftwards to grasp a bucket (peg runner); then pull up and grab the break (large *in-situ* thread runner). Easy jug-pulling over the next overhang at a fin (peg runner) gains an abseil station.

Above the half-height break hereabouts lies a grey slab.

★Up a Gum Tree   35 feet   E5 6b   (6.7.88)
Steep, intricate, and thuggish work to surmount the guarding overhang below the corner of the white slab. Although the route was at one time quite a popular E4, the disappearance of the peg under the roof has made the pitch much more serious. Start immediately left of the previous route. Pull awkwardly up to the overhang, move left a little, and launch through past a bolt runner to grab the break. Much easier climbing leads up a small corner (leftwards) past a bolt runner to an abseil station.

Utilizing Eucalyptus   35 feet   E4 6b F7a †   (11.8.91)
A debilitating eliminate where size and prowess count. Start immediately
left of the previous route.
Pull up to layaways under the roof (bolt runner above) and make a long,
long stretch to a flat jug on the arête. Another long, long stretch just about
reaches the main break with its welcoming rest. Clip the bolt of *SoFB
Country* on the left and the bolt of *Up a Gum Tree* on the right, and
proceed with patience up the centre of the thin, white slab to the abseil
station.

★SoFB Country   40 feet   E4 6a F6c+   (9.7.88)
A pitch that weaves through the intimidating barrier of overhangs at their
widest point. Start 15 feet right of *Violation of Trust*. Move up to the overlap
at 12 feet (inverted peg runner) just left of *Utilizing Eucalyptus*. Step left,
make some hard moves up past two peg runners to reach an *in-situ* thread
runner beneath the large roofs, and then shuffle right to a restricted
lie-down rest. With protection from a bolt runner, ease up around the
bulge above to grasp a thin crack (peg runner) and finish awkwardly to the
abseil station.

★Violation of Trust   35 feet   E2 6a F6b+   (26.6.88)
A quirky yet irresistible roof problem with user-friendly protection. You
either love it or hate it! [Photo p.224.] Start beneath an open
chimney/groove that breaches the upper series of overhangs in the centre
of the bay.
Boulder up the initial wall to the roof (and peg runner), get the bucket on
the lip (peg runner), and then power through (*in-situ* thread runner) to a
rest at the break. Continue up the chimney/groove (thread runner) to an
abseil station.

At the left side of the left-hand Overhanging Bay lies a deep chimney starting
from the mid-height break. Immediately right of this chimney is a slim,
feminine groove.

Lip Service   35 feet   E3 5c   (16.7.88)
A problematic crux provides the interest. Low in its grade. Start at a short,
bulging wall leading up to the deep chimney.
Climb the bulging wall (peg runner) and continue up to a peg runner at
the base of the slim groove. Stride right to a position on the lip of the roof
(*in-situ* thread runner); then power through the overlap using the obvious
undercuts. Abseil from the tree above.

So Gross   35 feet   E2 5b   (16.7.88)
A bit ugly but with a nice personality! Take plenty of protection. Start as for
Lip Service.
Climb the bulging wall (peg runner) and continue up to a peg runner at
the base of the slim groove. Follow the groove, and hand-traverse right

Nice and Sleazy (E), first ascent) Woodcroft Quarry, Wintour's Leap
Climber: Gordon Jenkin   Photo: Jenkin col.

Firefly (E2) Fly Wall, Wintour's Leap.
Climber: unknown   Photo: Chris Craggs

above its top to reach the tree belay shared with *Lip Service*. 'Have a cigarette' and then abseil off.

Crocker's Ash   35 feet   E5 6b †   (11.8.91)
A surprising line with a fierce, technical start that gets straight to the point. Low in its grade. Start just left of the deep chimney at a double tree-stump. Climb directly up the steep, bulging wall past a bolt runner and peg runner to the overhang. Pull through this on some precarious jams (crucial *Rock 4*) to better holds and a much-needed rest at the break. Finish straight up the wall above to an abseil station.

Gobbo Wuz Yer'   35 feet   E4 6a   (23.8.88)
Start immediately left of the double tree-stump.
A sequence of moves on undercuts and layaways leads up through the initial bulges (rusty *in-situ* wire). Climb the wall above to the break and exit slightly leftwards through the roof.

BONGO 'BUTTRESS'
This is the short area of rock that links the left-hand end of The Twin Overhanging Bays to the much more impressive Crawl Buttress. The left-hand Overhanging Bay turns a slight corner at a double set of roofs.

Let's Hear It for Lorenzo   30 feet   E1 5c   (3.7.88)
A direct line giving inconsistent climbing through the centre of the double roofs. Start 6 feet right of a big tree and a couple of feet left of *Gobbo Wuz Yer'*.
Having clipped a bolt runner on the right with difficulty (crux), climb straight on through to easier ground. The broken crack/groove through the capping overhang gives an easy finish.

Take the Wave   35 feet   E1 5b   (17.9.88)
A devious pitch with good gear. Worth the effort. Start by the large tree. Pull into the open scoop, and at the bulge traverse right along the break (peg runner) to gain the resting-ledge on *Let's Hear It for Lorenzo*. Step up and surmount the roof on the left; big holds now lead to the tree at the top.

A serious and badly-protected eliminate, **Gravitational Dyslexia** (E3 6a † 15.8.94), has been climbed through the overhang above the start of *Take the Wave*.

★**Genetic Engineering**   35 feet   Hard Very Severe 5a   (17.9.88)
Pleasant. Start at the deeply-pocketed scoop 5 feet left of the tree of *Take the Wave*.
Enter the scoop and pull straight up, rather steeply, to good holds on the slab (peg runner). Climb the slab past two *in-situ* thread runners, and follow a thin diagonal crack to a tree belay on the right.

★Genetically Engineered Super Mutant 35 feet Very Severe 4b (17.9.88)
A safe, varied, and enjoyable outing. A good introduction to the
lower-grade routes.
Enter the scoop as for *Genetic Engineering* (peg runner); then make a
difficult step out left to stand on a good ledge. Continue up more easily
and follow the slim corner above to a tree at its top. Abseil descent.

A Liberal Smear   40 feet   E2   5c   (23.7.92)
No protection on the initial part of the route – the part that counts! Start 6
feet to the left of the pocketed scoop of *Genetic Engineering*.
Pull up to the first overhang and step delicately left to below a steep,
shallow groove that breaks through the main bulge. Pinch grips and deft
footwork gain better holds, from where an obscured flake jug (out right)
brings an end to the difficulties. Move up easily (good protection – at last!)
and foot-traverse right to join *Genetically Engineered Super Mutant*. Finish
up the slim corner above to a tree at its top. Abseil descent.

The line of low bulges continues leftwards to where they abut an indistinct red
wall. A small, narrow slot (climbed by *A Date with David Mellor*) cuts into the
end of the bulges while *Get Them Out by Xmas* takes a direct line up the red
wall to the prominent, small yew tree.

A Date with David Mellor   25 feet   E1   5b   (23.7.92)
Better than you might think! Start 12 feet left *Genetic Engineering*, beneath
a slot in the overhang (which is immediately right of a more obvious little
groove).
Pull off the floor using a perfect oval pocket and move up to a peg runner.
Make a hard reach over the overhang and haul up on some big holds.
Belay immediately on nuts and a tree-stump. Abseil descent.

Raining Stones   30 feet   Hard Very Severe 5b †   (14.7.94)
Climb the little V-groove 3 feet left of the slot of *A Date with David Mellor*
past a peg runner to chockstones. Step right to the tree-stump on *A Date
with David Mellor* and finish up right to a yew tree.

Get Them Out by Xmas   30 feet   E3   6a   (23.7.92)
A trick crux, but ample protection invites? Begin beneath the right-hand
side of the red wall; an unusual flake/fin hold starts the pitch.
Pull up to the first break and make a wicked reach up right to grasp a jug
atop a thin crack. Span up leftwards to the second break and finish up the
easy seam above to the bushy yew tree. Abseil descent.

Nation of Shopkeepers   30 feet   E2   5b   (9.7.88)
A bit of fun. Start to the right of an unsightly gully.
Climb steeply (small *in-situ* thread runner) to the break and stand up in this
at a thin crack (*in-situ* thread). Make a long reach to the right to a good
hold and finish at the bushy yew tree above.

The Microwave Man   40 feet   E1   5b   (17.9.88)
Some satisfying climbing that proves to be much more difficult than it
looks. Start a few feet to the right of the gully.
Follow a weakness to the break, keeping left of *Nation of Shopkeepers*;
then step right and climb steeply up a thin crack (*in-situ* thread runner),
trending slightly left near the top to reach the terrace. Belay to a good tree
high up on the left.

The obvious gully is unpleasant and insecure, and is therefore not recommended as a line of ascent or descent. It has been used as a rubbish chute,
the most notable rejected objects being a considerable quantity of horse
manure and an unopened bottle of port!

Kalamazoo   25 feet   E1   6a   F6b   (17.9.88)
A tasty, technical titbit that tackles the short black pillar. An *in-situ* thread
runner and a bolt runner protect. Abseil station above.

Pooh Corner   35 feet   Hard Very Severe   4c   †‡   (18.9.94)
In the walls left of *Kalamazoo* lies a small tower of rock just right of the
main chimney/corner. Very vegetated.
Climb the wall right of the chimney and move up into a slim right-facing
groove. Climb this to a chained ring abseil station on the right.

CRAWL BUTTRESS
The biggest, the best, and the most obvious feature on The Left-Hand
Escarpment is undoubtedly Crawl Buttress. This imposing attraction gained its
name from the horizontal bedding-plane along which it was once necessary
to crawl and grovel. The original crossings were quite memorable, the drop
below giving it that extra 'edge'. Cleaning operations on the buttress quickly
neutered the experience, and more recently a traverse on a lower line of ledges
has been excavated.

★★Latest Craze   60 feet   E6   6b   (9.7.88)
An impressive route tackling the hanging right-hand arête of Crawl
Buttress. Sustained and strenuous. Start 10 feet to the right of the undercut
arête.
Pull over the initial bulge (*RPs* protect) to reach a bolt runner; then tip-toe
left along the lip of the roof to gain the arête. Layback up the right-hand
side of this past a second bolt runner to meet the break and a tree. Climb
the easier slab above to an abseil station at the top.

★Good 'Jab'   60 feet   E4   6b   †   (16.7.88)
An unusual pitch on very good rock. Start just left of the right-hand arête.
Pull up into the overhanging corner above the rectangular cave, and move
up to the roof before traversing right with difficulty (bolt runner) to a
foot-ledge just left of the arête. Surmount the roof on superb holds
(awkward wire placements) to gain the wide break, from where a clean

groove leads to the top.

★Lounge Lizard Leisure Suit   50 feet   E4   6a   (4.9.88)
An exposed route venturing onto the steep ground immediately left of the hanging corner. Low in its grade but still exciting stuff.
Pull up into the overhanging corner of Good 'Jab' to a concealed wire placement, and then launch out leftwards to a good hold and up to the slim break beneath the capping overhang (Friends 1 and 1½). Continue straight up (peg runner) passing a suspect block and large Friend placement to reach a large tree in the break. Struggle into the tree and finish up the open groove above.

★★Just Too Hot   70 feet   E5   6b   (3.7.88)
A superb hard route taking the bulges in the centre of Crawl Buttress. Belay on the lower traverse at a single bolt.
Climb up to an in-situ thread and make powerful moves (bolt runner) to gain a small shelf above the roof and another in-situ thread runner. Move blindly right into a tiny groove, and then go straight up to a good hold in the break above the roof (peg runner). Make a hard pull on a small pocket to gain the wide break, and step up to a system of curving grooves (peg runner). Follow these, moving right, onto the final wall before finishing straight to an abseil station.

★★★Too Hot to Touch   60 feet   E5   6b   (9.7.88)
A scorching pitch on immaculate rock that pushes through the roofs in the left arête of the buttress; marred only by the runout above the first bolt runner. Start beneath a good ledge at the left end of the 'crawl'. Peg and nut belay.
Pull over the first roof using a good, hidden finger-jug on the right (bolt runner), and then move up to the tiered roofs (two peg runners). Make a very long reach for the wide break above, swing left to the arête, and climb it past a bolt runner to an abseil station at the top.

★B'stard   40 feet   E4   6a   (7.9.88)
Some good climbing and amenable for its grade. Start as for Too Hot to Touch.
Surmount the opening bulge immediately left of Too Hot to Touch and climb the wall above past a pair of peg runners. Continue up to a projecting block hold and bolt runner (peg runner above); then step left and ascend the corner-line (peg runner) to the obvious break. Climb the crack above (peg runner) to reach an abseil station. The original line made hard moves and a very long reach up slightly rightwards from the bolt runner past the peg (and an in-situ wire) to gain the break (E5 6b).

CRAWL WALL
The last section of wall, Crawl Wall, stretches the short distance across to the large open gully. It has the highest concentration of 'E' points on the

Escarpment and (with its neighbouring buttress) provides the ideal spot for the serious enthusiast in search of a good day.

Sitting snugly between the end of 'the crawl' and the prominent yew tree is a set of roof stacks sporting three bolt-lines.

★The Forest 35 feet E5 6c F7b+ † (27.6.92)
A short, power-packed problem through the roofed barrier just left of *B'Stard*.
Start 17 feet right of the large tree. Make a series of debilitating moves past a bolt runner to grasp a narrow, rounded shelf. Pull up past a second bolt runner into an undercut position; then monkey left (*in-situ* thread), pull over, and climb a short wall to an abseil station.

★★Really Big Sur 35 feet E6 6c F7c (17.7.88)
A powerful pitch climbing the stack of five roofs 10 feet to the right of the large yew tree.
Trace a line through the roofs via a projecting pinch-grip (two bolt runners); then move up (hidden peg runner) to finish via a narrow groove (peg runner) breaching the last roof. Abseil station above.

★Frisco Disco 35 feet E5 6b F7a+ † (27.6.92)
Another stern test of muscle with a hair-raising second clip. Start immediately right of the large yew tree.
Climb the undercut wall (bolt runner) to gain good holds above the main overhang (bolt runner); then slip into overdrive and pull over the final overhang to gain a short corner. Exit rightwards from the top of the corner to an abseil station.

Trishna 40 feet E2 5b (6.9.88)
Commendable. Clamber into the arms of the yew tree: from its highest branch step onto the rock and climb a slim groove to the break. Carry on in a similar line to a large tree at the top.

★Craters of Mono 50 feet E5 6a (17.7.88)
Clean climbing with just sufficient protection. Start 10 feet left of the yew tree. Low in its grade.
Enter a smooth, square-cut recess above the roof (bolt runner) and gain a good hold up and right. Follow a line of holds to the next roof and surmount this on excellent holds. Finish up the centre of the tower above passing an *in-situ* thread runner.

Breast Stroke in a D Cup 40 feet E3 6b (4.9.88)
An intriguing and invigorating problem. Start 15 feet to the left of the yew tree.
Follow the obvious weakness up rightwards (peg runner with *in-situ* sling) to fondle a large undercut. A difficult move from the scoop (bolt runner)

gains better holds and a peg runner; then climb slightly left from the break and up to a convenient tree. Abseil descent.

The Gnarliest   40 feet   E4 6c †   (4.9.88)
Some vicious climbing, 'way gnarly'. Start 25 feet left of the yew below a weakness in the centre of the obvious roof.
Climb to the roof (peg runner) and reach out to gain a jug on the lip. Clip a bolt runner, whereupon a bitter struggle ensues to get established on the wall above (peg runner). Continue up the headwall passing a peg runner to a tree-stump in the break and finish at a small tree above. Abseil descent.

★Snaffel Attack   40 feet   E4 6b   (16.7.88)
An excellent and technical pitch. Start on the left side of the large roof by a small cave at ledge-level.
A hard start leads to good layaways in a niche in the roof. Move right around the lip (bolt runner) and then go up and slightly right (crux) to the break (*Friend 1½*). Continue up flake cracks to the top.

Damn Snaffelhounds   40 feet   E5 6a   (16.7.88)
A meaty excursion just left of *Snaffel Attack*.
Climb up to the roof (*in-situ* thread runner) and move right to fight a way through the roof via the layback crack. Finish up the easier crack and groove above.

★The Sac Gang   240 feet   E2   (2.9.88)
The girdle traverse of Crawl Wall and Crawl Buttress following the mid-height break. A good, fun outing. Start 5 feet left of those *Damn Snaffelhounds* on the right-hand side of a clump of trees.
1 20 feet 4c. Climb up right of an obvious short crack at ground-level and then move over a series of small ledges to a good ledge (*Friend* and nut belay).
2 80 feet 5a. Traverse right along the main break, mostly by keeping below it, to a tree belay on the jutting ledge above *Really Big Sur*.
3 90 feet 5b. Step into the corner and traverse out onto the exposed arête of the front face (thread runner and high bolt runner). Hand-traverse along the break (bolt runner) until good footholds on *Just Too Hot* give the arms a rest (peg runner). Continue more easily to the large tree in the break and belay here; or, better, carry on to a nut belay immediately before the arête.
4 50 feet 4c. Swing around the arête to the tree atop *Latest Craze*, thrash past this, and continue to a good ledge by keeping low (peg runner). Step down a few feet to a thread runner and follow the break to a sapling and bolt belay at the rib of *Kalamazoo*. Abseil off or continue as for the next route.

The Parallax Vision   610 feet   E2 †   (11.9.88)
A girdle traverse of the majority of The Left-Hand Escarpment. A good day out or a mammoth expedition depending upon your point of view. A full rack of *Friends* is required as well as one to belay you.

1-4 240 feet 5b. *The Sac Gang.*

5 50 feet 5b. Move right to a large, cleaned ledge; then traverse the break, standing up in it at the thin crack of *The Microwave Man* (*in-situ* thread runner). Make a long reach right for a good hold; then gain easier ground and a tree-stump belay.

6 70 feet 5b. Follow a series of small ledges until they peter out and a brief hand-traverse (*in-situ* thread runner) can be made across *Genetic Engineering* to a groove. Make a cramped traverse under an overhang to reach *Let's Hear It for Lorenzo*, and follow the break around the corner to a peg and bolt belay in a chimney.

7 50 feet 5b. Reverse pitch 2 of *High and Dry.*

8 50 feet 5a. Reverse pitch 1 of *High and Dry* as far as *Victimization* and from this point step up in the break at the 'biscuit hold'. Foot-traverse right (bolt runner) to belay on a large block.

9 50 feet 4c. Step down and follow the main break running across *Alienation*. From a ledge, a series of moves leads to a tree belay above the large roof of *Felt, Batten, and Smile*.

10 70 feet 5a. Foot-traverse right into a corner and step down a few feet before crossing a rib to a ledge on *Who Is This Man Dukakis?*
Hand-traverse boldly into the chimney of *Ugooloo* and belay on good nuts above the break.

11 30 feet 5c. Move right onto *Avidya*. Climb the roof and hanging slab (peg runner) and finish up easier ground just above.

Jurisprudence   30 feet   E2 5b   (25.9.88)
An interesting little snippet. Start on the left-hand side of the clump of trees growing from the base of a corner and climb the left arête of the corner.

THE LADDER GULLY AREA

The Left-Hand Escarpment finally ends at a large, open gully sporting two metal ladders. The Ladder Gully Area covers the two tiers of cliff that stretch across to, and eventually merge with, the unmistakable Main Crag. The routes on these tiers are described from **right to left.**

Immediately left of the first ladder is an isolated buttress with a prominent right-facing corner.

The Fat Controller   40 feet   Hard Very Severe   5b   (25.9.88)
Climb the right-facing corner to a peg runner in the left wall and swing out left past the peg to gain a resting-ledge. Finish easily up to a tree belay.

Standard Deviation   40 feet   E1 5b   (8.10.88)
A poor route up the front the buttress to the left of *The Fat Controller*; some

tricky initial moves.

THE LOWER TIER
The main (ground-level) track continues downslope, passing a low tubular cave entrance after 30 feet; then, after a further 100 feet, a step up above the path brings one to The Lower Tier routes. Immediately in front, another (this time larger) cave entrance sits at the base of *The Gates*, while to the left an obvious white, dirty corner provides inspiration for *The Corner*.

No Big Cigar   40 feet   Very Severe   4c   (8.10.88)
'Beware of ash!' Climb the crack on the right-hand side of the vague arête and abseil from the large tree.

Old Smokie   40 feet   E4   6b †   (5.5.93)
A thin and very technical crux.
Climb up just left of *No Big Cigar* past a bolt runner to a ledge (*Friend 1½*). Now climb the wall above, keeping just right of the arête (bolt runner) to finish at the obvious tree. Abseil descent.

Merthyr Bob   40 feet   E3   5c   (4.10.88)
Quite a tough pitch for its grade but worth some attention (and further cleaning); it climbs the vague arête.
Climb steeply up past a peg runner to a good hold and step up left to a resting-spot beneath a small overhang (peg runner). Move right using a layaway and pull dynamically over the overlap to easier ground. At the top, step right and abseil from the large tree on the right.

The Gates   50 feet   E1   5b   (18.9.88)
Something a little different. Start at the cave entrance.
Climb an easy hand-crack just right of *The Corner*; then step across right and follow the thin crack up the centre of the slab. At the top, traverse right and finish as for *Merthyr Bob* up through the vegetation; abseil from the large tree. A harder and more direct start looks possible but is as yet unclimbed.

The Corner   40 feet   Very Severe   4b   (18.9.88)
Climb the corner. Very dirty.

Left Wall   40 feet   E1   5b †   (13.5.89)
Climb the left wall (if possible) amidst the dirt and encroaching jungle.

Thirty feet further on is a small bay with a corner-crack on the left taken by *Top Cat*.

The Boss   40 feet   Very Severe   4c †   (10.2.89)
Climb the back of the bay, passing the overhang to its left, and finish at a single-bolt belay or a tree further out left. Abseil descent.

Officer Dibble   40 feet   E4 6b †   (10.2.89)
Climb the right-hand side of the right arête of *Top Cat* (bolt runner). Finish
at a single-bolt belay or a tree out left. Abseil descent.

Top Cat   40 feet   Very Severe 4b   (8.10.88)
Climb the corner-crack to a poor finish.

Amnesty   40 feet   E3 5c   (8.10.88)
A direct line up the wall and overhang to the left of *Top Cat*.
Power up the lower wall past a peg runner until big holds and a ledge are
reached at 30 feet. Pull up and left over the roof to a huge jug and belay
at a sapling. Abseil descent.

Further progress is halted as The Lower Tier now merges into the right-hand
end of The Main Cliff (traverse left and take a long look down!) Return to the
main (ground-level) track and continue downslope to reach the foot of The
Main Cliff.

THE UPPER TIER
The routes here are centred on a compact wall at the far end of the Upper
Tier and reached by carefully traversing the vegetated terrace around from
the base of the second ladder in Ladder Gully. This area is very close to the
houses above – **please climb quietly**.

★**High Treason**   40 feet   E3 5c   (2.10.88)
Climb the corner and overhang on the right-hand side of the compact
wall. Tough for its grade and with a hard start.

★**High Fidelity**   40 feet   E4 6a   (24.11.91)
The best route on the upper tier. Start 5 feet to the left of *High Treason*.
Climb up to a small flake (*in-situ* thread), swing up onto the headwall (bolt
runner), and finish direct past a peg runner. Tree belay above.

★**High Society**   40 feet   E2 5c   (2.10.88)
An intricate pitch up the wall starting to the right of the deep corner. Abseil
off a tree on the left.

★**James Mason**   35 feet   E3 5c   (24.11.91)
This climbs the smooth-looking wall immediately right of the deep corner.
Technical climbing on perfect rock; two peg runners protect.

Free Masonry   40 feet   Very Severe 4b   (2.10.88)
The obvious deep corner.

★**The Mason's Arms**   50 feet   E4 6b   (24.11.91)
Another worthwhile pitch; it takes the slim arête to the left of the deep
corner. The hard moves are concentrated in the middle section with a peg

runner (difficult to clip) providing some comfort. At the top, follow the arête direct taking care with an unsound block.

Stone Mason   40 feet   Very Severe   4b   (2.10.88)
Start 10 feet to the right of a steep, vegetated gully and climb the obvious crack, passing a tree at 10 feet. Abseil off a tree on the right.

★Stinging on a Star   45 feet   E2   5b   (25.9.88)
A fine pitch up the projecting face to the left of the steep gully.
Move easily up to a band of small ledges running across the face; then step left (peg runner) and climb steeply to the top past an *in-situ* wire.

★Rudolph's Roof Route   35 feet   E5   6b †   (25.12.91)
A superb little route taking a direct line up the roof-stacked arête to the left of *Stinging on a Star*. Three bolt runners mark the line. A *Friend 1½* helps calm the nerves between the first two bolts. Abseil from the tree at the top.

Rockin' Robin   35 feet   E3   5c †   (25.12.91)
Follow the obvious direct line up the wall just to the left of *Rudolph's Roof Route*, passing a sapling part way. Abseil from the tree at the top.

The Upper Tier now merges with the top right-hand side (Upper Tier) of The Main Cliff. Please respect the access note on page 176 and **do not climb beyond this point**. Return to the base of Ladder Gully, and continue down the main track beneath The Lower Tier to reach the foot of The Main Cliff.

THE MAIN CLIFF
The routes are described from **right to left**, as one approaches.

With the exception of The Continuation Wall at the far left end, all of the routes here are immediately accessible from the terrace path that follows the base of the crag. Once a difficult obstacle, this path is gradually improving with the passage of feet and time. At certain times of the year a dense bed of nettles may be encountered; however, a few minutes stomping about from your climbing partner will quickly sort it out. This ebb and flow of vegetation and the lack of any distinguishing landmarks cause problems in describing the location of the sixty or so routes since most of the crag's features become apparent only when they are viewed from a stance back from the wall. Stuck-on name plates resolved this difficulty but provoked objection; they were subsequently removed. So to preserve ethical purity the climber will have to endure the irritation of working out the relative positions of the climbs (and trying not to slide down the slope when stepping out from the wall).

The first route described in the text is a high-level traverse, best viewed from the foot of The Main Cliff but actually starting from The Lower Tier of the Ladder Gully Area. The purist will, of course, spurn such beta and head on-sight around the initial arête...

★★No Head for Heights   200 feet   E4 †   (8.9.90)

A high-quality, airy outing along the lip of the dramatic roofs that form the main feature of the first part of the crag. An impressive route requiring a full rack of *Friends* and both a steady leader and a steady second. Start at the left-hand end of the lower tier of The Ladder Gully Area where it begins to merge into the main crag.

1 80 feet 5c. Follow the corner-crack of *Top Cat* (or the wall to its left, *Amnesty*) for 15 feet to reach the first break, and hand-traverse left along this to a ledge above the roofs on *Gimme Back My Head* (bong runner). Stand up using a flake; then continue the traverse until moves up past a peg runner gain a good ledge. Swing down and left to a ring bolt (back-rope for second possible) and step down a few feet to a bolt and peg belay.

2 40 feet 6a. Move left on the very lip of the roofs to an arête (bolt runner), and then make some trying moves into a slim groove. Traverse left along the break (wires and a bolt runner) until some difficult moves (low peg runner and *Rock 3*) lead to the bolt belay of *The Drilling Fields* and *Almost Me*.

3 80 feet 6a. Move up left onto a ledge on the arête (peg runner); then traverse left along an obvious line of holds below some ivy (two peg runners) to where hard moves down left lead to the thread runner on *Hummin' Bird*. A wild traverse now ensues past a bolt and a thread runner to reach another bolt runner. Move awkwardly out left to a bolt belay. Abseil off.

HEAD SECTOR

Approach past the metal ladders (Ladder Gully Area) and follow the rugged track downslope for 100 feet until the right wing of The Main Cliff comes (quickly) into view.

The most immediate sight on arrival is that of the massive roofs that arch dizzily above your head. This sector extends past a conspicuous pillar to end where the roofs do, above a short dip in the terrace path.

★Open Head Surgery   70 feet   E4 6a F6c+ †   (23.5.93)

Excellent. Start by a tree just after the point where the approach path steps up to the base of the wall.

A tricky start through an overhang (peg runner and *in-situ* sling) gains a ledge and a bolt runner (belay possible, backed up by a second bolt to the left). Move up to the bolt runner above; then step right and climb a hanging arête to a protruding hold (bolt runner). Make technical moves to gain the break (*Friend 2*), from where moves leftwards above the void (bolt runner) gain an abseil station.

★★Gimmee Back My Head   75 feet   E5 6b F7a+   (16.2.89)

Powerful climbing through the right-hand end of the tiered roofs; a fine introduction to the style of climbing on this section of cliff.

As for *Open Head Surgery*, pull through an overhang (peg runner) to gain a ledge and bolt runner/belay. Climb a short wall to the wide break from where steepening, fingery climbing breaches the wall and right-hand side of the roof (three bolt runners). From a ledge (bong runner), step left and climb a short flake to an abseil station.

★★**Head Tennis**   75 feet   E6 6b F7c †   (28.5.89)
An impressive pitch tackling the initial set of roofs head on. Superb and improbable climbing made possible by the addition of a sacrificial artificial hold. Start beneath a slight ramp 12 feet to the left of *Open Head Surgery*.
Some difficult climbing up the ramp and short wall (two bolt runners) gains the left-hand end of a ledge (bolt runner – belay possible using a second bolt to the right). Move up a short groove to the wide break and then tackle the intricate wall (two bolt runners) to gain the lip of the first overhang by a flying leap (bolt runner). Strength-sapping moves above (bolt runner) lead to good holds and relief in the form of a ledge to the right. Clip a peg runner above and move right to an abseil station.

★★**Stitch That!**   65 feet   E6 6b F7b+   (28.5.89)
Yet more superlative roof-climbing. A power-problem that is well geared and low in its grade. Start 12 feet to the left of *Head Tennis* below a shallow, smooth-looking, white groove.
Climb the groove (bolt runner) to a ledge (*in-situ* thread) and then move up to the wide break (bolt runner). Pursue a direct and intimidating line up the technical wall (bolt runner) to the roof (bolt runner) from where a wide span gains a hidden pocket and the lip (peg runner). Struggle over to an immediate abseil station.

The next two routes, the show-pieces of the crag, start from a double-bolt belay atop the white pedestal situated beneath the most imposing section of the roofs. The belay can be gained by climbing the crack on the left-hand side of the pedestal (Severe).

★★★**The Drilling Fields**   75 feet   E6 6b F7c   (14.7.90)
A brilliant pitch, relatively short, but packing a strong punch. Well protected with five bolts and a peg.
From a ledge 10 feet above the belay, take the right-hand of the two bolt lines through the impressive roof-stack. Climb mainly on pinch-grips and pockets to reach a bucket on the final lip, from where a technical move to a huge jug is followed by intricate climbing up a thin flake. Abseil station slightly left.

★★★**Almost Me**   75 feet   E6 6b F7c   (15.7.90)
The left-hand route provides fine climbing in impressive positions. The main difficulties are passing the third of five bolts where strength and tenacity count most.
Climb to a ledge at 10 feet (as for *The Drilling Fields*); then step left and

follow a stunning line slightly rightwards through the tiered buttress via tufa pillars and pockets to gain a jug at the lip. Battle manfully over past the final bolt runner to reach an abseil station slightly to the right.

★★**Hummin' Bird**   75 feet   E5 6b F7b+   (28.5.89)
Another superb pitch taking the immaculate, snaking groove-line just to the left of *Almost Me*. Sustained and well-protected climbing. Start 15 feet to the left of the white pedestal below a vague, white ramp. Nine bolt runners.
Move up to pass the ramp by an awkward manœuvre and climb straight up to a cave at the half-height break. Pull out of the right-hand side of the cave to reach the groove, where awkward moves up gain a rounded hand-ledge leading rightwards into the upper section of the groove. Climb this, making a desperate final move to reach good holds alongside the thread belay.

★**Sea-King Me**   75 feet   E4 6a   (16.2.89)
Good climbing, but quite bold at one point, tackling the prominent, short corner high on the cliff. Start immediately left of *Hummin' Bird*, by a double-trunked tree.
Move up to an *in-situ* thread runner; step left, then up and back right to gain easier ground leading to the terrace. From a large flake (bolt runner) make bold moves directly up the wall to reach a ledge below the corner. Finish up this to an abseil station.

Chin Hooks   65 feet   E5 6a   (9.12.89)
A taxing eliminate and quite bold but with a contrived section at the top. Start immediately left of *Hummin' Bird*.
Move up to an in-situ thread (as for *Sea-King Me*); then pull out leftwards to gain positive ledges leading to the terrace. Here, climb directly up the short wall (two bolt runners) and enter a short, wide groove (peg runner). Pull straight over the overhang with difficulty and continue blindly up the wall to reach an abseil station on the left.

★★**Heady Days**   65 feet   E2 5c F6b+   (5.90)
The introduction to The Main Cliff. A superb, intimidating yet well-protected outing, offering a sensational finish through the jutting roof-capped corner. At the top of its grade. Start 25 feet to the left of the white pedestal where the terrace dips abruptly. Seven bolt runners.
Move up and then left to gain a prominent, suspect flake. Despite its appearance the flake is solid and leads to easier ground and the terrace above. Take the shallow groove above to meet the large roof, and then swing jauntily out right to gain the lip. Pull up and swarm over the next overhang via a thin crack to reach an abseil station above.

APEDEX SECTOR
This area starts where the roofs of the Head Sector finish, at the large (and largely!) vegetated, left-facing corner-line taken by *Nod if You Understand*.

The routes hereabouts are much more slabby in nature than their burly neighbours, requiring reliance more on technical merit than on brute force.

Nod if You Understand   75 feet   E2 5b   (9.12.89)
Fifteen feet to the left of *Heady Days* the terrace path steps back up. Start here, below a ribbed groove-line.
Climb the groove to a large ledge/earth mound and take a short, tricky wall (thread runner) to gain the big ledge. The obvious corner finishes the route. Abseil from trees on the right or from a bolt belay.

Maestro's Wall   65 feet   E4 6b   (10.2.90)
Start 15 feet to the left of *Heady Days*.
Climb the groove (as for *Nod if You Understand*) until just below the earth mound, and step left to a tree-stump. Climb a short wall to a large ledge. The smooth, upper wall is hard and technical; climb it past a bolt runner and an *in-situ* thread to reach an abseil station.

Yellow Taxi   70 feet   E1 5b   (10.3.90)
Reported to be excellent climbing if the route were to be recleaned. Start 6 feet to the left of *Nod if You Understand* beneath a short, open groove in a smooth wall.
Make some poorly-protected and committing moves up the initial groove to better holds, and then continue more easily up a short crack (the side of a huge block) to the half-height break. Continue up the wall past a tree-stump until a fine, smooth groove leads to an abseil station.

Fresh Fish   60 feet   E5 6a   (10.12.89)
Bold and committing. Start 15 feet to the left of *Nod if You Understand*.
Climb the wall via a tiny groove and then an easier groove to the terrace. Follow the shallow groove above with difficulty to gain the right-hand end of an overlap (*Friend 1½*); then pull through this leftwards and climb a small arête to a tree belay.

★In Apedex   60 feet   E5 6b F7b   (10.12.89)
A superb and well-protected test-piece giving clean and enjoyable climbing but requiring a telescopic reach. Start below an obvious, shallow groove 20 feet to the left of *Nod if You Understand*. Six bolt runners.
Climb the groove and wall above to gain the terrace. The smooth-looking wall is excellent and leads to the crux roof which is passed to a ledge. Finish up a short groove on the right to a tree belay.

The Motley Crew   60 feet   E3 6a †   (28.12.90)
Climb the initial groove of *In Apedex* and then trend leftwards up another groove to reach a good ledge. Climb a short, blocky wall to gain a groove, which provides a couple of awkward moves to reach an abseil station above an overlap.

★Muddy Waters   65 feet   E1   5b   (16.2.92)
A worthy and varied route starting 20 feet to the left of *In Apedex*, below a
grey groove just after a dip in the terrace is crossed.
Climb the groove (*RPs*) to ledges and continue direct up a compact wall
(*Friend 3*) to the large terrace. From the right-hand side of the terrace, step
up onto blocky footholds and climb carefully (crux) up to the thin break
above. Swing left and climb the slabby groove (*RPs*) to a crack and an
abseil station above.

★Slow Boat to Chepstow   65 feet   E3   5c   (16.2.92)
A disconcerting start and high in its grade. Start 5 feet to the left of *Muddy
Waters* below a fairly obvious, small, square-cut ledge in a shallow, whitish
scoop.
Move up onto the ledge. With an *RP 3* for protection use a (well-)hidden
hold on the left to reach some good jugs; then continue fairly easily (but
with no further protection) directly up to the terrace. A tricky move through
an overlap leads to cracks, good wires, and the right-hand end of a long
ledge. Climb straight up above the end of the ledge with some delicate
and awkward final moves to reach an abseil station slightly left.

★Up the Garden Path   80 feet   E3   6a   (16.9.90)
A disconcerting start and a technical finish. High in its grade.
Start below the small square-cut ledge as for *Slow Boat to Chepstow*, and
follow that route to where a step left gains a relatively easy groove leading
up to the terrace. Climb a shallow scoop above this (bolt runner) to reach
the left-hand end of a long ledge; then make further technical moves up
the shallow groove to an abseil station on the right.

★Cocotte   65 feet   E4   6a   (16.9.90)
A good direct route up the steep lower wall and then the prominent, blunt
arête above. Take small wires and *Friends* for the upper section. Start 6 feet
right of *On the Game*.
Climb straight up the centre of the fractured wall (three bolt runners) to
gain the terrace. Pull over the overlap on the right (bolt runner) and swing
up left to gain a pocketed crackline and a peg runner. Follow a series of
thin breaks above; then step right and climb the fine, blunt arête (*in-situ*
thread runner) to a thin crack and an abseil station.

CEMETERY SECTOR
The crag now rears up again to produce roofs and bulges in its upper section.
Cutting into the right-hand side of the roofs is a groove climbed by *On the
Game*. A prominent large flake that extends almost up to the mid-height break
is located just past the left end of the roofs – the starting-point for *You're My
Comic Strip Hero*. A bit further on, a fairly obvious shallow groove (*Helter
Skelter*) marks the end of this area and the beginning of Accuracy Sector. This
is a popular part of the crag, which may have something to do with the terrace
path's being at its widest here (and most comfortable?).

On the Game   65 feet   E5 6b   (12.11.89)
Serious.
Climb the shallow groove in the lower wall to the terrace. A stern pull over
the overlap leads up right to a thin crack and a peg runner. From here,
swing left into the hanging groove and follow it to an abseil station on the
left.

★★**Pet Cemetery**   75 feet   E4 6b F7a   (16.9.90)
An exhilarating route, mainly on good holds, that pierces the right-hand
side (and widest part) of the roofs. A good resting-ledge before the crux
permits a light-hearted approach, especially with the knowledge that the
roof itself is easy. Definitely your first E4 on the crag! Start just left of *On the
Game*. Seven bolt runners; one peg runner.
Climb the initial wall by a long reach, step left at the ledge, and follow a
shallow groove to the terrace. Step right to below a depression in the roofs.
Make hard crux moves to gain jugs above the first tier, and swarm freely
over onto the hanging arête. Some tricky moves going direct give access to
a ledge and an abseil station.

★★**Aerial Combat**   75 feet   E6 6b F7b+   (3.3.90)
Exciting roof gymnastics, perhaps technically harder for the short. Start 10
feet to the right of the large flake. Eight bolt runners.
Climb a diagonal thin crack to a ledge; then step right and continue up the
wall above to reach the terrace. The entertainment starts here. Move up the
short square-cut groove to gain a break; then cross rightwards through the
large overhang on undercuts and heel-hooks. Once gained, a slim groove
leads to an abseil station on the left.

★★**96 Tiers**   75 feet   E5 6b F7b   (10.3.90)
Superb technical climbing up the slim, hanging groove high on the cliff.
Perfect rock and excellent protection, but tough for its grade. Start at the
foot of the large flake. Seven bolt runners.
Climb a thin crack veering off to the right and continue up the wall above
to the terrace. A technical move up the wall gains the hanging groove and,
eventually, large holds on the right. Swarm through the final overhang to
good holds and an abseil station on the left.

★**A Gathering of Old Men**   70 feet   E5 6b   (8.3.92)
Yet another very technical offering where a long reach proves invaluable.
Superb rock on the upper section. Start at the foot of the large flake.
Climb the flake to the terrace and levitate up the wall just to the right past
two bolt runners to a jug in a break (bolt runner). Tackle the calcite pillar
above to reach an overlap (bolt runner) and pull through onto the
headwall where a thin crack (peg runner) leads to an abseil station.

You're My Comic Strip Hero   75 feet   E3 5c †   (28.12.90)
Start at the foot of the large flake.

Climb the flake-line and move left at the terrace to below the obvious groove. Pull through the overhang and follow the groove (peg runner) to an abseil station.

★★**Let's Celebrate**   65 feet   E5 6b F7a+   (10.12.89)
A very fine route with good climbing throughout. Start below a pillar 12 feet to the left of the large flake. Eight bolt runners.
Climb the centre of the pillar to reach the terrace. Pull over the roof to the right of the corner, ascend the blunt arête, and lunge for a flat hand-ledge. Pull straight up and step right to climb the upper wall via a thin crack to an abseil station.

★★**The Beauty of It All**   70 feet   E4 6b F7a   (28.11.89)
The fine, compact wall to the left of *Comic Strip Hero* provides quality technical face-climbing. Start at a slim groove 8 feet left of *Let's Celebrate*. Move up easily on big holds and step left to a peg runner. Proceed directly up past a bolt runner to the terrace and a second bolt runner. Follow a line up the centre of the wall above (three bolt runners) to reach the upper part of a thin crack-system. Hard moves with a final bolt runner by your waist gain an abseil station.

★★**Gunsel**   75 feet   E3 6a   (19.11.89)
Commendable open climbing. Start 6 feet to the left of *The Beauty of It All* at a prominent, low flake ledge.
Move up awkwardly onto the flake ledge and climb the smooth wall above with difficulty (crux) to reach a ledge; above this follow a thin crack to the terrace. Step left; then, using a layaway edge (bolt runner), climb up to the right-hand side of the overlap (peg runner) and pass this awkwardly by mantelling onto the ledge. Climb the shallow, right-hand groove above to reach some good ledges and an abseil station.

 ★**After Midnight**   75 feet   E3 5c   (29.11.89)
Worthwhile. Start 6 feet to the left of *Gunsel*.
Climb a short, thin wall and a prominent flake to reach the terrace. Continue up the obvious depression via a hanging 'lump' (bolt runner) to meet the overhang, where a stern pull over (peg runner) gains the wide break. Step right and climb a thin crack and shallow groove past a ledge to an abseil station (shared with *Gunsel*).

★★**Tier-Gas**   70 feet   E5 6b F7a+   (29.11.89)
Perfect climbing on flawless rock on the upper section of the wall. Start 6 feet left of *After Midnight*. Six bolt runners.
Climb the awkward lower wall and large flake to reach the left-hand end of the terrace. Take the centre of the wall above with difficulty to reach a wide break where some further technical climbing straight up leads to an abseil station.

It's a Sin   60 feet   E5   6a   F7a+   (10.12.89)
A short, hard section of excellent moves. Start 10 feet to the left of *Tier-Gas* and just right of *Helter Skelter*. Six bolt runners.
Climb straight up the wall to reach the terrace. Move up the smooth wall above and climb this on pinches and layaways to reach a break. Follow the groove above this to an abseil station.

ACCURACY SECTOR
Other than its mid-height ledge-system this section has few distinctive features until it meets with the large bounding corner of *Home Is Where the Heart Is*. A minor landmark at the start of the Accuracy Sector is a boulder across the path (sometimes obscured by vegetation). The boulder 'was dislodged with some glee' from *It's a Sin*. The obvious slender corner above the boulder is *Helter Skelter*.

In the middle of this area are four pitches that have become popular, as their upper sections (above the mid-height terrace) can be climbed as sport routes in their own right. These are *Accuracy* (F6b+), *Costner's Last Stand* (F6c+), *Boys Don't Cry* (F6b), and *No Way Out* (F6c). They are usually approached via the initial easy groove of *Object* to reach a belay on the mid-height ledge. (The groove of *Object* is directly in front of a tall clump of six slim trees set just down from the terrace path.)

Helter Skelter   65 feet   E2   6a   (3.3.90)
Climb the slim corner-line to a cave at the terrace. Steep pulls from here (*in-situ* thread runner) lead to easier climbing up the groove to an overhang. Pass this on the left and follow the continuation of the groove to a tree belay.

★★**Baggy Trousers**   65 feet   E4   6a   (9.12.89)
Varied and strenuous climbing on the slim, upper buttress. Start 5 feet to the left of *Helter Skelter*. High in its grade.
Follow the groove-system (thread runner) to the terrace. Climb a short, difficult wall (bolt runner) to a break and bolt runner; then make further awkward moves past a third bolt runner to a thin diagonal crack (wires). Some hard climbing to finish gains an abseil station slightly left.

The Correct Use of Soap   70 feet   E4   6b †   (10.12.89)
Start 15 feet to the left of *Helter Skelter*.
Climb a tiny flake groove and then an easier wall (all quite boldly) to the terrace. A short wall (bolt runner) leads to the roof where a desperate slippery battle through (bolt runner) lands you on the lip. Phew! Now wash your mouth out. Continue up the wall (peg runner) trending slightly left to an abseil station. (The route originally climbed rightwards to the belay of *Baggy Trousers*.)

Lux 65 feet E2 5c   (16.2.92)
Climb an open, rectangular-shaped groove starting from a tree-stump to
the left of *The Correct Use of Soap*. At the terrace, continue boldly up the
short groove above; then step left and pull through the overlap (bolt runner
on the left) to better holds. Finish pleasantly up the slabby wall to a bolt
belay. Abseil from the station on the left.

The next three routes all cross each other at the terrace; their upper sections
are not in line with their lower ones. They have been described in this somewhat
confusing state in order to achieve consistent standards of climbing throughout. To aid identification, these three routes are placed (right to left) in the
order that their main sections follow **above** the terrace.

★**Object** 75 feet Very Severe 4b   (1.2.92)
Start 25 feet to the left of *Lux*.
Climb the deep groove in the lower wall and move right along the terrace
until below a large corner (belay possible). An awkward start leads to
pleasant climbing and a ledge with an abseil station.

★★**Accuracy** 65 feet E2 5c   (1.2.92)
An excellent contrasting route; although poorly protected in its lower half,
the steep and strenuous upper arête has been equipped for popularity. Five
bolt runners, but definitely no soft touch. Start 10 feet to the left of *Lux*.
Climb directly up the lower wall on positive holds until a final, more difficult
move gains the terrace (small wires required). An awkward start just left of
the top corner of *Object* leads onto a juggy wall with a small groove
above; tricky moves here lead to an abseil station on the right.

Another Day 65 feet Hard Very Severe 5a   (1.2.92)
Start immediately right of *Object*, 20 feet to the left of *Lux*.
Some awkward initial moves up the wall right of *Object* lead to an easier
wall and the terrace. Pull into the slender groove in the left arête of
Accuracy, and bridge pleasantly up the open groove above; finish
rightwards to an abseil station.

The next four routes have a common start: a prominent thin crack in the wall
to the left of the initial deep groove of *Object*.

★**Costner's Last Stand** 60 feet E4 6a †   (23.5.93)
Start 10 feet to the left of the groove of *Object*.
Climb a thin crack, and continue up the wall above to the terrace. Step
right, and climb another wall via an overlap, a thin pull, and a finishing
arête (one peg runner and three bolt runners). Abseil station.

★**Boys Don't Cry** 60 feet E2 5c   (1.2.92)
An enjoyable top section.
Climb the thin crack, and continue up the wall above to the terrace. Pull up

to the left of the cave past a peg and a bolt runner to gain a jug on the left.
Pass a bolt runner to reach a flake which is followed by a long stretch.
Climb the crack above to an abseil station.

★No Way Out   60 feet   E3 6a   (1.2.92)
Climb the thin crack, and continue up the wall above to the terrace.
Proceed on layaways past a bolt runner to gain better holds (and a bolt
runner) beneath a slab/groove. Pull awkwardly into this groove; then move
right below a roof (*Friends* or medium-size wires) and continue up to an
abseil station.

The following three routes all climb to the top of this section of wall before
traversing left to a large tree on the main terrace. Descent is by abseil. Please
respect the access note on page 176 and **do not climb any higher**.

To Bee or Not to Bee   80 feet   E1 5b   (8.7.90)
Originally quite pleasant climbing but now in need of recleaning. Start 10
feet left of the groove of *Object*.
Climb the thin crack (hard) and continue via a small groove in the
right-hand side of an overhang to the terrace. Take the wall above slightly
rightwards to a hole in the break (peg runner on the left), and pull through
the overlap on the left via good holds to a flourishing bush. Trend
diagonally left across the nice slabby face (*in-situ* thread) to reach the top
of the obvious corner and a friendly exit onto the terrace. Walk left to abseil
from the obvious tree.

In My Hour of Need   75 feet   E2 5b   (7.7.90)
An enjoyable pitch, low in its grade and offering some good climbing, but
with a poorly-protected start. Worth a star if recleaned. Start 10 feet to the
right of *Home Is Where the Heart Is*.
Climb a slim groove to an overhang and pass this to the left via another
groove to reach a ledge. Climb a thin flake and juggy wall (peg runner) to
the final slab (*in-situ* thread) where moves left gain the top of the corner
and the terrace. Abseil from a tree over to the left.

WYE SECTOR
The most useful defining feature here is an easy weakness leading up to a
right-facing corner high on the cliff – this is *Home Is Where the Heart Is*. The
terrace path now drops down to a broken tree-stump before continuing more
awkwardly under yet more good routes to end at a tree marking the common
start of *Kiss of Death*, *Goodbye Kiss*, and *Perfect Kiss*.

Home Is Where the Heart Is   75 feet   Very Severe 4c   (4.90)
This prominent corner-line is becoming very dirty again. The crux is low
down and well protected.
Climb the line of the corner past a tree to the terrace. Abseil from a tree on
the left.

Barbaracue 75 feet E5 6a (4.90)
Very serious. An *in-situ* wire used on the first ascent fell out on the second ascent.
Climb *Home Is Where the Heart Is* to its tree; then break out left and climb the buttress (*Friend* protection and poor wires) until harder moves leftwards gain the front of the buttress. Continue directly up this to an easy exit onto the terrace. Abseil from a tree on the left.

Wye're Less 75 feet E3 5c (7.7.90)
Start 20 feet to the left of *Home Is Where the Heart Is*. Worth a star when recleaned.
Climb the rightward-trending crack to reach a ledge at half height. Step left and pull through the overhang (peg runner) to ledges; then continue up the front of the buttress (bolt runner) and climb the rib on its left to pass the overhang to the left. Easy ledges now lead to the terrace. Abseil from a tree on the left.

*Wye Not 75 feet E3 5c (26.11.89)
Varied climbing taking the obvious high-level corner. Start 3 feet left of *Wye're Less*.
Ascend a scoop with a flake to reach easier ground and a thin crack leading to the terrace. Climb rightwards across the wall towards a corner and move up into it (peg runner). Continue out rightwards onto the front of the buttress and exit easily to the top terrace. Abseil from the tree on the left.

**Wye Me 75 feet E4 6b (3.3.90)
A high-calibre route with an engaging sequence through the top bulges. Start immediately left of *Wye Not*. High in its grade.
Climb the wall past a bolt runner to easier ground (*in-situ* thread) and the terrace above. Attack the blunt rib using a sharp layaway (bolt runner) and then gain the bulge (bolt runner) from where hard moves (bolt runner) enable a flake to be grasped. Pull up (bolt runner) and go left to the arête to finish at a convenient tree. Abseil off.

Why Should I! 65 feet E5 6a/b (3.3.90)
This tackles the centre of the large, rounded buttress – some holds have come off and it is still a bit loose in places. Start below a shallow groove 6 feet right of a pair of more obvious grooves.
Climb the relatively easy shallow groove to the terrace. Above, a short problematic wall (bolt runner) gains the overhang (peg runner), from where harder moves on spaced holds (peg runner) lead into a slim groove (*Friend 2*). Exit left and go up to an abseil station.

*If So, Wye 65 feet E3 5c (3.3.90)
An attractive line with some splendid climbing. Hard for its grade. Small *Friends* useful. Start at the main shallow groove leading to the open corner above.

Follow the groove with small wires for protection to get to the terrace. Pull into the depression (bolt runner) and exit (bolt runner) into the corner; climb this on positive holds (small *Friends*) to an abseil station on the right.

All Ten Mill   65 feet   E5   6b   (8.7.90)
Some fine moves. Start at the next shallow groove-system by a stump 5 feet left of the previous route.
Climb the groove to a ledge and move up the left side of the tricky depression (peg runner). Continue up the right-hand side of the rounded buttress above on pinch-grips and undercuts (three bolt runners) to gain a flake and an abseil station further up.

★Save Your Kisses for Me   65 feet   E5   6b   (2.9.90)
Lovely clean climbing up the centre of the bulging buttress. Start 12 feet to the left of *All Ten Mill* and just right of *Kiss of Death*. Low in its grade.
Take a direct line up the fairly easy lower wall to reach a good flake crack and then the terrace. Climb a short corner (small wires) and gain the front of the buttress (bolt runner). Climb the buttress slightly rightwards on hidden holds (two bolt runners) and then follow a large flake to an abseil station.

The next three routes have a common start.

Kiss of Death   60 feet   E2   6a   (19.11.89)
Bold and sparsely-protected climbing but with a safe crux. Small wires essential. Start beneath a prominent flake at head height.
Climb past the flake on the lower wall and follow the square-cut groove above (*RPs*) to the terrace. Pull over the overlap (bolt runner) and continue up to better holds and poor protection in the base of the deep groove. Follow the groove fairly easily (difficult to protect) to reach a peg runner at the top; then step left and up to a good ledge and an abseil station.

★Goodbye Kiss   60 feet   E4   6a   (2.9.90)
Some unlikely and demanding technicalities up the slender buttress. Worth seeking out.
Follow *Kiss of Death* to the terrace, step left, and pull up the crack. Swing delicately right and proceed straight up (two bolt runners and a peg), utilizing the layaways to the full, to where more relaxed climbing gains an abseil station.

★★Perfect Kiss   60 feet   E2   5c   (26.11.89)
Sustained and rewarding. The crux bulge succumbs to a motivated approach.
Follow *Kiss of Death* easily to the terrace and then climb the thin crack to beneath an overlap (peg runner). Pull strenuously up on layaways (crux) into the upper groove, which does not let up until the abseil station is reached.

THE MAIN CLIFF – CONTINUATION
The final selection of routes all start from a high-level ledge and are best approached by climbing *Kiss of Death* to the terrace and traversing easily across. The routes at the extreme left-hand end may be reached by continuing along the vegetated path at the bottom of the cliff and clambering up the dirty slope, pulling very carefully onto the narrow end of the ledge.

The routes are described from **right to left**, starting at a cave (at the widest part of the ledge) located to the left of *Faithful Couple*.

Faithful Couple   30 feet   E3 5c   (3.3.90)
From the cave, traverse around to the right and climb the clean, white wall (bolt runner) to reach a thin crack; continue up to an abseil station.

Slave to the Cave   25 feet   E2 6a   (13.10.90)
Pull steeply out of the right side of the cave to clip a bolt runner (first crux); then make some butch moves (second crux) to grasp better holds above. Follow the crack (*in-situ* thread) to a tree with a sling. Abseil off.

Which Poison?   30 feet   E3 5c †   (13.10.90)
Climb the wall 10 feet to the left of the cave, just right of a prominent flake, via a thin crack and slight groove to a peg belay. Abseil off.

What Presence?   30 feet   E4 6b   (16.9.90)
Short but stressful. Start 10 feet to the left of *Which Poison?*
Climb the wall boldly (*RP* protection) and make a gripping, long reach to clip a bolt runner. Hard moves past the bolt gain poor holds in the shallow groove and a bolt belay. Abseil off.

No Chance   25 feet   E3 6a   (13.10.90)
An amenable little pitch with reasonable protection. Worth doing. Start by a tree at the left-hand end of the main part of the ledge.
Make some technical moves (peg runner) to gain a short groove (*RPs*) and then climb directly up the wall above (peg runner) to a bolt belay. Abseil off.

Some Chance   25 feet   E4 6b   (13.10.90)
A good sequence. At the bottom of its grade.
Pull out left from *Last Chance* via a flake to a bolt runner; then move up on a pinch (bolt runner) and make some desperate moves (*Rock 4*) to grasp jugs. Bolt belay to abseil off.

The next route starts 15 feet down to the left below a step in the terrace. Stay roped up to get across the awkward step.

★Sausage Dog   45 feet   E3 5c †   (16.9.90)
Quite good and quite bold. Start by a tree-stump.
Climb straight up via a slim groove to reach a shallow groove and crack

(*Friends*) leading to an abseil station.

Pocket Tarantula   45 feet   E2 5c †   (13.10.90)
Follow *Sausage Dog* for 10 feet and then climb the slabby wall to the left
on good holds until tricky moves lead rightwards to an abseil station.

The terrace now narrows, and this necessitates care in moving about. The
following routes are more easily reached from the vegetated lower path.

Goebbels, Moseley, God, and Ingrams   30 feet   E4 5c †(13.10.90)
A bold route – serious. Start just left of a large tree.
Pull over the overhang on good holds and make difficult and committing
moves to gain a crack leading to an abseil station above.

★There You Go Again   30 feet   E4 6a F6c+   (13.10.90)
By far the best pitch in this vicinity. Low in its grade. Start to the left of the
tree.
Climb the centre of the fine wall, passing two bolt runners to reach a small
overhang and *in-situ* thread runner. Pull straight over to an abseil station.

Snake Flake   30 feet   E2 5c   (13.10.90)
Start to the left of *There You Go Again*.
Climb the prominent flake boldly to reach a break at its end; then step
right and make some difficult moves to the abseil station.

At the extreme left-hand end of the terrace wall lies a large, open
scoop/groove. The final two routes start from a poor belay at a small,
contorted oak at the bottom left-hand side.

Free the Radicals   30 feet   E3 5b †   (13.10.90)
An awful (and deadly!) little number. Trend rightwards up the wall (bold) to
reach a small ledge (*Friend 1*). Here, difficult moves left to stand up on a
hand-ledge lead to an abseil station.

★Mouchette   30 feet   E3 6a   (13.10.90)
Excellent 'macho' climbing.
Move up above the sapling to a break (*Friends*); then step left to a
shattered crack-system (*in-situ* thread). Move up to a large hole decorated
with two *in-situ* threads, whereupon steep thuggery on hidden holds leads
past a second hole in the bulges to an abseil station.

Tintern Quarry

INTRODUCTION

Tintern Quarry lies on the east bank of the river Wye about two miles upstream from Wintour's Leap. The upper walls can be glimpsed from the main Chepstow to Tintern road but the huge scale of the place is not apparent until viewed from close quarters.

The Quarry has been cut far back and deep into the steep sides of the Wye Valley gorge. From the sunken floor to the back of the east wall the limestone towers over 500 feet. Viewed from above, the Quarry is roughly triangular and is some 900 feet across.

It might appear surprising that such a large and obvious crag should have remained neglected for so long. There may have been uncertainty amongst casual visitors regarding the access situation but for the Wye Valley's main activists it was the considerable work and uncertain returns that dissuaded them from taking time off from the easier pickings to be found elsewhere. Anyone aspiring to create routes here should be aware that the process can be prodigiously time consuming. This is not the land of the on-sight lead!

Of necessity, the majority of the climbs here are either entirely bolt protected (good news for sport climbing enthusiasts) or make substantial use of bolts for protection. In this respect Tintern Quarry is unique in the Wye Valley, offering as it does the opportunity to do big pitches (on sectors like the Triassic and Jurassic Walls) with just a rack of quick-draws and perhaps the occasional *Friend* or nut.

A large proportion of the rock is blatantly unstable, but owing to the size of the Quarry there remains a considerable area to interest the climber. The mixture of good and very bad rock juxtaposed in a spectacular manner gives the secluded setting of Tintern a distinctive atmosphere. On a calm day, voices carry easily across the Quarry, somehow heightening the atmosphere, especially when you are perched high up on one of its retaining walls.

The Quarry is divided by several horizontal access terraces and the height of the intervening walls varies between 30 and 150 feet. There is something to suit most tastes – classic crack- and corner-lines, finely situated arêtes, delicate wall-climbing and, of course, some big single-pitch routes.

As is the case with certain other recent discoveries, no formal permission has been sought to climb here and climbers should remain as discreet as possible in their comings and goings. Despite full-time activity throughout the summer of 1993 and sporadic visits since, no opposition has been encountered to date.

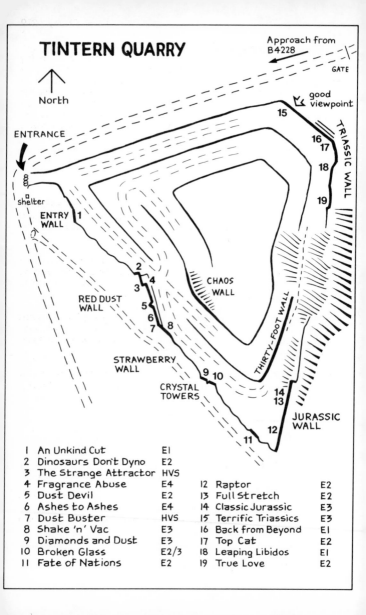

TINTERN QUARRY

↑ North

Approach from B4228

GATE

good viewpoint

ENTRANCE

shelter

ENTRY WALL

RED DUST WALL

CHAOS WALL

TRIASSIC WALL

THIRTY-FOOT WALL

STRAWBERRY WALL

CRYSTAL TOWERS

JURASSIC WALL

1	An Unkind Cut	E1
2	Dinosaurs Don't Dyno	E2
3	The Strange Attractor	HVS
4	Fragrance Abuse	E4
5	Dust Devil	E2
6	Ashes to Ashes	E4
7	Dust Buster	HVS
8	Shake 'n' Vac	E3
9	Diamonds and Dust	E3
10	Broken Glass	E2/3
11	Fate of Nations	E2

12	Raptor	E2
13	Full Stretch	E2
14	Classic Jurassic	E3
15	Terrific Triassics	E3
16	Back from Beyond	E1
17	Top Cat	E2
18	Leaping Libidos	E1
19	True Love	E2

The owners have, however, obtained planning permission (early '94 ?) to restart quarrying here. Although this may eventually mean an end to climbing activities, certain obstacles stand in the way of the owners. In particular, the permission has been granted on the condition that the rock be extracted via the railway tunnel which serves the lower quarry. It is believed that making this serviceable will be a costly business and that this may not happen for an unspecified number of years. Following the granting of planning permission, the Quarry was 'mothballed', a wire fence appeared around its perimeter, and the entrance was loosely blocked. This fence should not be disturbed. Meanwhile, the owners would almost certainly not appreciate the attention of climbers and, if you are requested to leave, you are asked to do so as respectfully as possible.

APPROACH

Pass by the green steel gate (page 13) and follow the straight track gently downhill until the Quarry opens out on your left. From this standpoint (step through the fence) a panoramic view of the Quarry is available and it is worthwhile pausing to take stock of the general layout.

Directly beneath the viewpoint is Triassic Wall. At its top are a mound of scree topped by some large boulders, and several embedded steel posts. The wall occupies a large area of rock some 130 feet high and extending 150 feet to your left (south) until obstructed by a large scree slope.

On the opposite side of the Quarry lies the distinctive jutting prow of the Red Dust Wall. This wall is split at one-third height by a small terrace which gives access to the numerous routes now in place on the main upper walls and arêtes. The huge slanting crackline of *Dust Devil* is clearly visible.

Over to the right of the Red Dust Wall is a 60-foot-high wall which contains a few routes and which is the first feature on the right after entering the Quarry. This is the Entry Wall.

To the left of the Red Dust Wall is Strawberry Wall, (so named because of the carpeting of alpine strawberries which cover the access road at its top). This wall is fairly broken and currently sports only one impoverished route.

Further left, the sandy-coloured and quartz-adorned Crystal Towers can be seen. Continuing leftwards, the rock is very broken and offers little potential.

Near the left end of the wall is a lighter-coloured stripe of rock which provides the large single pitch of *Fate of Nations*. The wall terminates in a massive and crumbling corner, at the top of which are two steel posts and a connecting rail.

Adjacent to the huge crumbling corner and facing west is the 150-foot-high, massive and continuous grey-coloured Jurassic Wall. Below Jurassic Wall is a short but good-quality tier (Thirty-Foot Wall) where a few short problem pitches have been created with relatively brief efforts.

Directly below the Red Dust Wall the track forks to give access to the lower tiers. Immediately beneath the fork is another shorter tier of a reddish colour and known as Chaos Wall, the deepest in the Quarry.

To enter the Quarry, continue down the approach road to where a track doubles back to the left. Step over some blocks and through the fence and enter the Quarry at its north-western corner.

Routes are described from **right to left** (the normal direction of approach) unless otherwise stated.

ENTRY WALL
On entering the Quarry, the path curves around to the right beneath a crumbling buttress. After some 150 feet the quality of the rock improves considerably offering short, technical climbs on a reddish-coloured steep wall which is split by a narrow ledge at half height.

An Unkind Cut   60 feet   E1   5b/c   F6a+   (8.6.94)
A somewhat dull pitch and one that sees more traffic than its worth warrants. Start beneath the obvious clean wall situated on the right after the entrance to the Quarry. Five bolt runners.
Move up to a ledge and follow the diagonal corner-crack up rightwards to a useful large *Friend* slot protecting an awkward mantel onto a large, cleaned ledge. Climb the slab above to a narrow crevassed ledge (optional medium wires) and pull directly up the wall and bulge above. Hand-traverse left a couple of moves to reach a double-bolt abseil station.

Dispossessed   55 feet   E3   6a   (23.7.93)
A surprisingly tough proposition. Start as for *An Unkind Cut*.
Move up to a ledge (bolt runner) and then climb straight up past a second bolt runner to reach a large sapling (a welcome rest and some reasonable wires). Pull steeply up leftwards and tackle the tricky wall above (sustained) past two peg runners until a move right gains a double-bolt abseil station shared with the previous route.

RED DUST WALL
The enormous and striking reddish/orange-coloured wall which dominates the centre of the western side of the Quarry. The wall is split at one-third height by a terrace which has been cleaned to provide access to its more worthy upper tier. The climbing here is characterized by powerful crack- and corner-lines, and also sports two exposed arêtes.

The main features as one approaches are the unmistakable prow climbed by *Fragrance Abuse*; while immediately to is right lies the right-angled vertical corner taken by *The Strange Attractor*. As one comes around underneath the prow, the wall is dominated by the rising, large stepped crack of *Dust Devil* emerging from the back of the wall's central cavity, while to its left a bare wall peppered with a line of bolts is the backdrop for *Ashes to Ashes*. At the left end the steep, pencil-straight crack is *Sauropods* along with its accompanying corner *Dust Buster*.

The first six routes all start from a twin 8mm bolt belay at the far right-hand end of the terrace. The belay is located at the foot of the prominent arête that is climbed by *Dinosaurs Don't Dyno*. Access to this belay (and its neighbouring climbs on the terrace) is via an initial scruffy 30-foot wall with four bolts (grade about Severe).

For the other routes on the Red Dust Wall (*Man in Tears* across to *Shake 'n' Vac*), approach via the first pitch of *Dust Devil* or by abseil from the big trees atop *Ashes to Ashes*. (Note: to reach the top of the wall continue past the Quarry entrance, step over a mound, and walk up the wide diagonal track to reach the cliff edge; then cut back left).

All routes start from the terrace and are described from **right to left.**

Chossticks 70 feet Hard Very Severe 5a † (16.5.94)
Bold climbing up the split crackline at the extreme right-hand end of the Red Dust Wall.
From the bolt belay at the start of *Dynosaurs Don't Dyno*, move up right past a drilled peg. Continue up and keep trending right over ledges to the base of a large pillar. Climb up carefully to the start of the wiggly crackline. Layback and bridge up the cracks, with more difficulty towards the top. Hand-traverse left past a bolt runner to the double *Eco-bolt* abseil station on the arête of *Dinosaurs Don't Dyno*.

Megabyte 60 feet Hard Very Severe 5b † (16.5.94)
Carry hexes for this one! A nice traditional route, with good moves up the top wall.
From the bolt belay at the start of *Dynosaurs Don't Dyno*, move up right past a drilled peg. Continue up and keep trending right over ledges to the base of a large thigh-deep crackline. Climb the crack, awkwardly at first, with more delicate climbing towards the top. Hand-traverse left to the double *Eco-bolt* abseil station on the arête of *Dinosaurs Don't Dyno*.

Bad News for Druids 60 feet Hard Very Severe 5b † (16.5.94)
Unusually satisfying crack-climbing in good positions. Well protected.
From the bolt belay at the start of *Dynosaurs Don't Dyno* move up right past a drilled peg. Climb up into the corner with a capping roof and make exciting moves (good small wires) over this to a superb crack just right of the arête. Follow the crack to the double *Eco-bolt* abseil station shared with *Dinosaurs Don't Dyno*.

★Dinosaurs Don't Dyno   60 feet   E2   5b   F6a+   (7.7.93)
An airy outing up the detached fretwork of blocks that comprise the arête
at the right-hand end of the Red Dust Wall. Start at a double-bolt belay at
the far right-hand end of the terrace. Eight bolt runners; two peg runners.
Move up rightwards a bit and then back left until underneath a jutting
overhang that forms the base of the arête. Ease up to good holds and
heave decisively to jugs and easy ground above. Continue up the stacked
block arête to a drilled-peg runner and the start of some more meaty
climbing. Surmount the bulge above and savour the fine position up the
edge of the top arête past an unnecessary drilled peg to reach an *Eco-bolt*
abseil station.

Boltisaurus   60 feet   E1   5b   (7.7.93)
A 'traditional' crack-climb taking the curving crack- and corner-line formed
by the left side of the stacked block arête of *Dinosaurs Don't Dyno*. Start in
the centre of the buttress at the right end of the Red Dust Wall.
Climb straight up (bolt runner) until it is possible to move across rightwards
to gain the crack and groove which is followed with some semi-layback
moves to a small roof and bolt runner. Romp over the roof and follow the
layback-crack to the top. Double *Eco-bolt* abseil on the right as for
Dinosaurs Don't Dyno.

★Pocketful of Kryptonite   60 feet   E1   5b   F6a   (22.7.93)
A good pitch, well protected, but no push-over at its grade. By far the best
of the easier routes on the crag. Start in the centre of the buttress at the
right end of the Red Dust Wall (as for *Boltisaurus*).
Follow the central crackline up the middle of the wall (five bolt runners –
the timid will also find small wire placements); then exercise your arms
swinging over the steep bulge above using large pockets, passing a further
two bolt runners and an *in-situ* thread. Pull up (bolt runner on the left) to
the break and then step left to the peg and *Eco-bolt* abseil station of
Ammonite.

Ammonite   60 feet   E2   5c   F6b   (22.7.93)
This takes a very tight eliminate line between the big corner of *The Strange
Attractor* and the centre-line of *Pocketful of Kryptonite*. Seven bolt runners.
Climb up rightwards to gain the central line of *Pocketful of Kryptonite*; then
break left and pursue a constrained line up the edge of the buttress to
where some delicate and dynamic final moves lead directly to a peg and
Eco-bolt abseil station.

The Strange Attractor   60 feet   Hard Very Severe   5a   †   (31.7.94)
The unmistakable vertical corner provides a powerful yet dusty line that
succumbs awkwardly to the thuggish, yet elegantly to those who can open
their legs. Quality, protection, and enjoyment all improve with height.
Climb up to ledges (bolt runner on the right on *Ammonite*, then a *Friend*
and wires) until some bridging passes some flake cracks (good holds on

the right, peg runner on the left) to gain the corner proper. Follow the corner past various nut placements, an *in-situ* thread runner, and five of the bolts on *Ammonite*. Peg and *Eco-bolt* abseil station.

Fragrance Abuse   80 feet   E4   6b   (30.6.93)
The dominating prow of the wall provides a compulsive and rewarding outing marred only by the poor rock on the crux, and the need to leave a rope at the top. Start on the terrace at the foot of the big arête.
Climb the arête, passing a bolt runner, to a good hand-ledge and a second bolt runner. Ease up over the bulge above on its right-hand side (third bolt runner) and make a hard move to poor holds and a drilled-peg runner (with *in-situ* sling). A small, blind layaway on the left side of the arête eases the situation, whereupon better holds above permit moves right to a comfy ledge. Follow the crackline (peg runner) on continually surprising holds (*Friends* and wires) until near the top (peg runner), where a swing left onto the arête brings the airy finishing jugs within grasp. From the ledge atop the arête, belay on a rope preplaced on the lone tree above (take care to place the rope over the front of the arête). Alternatively, in keeping with the first ascent experience, pull up *leftwards*, carefully, using the tree roots (sling runners).

★**Man in Tears**   60 feet   E6   6b   F7b+   (28.8.94)
A sustained pitch that tackles the stunning, leaning crack. Start at the back of the terrace next to a large block. Five bolt runners.
Make some steep opening moves (good wire runner) to poor holds, and then a difficult pull to better handholds. Move left and up to a hidden hold and continue to a shake-out jug beneath the roof. With a powerful reach, grasp the first of a series of shallow finger-jams which lead tenuously up the crack (wires possible) to a welcome rest in a scoop and the abseil station just above.

Dust Devil   110 feet   E2   (6.93)
The impressive deep crack and overhangs in the centre of the upper tier. The first route on the Red Dust Wall. Start below the main crack at the right-hand side of a triangular slab of rock which points to the terrace. The second pitch is well protected with mainly large nuts and hexes. The rock, although still dusty, is sound and will improve further with traffic.
1   30 feet   5a. Climb the right-hand side of the triangle until a delicate move across leftwards gains a short crack which leads to the cleaned and spacious terrace. Block and nut belays. A somewhat disconcerting little pitch.
2   80 feet   5b. Follow the obvious corner-crack strenuously over several overhangs to a cramped position under the final roof. Make determined moves to bridge out beneath this and take it direct to good jugs up the final short wall. Tree belay beyond.

★★Ashes to Ashes   80 feet   E4 6a F6c+   (5.9.93)
An excellent, enticing pitch. Continually interesting and on surprisingly
good holds throughout. Double ropes needed. Start on the terrace at a
bolt and nut belay at the foot of a crack-system in the left arête of *Dust
Devil*. Nine bolt runners.
Step left and climb directly up into a short right-facing corner; then swing
out left to grab the end of a good handrail. Hand-traverse left a couple of
moves to where a delicate mantel up left regains balance, harmony, and a
bolt runner just above. Swing steeply back right to a good jug, stand up
with difficulty and then pull up and step right. Some good jugs now lead
back horizontally left, whereupon a final bulge and short wall provide a
fitting finale. Cleaned ledges permit an easy top-out to substantial tree
belays.

★Sauropods   60 feet   E3 5c   (31.7.93)
The prominent, vertical crackline at the left end of the Red Dust Wall. Start
as for *Dust Buster*.
Climb the corner of *Dust Buster* for 15 feet until it is possible to step right to
the base of the steep crackline. Follow this with increasing difficulty past
several peg runners, using small holds on the wall to supplement the crack,
to an excellent pocket and make a hard finishing-move to the top. Belay
on trees.

Dust Buster   60 feet   Hard Very Severe 5b   (23.6.93)
This takes the fine corner-crack. From the terrace (peg and nut belay),
climb the corner-crack with surprising subtlety past the final overhang to a
difficult finishing-mantel onto a cleaned ledge. Tree belays.

★Shake 'n' Vac   50 feet   E3 6a F6c   (24.6.93)
This route takes the slab of clean rock at the extreme left-hand end of the
Red Dust Wall terrace. Absorbing technical climbing on predominantly
good rock. Belay as for *Dust Buster* (peg and nuts) at the foot of the corner.
Move up leftwards until behind an elder bush; then climb directly up the
wall on small positive holds (avoiding the dirty crack on the left). Four
drilled pegs protect. Tree belay behind.

STRAWBERRY WALL
This is the section of dark rock to the left of the Red Dust Wall which extends
leftwards until bounded by The Crystal Towers.

Footloose   90 feet   Hard Very Severe 5a   (19.6.93)
The first route in the Quarry. Start 20 feet right of The Crystal Towers below
an obvious large recess leading to an overhang at 30 feet. The route is
good in its upper half but the left-hand side of the recess, despite vigorous
cleaning, has refused to stabilize and should be treated with some care.
Climb the left side of the recess, and then the pillar on the left until it is
possible to step across right to the lip of the overhang (peg runner). Move

Violation of Trust (E2) Left-Hand Escarpment, Ban-y-gor
Climber: Matthew Bond   Photo: Bond col.

Pussyfoot (E4) Triassic Wall, Tintern Quarry
Climber: Jeremy Hutchings   Photo: Martyn Cattermole

up to a ledge and take the wall above direct (peg runner) to gain a large ledge before the final deep V-groove. Climb this to finish. Belay on the fenceposts and bushes behind.

THE CRYSTAL TOWERS

These are the prominent, twin pillars at the left end of The Strawberry Wall characterized by a random veneer of quartz intrusions. The lightly-coloured rock on the lower half of the pillars has a somewhat sandy texture.

★Diamonds and Dust   70 feet   E3 5c F6b+   (7.8.93)

A difficult, sustained and technical pitch, worth doing despite its poorish start. Begin behind a tree at a thin crack in the right-hand pillar.
Climb the awkward crack (easing with height) past two bolt runners to a good rest and optional medium wires. Step up rightwards (bolt runner) and make some tricky moves to get established on the wall above (bolt runner). Proceed with continuing interest up the centre of the pillar, passing a further three bolt runners. Pull over the top onto easy ground and fencepost belays behind.

★Broken Glass   75 feet   E2/3 5c   (29.6.93)

An intricate and quite varied route with a hard first part, then a more enjoyable, open top section. Start at the base of a vague crackline leading to an obvious overhang in the centre of the left-hand pillar.
Make a stiff move to get started (small wires) and reach a large jug and drilled peg runner (nut-slot on the left). Some hard moves (crux) are required to gain a good nut crack and a rest beneath the prominent overhang. Pull up carefully to and around the right-hand end of the overhang (peg runner, and gear just above); then climb up rightwards (drilled-peg runner) to a dusty hand-crack where the climbing eases. Step up and back left to a peg and a bolt runner; then follow the centre of the face above past a final peg runner to an easy finish. Belay behind on the fenceposts.

JURASSIC WALL

This is the impressive (150-foot-high) west-facing wall of dark-coloured rock to the left of the massive crumbling corner. The lower half is dark and compact; this is where the technical difficulties are concentrated. The upper half is sandy-coloured and is crossed by occasional breaks of more friable rock. The top section gives relatively easy but spectacular access to the service road at the top of the wall.
The first route is not on the Jurassic Wall itself but about 30 feet to the right of the massive crumbling corner on a tapering pillar of whitish-coloured rock with a distinctive square of quartz at 25 feet. The pillar is bounded by rubbish-filled cracks on both sides.

Fate of Nations   150 feet   E2 5b   (4.9.93)

A much better route than appearances might suggest, but nonetheless best suited to members of the Tintern Appreciation Society! After a shattered start, the rock gradually improves (honest!).

Climb tentatively past two bolt runners, and reach awkwardly up right to the base of a short finger-crack (peg runner). Follow the crack (good wires) to its end (peg runner) and make a difficult move up left to the base of a hanging pillar (bolt runner). From the top of the pillar, step up to a large pocket; then move out left (bolt runner) to a shallow groove on the left side of the tower. Climb on up (bolt runner) to more positive holds from where it is possible to follow the centre of the tower past five bolt runners until below the top roof. Place nuts in the break and pull over rightwards to jugs above; then follow the short final groove easily to an exit onto the top path. Belay on the fenceposts.

★★**Raptor**   130 feet   E2 5c F6b   (31.8.93)
Well protected and with the hardest climbing low down. At the top of its grade. Start at the base of a shallow, right-facing groove 15 feet left of the huge crumbling corner. Ten bolt runners.

Climb the groove and exit onto a sloping ledge. Make some thin moves (crux) to gain an obvious large pocket; then follow a line of smaller pockets until it is possible to swing left and surmount a bulge to gain easier ground at the base of a short, left-facing groove. Climb the groove (optional small and medium wires) and step up onto the top of a large block. Pull over the overlap above and continue to a sandy-coloured scoop. Climb the right wall of the scoop passing a bolt runner over on the left to reach a series of larger ledges and bands of shale. Step left to a double *Eco-bolt* abseil station.

★**Full Stretch**   130 feet   E2 5b/c F6b   (5.9.93)
Mostly amenable climbing with a short hard section on the bulging pillar at two-thirds height. Start on the leftward-rising mound of scree at a thin vertical break 6 feet to the left of a semi-circular roof at 30 feet. Fourteen bolt runners; one thread runner.

Follow the thin crack for 15 feet until a step right starts a walk up the large cleaned flake. At the end of the flake, pull up leftwards past an *in-situ* thread to ledges. Continue easily to the right-hand end of a good ledge beneath the conspicuous arête (taken by *Classic Jurassic*). Now climb up rightwards to a rest (long sling required on the bolt over on the right) and tackle the imposing bulging pillar (crux). From a roomy ledge atop the pillar, pull up rightwards and follow easy ground to a change in the strata. Clip a bolt runner and step left to a double *Eco-bolt* abseil station perched on the lip of an overlap.

★**Classic Jurassic**   130 feet   E3 5c F6b+   (5.9.93)
This climbs the lower half of *Full Stretch* before launching up the prominent arête and headwall above. Fourteen bolt runners; one thread runner.

Follow *Full Stretch* until below the arête. Tackle the arête: its left side gives tenuous and thoughtful moves to grasp a well-hidden hole with a tricky mantel to finish; alternatively the difficulties may be avoided by much easier climbing in the scoop on the right side of the arête. Continue easily and then trend slightly left to reach a hand-ledge beneath the headwall. Make a difficult move up and continue to reach a double *Eco-bolt* abseil station shared with *Full Stretch*.

THIRTY-FOOT WALL
This wall takes the short tier below Jurassic Wall and contains a number of bolt-protected problem pitches. At the extreme right end of the wall is a scree-slope. Some 45 feet left of this is a tottering buttress comprising large, shattered blocks with a jutting and shattered nose at two-thirds height. The first route starts on the 12-foot-wide, clean black wall just to the left of this, by a small elder.

Dinomania 30 feet E1 5b F6a (7.9.93)
Start in the centre of the clean black wall by a faint grey groove.
Move up the wall past three bolt runners to a bulge. Clip a bolt runner on the lip of the bulge before making a final mantelshelf onto the top. Exit carefully onto the road above. Block belay on the right.

To the left of the clean wall is a shattered buttress. The next route is to the left of this and takes a grey recess with a crack and corner on its right and a series of overhangs stepping in from the left.

Dinofever 30 feet E1 5b F6a (7.9.93)
Quite hard for its grade. Start at the left side of the recess.
Move up to a bolt runner (it is also possible to place nuts in the crack up on the left). Move back to the centre and go up past a bolt runner to a roof. Clip the bolt runner above the roof and take the roof direct to the short wall (bolt runner on right); finish very carefully onto the road. Poor belays.

Sixty feet further on is an easy-angled, protruding buttress (that appears to be slipping away from the face). Immediately left of this is a slabby wall of decent rock.

Just a Mo 30 feet Very Severe 5a FV (16.6.96)
Some tricky moves to pass the last bolt runner; the easier left-hand finish may prove tempting. Start at the base of a short undercut arête.
Step right and climb on good holds to get established on the slab above. Continue up (just left of the next three bolts) and exit direct onto the terrace.

The last route here is located on an innocuous-looking clean slab at the extreme left-hand end of the tier just prior to the huge scree slope that separates the Thirty-Foot Wall from the Triassic Wall.

Déja Vu   30 feet   E2   6a   F6b+   (16.6.96)
A very short but hard piece of slab-climbing. The proverbial technical tit-bit.
Scramble up the slab and clip the fourth bolt runner. Either make a difficult
move directly up the centre or go for the softer option using holds out left.
Exit leftwards up, over, and onto the terrace above.

TRIASSIC WALL

This is the area which is immediately below the viewpoint on the main
approach path and which extends for about 150 feet until terminated by a
massive scree-slope.

On entering the Quarry, proceed directly ahead along a wide terrace to where
the rockface makes a right-angled turn. The dominating feature here, up
above you, is a steep and strangely-featured orange wall – The Lunar
Landscape, offering *Terrific Triassics* and *Supersaurus I, II, and III* up its left and
right flank respectively.

To the right of The Lunar Landscape, the full height of the cliff is split into three
equal-sized tiers by two rubble-strewn terraces; there is a single clean line just
right of centre – *Back from Beyond*.

To the right again, the Triassic Wall now forms a poorly-defined yet dominating
buttress. In its middle, and starting from above mid height, is a distinctive
tower on the left side of a compact grey sheet that is itself bounded by a
prominent left-facing, stepped corner formed by a massive flake.

Leaping Libidos climbs straight up to and on top of this tower before it tackles
a short but intimidating arête above; the compact sheet provides the setting
for this sector's hardest route, *Pussyfoot*, while the stepped corner is the line
of *Quip-U for Leisure*. All three routes share an abseil station on the lip of the
wall (atop *Pussyfoot*).

Further right, the Triassic Wall ends at a large scree slope; scrambling across
this brings you to the left end of the Thirty-Foot Wall.

The first route, *Terrific Triassics*, begins next to the rubbly right-angled corner
and takes a fairly straight line up to and through the white bulges in the top
left-hand corner of The Lunar Landscape.

Routes on this wall are described from **left to right**.

Terrific Triassics   120 feet   E3   F6b, F6c   (16.8.93)
An innocuous-looking but troublesome and tiring start is followed by very
easy climbing until one is left grappling with the top bulge on the second
pitch. Difficult for those of lesser reach. Start at the extreme left-hand side
of the wall, avoiding the obvious choss.
1 75 feet 5c. Make hard moves up the bulging wall for 12 feet to a good

hold by the second bolt runner. Move up on this good hold to a square niche (bolt runner) capped by a small roof. Break out up and right onto the arête (bolt runner on left). Easier moves up the sloping arête past two bolt runners lead to a ledge. Clip the bolt runner on the left and climb the corner past a further bolt runner to another ledge. Climb the wall above past a final bolt runner and exit onto the main ledge. Double 8mm bolt belay.

2 45 feet 6a. Climb up steep ledges past two bolt runners to reach a pair of bolt runners beneath the final sandy bulge. Step up (bolt runner) and make some hard strenuous moves (bolt runner off-line on the left) straight up to grasp the ledge above (bolt runner). Double 8mm bolt belay. Do not abseil from the linking chain; instead thread the bolts with spare tape and abseil appropriately.

The right-hand flank of The Lunar Landscape has been completely carpeted with bolts to produce three poor isolated pitches only one of which may repay the effort in reaching it. Although they are crammed together, each pitch has its own twin 8mm bolt belay linked with a chain. Do not abseil from these chains; instead traverse off to the right and scramble over the top to block belays. All three pitches start from the same double 8mm bolt belay where the orange rock merges into the grey. Only quick-draws are required for these routes.

Choose one of the three possible approaches outlined below (any of which will take longer than doing the routes!):

1. Climb the first pitch of *Terrific Triassics* (judicious use of aid will neuter any difficulty) and then traverse easily across beneath The Lunar Landscape (bolt runner).

2. Abseil from blocks atop the wall, re-belaying at one of the bolt belays on the way down.

3. Climb the first two-thirds of *Back from Beyond* and traverse left across the gravel slope (bolt runner).

Supersaurus I 30 feet E2 5b F6a+ †   (19.9.93)
The best of this bunch. Climb straight up above the belay, slightly left at first, then back right to a ledge and double-bolt belay. Seven bolt runners – no runouts here! Exit to the right.

Supersaurus II 30 feet Hard Very Severe 5b FV+   (19.9.93)
Step 3 feet to the right of the belay and climb up the edge of a tiny grey slab before following a constrained line up the steeper orange rock to a ledge and double-bolt belay. Six bolt runners – an extremely safe pitch. Exit to the right.

Supersaurus III 35 feet Very Severe 5a/b FV   (19.9.93)
Step 3 feet to the right of the belay, climb easily up the centre of the tiny grey slab, and mantel onto a rectangular block. Make a single very difficult

move to better holds and grovel over to a double-bolt belay. Five bolt runners – wasted on a pointless piece of climbing. Scramble up to the right.

Back at ground-level, and standing next to the rubbly corner (down and left of The Lunar Landscape), walk 60 feet to the right beneath various choss to the first of two grooves. The first groove is climbed by *Top Cat* while *Leaping Libidos* starts immediately right of the second groove.

Back from Beyond   110 feet   E1   5b   F6a   (19.9.93/20.6.96)
Surprisingly clean and open climbing up three distinct tiers, each of which sports a single hard move. Somewhat spoilt by the need to scramble across two scree-covered terraces; worth doing nonetheless. Start 50 feet right of *Terrific Triassics* and 10 feet left of the opening groove of *Top Cat*. Climb the first tier past four bolt runners, continue up the easy-angled gravel, and climb the central (reddish) tier on spaced but positive edges past a further three bolt runners. Ascend the second gravel bank to the final tier (belay possible) and climb this immediately right of a line of five bolt runners (crux) to a final reachy clip of the double *Eco-bolt* abseil station at the top of the wall.

★Top Cat   120 feet   E2   5b   F6b   (16.8.93)
A good outing sadly marred by the rubbish on its first third, but thereafter continually interesting and absorbing. Start at the foot of an open groove. Twelve bolt runners.
Step up on loose material and pull into the groove. Move up leftwards onto a narrow ramp and scramble carefully over poor ground to the base of the steep wall/rib (hidden bolt runner). Climb directly up the intimidating rock above until an awkward move diagonally leftwards enables a scoop to be entered. Pull up leftwards and make a delicate step back right; then finish up the corner above to reach a double *Eco-bolt* abseil station (and redundant chain anchor). Take an uncomfortable stance here; then either abseil off or step over the top to finish.

Between *Top Cat* and *Leaping Libidos* is a very distinctive line of bolts going up unappealing rock to the chimney that forms the left side of the prominent tower. From the top of the tower the bolts go left and finish up a steep, bare headwall. At the time of writing this line remains unclimbed…

★Leaping Libidos   120 feet   E1   FV, F6a+   (15.6.96)
A dramatic line that climbs up to the top of the eye-catching tower before harder and more testing climbing joins with the short upper arête. An excellent top section makes up for the poor quality of its initial easy half. Fairly high in its grade. Start 15 feet to the right of *Top Cat*.
1 70 feet   5a. Mantel onto the initial ledge, clip a high bolt runner, and step up, taking care with the loose material on the right. Move awkwardly back left and up to a second bolt runner before stepping out right and ascending gravel-strewn ledges to a third bolt runner at the base of a

clean slab. Climb the slab, and belay at the base of the tower utilizing the
two bolt runners above plus an optional *Friend* 1½ beneath the overlap.
2 50 feet 5b/c. Climb the wide crack formed by the right side of the
tower to an airy resting-ledge on its summit. Now for the crux: make some
cunning moves up a tiny corner past two bolt runners and cross the
overhang with difficulty to grab big jugs out right. Make a final heave to
attain another rest-ledge, a bolt runner, and a reduction in your heart-rate.
Follow the arête above past the final bolt runner to a clean-cut edge atop
the crag, and reach across to the right to a double *Eco-bolt* abseil station.
Fifty-metre ropes will permit the leader to be lowered directly to the ground.

★★**Pussyfoot** 120 feet E4 FV, F7a (15.6.96)

A choice pitch that forces an appealing line up the middle of the exposed
sheet on intricate small holds. [Photo p.225.]
1 70 feet 5a. *Leaping Libidos* pitch 1.
2 50 feet 6b. Step right from the belay; then pull up to and balance up
on a small ledge (with a bolt runner above). Difficult moves diagonally left
to a second bolt runner are followed by a long reach back right to a
positive edge below the third bolt runner. Now climb straight up and
fractionally right (the crux) and grasp some welcome holds by the fourth
bolt where a final tricky move allows you to stand in balance at last. It's in
the bag! – just continue up past a final bolt runner into a slight scoop and
span out left to a double *Eco-bolt* abseil station. Fifty-metre ropes will
permit the leader to be lowered directly to the ground.

★**Quip-U for Leisure** 150 feet E3 (15.6.93)

The left-facing, stepped corner-line provides a strong challange and
necessitates a forceful approach. Get stuck in! Double ropes useful.
1 90 feet 5a. Follow *Leaping Libidos* to the base of its tower; then
traverse 20 feet carefully to the right (underneath *Pussyfoot*) to a double
8mm bolt belay on an excavated ledge at the base of the massive flake.
2 60 feet 6a. Move back left to the base of the wide dusty corner and
climb this (optional *Friends*) past two bolt runners to the jutting roof.
Undercling this to the left to meet a third bolt runner and layback
strenuously (*Friends* and wires) up the flake crackline to where the holds
disappear by a bolt runner on the arête. Climb directly up through the
blank bulge above (crux) and stretch thankfully for a flat jug. Clip a high
bolt runner on the right and traverse delicately left to a rest on *Pussyfoot*.
Continue straight up past a final bolt runner into a slight scoop and span
out left to a double *Eco-bolt* abseil station. Either move left and top out or
lower the leader to the belay on *Leaping Libidos*.

The corner of *Quip-U for Leisure* is formed by a massive flake. The right side
of this flake is less distinct (when viewed from below) but provides the climber
with a steep line of bucket edges taken with a firm grip by *True Love*, and which
escapes out right along a prominent ramp at the top.

True Love   150 feet   E2   (20.6.96)
An unusual, varied and worthwhile pitch with an airy and insecure finish.
1 90 feet 5a. Follow *Leaping Libidos* to the base of its tower; then
traverse 20 feet carefully to the right to a double 8mm bolt belay shared
with *Quip-U for Leisure.*
2 60 feet 5b. Pull up rightwards from the belay to stand on a small ledge
(bolt runner) and climb the steep jagged flake crack past a second bolt
runner with an awkward move to reach an undercut in the bulge above.
Step left and arrange additional protection before heaving over into the
scoop above (bolt runner). An unnervingly delicate step up onto the base
of the ramp is required to grab a jug up above from which it is possible to
clip a high bolt runner. With protection from this, pad gently up the
ramp-line for a disquieting reach (possible wire on the left) to grasp flat
jugs and the double *Eco-bolt* belay above. Abseil retreat.

CHAOS WALL
Below the Red Dust Wall, on the lower tier, is a somewhat scrappy-looking
wall which does contain some good sections for those with an eye for a line.
In the centre of the wall is a reddish area of rock, with a huge pile of chippings
at its base. In the centre of this section is an obvious broken and vertical crack.
This is *Chaos Crack.*

Chaos Crack   60 feet   Hard Very Severe 5a †   (10.7.93)
The obvious crackline with good natural protection.
From the top of the mound of chippings, move up to gain the crack and
climb it to a bulge. Make an awkward move over this and follow the crack
more directly to a good finishing-move up the final wall to the terrace.
Belay on a huge block.

Fractal   55 feet   E1 5b †   (27.7.93)
To the right of *Chaos Crack* is another crackline. Start at the right-hand side
of the reddish wall at a loose bay.
Climb into the bay and up left over loose but easy ground to a small pillar
(bolt runner). From the top of the pillar, follow the steep crack to the
overhang past bolt runners. A difficult move right leads to ledges. Awkward
moves up and left past a bolt runner lead to easier ground (peg runner)
and the top. Belay on a small block backed up with bushes beyond.

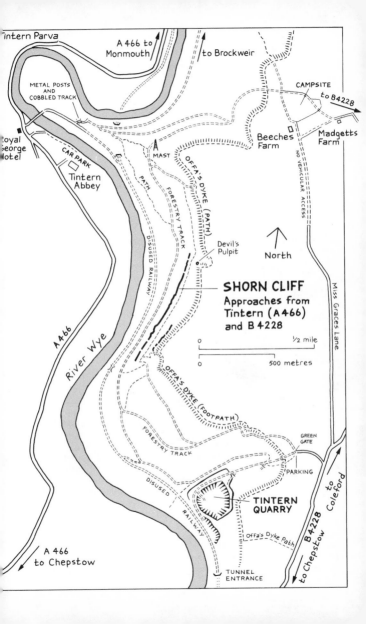

Shorn Cliff

INTRODUCTION

Shorn Cliff is situated in the most substantial wooded area on the east bank of the lower Wye. The woods themselves are rather drab and uninteresting, and the extensive leaf canopy in summer obscures the views except from a few vantage points (the upper sections of the climbs being fortunately amongst them). The network of Forestry tracks and public rights-of-way provides pleasant and easy approaches to this, the most remote crag in the guide, but the (mercifully short) paths up to the rocks and the one along the base are less appealing, and straying onto unpathed territory is invariably even worse. Things are at their best on a crisp winter's day when the vegetation is dormant and the impressive surroundings can be properly appreciated.

The crag provides an excellent selection of single-pitch, middle-grade (VS to E2) climbs, many of real quality, and just a few harder and easier ones. The rock is unquarried limestone with a greater variety of rock features than is commonly found in the Valley. The majority of the routes can be well protected naturally, but a number of pegs and threads and a few bolts are in place. Some of the shorter and more broken buttresses suffer from seepage in wet spells, especially in winter, but the larger slabby areas are usually climbable year round.

APPROACH

First, it is necessary to reach the central section of the main Forestry track that runs below the crag, and from which the rocks are only partially visible. This takes 20 to 30 minutes.

1a. From Tintern Abbey (see pages 12-13), walk upstream along the river bank and back to the road at the *George Hotel*. Then turn right, cross the footbridge onto the peninsula, and follow the level track ahead until a cobbled path protected by barriers rises from it on the left. This goes up a wooded ridge with remarkable views of the river on both sides (resulting from its tightest ox-bend). Soon, two forks are reached; keep right at both (following signs to The Devil's Pulpit). At a third fork a little further on there is a choice: the left-hand branch is the well-made tourist track which rises steeply up the left side of the ridge until it emerges at a multi-junction on the Forestry track – turn right along that to reach the paths up to the crag in about half a mile; the right-hand branch meanders along the right-hand side of the ridge before rising to meet the Forestry track about half-way. There is little to choose – probably the former is quicker in ascent and the latter in descent.

1b. From Tidenham Chase (see page 13), pass the barrier and keep to the wide track, which crosses Offa's Dyke path and later forks twice; always keep going ahead, left at the first fork, right at the second.

1c. From The Beeches campsite (page 13), pick up the track that runs from the gate, behind the toilet block, and down below the site; pass two gates/stiles

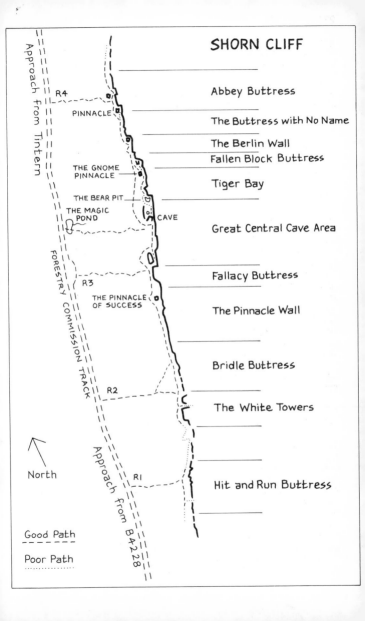

into the woods and follow the track, keeping ahead (left) at the fork just after a gully and stream are crossed, and ahead again at the multi-junction where the Tintern–Devil's Pulpit path crosses.

From the Forestry track, five paths, four of them clearly marked by *Forest Enterprise* for the rescue services, lead up to the rocks.

2a. R1, the first to be reached from the Tidenham Chase end, leads up to the right-hand end of Hit and Run Buttress.
2b. R2 divides half-way: the right fork finishes under the smaller (left-hand) of The White Towers; the left fork leads to the hooped tree against Bridle Buttress.
2c. R3 lands you between The Pinnacle Wall and Fallacy Buttress.
2d. R4, the best, makes straight for the obvious crackline of *Tigers Don't Cry* on Abbey Buttress.
2e. Between R3 and R4 (but nearer the former), another path can be used to reach The Great Central Cave Area.

A path of sorts runs along the base of the crag, with diversions to avoid Tiger Bay and the right-hand parts of The Great Central Cave Area. This is good at the left-hand end as far as Tiger Bay, but then deteriorates progressively; the final section, from The White Towers to Hit and Run Buttress, is awful – it is easier and quicker to descend R2 and reascend by R1.

DESCENTS
Apart from the repulsive possibilities mentioned in the sections below, there is little option but to abseil from the trees at or near the tops of the routes, and this practice has been universal. However, please read the section on trees in the General Introduction (page 17).

Beware of loose rock in the leaf litter at the cliff-edge.

ABBEY BUTTRESS
Marking the northward limit of Shorn Cliff, this is the first significant buttress seen from the Tintern approach track. From above, it is possible to scramble down the rocky slopes here, although the looseness of the terrain makes this unpleasant. The cliff is at first short, scrappy, very vegetated, and with no worthwhile climbs.

Take path R4 to reach the unmistakable white-stained crack of *Tigers Don't Cry*, 100 feet right from where the cliff disappears into the earth. Another feature is a squeeze-chimney (*Beeline*) some 20 feet left of *Tigers Don't Cry*. Thirty feet left again is a large cluster of trees close against the rock, with the groove-line of *Lazy L* just behind on the left.

Petit Mort   40 feet   E3 5c ‡   (4.87)
At the extreme left-hand end of the buttress, past a jungle of vegetation

and fallen trees, is a short arête and corner; this climb takes the
unprotected arête.
Start on the right, and at half height traverse around the arête and up the
face. Finish past vegetation to a tree.

On Reflection   35 feet   Very Severe 4c ‡   (25.3.90)
Vegetated. Start 20 feet left of the cluster of trees and climb the thin crack
on the left edge of the slab to the notch; traverse right at the top to finish at
a tree.

One-Way Glass   35 feet   E2 5c   (20.10.85)
Short and hardly worthwhile. Start at the centre of the triangular buttress,
just left of another clump of trees situated 5 feet left of the groove of *Lazy L*.
Climb straight up to a horizontal break at 12 feet (good wires), and then
make a difficult move up the shallow scoop to gain good holds at the base
of a short broken crack. Climb this to a tree.

Gorillas in the Garden   60 feet   E1 5b †   (25.5.96)
Bridge up the wall using the large forked tree. Climb the slab delicately
and climb up and right of a sapling. Step back left onto the arête and
follow it to the top. Finish rightwards to a large tree.

Lazy L   60 feet   Very Severe 4c   (2.11.85)
Start at the groove just left of the cluster of trees.
Follow the groove for 20 feet and then the left arête for 10 feet. Regain the
groove and climb it until a ledge on the left is reached; finish right.

A large thin flake just right of the cluster of trees close to the cliff gives a useful
marker for the next two routes. Above and slightly left of this flake is a groove
(*Wet Sunday*), while to the left there is an arête.

Edge Game   60 feet   Hard Very Severe 5a   (23.6.85)
The left arête of the groove. Start at the large thin flake below the groove.
Gain the flake, and then move left along it to the arête. Use several thin
cracks to start, and carry on up the same line, passing the top overhang
direct to a dirty finish.

Wet Sunday   60 feet   Very Severe 4b   (23.6.85)
Start as for *Edge Game*.
Gain the flake. Step left and climb up a steep wall to the base of the
groove. Easy climbing up the groove leads to a loose exit on the left.

Birth Canal   50 feet   E3 5b   (5.7.85)
For masochists only. Minimal protection. Twelve feet right of *Wet Sunday* is
a large block; start just left of this.
Climb easily up the wall. If feeling bold, make committing moves up to a
faint groove below a sapling; there is then a loose finish to a tree.

Gargoyle   40 feet   Severe   4b   (22.9.84)
Short, but a good route for novices; excellent protection.
Start below the large block 20 feet right of *Wet Sunday*, surmount the
block, and then climb a series of broken cracks to a tree.

Alta Vista   40 feet   Very Severe   4c   (25.5.96)
Start just right of the block under the *Gargoyle* cracklines.
Bridge up the corner to below the break. Reach up and layback the crack
for 10 feet. Continue up the crack to the tree.

★Party Piece   50 feet   E3   6a   (30.6.85)
Exciting climbing up the arête and wall left of the *Beeline* squeeze-chimney.
Climb boldly up left on red rock to a shattered crack (wires). Using positive
finger-jams and pockets, climb straight past a peg runner and then steeply
up the wall above (peg runner) to finish up the hanging arête on the right.

Beeline   50 feet   Very Severe   4c   (c.1975)
A pleasant route at the grade. Swarm up the squeeze-chimney to finish
past a chockstone.

Rumble in the Jungle   55 feet   Hard Very Severe   4c   (30.6.85)
Nice, and well protected. Start right of the chimney.
Climb awkwardly up into the square corner. Finish up the crack and easy
corner above the ledge.

★The Bone   60 feet   E1   5b   (15.7.84)
An invigorating route requiring concentration. The clean white wall right of
the chimney provides some quite technical moves. Start at the cracked wall
12 feet right of the chimney.
Climb straight up the wall to a small ledge with good protection (small
wires). Make several difficult moves up thin cracks to gain good
finishing-holds. Trend right, up towards a tree.

★Pooh Sticks   60 feet   E1   5b   (20.7.84)
This and *The Bone* make a nice matching pair! An enjoyable pitch up the
rib and wall, just right of *The Bone*. Start just left of the foot of the blunt rib.
Climb the rib until a reachy move gains a ledge at 15 feet. Climb up and
slightly leftwards to the wire-slots on *The Bone*. Finish up right to a tree.

A Bolt from the Blue   50 feet   E3   5c   (8.9.85)
An eliminate, with a dubious bolt for protection. Start just left of *Tigers
Don't Cry*.
Climb the thin, shallow groove before moving up and left on small holds
to the old bolt runner. From this, continue direct to a ledge. Finish up the
corner as for *Pooh Sticks*.

★Tigers Don't Cry   60 feet   Hard Very Severe 5b   (15.7.84)
This brilliant route deserves its Wye Valley classic status! The inspiring
straight crack gives a superb pitch with even better protection. Climb the
crack and groove above to the trees.

★Three Score Years and Ten   60 feet   E5 6b   (20.10.85)
The smooth wall right of *Tigers Don't Cry* provides a very bold and
intensely technical problem. Start 10 feet right of *Tigers Don't Cry*.
From the obvious undercut at 10 feet, step right (good wire in a pocket).
Make a dynamic move for the obvious jug up right. Swing back left and
climb the centre of the face to a large flake. Finish easily above this.

Acoustic   65 feet   Very Difficult   (8.9.84)
A deservedly popular route up the obvious central weakness. Start directly
below a corner at 40 feet, some 20 feet right of *Tigers Don't Cry*.
Climb up the corner via ledges (alternatively, take the short crack on the
left). Follow the corner-crack past a large jammed block at its top. Take the
broken groove past a tree and exit with care.

Intravenous Feeding   65 feet   Very Severe 4c   (16.9.84)
Enjoyable climbing up the wall and crack right of *Acoustic*.
Start as for that route and follow it to a ledge below the cracked wall to the
right. Climb this to a second ledge. Finish left of the large tree at the top.

The next two climbs start from an obvious layback flake at the right-hand side
of the buttress.

★Social Criticism   65 feet   E1 5b   (7.9.84)
Formerly an excellent climb, but the top overhang is now unstable.
Layback the large flake to the overhang. Climb up and step across with
difficulty into the V-groove. Climb this for 25 feet; then move right for 10
feet and follow a system of shallow cracked corners to the left-hand side of
a downward-pointing overhang. Turn this on the left with care, and finish
at the large tree.

★★Side Effects   65 feet   E1 5b   (9.9.84)
A delicate and bold pitch following the arête of the buttress.
Layback the flake to the cracked block, and then climb up and right into an
awkward niche under the overhang. Place good small wires blind on the
right, and climb the arête up to a resting-position. Continue up the arête,
placing gear creatively, until the trees are reached.

Right of *Side Effects* is a massive leaning pinnacle.

★Hydraulic Jump   60 feet   Very Severe 4c   (8.9.84)
Satisfying moves up the corner.
Scramble up behind the pinnacle to the base of the corner, and climb it

past some layback flakes to the top and a tree.

Brain Washed   60 feet   E4   6a   (5.9.85)
Not the most popular of routes at Shorn Cliff! Extremely bold. Start at the
foot of the left arête of the pinnacle.
Climb the pinnacle (thread around top block). Use pockets (poor wires
twisted in these) to get established on the wall. Climb direct with one hard
move until it is possible to step left to a tree and relax.

Self Defence   60 feet   Very Severe   4b   ‡   (3.9.84)
Unpleasant. Climb the pinnacle (thread at top) as for *Brain Washed*. Step
right and climb a thin, dirty crack to a ledge and tree.

THE BUTTRESS WITH NO NAME
The first buttress right of Abbey Buttress starts 30 feet right of the pinnacle,
and is best identified by means of a vague cracked tower at its left-hand side.
While none of the routes here is of brilliant quality, most are worthwhile despite
being short. At the extreme left side of the buttress and just right of the pinnacle
of *Brain Washed* and *Self Defence* is a square-cut corner.

Rule the Roost   45 feet   Very Severe   4b   ‡   (5.8.85)
Only for the desperate. Climb the corner to a chossy finish.

The Orphan   55 feet   Hard Very Severe   5a   (8.9.84)
Reasonable although short. Start below the left-hand crack of the vague
tower on a ledge at 5 feet; a tree above gives a convenient belay. Climb
straight up the crack above the tree.

Heavy Plant Crossing   55 feet   Very Severe   4c   (17.8.84)
Quite satisfying. Climb the right-hand crack up the tower to the top.

Alone in a Crowd   50 feet   Hard Very Severe   5b   (17.8.84)
Good moves to start. Fifteen feet right of *The Orphan* is a crack leading to
the widest part of the overhang at 15 feet; start here, between *The Orphan*
and the crack.
Make a hard move up to the break beneath the narrow overhang. Pull
over rightwards on positive holds; then step left into the groove using some
pockets. Continue up the easy groove and step left to belay.

★Breech Birth   35 feet   E2   5c   (29.8.84)
Short but with good moves at the bottom. A bit frustrating if you have short
arms!
Climb the obvious flake crack to the overhang. Stretch to gain good crimps
well above the lip. Struggle over on these and stand up awkwardly.
Scramble rightwards to finish.

The Long Reach   35 feet   Hard Very Severe 5b ‡   (5.9.84)
A short climb with interesting moves to start. Start 5 feet right of *Breech Birth*.
Climb directly up the slabby wall to the overhang, taking it at its narrowest. Scramble to finish.

Artificial Insemination   40 feet   Hard Very Severe 5a   (22.9.84)
The more continuous steep wall 10 feet right of *The Long Reach* gives a reasonable pitch.
Climb up to the centre of the overhang. Turn this on its right, and pull back left above it onto the arête. Go straight up the wall to a thread and big holds. Climb up to a tree.

Indecisive Victory   50 feet   Hard Severe 4b   (22.9.84)
Right of *Artificial Insemination* is a good corner.
Climb the wall to a tree at the foot of the corner. The corner is quite awkward at first but soon leads to a tree just below the top.

Llamas in the Loft   50 feet   Hard Very Severe 5a ‡   (11.10.87)
Start 10 feet left of *Thread Security*.
Make an unprotected move up the wall to a break; then follow the crack on the left. Move left around a tree and trend right to an earthy finish.

Thread Security   50 feet   Hard Very Severe 5a   (27.7.85)
The black wall right of *Indecisive Victory* gives an interesting, if short-lived boulder-problem. Boulder out the black wall to reach a break. Bop on up the arête to a dirty finish.

Probing in the Dark   50 feet   Hard Very Severe 5b   (5.9.84)
Bold, with awkward moves at the top. Twenty feet right of the *Indecisive Victory* corner is a white-stained scoop with a capping overhang.
Climb just left of the groove to a small ledge. The thin crack above is difficult to start. Exit right to trees.

Secret Identity   50 feet   Hard Very Severe 5a   (29.8.84)
Good, with tricky moves. The obvious pod-shaped groove on the right-hand side of the buttress of *Indecisive Victory*.
Climb the wall, pod, and crack. Sustained, but well protected.

Dirty Harry   50 feet   Hard Severe 4a   (31.5.84)
A nice crack leading to a dead tree, then loose rock above.

Aquatic Cyclist   55 feet   Hard Very Severe 5a ‡   (9.8.87)
Start 10 feet right of *Dirty Harry*.
Climb the white bulging wall to a ledge, and continue up the pocketed wall, trending left to finish up a crack.

Right of *Dirty Harry* the cliff is vegetated. The path descends slightly for a few yards to a cleaned white wall, the left-hand side of the Berlin Wall.

THE BERLIN WALL
This is the rather broken buttress just before Fallen Block Buttress is reached. Towards the left-hand side of the wall a slender, detached pinnacle stands in a corner. The obvious flake crack to the right of this, and just behind a fine ash, is *Organ Grinder*. The first climb takes the cleaned white wall 15 feet to the left of the slender pinnacle.

Name in the Book   55 feet   E1   5b   (13.7.85)
Good climbing with a hard crux. Start 5 feet left of the arête.
Take a direct line to some good holds below a bulge. Using poor holds above this, make tricky moves to pockets above a small overlap. Continue more easily to a cleaned ledge and tree belay.

East to West   60 feet   Hard Severe   4b   (8.9.85)
Not the best of routes. This climb takes the corner-line above the slender, detached pinnacle.
Climb the wide crack on the right of the pinnacle, or the easier one on the left, to a ledge. Take the left wall until a dirty finish leads leftwards to a tree.

The Iron Curtain   50 feet   Very Severe   4c   (15.8.84)
Skirted by vegetation on the left, but the best route on this area of wall. Start 10 feet right of the corner.
Climb the wall via some good pockets to the easier-angled section of the slab. Go straight up to a thread runner in a horizontal break. Step up from this using a hidden pocket to reach good holds. Lean rightwards to a short crack, which is followed to a ledge and tree.

Another Brick in the Wall   50 feet   Very Severe   4c ‡   (15.8.84)
Heavily vegetated. Start 20 feet to the right of the pinnacle of *East to West* and climb up into the scoop. Follow the crackline to the left of the yew.

Defection   50 feet   Very Severe   4c ‡   (15.8.84)
Heavily vegetated and insignificant. Broken climbing up the walls and ledges right of *Another Brick in the Wall*. Start 5 feet right of that route at the lowest, easiest-angled part of the wall.
Climb straight up the centre of the walls to finish at an obvious groove with poor quality rock.

Dictator   55 feet   Hard Very Severe   5a   (9.9.84)
Start just right of an ash tree on a ledge.
Climb up to some small ledges on the left behind the tree. The tricky wall above is best taken trending leftwards to a good ledge. From this, step left to a crack (awkward to start with) to finish at blocks and vegetation.

Traitor 55 feet Hard Very Severe 5a (15.9.84)
Interesting, with sustained climbing.
Start as for *Dictator* and follow it to the good ledge. Move right from this to
climb the wall to an obvious short crack and final overhang.

Temporary Truce 55 feet Very Severe 4b (15.9.84)
Start as for *Dictator* and climb it to the small ledges on the left. The obvious
rightward-trending crack leads to the finish of *Organ Grinder*.

★★**Organ Grinder** 55 feet Hard Very Severe 5a (21.8.84)
A popular climb, with a powerful and strenuous lower section.
Layback the massive flake to an awkward move where it forms a small
overhang. Circumvent this with a difficult sequence before entering a short
corner on the left, and climb this to easier ground.

Five Pints 60 feet E3 5c (2.8.85)
The overhang and wall right of *Organ Grinder*. Strenuous and bold.
From the obvious niche, pull over the roof at its widest (peg runner) with
considerable difficulty, and layback the leftward-facing crack. Climb the
wall, deviating slightly leftwards to a thread. Trend back rightwards to finish
up the final wall on pockets to an awkward exit.

A strip of vegetation now separates this wall from Fallen Block Buttress.

FALLEN BLOCK BUTTRESS
This clean buttress starts about 30 feet right of *Organ Grinder*. It is easily
identified by means of a huge fallen block leaning against the cliff about 20
feet below an overhang. A tall yew tree grows nearby on the right.

Jug? What Jug?! 100 feet Very Severe 4c ‡ (27.7.85)
Start immediately right of the worst vegetation at a small right-facing corner.
Battle up the corner until a small ledge on the left can be reached at 15
feet. Continue direct via a faint crack until a bold move gains a good
ledge. Traverse delicately left (peg runner) to the base of the large flake
crack. Climb this.

★**One Less White Nigger** 100 feet Hard Very Severe 4c (17.7.84)
Enjoyable and well-protected climbing up the obvious system of grooves
on the left-hand side of the buttress. Begin 15 feet left of the fallen block
and directly below a tree growing out of the cliff at 60 feet.
Step up beneath the overhang. Make a long reach for a jug; climb up
using this and holds in the crack. Trend left to the groove and follow it to
ledges level with the tree on the right. Cross the slab to a groove; finish up
this carefully.

★★**Emotional Dyslexia** 90 feet Hard Very Severe 5a (1.7.84)
A good pitch, taking the wall left of the overhang. Start at the left edge of

the block.
Climb the block to a ledge. Step across left onto the face and climb boldly up the centre of the wall to a small ledge and peg runner. Follow the thin black groove on some surprising holds until it is possible to pull up left to finish. (A direct start at E1 5a is possible from the fallen block up just left of the overhang.)

★**Night Rider**   100 feet   Very Severe 4b   (17.7.84)
This takes the flake directly above the overhang by some fine climbing. Another very worthwhile route.
Start as for *Emotional Dyslexia* (at the left edge of the block) and follow it to the ledges on the face. Step up, then right to a ledge above the overhang. Gain the flake; climb this and then go up behind the pinnacle to find a good tree.

The Green Meanie   90 feet   E3 5c   (5.8.85)
A challenging route with exciting moves but needing dry conditions. Start from the right edge of the block.
From this, climb to the overhang using a shaky crack. Undercut rightwards beneath the overhang until it is possible to pull easily over to a ledge. From its left side, climb straight up for a few feet, and then traverse rightwards for 10 feet to an obvious and crucial peg runner in the break. Difficult and tiring moves enable a resting-position above the break to be reached. Move up more easily to finish at the tree of *Night Rider*.

The next climbs start on the small terrace level with the overhang and right of the yew tree; these are described under the Tiger Bay section. This is convenient, since the path divides here, the lower one continuing to The Great Central Cave Area.

TIGER BAY
This section covers the extensive area between Fallen Block Buttress and The Great Central Cave Area. From Fallen Block Buttress, take the higher-level path, which rises to a semi-circular bay. The first routes start on the small terrace level with, and right of, *The Green Meanie* overhang on Fallen Block Buttress. A square-topped, detached pinnacle, 'The Gnome', should be an obvious feature.

★★★**Motion Pictures**   70 feet   E1 5b   (1.9.84)
A superb route on excellent rock, starting at the left-hand end of the terrace. Climb up a faint depression in the wall (small wires) to a peg runner visible at 20 feet. Above, a long reach gains some good small pockets. Climb positively up the vague depression on improving holds to easier ground. Finish with care up the cleaned exit above.

★★**Touch the Fire**   70 feet   E2 5c   (14.9.84)
Another good climb, with a tricky and bold boulder-problem start.

Levitate up the lower wall with confidence until able to clip the *in-situ* threads on the first concretion. Climb carefully straight up past the second concretion (with threads) at 30 feet, and then up and left to finish as for *Motion Pictures*.

Last Call   70 feet   Very Severe   5a   (1.9.84)
Well protected and enjoyable. The obvious crack just left of The Gnome pinnacle.
Climb the crack for 50 feet until it is possible to transfer to a flake crack in the right wall, and go up to finish at a tree.

Cruisin' for a Bruisin'   55 feet   E1   5b   ‡   (27.7.85)
Climb onto The Gnome and, from its top, pull into a scoop on the main face. Climb up (peg runner out right) and continue with difficulty to gain a vegetated ledge. Swing left past a peg runner (not seen from below) to a crack for thin fingers. Follow the crack awkwardly to a ledge, and then finish direct.

Intermission   50 feet   Hard Severe   4b   (16.9.84)
Climb the layback flake right of The Gnome, and mantelshelf onto a ledge. Finish direct.

Wolf Whistle   50 feet   Very Difficult   ‡   (13.9.84)
Climb the curving crack right of *Intermission* to a ledge. Finish up the wall, trending back left towards a holly.

Trouble Brewing   50 feet   E3   5c   (3.9.85)
Start 15 feet right of *Wolf Whistle*.
Climb onto the slab towards the thin horizontal break; arrange protection here (good wire just above). Tip-toe delicately right into a very shallow scoop and climb it boldly; good holds appear when most needed. Finish easily.

Cry Wolf   50 feet   Very Difficult   (16.9.84)
Climb the wide crack 5 feet right of *Trouble Brewing* to a ledge. The corner and wall lead to the top.

Further right the terrace drops down slightly. A thin hanging crack is visible in the wall.

Pump It Up... Again   50 feet   E2   5b   ‡   (31.7.84)
Vegetated. Start at a flake to the left of the hanging crackline.
Climb onto the flake and grope blindly for holds which provide an entry to the crack. A determined assault is now necessary for a few feet until a hold on the left wall allows more accommodating jams to be reached. Finish at the first good tree.

★★Renaissance   65 feet   E1   5b   (13.8.84)

This is the flowstone wall with stalactite-type formations. A good route with a fairly bold start, which is from a boulder at the foot of the wall.
Get onto the wall, and then climb to the second of two obvious good handholds. Make one move right towards the arête to a good small wire placement in a horizontal break. Trend back leftwards to a faint groove; follow this and then the crack above.

★Bursting the Renaissance Bubble   65 feet   Hard Very Severe   5b †   (25.5.96)

Well protected. From the same start as *Renaissance*, climb up to a flake.
Climb over the bulge and right onto the arête. Climb the arête for 30 feet into the final scoop, and move up through the overlap to a tree.

★Bubble Memory   65 feet   Hard Very Severe   5a   (30.6.84)

An attractive climb. Start on the ledge right of *Renaissance*, at the base of the arête.
Climb up on good holds to a thread at 15 feet. Follow the arête above.
Continue directly to a small pocket; step left, up, and then right to a small corner-crack. Go up this and past a block to a tree.

One Step Down   80 feet   E1   5b   (8.9.84)

Start at some fallen blocks at the lowest part of the buttress.
Climb straight up just right of *Bubble Memory* for 50 feet to a good ledge at the base of a shallow depression. Crimp up on small holds (peg runner out right) to better holds in a short groove. Exit right.

Right of *One Step Down* is a large open hole/cave – The Bear Pit. The flake of ...*Think of England* emerges from it.

Streaker   55 feet   Hard Very Severe   5b   (30.6.84)

An interesting route. Start on the left edge of The Bear Pit.
Climb the slab 10 feet left of the flake. When below a thin groove, bear right for a few feet. Climb the wall and then trend back left to a tree belay.

...Think of England Direct   90 feet   E1   5b ‡   (30.6.84)

Vegetated, green, and dirty. A route for cavers? Start at the bottom of The Bear Pit, reached by abseil or a claustrophobic crawl though a hole below its left edge.
Attack the steep section of the flake by an energetic layback – a good wire in the right wall protects. Carry on easily up the remainder of the flake.

...Think of England   70 feet   Very Severe   4b ‡   (c.1975)

Start at the right edge of The Bear Pit.
Traverse delicately left to reach the flake, and climb it to the top.

The climbs starting off the terrace to the right are described under The Great Central Cave Area.

THE GREAT CENTRAL CAVE AREA

This area has some of the best middle-grade climbs at Shorn Cliff, offering a perfect introduction to the joys of climbing on natural Wye Valley limestone. Protection is usually excellent, with the water worn-rock providing a profusion of bomb-proof nut placements.

A good place to start is the large expanse of slabs close to an obvious cave at the foot of the cliff. The area is best reached by following the low-level path which descends slightly from Fallen Block Buttress (thus avoiding the scramble around Tiger Bay) or by the unmarked path between R3 and R4 from the Forestry track. The Great Central Cave itself is formed by a huge leaning boulder and provides a convenient place to leave gear.

Directly above the cave is a terrace, which eventually leads back to The Bear Pit. At the back of the cave is a classic chimney/shaft which leads onto this terrace. Rightwards from the cave, the cliff attains its maximum height. The crack just left of a pinnacle flake here is …*One for All*.

The recessed wall is the obvious, slightly set-back wall bounded by two corners, the right one being *The Phoney War*. Further right again, the path divides; the lower branch continues to Fallacy Buttress, whilst the higher rises onto a terrace. The steep white wall above this terrace is taken by *Complex Variable*, amongst other routes, and is terminated by the loose-looking corner of *Wet Dreams*.

The first climbs in this section start from the left-hand end of the terrace above the cave. This is best reached by scrambling up easy ground left of the cave and then along the terrace.

Damsel in Distress 55 feet Very Severe 4c (c.1975)
Start 10 feet right of The Bear Pit and climb to a bulge with a thread runner. Climb past this and then leftwards towards the top of …*Think of England* to finish.

Lucky Star 60 feet E1 5c (5.7.87)
Bold. Climb the shallow groove between *Damsel in Distress* and *Yer Money or Yer Life*, entering via a mantelshelf (poor thread runner) and exiting left.

Yer Money or Yer Life 60 feet Hard Very Severe 5a (14.8.84)
Start 20 feet right of The Bear Pit.
Climb up, slightly rightwards at first, and then more boldly up to a faint groove. Move right at the top to an obvious tree overhanging the cliff.

★**Ché Guevara** 200 feet Hard Very Severe (20.8&22.9.84)
A high-quality left-to-right girdle traverse of the slabs taking in much of the best they have to offer. The first pitch is particularly delightful.
1 120 feet 4c. Follow *Yer Money or Yer Life*. for 20 feet. Traverse right to

a grassy flake (on *Ironside's Men*). Step down slightly (at *The Spanish Inquisition*) and then back up to a rock scar by a rib (thread runner not in place). Descend the groove of *All for One...* for a few feet to the thread on that route. Tip-toe rightwards (thread runners on *The Bitter Battle Tears* and *The Laughing Cavaliers*) to belay at the crack of ...*One for All*.

2 50 feet 4c. Traverse easily to the arête. Cross the recessed wall by descending slightly towards its centre. Gain the corner of *The Phoney War* and climb this to a tree-stump.

3 30 feet 4a. Finish up the left wall as for *The Phoney War*.

Stand and Deliver   60 feet   E1 5b   (14.8.84)

A good climb with a steep start. Begin just left of the shallow depression taken by *Ironside's Men*, and below some thin cracks in the bulging wall. Climb straight up for 20 feet. Move up left to gain some good pockets, and then back right at a large pocket. Continue more or less direct to the tree overhanging the cliff-top.

The next two climbs start from a pedestal on the terrace above the cave. This can reached by the classic chimney leading up through the back of the cave.

★★Ironside's Men   60 feet   E2 5b   (3.6.84)

An excellent and technically testing route. Start just left of the shaft entrance on the terrace at a shallow depression.
Hop onto the rock from a boulder and climb the depression via a thin crack to good pocket holds up and left. Stand up in these; then go direct up the wall to finish.

The Spanish Inquisition   65 feet   E1 5a   (3.6.84)

More enjoyable climbing right of the previous route. Sparsely protected, though the rock is quite sound. Start on the pedestal just right of the shaft entrance, and left of a tree.
Climb the wall past some 'attached' concretions to a ledge after 25 feet. Climb thin flakes and the slab until able to finish at the trees.

Treason   80 feet   E1 5b   (23.8.86)

An eliminate, but with fine and continuously interesting climbing. Start behind the tree on the terrace.
Move up onto a cleaned ledge at 10 feet, step right, and go up to a peg runner beneath a small overlap. Pull over to good holds, and move up some cracks to a small ledge. Climb the faint rib, boldly at first, trending slightly left, and then direct to a sapling. Make a delicate traverse rightwards to a tree.

★All for One...   95 feet   Hard Very Severe 5a   (3.6.84)

Worthwhile and on good rock. Start immediately by the cave entrance. Climb the crack and then move up and rightwards to a ledge level with the terrace. Go up steeper rock to another ledge. Trend left via good holds to a thread runner in a faint groove; then climb directly to a small tree. Abseil from the good tree above.

★★★The Bitter Battle Tears   95 feet   Hard Very Severe 5a   (3.6.84)
A Wye Valley classic! A beautiful slab route with neat technical climbing. Very well protected. Start 5 feet right of the cave.
'Thug' onto the face at a nose, and then climb up, trending slightly right onto the easier-angled section of the slab (thread runner on right). Carry on to a small, ill-defined pedestal. From this, climb up using superb deep pockets to a thread runner. Continue direct past it, and then finish carefully up the wall.

A King's Ransom   90 feet   E3 6a   (30.6.85)
A contrived eliminate. Start at a slight groove just left of *The Laughing Cavaliers*.
Climb the groove, and then move immediately left to a short, leaning wall. Make an awkward reach to good holds at its top and gain the easier ground above (thread on *The Bitter Battle Tears*). Climb carefully up above to the blanker section of rock (poor peg runner) and continue directly above this to gain pockets and a junction with *The Laughing Cavaliers*. Exit left.

★★★The Laughing Cavaliers   100 feet   Hard Very Severe 5b   (3.6.84)
Another brilliant route, typifying the best of Shorn Cliff, and quintessentially British climbing! Exquisite climbing with perfect protection up the very centre of the slab. [Photo p.256.] Start at a slight groove 15 feet right of the cave.
Climb the shallow groove onto the easiest-angled section of the slab (thread runner on left). Go straight up with a thread on the right. From this, move up and left for 10 feet to a juggy flake. Climb up and then right past a large flake to a tree belay.

★★★No Musketeers   100 feet   Hard Very Severe 5a   (9.6.84)
An excellent combination of nice moves on good rock. Start 5 feet right of *The Laughing Cavaliers*.
Climb straight up the wall past a good ledge and thread runner on the left onto the upper slab. Climb directly up this (thread slightly left, on *The Laughing Cavaliers*) to an undercut flake. Tip-toe delicately rightwards, and then climb up just left of the crack taken by *...One for All* until it is possible to move back left above the bulge to finish at a tree. A fine alternative finish is to climb directly through the bulge by some thin cracks (E1 5c).

★★...One for All   100 feet   Hard Severe 4a   (8.9.84)
A wonderful route for the grade, taking the crack in the slab by some delectable climbing. Start 40 feet right of the cave, below the left end of a ledge at 20 feet.
Climb straight up to the left end of the ledge on superb holds. Step left from this and go up to the left of a large pinnacle flake. Climb the crack to a ledge 15 feet below the top. Step right to finish up the continuation crack

on the arête.

Two climbs take the slab to the right of *...One for All*, passing an obvious pinnacle flake at 40 feet.

War Is Declared   90 feet   E1 5b   (10.7.84)
An eliminate with enjoyable climbing. Start 5 feet right of *...One for All*. Climb the easy wall to the ledge at 20 feet. Go up and right into the scoop. Place a good wire at half height on the right, and make very bold moves up on good holds to stand on the small ledge. Move up positively to the narrow overhang and crack (good wires). Pull over on good holds and finish left to a tree belay.

★The New Republic   95 feet   Hard Very Severe 5a   (10.7.84)
Similar to, but finer and more independent than *War Is Declared*. Start 20 feet right of *...One for All*, just right of a shallow cave at foot-level. Climb the boulder-problem wall to the right-hand end of the ledge at 20 feet. Make bold moves up to gain a thread runner right of the pinnacle flake. Continue direct to the centre of the narrow overhang and make a thin move over to superb holds. Finish as for *...One For All*.

Just to the right of *The New Republic* is a four-trunked tree and a vegetated wall bounded by two corners.

Armistice   90 feet   Very Severe 4b ‡   (21.8.84)
Vegetated. The climb took the left-hand corner.

No Surrender   90 feet   Very Severe 4c ‡   (9.9.84)
The available rock between *Armistice* and *War of the Worlds*.

★★War of the Worlds   90 feet   Very Severe 4c   (15.9.84)
Very enjoyable, and well protected. Exquisite climbing on small holds giving a very direct line. Exceptionally good wire protection, and sustained for the grade.
Climb up from the pedestal in the centre of the recessed wall, taking a direct line to the tree above the centre of the bay, with a mantelshelf into a depression just below the top. Earthy finish.

Peace in Our Time   90 feet   Hard Very Severe 5a   (9.6.84)
Worthwhile. Climb 6 feet up onto the pedestal in the centre of the wall and move right to a crystalline crack. Where the crack fades, favour the right wall to finish as for *The Phoney War*.

★★The Phoney War   90 feet   Hard Severe 4b   (31.7.84)
A satisfying route. Climb the right-hand corner and crackline, and then the left wall 30 feet from the top to avoid a loose section in the corner.

Rebellion 60 feet E1 5a ‡ (28.7.84)
The slender face of rock right of the corner gives an absorbing lead with little in the way of protection.
Climb directly up the centre of the face with escalating difficulties (thread runner not *in situ*) to crux moves on small holds which reach a ledge.

★**State of Independence** 60 feet Very Severe 4c (31.7.84)
Interesting and enjoyable. Start on the mini arête 10 feet right of *Rebellion*. Climb the wall, trending right to the overhang. Pull over on the large concretions (two thread runners), and climb boldly and delicately for 15 feet up the wall to the next protection (tape round tree). Large finishing holds on the right.

Just right of *State of Independence* is a massive flat block lying at the foot of the cliff – 'The Table'. From The Table, the path rises steeply through brambles onto an earthy mound. The following routes start from the mound.

Seven Chinese Brothers 50 feet E1 5a ‡ (28.7.84)
A nasty little route, unprotected to start.
From the left-hand side of the terrace, scramble up vegetation and then climb boldly to a thread runner. Trend leftwards along a vague ramp and then up to a thread runner. Loose rock to finish.

Oogmuts 50 feet E3 5b (2.5.88)
An eliminate between *Much Ado about Nothing* and *Seven Chinese Brothers*.
Start just left of the former and climb directly up the wall past a small pocket (crucial *Hex 4*) to meet the thread of *Much Ado about Nothing*. Traverse left and climb the wall above; avoid the top earth bank by traversing left to a small tree.

Much Ado about Nothing 60 feet E1 5a (5.7.85)
Bold. Start 10 feet right of the tree on the terrace, and directly below two slings at half height.
Make one move onto the wall, and then bear right to a poor thread on *Complex Variable*. Cautiously balance up leftwards to the right-hand of the two slings, which is on a hidden peg runner. Step left to the other sling (thread) and pull round the edge of the flake (thread runner). Move back right on top of the flake and climb dirty rock to the final corner of *Complex Variable*.

Complex Variable 60 feet E1 5a (14.9.84)
The cleanest and best route on the white wall above the terrace. Bold and with sparse gear. Start 20 feet left of the large corner at the extreme right-hand end of the terrace.
Climb direct to a poor thread runner at 15 feet; then climb up and left to a second thread (shared with *Much Ado about Nothing*). Bold moves lead

rightwards to a third thread at a small undercut overhang. Traverse left to a sapling and take the groove behind this to the top.

All in a Day's Work   55 feet   E2 5b   (7.5.88)
A serious pitch featuring concretion climbing. Start 15 feet left of *Wet Dreams*.
Climb a slight bulge to a resting-position at some good footholds (two peg runners). Use a series of fragile holds with care to attain the undercut flake of *Complex Variable* (thread); then pull straight over the bulge (peg runner) and move quickly right to the bolt belay of *The Land of Nod*.

★The Land of Nod   55 feet   E2 5c   (7.5.88)
The wall immediately left of *Wet Dreams*. Start 5 feet to its left.
A series of small holds leads to an obvious ledge and an awkward mantelshelf (bolt runner). Climb over the slight black bulge (bolt runner) to gain a good nut-slot. Continue until the steepness begins to ease off (two threads) and a bolt belay can be reached.

Wet Dreams   55 feet   E1 4c ‡   (c.1975)
Avoid like the plague. The loose and vegetated corner at the right-hand side of the terrace.
Enter the corner via loose rock, climb upwards, and exit right at a ledge on the arête. Climb carefully right to the finish of *Fallacy*.

FALLACY BUTTRESS
To reach this buttress, either traverse beneath the crag on the poor and overgrown main path, or take path R3 up from the Forestry track.

Fallacy   70 feet   Hard Very Severe 5a   (c.1975)
Take your hexes!
Climb the obvious large crack on the left side of the buttress, taking care with loose rock at the top.

Expectant Chimp   80 feet   E4 5c   (3.9.91)
A testing, though constricted, eliminate.
Climb the shallow groove just right of *Fallacy* to two small pockets. Make a rising traverse to a junction with *Lundy Calling*. Climb up and left into the groove past a bolt runner. Trend right to the top of the groove, step left, and finish easily to a tree.

★★Lundy Calling   70 feet   E4 5c/6a   (20.7.84)
The striking white-stained face right of *Fallacy* gives some very thin moves requiring a bold approach. Start 10 feet right of *Fallacy*.
Climb up to the overhang and pull over using positive holds in the break above to gain a small resting-ledge. Above are thread runners; climb past these and then directly up a shallow scoop (peg runner). Climb straight up past the peg to finish at the trees.

★★The English Opium Eaters 70 feet E4 6b (22.5.88)
Brilliant climbing up the wall right of *Lundy Calling*. Start under an overhang 10 feet to its right.
Make a long move up; then pass awkwardly right of the overhang (peg runner) to reach a break (peg runner). Pursue a direct line up the face above (three bolt runners) with escalating difficulty until a harder move finally gains better holds (peg runner). Finish as for *Lundy Calling*.

★Cool Heat 70 feet E2 5b (15.9.84)
A safe and enjoyable route, which should be more popular. It takes the wall left of the horrible corner. Some good climbing as long as the corner is avoided. Start 10 feet left of the corner.
Climb a slim groove to the overhang. Pull over this using good holds, and climb up to a thread in a concretion. Go boldly up the wall for 15 feet, and step left onto more concretions (peg runner up and left). Exhilarating moves on the wall to finish.

Colour Dreams/Dream Topping Finish 70 feet E1 5a (c.1976)
For lovers of loose blocks.
Climb the obvious corner up towards the blocky, trembling overhang. Gingerly keep on trending up and left until able to step right and finish straight up.

Protoplasm 30 fee E4 6b ‡ (22.5.88)
The hard problem roof right of the start of *Colour Dreams*.
From the narrow slab, extend 'forever' to a jug (and a peg runner) over the roof. Struggle over and move up to a tree.

The Numbers Game 30 feet E1 5c ‡ (22.5.88)
The name says it all.
Climb the obvious crack from the start of *Protoplasm* past the right side of the roof and then cross left above it to the tree.

Paroxysm 60 feet E2 5b (14.6.85)
Of little merit. A serious line on the wall left of a loose corner. Friable rock.
Climb steeply to a ledge at 12 feet. Follow the crack of *White Water*; descend to a point just above the ledge, and then break out onto the wall and climb steeply for 20 feet to easier but unstable ground and a tree.

White Water 60 feet Very Severe 4c ‡ (14.6.85)
Scrappy and dirty. Start at the left-hand side of the roots of a fallen tree.
Climb up to the left-hand side of a ledge at 12 feet. Walk along the ledge to a crack. Climb the crack and then loose ground above.

THE PINNACLE WALL

This is a fairly long section of cliff marked by a large pinnacle, *The Pinnacle of Success*, which stands close to the cliff. The first routes start between the pinnacle and *White Water*. On the other side of *The Pinnacle of Success* is an expanse of wall giving several worthwhile routes. An obvious break marks the boundary of this wall and the start of Bridle Buttress.

Walk Don't Run   50 feet   Very Severe   4c   ‡   (2.11.85)
Hardly worthwhile; a loose finish. Start 35 feet left of *The Pinnacle of Success*. Climb a clean crack with an awkward move at the top.

A Is for Apple   50 feet   Severe   ‡   (2.11.85)
The serious loose crack 20 feet left of *The Pinnacle of Success*. Climb this and move right at the top.

B Is for Bag   50 feet   E3   5c   (22.5.88)
Serious. Start below the open groove left of *The Pinnacle of Success*. Climb directly and boldly up the scoop, pull over the bulge (bolt runner) past some good concretions and finish on big holds.

The Pinnacle of Success   60 feet   Very Severe   4b   (14.6.85)
Hardly worthwhile. Ascend to the pinnacle's summit. Climb the wall above until level with the multi-trunked tree on the left and traverse to it.

★Stuck On You   65 feet   E1   5b   (12.7.86)
Strenuous and satisfying at this grade. The wall right of *The Pinnacle of Success*, clearly marked by a line of *in-situ* gear. Start immediately right of the pinnacle.
Climb past a thread runner with a bold move to a peg runner at 20 feet. Make a tricky move to gain a thread slightly to the right. From two threads above, climb straight up the wall and traverse left at the top to the trees.

★A Stitch in Time   65 feet   E1   5b   (27.4.85)
An enjoyable route with some enervating moves. Start below the shallow left-facing corner.
Climb the corner until it begins to curve left. Swing right and pull over the overlap on a jug. The wall above needs to be climbed on the left with a little sensitivity.

★★The Hit   65 feet   E3   6a   (29.9.85)
Very bold and technically sustained with a thrilling top section, it takes good rock in the centre of the buttress, right of *A Stitch in Time*. A low runner in that route may be advisable to protect the first overlap. Climb up the centre of the buttress to a *Friend*-slot under the first overlap. Surmount this ingeniously. Climb up the wall (two peg runners) to below the next overlap. Overcome it at its narrowest point with difficulty. Crimp up on small but very positive edges with sparse *RP*/wire protection. Find a tree!

Freak Brother Convention   65 feet   E1   5a   ‡   (15.9.85)
Unpleasant and of little value, this route climbs the red recess right of *The*

Hit. Start 10 feet right of *The Hit* at a short left-facing corner.
Climb the corner to a small overlap. Climb past it (peg runner out right), and then up into the red recess (peg runner above). Exit this by pulling up to the left until it is possible to step into the foot of a corner.

Relics   60 feet   E1   5b   ‡   (8.9.85)
Redundant and horrible. Start 10 feet left of *Second Wind*.
Climb dirty rock to the bulge and pass it at a small triangular block by an awkward move. Either climb directly up the wall or step left and follow the final corner of *Freak Brother Convention*.

Second Wind   75 feet   E2   5c   (8.9.85)
Not a bad route for its grade, though vegetated to start. The conspicuous left-to-right overlap; well-protected with a good crux. Start directly below the left-hand end of the overlap.
Follow the overlap to a peg runner up and right. Use a layaway to move left (peg runner) – difficult for shorties; then continue directly up the wall.

Over the next 30 yards, routes have become seriously vegetated, with loose rock apparent and eroded exits. **Higher Flier** (65 feet E1 5b ‡ 27.4.85) and **Femme Fatalé** (65 feet E1 5a ‡ 12.5.85) start beneath a black scoop right of *Second Wind* and climb up and then right to a small corner, finishing either side of it. **Smart Arse** (65 feet E2 5b ‡ 12.5.85) takes a gap in the overhangs at 15 feet and finishes up a thin crack. **Insurrection** (65 feet E2 5c ‡ 11.5.85) starts 10 feet left of a multi-trunked tree near the cliff and climbs over the overhang, up another thin crack to a corner in the overlap, then 5 feet left and to the top. **Symbiosis** (70 feet E1 5a ‡ 10.5.86) and **Jungle Rock** (70 feet E2 5b ‡ 10.5.86) both climb the multi-trunked tree and the face above. **Doing the Bop** (70 feet E3 5c ‡ 12.7.86) starts 25 feet further right and takes a rightward-trending line.

BRIDLE BUTTRESS
The tall white buttress with a conspicuous concave face sprinkled with threads and concretions, some 100 yards south of Fallacy Buttress, is Bridle Buttress. This area includes the short broken section of the cliff leading up to The White Towers. Approach by path R2, taking the left fork half-way, or by a poorish path from either neighbouring area. A tree painted with two white hoops gives a useful reference point. The first two routes start on the left of the wall.

Blood Brothers   60 feet   E1   5b   (27.5.96)
Start from the slight mound on the left of the buttress, just left of a small corner.
Climb into the scoop (crucial horizontal *Wallnut 1* placement high on left). Make a bold and testing move up onto the bulge towards two threads above on the right. Climb up large holds, following the line of threads and concretions to a cleaned exit.

Heart of Stone   65 feet   E1   5b   (27.5.96)
Starting as for *Blood Brothers*, traverse up and right to an enormous concretion. Climb straight up the rib (peg runner) on large holds to the top; exit right of the cleaned groove of *Blood Brothers*.

The next route starts at a small detached pedestal below an open scoop in the centre of the concave face.

Nosey Bleeder   70 feet   E3   5c   (29.9.85)
A badly-protected start with poor protection and dubious rock.
Step off the pedestal and up into the depression. Move left and then pull back rightwards to get to several thread runners just above a small overlap. Climb cautiously past this to a thread runner by a hollow block (thread runner in *Run for Home* recommended here). Climb the difficult wall above on crimps to two thread runners. Traverse carefully left to an exit and trees.

★★Run for Home   100 feet   E2   5b   (11.5.85)
Challenging and unusual climbing with protection mainly from *in-situ* threads. Start 15 feet left of the tree with the white painted hoops.
Climb a short wall and then pull up left to a flake crack. Follow the crack, and then climb to a small thread in the depression. Continue up, taking care with the rock, to two threads in the wall above. Climb the wall decisively (three more threads) until level with the highest thread. Make one more move up and swing right to a good ledge. Climb the flake on the left, and then take a direct line up to finish.

Running on Empty   100 feet   E3   5c   (8.9.85)
A bold undertaking. Start as for *Run for Home*.
Climb the short wall and go directly to a small blocky ledge at 30 feet. With protection from a thread out left and a peg runner in a vague groove near the arête, climb the wall, taking care with loose holds. Continue up the wall using a thin flaky crack to ledges and move up to a tree.

★★Easy Rider   105 feet   E1   5b   (16.9.84)
Excellent and impressive climbing. One of the longest routes on the cliff, it deserves popularity. Start below the right arête of the concave face, 6 feet left of the hooped tree.
Climb a short groove, exit left onto a steep slab, and move up and back right with small wires in the thin layback crack. Climb to the overhang and pull over it positively. Climb the groove to the right of the arête to the top. Traverse out left, until good holds and protection lead up to a tree.

★★Running Hot   100 feet   E2   5c   (10.5.86)
Start behind the tree with two painted white hoops. An enjoyable route with some quite bold moves on the upper wall.
Move straight up to a peg runner at 15 feet and then right with difficulty

The Laughing Cavaliers (HVS)
The Great Central Cave Area, Shorn Cliff
Climber: Chris Craggs   Photo: Craggs col.

Rainmaker (E1) Shakemantle Quarry, Ruspidge
Climber: Alan Moore · Photo: David Moore

towards the crack. Take the overhang direct on big holds and move past the trees on the left. Step back left and climb the wall, just right of *Easy Rider*, for 15 feet to a peg runner in a faint groove. Carry on direct on positive holds to reach a small niche by a rockfall scar (marginal wire placement here). Exit slightly leftwards from the niche with further marginal protection, climb to the final thread of *Easy Rider*, and finish up right.

★★Loss of Innocence   110 feet   Hard Very Severe 5b   (11.7.85)
Delicate and enjoyable wall-climbing with good protection. Start 5 feet right of the white-hooped tree.
Climb to a shelf on the right at 15 feet, and continue up and left to a thin flake crack (thread runner). Climb the wall above, and directly on up to a thread runner above a small ledge (good wires out right). Using the concretion, make an engaging move up over a small overlap to clip a thread directly above; then move up to the last thread and the finish of *Easy Rider*.

A route taking the flake crack 15 feet of the hooped tree called **Squirrel** (50 feet Hard Very Severe 4c ‡ 22.9.84) is now vegetated. (Does it take nuts?)

★Fat Man in Ethiopia   55 feet   E1 5b   (27.4.85)
Start 30 feet right of the white-hooped tree. An enjoyable and engrossing little route with good protection from *RPs*. Start 15 feet right of *Squirrel* and 10 feet left of a semi-detached pedestal.
Move up onto the wall and left to a ledge. Climb to a higher ledge to the right in the centre of the wall. From this ledge, climb delicately up the wall directly to a tree.

Turn to Stone   50 feet   Very Severe 4c   (2.11.85)
Begin at the corner, just right of the semi-detached pedestal.
Climb the corner and crack trending right. Climb up carefully to the trees.

Character Assassination   50 feet   E1 5a   (2.11.85
An enjoyable route with bold moves to start. It takes the centre of the wall right of *Turn to Stone*.
Climb the wall direct, passing a peg runner at 35 feet.

Pink Ticket   40 feet   Very Severe 4c   (2.11.85)
After an awkward start, take the left-facing crack below a small sapling for 15 feet, traverse right into a corner, and follow it up to a disappointing finish at the tree in the crack.

Further right, the cliff becomes increasingly scrappy. Thirty yards right of *Pink Ticket* a cleaned white pillar gave **At the Hop** (60 feet Hard Very Severe 5a ‡ 12.7.86), now vegetated.

Just beyond, the left-hand White Tower is reached. The right-hand branch of

R2 emerges here.

THE WHITE TOWERS
The two buttresses with stepped overhangs called The White Towers are one of the most conspicuous features of Shorn Cliff when seen from the Chepstow to Tintern road. A wide, loose gully separates the towers and can be used as an easy way up or down. Close up, a multi-trunked tree crowns the White Tower.

The quality of the rock on the left Tower is poor, and there are loose flakes.

The Little White Tower   65 feet   E2 5b
Poor rock and protection. The obvious and direct line up the left Tower.

Blanc Wall   60 feet   Hard Very Severe 5a   (10.5.86)
An interesting route, but the marginal protection demands extreme caution. Start on the right-hand side of the left Tower to gain a ledge. Climb directly up a faint groove until below a smooth headwall. Move delicately up to the overlap, hand-traverse left, and pull up by the tree.

On the right Tower, **Pretty Baby** (75 feet E1 5a ‡ 22.9.84) is now covered with ivy. The route took the left side of the Tower.

The White Tower   75 feet   E1 5b   (c.1975)
Start from a ledge left of a large multi-trunked tree and left of the groove on the right-hand side of the Tower.
A difficult and bold start gains the groove. This gives sustained climbing, with improving protection, to the top. The right arête has also been climbed, using a vibrating spike to pass a bulge at 15 feet. Step left near the top to finish as above.

The path ends here although a horrible 'jungle bash' can be made to Hit and Run Buttress. It is probably easier to descend R2 to the Forestry track and go back up R1.

HIT AND RUN BUTTRESS
From the A466 road near Tintern, the striking height and multiple stepped overhangs clearly mark this buttress, situated some 150 yards south of The White Towers. It is worth a visit for some reasonable higher-grade climbs. Reach it by path R1, which goes straight up to *Hit and Run*.

The first climb described takes a line up a pillar separated from the main part of the buttress by vegetation. This route begins with a scramble to the base of an obvious crack at the right-hand side of the pillar.

End of the Line   80 feet   E1 5b † ‡   (16.12.92)
Loose and unattractive. This route takes the arête.

Pull over the bulge on jugs and move up to the large leftward-facing flake.
Climb this and finish with great care.

A Claim to Fame   60 feet   Very Severe   4b ‡   (30.6.85)
A vegetated and badly-cleaned route.
Climb steeply up the crack and move leftwards to gain an obvious groove.
Climb this, taking care with the rock, to some large ledges and a tree.

★Hit and Run   80 feet   E2 5b   (19.10.84)
An excellent and generally well-protected route taking the crackline in the
buttress left of the barrier of overhangs at half height.
Climb a shallow groove, passing to the left of an overhang. Step out left
onto the arête and climb it for 15 feet before returning right to follow the
crack in the headwall, with increasing difficulty at the top, to a ledge and
tree.

The next four climbs weave intricate lines through the imposing overhangs at
half height.

★Chappell of Rest   70 feet   E5 6c †   (23.2.92)
The overhang and steep buttress immediately right of *Hit and Run*.
Problematic and strenuous; the hardest route on the crag to date.
Climb easily up the slab right of *Hit and Run* to the first roof. Surmount the
roof by hard moves (10mm bolt runner), and pull up left to a good resting
foot-ledge (small wire). Pull over the next roof (peg runner); then pursue a
direct line up the buttress (peg runner) on improving holds to a short crack
and good flake holds on the left that lead to a tree.

★Touché Pussycat   80 feet   E1 5c   (28.9.85)
A fine, intimidating climb, well protected at the crux. Start 20 feet right of
Hit and Run.
Take the corner for 15 feet to a small undercut roof, and move right for a
couple of feet under this to a short crack. Overcome the overhang by
making a long reach to gain high holds right of the obvious groove. Pull
up to the next ledge and larger roof and then left over this to a groove.
Stride left to a small platform and then return to the groove for a while.
When this begins to become chossy, transfer left to the wall and finish up it
to reach the first good tree.

★Colin's Apprentice   60 feet   E4 6b †   (23.2.92)
The quite striking line of the roofed groove that is avoided by *Cat Be
Nimble, Cat Be Quick*. A safe crux.
Follow *Cat Be Nimble, Cat Be Quick* past the peg runner, but go direct to a
projecting block-jug below the roof. Reach for the jug over the lip (peg
runner) and make a fierce pull into the groove above. Gain the massive
jug over the final roof (junction with *Cat Be Nimble…*, peg runner on the
left) and descend from the abseil station just above.

★Cat Be Nimble, Cat Be Quick   75 feet   E2   5c   (28.9.85)
This route is more sustained than *Touché Pussycat* and the protection is a
little more spaced. Well worthwhile. Start 10 feet right of *Touché Pussycat*.
Climb the short arête to the cracked block on *Touché Pussycat*. Break right
and pull past a poor peg runner with difficulty. Climb up towards the large
roof until it is possible to make a delicate traverse right to a small ledge
(peg runner). Gain this awkwardly; climb steeply back left and then up a
vague, shallow groove. Where it peters out, hand-traverse left (peg runner)
and pull up on good holds after a few feet. Go up pocketed rock past a
sapling to the first good tree.

The First Crusade   80 feet   Hard Severe   4b   (30.6.85)
Start 12 feet right of *Cat Be Nimble, Cat Be Quick*, at a corner-crack with
an overhang at 15 feet.
Climb to the overhang and traverse right on undercuts before pulling into
the corner. Follow the corner, passing a ledge after 20 feet and an
immense detached block close to the top. An easy, though dirty exit is also
possible to the left 20 feet from the top.

Incredible Voyage   80 feet   Very Severe   4c   ‡   (30.6.85)
Dubious rock makes this route a rather serious proposition for the grade.
Start 10 feet right of *The First Crusade*.
Climb the short corner and then straight up the groove. Follow the groove
until it is possible to move diagonally right to broken ground. Go past a
small suspect overhang and a sapling, and then make a series of steep
moves right to another groove, which is climbed to a tree belay.

★Poka Dot   80 feet   E2   5c   (24.6.85)
The fine grey wall right of *Incredible Voyage* gives some absorbing
climbing which is deceptively steep. Start at a crack 10 feet right of
Incredible Voyage.
Step right and follow the crack slightly leftwards to a rocking flake. Move
right from this onto a narrow ledge. Climb boldly up the wall, using a
good layaway out right, to a peg runner with *in-situ* sling. Move directly to
a short, steep crack, step into this, and struggle up it on jams (thread
runner) and so on to jugs. A dirty scramble leads to a tree.

This Space Reserved   80 feet   Hard Very Severe   5b   ‡   (24.6.85)
The steep groove-line right of *Poka Dot* is barred by several overhangs.
Climb easily to the first roof and manœuvre cautiously past it on
hollow-sounding holds. Climb the continuation groove to the next roof via
an awkward move. Overcome this more easily to reach a tree.

★Synapse Collapse   90 feet   E3   6a   (21.9.86)
A ferocious pitch, steep, strenuous, and sustained. Start 5 feet right of *This
Space Reserved*.
Follow a steep, right-facing crack to its closure at 20 feet. Move up right

(peg runner) until it is possible to move back left using flakes to a hollow-sounding block (this is just right of the corner of *This Space Reserved*). Go up directly to the overhang (peg runner) and haul over with difficulty (peg runner). Pull up right into a short groove (peg runner) and climb it to easier ground. Finish up the obvious crack.

★**Ramraider**   60 feet   E5 6b †   (23.2.92)
A highly technical route which climbs the overhanging scoop right of *Synapse Collapse*. Reasonable protection. Start 6 feet right of *Synapse Collapse*.
Pull up to a horizontal break (good wires). Reach jugs above and then more on the left in a small groove (peg runner). Climb up into the scoop (peg runner of *Synapse Collapse* on the left). Climb the increasingly severe scoop (peg runner) until fingery pulls over a bulge (peg runner) lead to a brisk layback crack (*in-situ* wire) to finish. Belay on the first tree.

A Great Day for Gravity   120 feet   E1 †   (30.8.95)
A traverse of the buttress. Start 12 feet left of *Mister Angry*, at a fallen tree.
1 40 feet 4c. Climb up to clip a peg runner and step left across to a flake. Traverse across to a groove. From the groove, move left to a ledge on *This Space Reserved*.
2 30 feet 5b. Descend from the right-hand end of the ledge and hand-traverse left to a peg runner. Climb diagonally across the wall to an obvious large foothold. Move left towards the overhang.
3 50 feet 5b/c. Climb up and left. Move along the obvious traverse-line above the overhangs towards a peg runner. Continue across towards *Hit and Run* and climb it to the top.

Nobby's Piles   80 feet   E1 5b †   (30.8.95)
Start in front of the large tree, at the wide crack.
Climb up onto the block. Make a hard move out left into a groove and crack. Well-protected moves up left of the overhang lead to a loose finish at a tree.

Mister Angry   90 feet   E2 5c   (21.9.86)
A reasonable route at this grade with a problematic crux. Start 6 feet right of the large tree and 20 feet left of the obvious broken chimney of *Angry Young Men*.
Use a short corner (above an earth bank) to boulder out the lower wall, and reach a ledge at 10 feet. Shuffle 3 feet left along it and climb directly up the wall (peg runner). Continue in this line until forced towards the left-hand side of the wall. Now make a hard move rightwards to get established by a ring-peg (good runners high up on left before reaching it). Another hard move attains good holds under an overhang. Finish over it with care. (An E1 variation finishing up *Blind Rage* has been done.)

Blind Rage   90 feet   E3 5c   (21.9.86)
Committing, though the climbing is in similar vein to the previous route.
Start 10 feet right of *Mister Angry*.
Climb the broken crackline to a peg runner at 20 feet, with another at 25
feet. Pull up right with difficulty before returning left to beneath an
overhang (peg runner above). Use a flake on the left to pass this, and then
move up to gain a faint groove, which is followed easily to a tree.

Flatlander   70 feet   E2 5c †   (11.5.96)
Start 3 feet right of *Blind Rage*.
Climb boldly but delicately up onto the wall and into a faint scoop.
Continue up the wall with difficulty (peg runner) towards the top bulge.
Tricky moves are required to pass a thread. Finish to a tree.

Angry Young Men   60 feet   Severe 4a   (30.6.85)
The obvious broken chimney and wall.
Climb the chimney and step up left to enter the groove. Alternatively, climb
the crack a few feet to the left (Very Severe 4c). Follow the groove to the first
good tree.

Santorini   50 feet   Very Severe 4b †   (11.5.96)
Start just right of *Angry Young Men*.
Climb up onto the ledge to the right and take the very large crackline on
the end of the buttress direct (care needed at the top). Finish up to the left
to a tree.

The Forest of Dean Quarries

In the 1987 guide, David Hope listed all known quarries (except, strangely, Point Quarry) that could possibly be of any interest to climbers. Of these, only Spion Kop had any recorded routes. Over the next year they were all investigated and those with potential were largely worked out; the results and some subsequent activity are recorded here, but the still-routeless quarries are omitted. There are two areas of interest and a couple of outliers. All of them lie on Forestry Commision property.

First and most important is the central sandstone area east of Coleford and north of Parkend. Unfortunately, Point Quarry is no longer open to climbing (if it ever was). It is part of the Nagshead Nature Reserve, a joint project between the Forestry Commission and the RSPB, and is a sanctuary for various species of birds (including kestrels and ravens), wardened by an RSPB officer. Although a local field-studies centre had been permitted restricted use, when the rock was subjected to more intensive development all access was withdrawn. A record of all the lines climbed is preserved in BMC *New Climbs 1988*, but be aware that almost all the pegs have been removed.

Higher on the hillside to the north is the secluded Spion Kop, which contains the finest sandstone climbing in the Forest, also a Nature Reserve but with

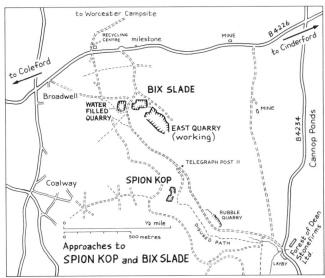

Approaches to
SPION KOP and BIX SLADE

limited access; and further north again are the three Bix Slade quarries. One of these is highly vegetated and its bottom is water-filled; it is of no use to climbers. Another, the most easterly, is still being worked. The central quarry, recently retired, has been designated an instructional area by the Forestry Commission; however, discreet use for recreational climbing is possible.

The second area comprises two quarries on the outskirts of Cinderford: a secluded sandstone one, rather different from those described above, and a large (though with a limited area of climbing) and public limestone one (Shakemantle).

Finally, another small sandstone quarry outside Bream gives two short routes on quite good rock, and Plump Hill gives some rather loose slab routes above Mitcheldean in pleasant, open surroundings.

Three short routes of a rather similar nature at Stony Green Quarry, near Mallard's Pike, were also recorded in BMC New Climbs 1988. However, as this faces north-west and is surrounded by trees the lines have mossed back over, and it seems inconceivable that anyone should want to clean them off again for so little reward. Parties under instruction keep the abseil strip free of vegetation but not of mud; things seem destined to stay this way!

The sandstone routes have seen very little traffic and have not been reclimbed for this guide. The grades are those suggested by the last known (in many cases the first) ascensionist; some of the 'easier' climbs may be found under-graded. However, the condition of each climb and the general accuracy of the descriptions have been checked, and the latter modified also for consistency and clarity in their context.

SPION KOP   OS Ref 598 103
This secluded little quarry is a Nature Reserve managed by the Gloucestershire Wildlife Trust. It is a nesting-site for species of birds uncommon to the area and is preserved as an isolated 'wild place' in the Forest. Climbing is tolerated **provided** it is restricted to the areas shown clearly on the map, and to the period from August to February inclusive; there is an absolute ban on all activity during the nesting-season from 1st March to 31st July.

The strange name is that of a South African hill, the site of a Boer War battle at which the British suffered heavy casualties.

APPROACH
Despite earlier reports and confusion, this is a pleasant and simple 20-minute (or less) walk by either of the following routes.
1 Drive north out of Parkend, and turn left onto the B4234 (signposted 'Lydbrook'); in just over one mile there is a pronounced right-hand bend with the Forest of Dean Stonefirms works on the right and a good lay-by on the left; park in the latter. Take the hard-surfaced Forestry track (the 'old tram-

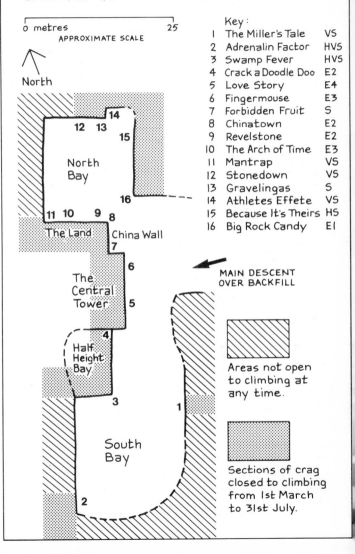

SPION KOP QUARRY NATURE RESERVE

0 metres 25
APPROXIMATE SCALE

North

Key:
1 The Miller's Tale   VS
2 Adrenalin Factor   HVS
3 Swamp Fever   HVS
4 Crack a Doodle Doo   E2
5 Love Story   E4
6 Fingermouse   E3
7 Forbidden Fruit   S
8 Chinatown   E2
9 Revelstone   E2
10 The Arch of Time   E3
11 Mantrap   VS
12 Stonedown   VS
13 Gravelingas   S
14 Athletes Effete   VS
15 Because It's Theirs   HS
16 Big Rock Candy   E1

North Bay

12 13 14
15
16

11 10 9 8
The Land   China Wall
7
6
The Central Tower
5
4
Half Height Bay

3   1

South Bay

2

MAIN DESCENT OVER BACKFILL

Areas not open to climbing at any time.

Sections of crag closed to climbing from 1st March to 31st July.

road') which follows the telegraph posts; these are numbered in descending order from 29. In another mile, immediately beyond post 11, turn back sharp left on a grassy track. After a short rise this levels out, and the perimeter fence is soon encountered on the right. (This track then continues in a generally southerly direction back to the starting-point. However, it has now become disused and route-finding in ascent is confusing. Although it looks more direct on the map it is not recommended.)

2 Slightly quicker, but with less good parking. Reach the Bix Slade quarries (see page 272). Take the track between the western and central quarries, and keep going downhill on this instead of following the perimeter fence (ignore also a path going ahead up into the woods); it turns out to be the upper end of the old tram-road, and the telegraph posts soon appear above you on the right. You probably cannot see the numbers until 10; anyway, 11 is the first one on the left-hand side. Fork right between the two.

TOPOPGRAPHY
Enter the quarry without damaging the fence which has, by law, to be maintained for public protection. The descent and moving around the floor of the quarry are somewhat treacherous, especially in damp conditions: moss, leaves, rotten branches, and various rubbish conceal greasy slabs and ankle-breaking potholes. However, the impressive Central Tower is straight ahead. To the left and right respectively are the almost enclosed South and North Bays. Abseil descents from trees are often possible, but it is better to walk down beside the perimeter fence (on either flank) where the top of the cliff is easily reached.

As noted above, the quarry has been little frequented, and many of the earlier routes, especially those in the two bays, have become heavily revegetated. In contrast, The Central Tower and its satellite walls are largely clean, though they benefit from an occasional light brushing, especially after a wet closed-season. However, it is suggested that considerable heart-searching should take place before removal of the moss and ferns from the routes in the outer wings of the two bays, and there is very little, if any, scope for genuine new lines in the permitted areas.

THE SOUTH BAY
The twin-crack in the middle of the eastern (west-facing) wall, **The Miller's Tale** (90 feet Very Severe 5a ‡ [R] 27.6.86), is now completely moss-covered.

At the left-hand end of the western (east-facing) wall is a crack-system starting behind the remains of a broken tree: **Adrenalin Factor** (90 feet Hard Very Severe 5a ‡ [R] 14.5.78). The main rock section is in reasonable condition, but the finishing-moves and earthy slopes above are desperate.

HALF-HEIGHT BAY
Well to the right there is a two-sided area of rock no more than 25 feet in height, on top of which is a large terrace. **The Mad Russian** (25 feet Very

Difficult [R] 3.8.82) climbs the crack-system on the south wall with a choice of finishes (the right-hand being the normal, safer, and easier). **Swamp Fever** (20 feet Hard Very Severe 5c [R] 6.10.87) is the sharp arête at the junction of the two faces. **Jive 'n' Bop** (20 feet Difficult [R] 23.4.78) takes the obvious greasy chimney above a raised ledge near the left-hand end of the east-facing wall, and **Firedamp** (25 feet E3 6b † [R] 6.10.87) gives a few excellent technical moves up the wall just to its right (three peg runners).

THE CENTRAL TOWER

The Central Tower is the crag's showpiece, giving several fine routes of up to 90 feet on vertical, mainly clean and sound rock.

There are two cracks in the south wall which start off a pillar/block on the terrace above the Half-Height Bay. The sun occasionally penetrates here! The block is reached by climbing one of the above routes or by a few 'moves' and a scramble from directly below.

Twist of Fate   50 feet   E1 5b † [R]   (6.10.87)
Climb the left-hand crack past a couple of jammed blocks. Move right up the middle section of the wall and regain the crack to finish steeply.

Crack a Doodle Doo   60 feet   E2 5c [R]   (15.8.86)
Climb the right-hand crack and wall until forced right at the top to the arête.

★**Heartbreaker**   80 feet   E5 6a † [R]   (24.10.87)
The fine upper arête between the south and main faces of the tower. Start (at ground-level) below and slightly right of the arête.
Pull up the wall to a good finger-edge (peg runner); move left to a crack and up onto a ledge. Avoiding the pillar, climb the arête direct with a long reach on the right (peg runner) to gain a small ledge (peg runner). Move up (peg runner) and continue up the arête using small pockets on the right to a horizontal crack (*Friend 1½*) and an easier finish.

★**The Power of Love**   90 feet   E5 6b [R]   (2.9.86)
A serious and committing climb of continuous quality. Start in the centre of the main face on a flat-topped block.
Climb the wall past three peg runners to the foot of the central crack and an old iron spike. Step down and transfer to handholds in a leftward diagonal crack which leads to a thin vertical one. Climb this and continue over delicate ledges to twin thin cracks. At the top of these, move left to good finishing-holds.

Love Story   90 feet   E4 6a [R]   (30.6.86)
Climb to the spike as for *The Power of Love*, and move up past it and then up right to a small niche, from where an awkward pull into the cave is made. Climb the crack above, and hand-traverse right to finish up a crack

through the final overhang.

★★Labour of Love   80 feet   E6 6b [R]   (28.8.87)
Brilliant sustained, strenuous, and direct climbing up the wall just right of
Love Story. Well protected: take a selection of smallish wires in addition to
enough quickdraws. Start on the next block to the right of the flat-topped
one.
Climb the wall past a wide break and two peg runners to a small diagonal
undercut flake (peg runner). Use this to launch upon a series of hard
moves to and up a thin crack (peg runner) and gain better footholds (peg
runner). Continue on and climb the headwall (three more peg runners) to
the top wide break (bong runner). Reach over and mantel to finish.

★Fingermouse   90 feet   E3 5c [R]   (24.8.86)
The bold and strenuous rightward-slanting crack starting 10 feet left of the
right edge of the face.
Climb the crack past a metal spike to the large ledge at two-thirds height,
and finish up the wall just right of the arête.

Hey Diddle Diddle   90 feet   E2 6a [R]   (24.8.86)
Climb the broken crack just left of the edge of the face to a ledge on the
arête. Step back left and climb a thin crack until moves on the right enable
the large ledge to be reached. Finish on the right as for *Fingermouse*.

Universal Bond (110 feet E5 6a [R] 24.10.87) is a right-to-left diagonal
across the main face: a good strenuous outing but with little independent
climbing. Climb *Hey Diddle Diddle* for 20 feet, swing left into *Fingermouse*,
and follow that to the metal spike. Traverse left along the horizontal crack to
the metal spike on *Love Story*. Take the diagonal crack of *The Power of Love*,
continue in the same line to the arête, and finish up *Heartbreaker*.

The slim, north-facing wall right of the arête is revegetating badly. You may
get the first route in if you hurry, but forget the other two. **Honeydew** (80 feet
E1 5c † [R] 18.10.87), mostly just free from the encroaching moss, climbs just
right of the arête via the first ledge (one peg runner below, three above) to the
second, and the finish of *Fingermouse*. **Thar He Blows** (90 feet Very Severe
4c ‡ [R] 27.3.86) takes the crack-system just to the right, again finishing on
the two-thirds-height ledge. The corner is **Forbidden Fruit** (90 feet Severe
4a ‡ [R] 21.8.83) – no apples available!

CHINA WALL
The wall to the right of the corner is a replica of the main face of the tower,
but slighter in both stature and quality. The vegetation is spreading in this
direction as well; the first two routes are currently unclimbable but could well
be reclaimed. **Slow Boat to China** (60 feet E2 6a ‡ [R] 28.9.87) takes a
direct line up the wall just right of the corner via a narrow ledge, a thin flake
crack, and three peg runners to the left end of an obvious ledge (peg and

thread belay). **All the Tea in China** (60 feet E4 6a ‡ [R] 15.9.87) starts at a deep letter-box slot and climbs the wall past four peg runners to enter a niche from the right. The belay ledge is just above.

Pensioner's Puzzle   90 feet   E2 5c [R]   (28.9.86)
The obvious crackline in the wall. Clean except for some brambles at 20 feet. Take the secateurs with you!
Climb the crack, awkward at first, to a good ledge. Continue up the upper crack until 10 feet below the top and then traverse the break rightwards to finish up the arête.

China in Your Hands   80 feet   E3 6a † [R]   (15.12.87)
The first 40 feet offers good wall-climbing with even better protection. From a layaway hold just right of the crack of the last route, make a long reach to a tiny edge (peg runner) and move up to a break. Climb directly up the wall (four more peg runners) until an awkward move gains the shelf. The upper crack of *Pensioner's Puzzle* is just above, and that route is followed to the top.

★**Chinatown**   80 feet   E2 5b [R]   (28.9.87)
The arête forming the right edge of China Wall.
Climb the right side of the arête (two peg runners) to the ledge. Climb the upper arête direct (two more peg runners).

Kerb Crawler   165 feet   E3 † ‡ [R]   (24.10.87)
A longer girdle/diagonal traverse. Pitch 2 is probably not currently possible. Take plenty of *Friends*.
1 50 feet 5b. Climb *The Arch of Time* (see next page) for 25 feet and traverse left to the *Chinatown* arête. Climb this (peg runner) to its ledge (peg and *Friend* belay under the overhang).
2 70 feet 6a. Move left to a *Friend* slot; then step up and make a thin finger-traverse (peg runner) to the top peg runner on *Slow Boat to China*. Step into the corner at a jammed block (thread) and traverse towards the arête (peg runner). Reach for a good jug on the arête and pull onto the ledge (peg belay with good wires behind).
3 45 feet 6a. Pull onto the left arête and reach a deep pocket on *Labour of Love*. Move up again (peg runner) and finger-traverse an edge leftwards to the crack of *Love Story*. Continue up this until it traverses right, and finish direct to the top (peg runner).

THE NORTH BAY
There are two distinct climbing areas here: the impressive north-facing wall right of the *Chinatown* arête, known as 'The Land', is the final section of The Central Tower complex; while the smaller south- and west-facing walls are now revegetating.

In the former, there are three obvious crack-systems running up the wall.

★Revelstone   100 feet   E2 5b [R]   (8.2.81)
From a tree 5 feet right of the arête, climb the erratic, left-hand crackline,
taking care at a broken section below the upper zigzag. Above this trend
slightly right to finish up the broken wall.

Landwaster   100 feet   E1 5a [R]   (15.8.86)
Climb the central crack-system to a small oak in the middle of the wall.
Take care with suspect rock in the cracks above and make a pull out right
to a large square ledge. Step up right and climb the wall to the top.

★★The Arch of Time   100 feet   E3 5c [R]   (2.9.86)
Climb the right-hand crack to reach the left-hand side of the large
overhang. Traverse right to achieve an uncomfortably sandwiched rest
under the keystone. Pull through the roof via the keystone and continue up
the wide crack in the wall above to reach trees and the top.

Triumph of the Bourgeoisie ([R] 18.11.87) provides an equally good
lower section to *The Arch of Time* at the same grade (though at its upper limit).
Climb the right-slanting cracks just to the right and move right under an
overhang (peg runner). Make a long reach for a jug (on *Mantrap* – peg runner
on the left) and pull over. Climb directly up via a vertical crack to join *The Arch
of Time* under the keystone.

The corner is ferny, though an uncomfortable ascent may still be possible.
Mantrap (100 feet Very Severe 4c ‡ [R] 23.4.78) takes this, passing left of
the large jammed block and then right of the overhang to a ledge, with a
finish up the crack and wall above.

The east-facing wall immediately right of *Mantrap* and the left-hand half of
the south-facing wall are off-limits. The next *permitted* route takes the latter
wall's central crackline, which starts with a distinctive S-shaped bend. The
cheekily named **The Dividing Line** (40 feet E1 5c † [X] 28.11.87), the crack
just to its left, is unfortunately nothing of the sort.

Stonedown   50 feet   Very Severe 4c [R]   (19.7.81)
Climb the S-bend crack.

Woody Ward Pecker   40 feet   E1 5b † [R]   (15.11.87)
Good steep climbing up the thin cracks between *Stonedown* and
Gravelingas.
Follow the jagged crack past the left end of the low overhang and continue
straight up over a narrow roof to short twin cracks. Climb these and trend
right to a niche near the top of the wide crack of *Gravelingas*.

The arête at the right-hand end of this wall is clean. At its foot is an overhung
groove; on the left is a high crack, and left again is a broken crack-system
slanting slightly left up the wall.

Gravelingas 50 feet Severe 4a [R] (8.2.81)
Climb the crack-system past an overhang, and on above as it becomes more broken.

★**Crusaders** 50 feet Hard Very Severe 5a [R] (19.7.81)
Start in the overhung groove and climb strenuously up and out left past the overhangs to reach the right-hand crack.

★**The Outlaws of Physics** 40 feet E3 6b † [R] (15.11.87)
The fine arête gives gritstone-like climbing. Start in the overhung groove, pull directly over, and layback up the tip of the arête to exit left onto *Crusaders* (two peg runners).

Athletes Effete (40 feet Very Severe 4c ‡ [R] 8.2.81) climbs the revegetating corner just right of the last two routes, and the overhang at its top. The slab just to its right, becoming mossy at the bottom, is a one-move wonder: **The Snails of Justice** (40 feet Hard Very Severe 6a † [R] 28.11.87). Dyno for the obvious slot. Two peg runners.

The wall now turns a right-angle to become west-facing. The moss is encroaching and, except for the very last one, these routes may not be viable. That, however, could be climbed with *minimal* cleaning.

Because It's Theirs (40 feet Hard Severe 4b ‡ [R] 14.5.78) climbs up over a ledge to and then a wide crack at the left-hand end of the wall. **A Snail of Two Cities** (40 feet E1 5c † ‡ [R] 28.11.87) takes the broken cracks to the right with a hard move (peg runner) to finish at a tree root.

Near the right-hand end of the wall is a crack leading to a tree at 20 feet. Five feet left of this, **Snails of the Unexpected** (40 feet E1 6a † ‡ [R] 28.11.87) gains the narrow shelf and then climbs directly to the top (two peg runners), thus crossing: **Spyin' Cop** (50 feet Hard Severe 4b ‡ [R] 23.4.78), which takes the crack to the tree, traverses 10 feet left along the shelf, and moves up over a bulge to a final crack.

★**Big Rock Candy** 40 feet E1 5b [R] (6.10.87)
The obvious arête.

THE BIX SLADE QUARRIES OS Ref 595 109
Bix Slade is a large area, but seems now the official name for what has previously been called Purple's Hill Quarry. The central quarry, in which the recorded routes lie, has in the past been referred to as 'the crane quarry', but its crane has now been removed and, to confuse matters further, the working quarry just to the east still *has* a crane!

The quarry returned recently to Forestry Commission management and has been designated as an instructional area in an attempt to take some of the pressure off Symonds Yat. The latter should be welcomed by all climbers and must be worth any limitation on access here. In fact, although recreational climbing is not allowed officially, climbers are likely to be tolerated **provided** they do not in any way disrupt or interfere with the activities of approved users (who pay a nominal fee to cover administration costs); and the topography of the quarry is such that there need be no conflict. Groups who wish to book should phone the Forestry Commission Office in Coleford (01594 833057) and ask for the Public Affairs Department.

The four routes on the north wall and the first two on the east tower are bolt-protected sport climbs, but the hangers (8mm) have been removed. Placing hangers and carrying out a light brushing if necessary on an abseil rope from convenient cliff-top trees are unproblematic.

APPROACH   (Map page 263)
This takes five minutes from the road. Although there are numerous ways in from the Broadwell area, the simplest to describe and find is as follows. Drive a mile and a half east of Coleford town centre on the B4226 *Speech House Road* to Cinderford. After exiting the 30mph speed limit of Broadwell, continue down the hill a short way to a tarmac track on the left which is the drive to the Worcester Lodge Caravan Park. There is parking space for two or three cars immediately on the left just opposite the small water pumping-station. Take the obvious track on the opposite side of the main road past a track junction on the brow of the short rise to another junction beyond. Turn left here, on either the track or the smaller path to its right. Both take you to the perimeter fence of the western quarry, and the central quarry is just beyond. For Spion Kop, continue downhill between two large boulders.

Further down the main road, just past the Recycling Centre, there is a small lay-by with a more direct gated track opposite. You can park here on Sundays only. During the week (including Saturdays) it **must** be kept clear for vehicles to turn in and out of the quarry. It is not permitted to drive up the track.

TOPOGRAPHY
The central quarry is more-or-less a rectangular hole in the ground, with the climbing potential centred mainly on the north and east (i.e. south- and west-facing) walls; the west end consists of vegetated scree and boulder slopes, while the south wall has two small rock features amidst more jumble and jungle.

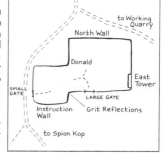

The quarry must be entered without damage to the surrounding fence or the new gates, which are kept locked.

This is best done by following the fence anti-clockwise past the first, small gate and traversing rough ground just above it to reach the second and wider gate in the south side. There is plenty of room to crawl underneath and a track leads down. The climbs are described clockwise from here.

The first feature thus encountered is a short, clean, undercut arête.

Grit Reflections   50 feet   E4 6a †   (27.5.96)
Grit-like in appearance and execution, with the prospect of an (albeit reasonably soft) crater from the crux.
Boulder straight up the arête, and then make a couple of thin moves to jugs (*Rock 8* placement – the first protection). Continue rather more easily up the left side of the arête passing a solitary *Friend 2* placement.

The next short wall to the right is currently the instruction area, mostly for abseiling, but a series of holds[!] have been carved up it. Immediately opposite the *Grit Reflections* arête is another, jutting out of the opposing north wall near its left-hand end.

Donald   60 feet   Hard Very Severe 5a †   (17.4.94)
Something of a struggle to reach and a struggle to start. Above the ledge, the upper section is loose and easy.

The wall joining the arête to the main wall is largely vegetated, but a cleaner strip 25 feet left of the corner between the two allows:

Digital   70 feet   E1 5b †   (17.4.94)
Make committing moves to a small ledge and launch up the blank-looking wall above on crimps and slots to a tree belay at the top.

The left-hand half of the main north wall is also vegetated and sports some interesting metallic relics. Half-way along is an obvious short corner leading to a roof at 25 feet that extends rightwards. To the right of the corner there is a quarry stake where the ground slopes away into the pit. The rock above is in much better condition..

Get On Up   70 feet   E5 6a F7a †   (30.6.96)
Some splendid roof-work – unusual for Forest sandstone. Six bolt runners. Start 10 feet right of the corner.
Climb the wall direct to the roof. Gain a sloper on the lip, lock (or lunge) over, and so reach the small ledge above. Climb the face above more easily, and then go diagonally right, joining *Mutant*, to retreat from the abseil trees.

Mutant   70 feet   E5 6b/c F7b+ †   (30.6.96)
Extremely ferocious, as one might expect. Seven bolt runners. Start 15 feet right of the corner.

Mantel up and left onto the hand-ledge and get established on a leftward-pointing flake. (At this point you should be eye-balling the face of the mutant – a remarkably symmetrical natural imprint upon the rock.) Using the fingery undercut in the roof, power over and continue direct up the face to the abseil trees on the right.

★Nice Noddy Holder   70 feet   E3 6a F6c †   (19.5.96)
The leading route of the quarry: thoroughly enjoyable climbing packed with more variety than most on sandstone. Seven bolt runners. Start below the right-hand end of the roof.
From the iron spike, foot-traverse right to below a compact scoop. Enter the scoop, and go up to the right-hand end of the roof. Pull leftwards through it on surprising holds and reach a good pocket above. Continue direct and gain the abseil trees slightly right.

Get Down and Get with It   70 feet   E3 6a F6c+ †   (19.5.96)
Sustained face-work right of the last route. High in the grade. Seven bolt runners.
Climb to the right-hand end of the roof (and third bolt) as for *Nice Noddy Holder*; then step right and move up to a blind break. Go up direct with two hard moves, and then climb the easier wall above before swinging left to the abseil trees.
At the right-hand end of the east wall is the obvious square-cut tower. The corner-crack to its right is that referred to in the 1987 guide.

Chimes of Nausea   60 feet   E5 6a F7b †   (30.6.96)
The left-hand arête of the tower (but gained from the right): soft, ball-bearing sandstone. Six bolt runners, and a good *Rock 4* placement between the third and fourth bolts.
Climb 10 feet up the outside of the crack and transfer left onto the wall using a finger-pocket; then move up and left strenuously to a coal-filled hole at the foot of the left arête. Follow the arête, using a good slot on the left, to trees at the top.

Desert Planet Kidz   50 feet   E2 5c F6b+ †   (19.5.96)
Sensational soft sandstone on the zany right-hand arête. Five bolt runners. Climb the outside of the crack, swing left, and then cruise up the left-hand side of the sharp arête to arrive on a narrow horn at the top – heart-thumping. Escape left to a tree belay.

Crash Dummies' Day Out   60 feet   E1 5b †   (17.4.94)
Some of the loose blocks in the lower crack have moved or been removed, but watch out for more. Climb the lower crack easily but carefully; then layback the main one to the overhang and escape leftwards to a tree belay.

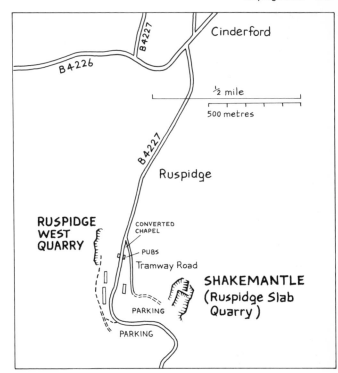

RUSPIDGE WEST QUARRY

OS Ref 648 117

Sandstone with a difference: the features resemble more a granite or grit outcrop. (Bad news for those who like their crags to be climbing-wall clones!) The rock is harder and lighter in colour than that in the afore-described quarries. In *New Climbs 1988* this quarry was incorrectly named Ruspidge East.

APPROACH

As you drive south out of Ruspidge, the last buildings on both sides of the road are part of a paint factory complex. Park immediately beyond, on the wide grass verge (or in lay-bys further on if you prefer). On the right-hand (west) side of the road, find a small path cutting back up rightwards through gorse and join a wider track which promptly narrows again. Follow this undulating path only a little above the factory to an isolated telegraph post where the path turns sharply left uphill. Descend steeply straight ahead or less steeply to the right into the floor of the quarry. This all takes less than ten minutes and there are no problems, but it is thought that the quarry may be reworked at some time in the forseeable future.

In the centre of the quarry is an obvious straight runnel flanked by twin slender arêtes. Just left of the left arête is a corner capped by an enormous projecting roof: The Horn.

Round the Horn   90 feet   E1 5c †   (1.5.88)
The left arête gives a spectacular finish.
Follow the rounded rib to the base of the corner, and then swing right along a handrail to gain a projecting ledge on the arête. Continue easily at first, and then make airy moves leftwards up the final undercut section (peg runner). Abseil from a tree.

Del Fuego   90 feet   E1 5b †   (1.5.88)
Elegant climbing up the clean-cut right arête on superb rock.
Climb the rounded lower arête with a tricky move to start, and then more easily to where it rears up. Move up and left (peg runner) and gain some ledges above with a long reach. Abseil from the tree on the right.

SHAKEMANTLE (RUSPIDGE SLAB QUARRY)   OS Ref 653 114
This is the set of slabs that can be seen from the B4227 Ruspidge to Soudley road. There are substantial areas of generally poor rock, but most of the routes are situated on the attractive slab in the north-east corner of the Upper Lift. The crag is quick drying in summer but can be a little greasy in winter. The holds range from small edges to cracks and the odd pocket. Some of these edges are fragile and frequently break off; but don't worry – there is usually another underneath!

The quarry is approached from Ruspidge Road by taking the last turning on the left before the twin pubs, Tramway Road, at a small converted chapel. Go along this until you reach a small parking-bay on the right (past the one that says Residents only). Walk along the track until you enter the quarry on the Upper Lift.

The approach road is owned by the residents, and climbers are asked to take especial care not to cause disturbance or inconvenience. The quarry itself is Forestry Commission property and there is no access restriction. However, parts of it may at some stage be developed, like Bixslade, for group instruction.

Shakemantle has been of interest to climbers for some while, as it has to the younger residents, many of whom have perfected the art of trundling! It is split into two lifts, the main routes being on the far slab on the upper.

LOWER LIFT
From the big block at the entrance, descend to the Lower Lift. The three routes so far recorded are on the long right-hand (east) wall, below and right of the main Upper Lift slab. In the corner at the left end of the wall is a huge pile of quarry debris. The first route starts on a tiny mound half way down the slope of this pile, and about 50 feet left of the corner.

Trash   50 feet   E1 5a   (23.4.88)
Climb the clean slab between two messy cracks.

In the centre of the wall is a ridge of huge tottering blocks. On its left is a clean strip taken by *Garbage Grinder*. Left of this is a roof above a slab, and left again is a lower large overhang with a crack running through it.

Thin Air   40 feet   E1 5b   (4.5.92)
Climb the crack in the large overhang direct. Good protection.

Garbage Grinder   50 feet   Hard Very Severe 4c   (23.4.88)
Climb the clean slab to the footpath.

UPPER LIFT
To lessen the erosion and polish on the climbs and the impact on the trees, it is recommended that the routes are finished at the top of the slab and that descent is made by the scree path along its bottom edge. It may be worthwhile checking the top of the crag for possible belays before starting your climb.

Around to right of the right edge of the main slab are two close cracks which have been climbed. The left-hand crack is 'so loose' and the right is very contrived.

It's so Loose!   60 feet   Severe 4a   (4.5.92)
Climb the obvious crack directly; well protected despite the rock.

Sign of the Times   60 feet   Hard Very Severe 4c   (4.5.92)
Climb the right hand crack without assistance or protection from the left-hand one.

The routes on the main slab are shown overleaf. They are described from **right to left.**

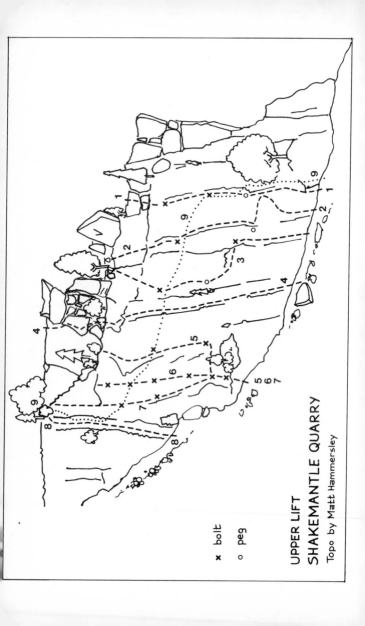

UPPER LIFT
SHAKEMANTLE QUARRY
Topo by Matt Hammersley

× bolt
○ peg

1 Acid Rain 60 feet E1 5a (23.4.88)
Spaced protection. From 5 feet left of the big tree at the right-hand end, climb directly past a peg runner and two bolt runners. to the top, and belay well back.

2 Rain Maker 60 feet E1 5b (23.4.88)
Good climbing on small holds. Start 10 feet left of Acid Rain. Climb up and clip the peg runner on Acid Rain, trend left to a peg runner, and continue directly up past another peg to some pockets. From these, climb directly (bolt runner) to a tree.

3 Rain Dance 60 feet E2 5b (23.4.88)
Harder and more sustained than the Rain Maker. Start in the centre of the slab. Climb right of the vegetated cracks to a bolt runner, continue left (peg runner) and up (bolt runner). Run it out on good but fragile holds to easier ground and continue to the tree.

Variation
Ruth Is Stranger than Friction 60 feet E1 5b (27.5.91)
From the first bolt runner of Rain Dance, climb directly until it is possible to lean right and clip the last bolt of Acid Rain. Continue up the same line about 5 feet right of the pine tree to easy ground. Step left to the pine to finish.

4 Dust Storm 60 feet VS 4b (9.8.90)
Follow the obvious crack and its continuation left of Rain Dance past the peg to the top of the slab.

The next routes were protected by bolts that have been stolen from the routes by some local cavers. They will be replaced but be prepared to place your own hangers. The routes start left of the overlap, further up the scree slope.

5 The Rain in Spain Falls Mainly on the Plain...
60 feet HVS 5b (23.4.88)
From the second bolt runner on Rain Shadow, traverse right and along the lip of the overlap to reach a shattered crack (bolt runner). Climb the crack to a lone pine tree in a diagonal break.

Rain Machine (E2 5b 4.5.92) is a direct start to the above route from the obvious tree-filled hole. Climb directly out and over the overlap onto the slab (small wires).

6 Rain Shadow 75 feet E2 5c (23.4.88)
Climb to the right of the centre of the smoothest part of the slab (six bolt runners) to reach a belay station at the diagonal break.

7 Eczema 80 feet E2 5c (23.4.88)
Technical climbing on small edges and plenty of smears. From the second bolt runner on Rain Shadow, move left onto thin delicate climbing. Pass two bolt runners and reach the thin cracks. Climb slightly left to finish at a convenient tree above.

8 Phlebitis 80 feet E1 5a (23.4.88)
Start at the thin cracks at the side of the slab. Small wires useful. Start a few feet up the slope from the previous routes. Climb up the thin cracks, sustained, until the angle eases and continue to the tree.

9 Rain Drops Keep Falling on My Head
150 feet E2 5b (7.5.88)
A fine, sustained, but well-protected rising traverse of the slab. Climb Acid Rain to its first bolt runner of and move up 10 feet to a small nut placement. Traverse left to pockets on Rain Maker (bolt runner above) and across left again into Rain Dance (bolt runner). A series of small edges lead on above to some broken ground (peg runner). Reach The Rain in Spain... (bolt runner); move up for 5 feet until you can step left into Rain Shadow (bolt runners); and tiptoe across at the level of its crux. Climb left to Eczema (bolt runner) and then onto the thin cracks leftwards on Phlebitis. Continue up this route until the angle eases and a convenient tree is reached.

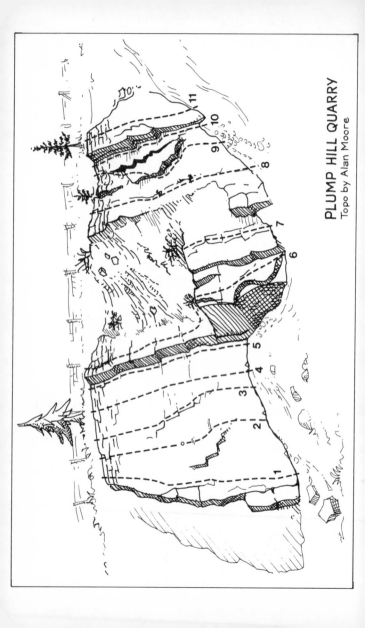

PLUMP HILL QUARRY
Topo by Alan Moore

PLUMP HILL QUARRY
OS Ref 661 168

The exfoliating slabs may appeal to climbers of an esoteric bent.

The crag is located on the outskirts of the village of Plump Hill, on the A4136 Coleford to Gloucester road. At the top of a hill a mile west of Mitcheldean, there is a signpost on the left to 'The Wilderness'. Take the track immediately opposite this and park anywhere convenient where it divides. The Quarry is a few minutes walk over grass to the left.

1 Dusty Springfield 50 feet VS 4b (12.8.91)
The left edge of the slabs.

2 Dustin Hoffman 50 feet VS 4b (7.5.88)
The darker rock provides the Quarry's best route. One peg runner.

3 Dust Devils 50 feet HS 4a (7.5.88)
A line of flaky edges leads diagonally left. Unprotected.

4 Follix 45 feet HVS 4c (25.11.96)
The rickety slab direct.

5 Day Tripper 45 feet VS 4c (2.2.92)
Follow the corner, with holds and runners in the next route.

6 Sandy Gall 60 feet S (12.8.91)
Two slabs, one above the other.

7 Little Treasure 25 feet VD (12.8.91)
Solid cracks.

8 Get on Your Zimmer Frame 50 feet VS 4c (15.4.93)
Plough up the chossy crack.

9 Dirt Bogart 40 feet VS 4b (12.8.91)
Climb the flaky crack quickly before it falls down!

10 Dirty Harry 40 feet HS 4b (12.8.91)
The corner to the right.

11 Flat Landers 35 feet HVS 4c (15.4.93)
The finely-featured final slab.

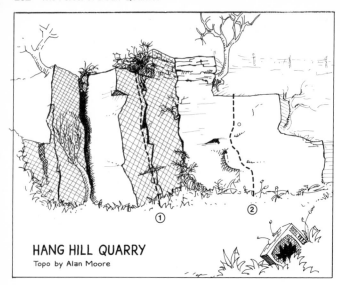

HANG HILL QUARRY
Topo by Alan Moore

HANG HILL QUARRY OS Ref 604 065
A small quarry with walls of tough Forest
sandstone lying hidden in the woods behind
the village of Bream. There are so far only two
routes, one each side of a central corner containing a birch tree.

Turn east at the cross-roads next to the school in
the centre of the village. Take the first right (Hang
Hill Road), and follow it and its track continuation
to a parking/turning-space in front of a row of
bungalows. A path leads into the woods, arriv-
ing in 100 yards at a fence marking the cliff-top.

1 Going for Gorse
30 feet HS 4b (4.12.91)
The obvious crackline 10 feet left of the
birch-tree corner.

2 Heart of Glass
30 feet VS 4b (4.12.96)
From a pair of white hands 20 feet right of
the corner, pull onto the wall and follow a
line of holds diagonally left to a ledge on top
of a faint nose (peg runner) Crimp for the
top.

Cleeve Hill – Castle Rock

This section is largely the work of James Collier and Roland Helps who died together in a fall while descending the north ridge of the Alphubel in the Swiss Alps on 29th July 1987, and it was published in their memory in the following year by their parents.

The booklet proved to be definitive and has been continuously in print and in demand since. After ten years, modest reappraisal of the grades and in a few places the descriptions was necessary owing to the continued polishing of holds and some minor falls of rock; but the text in essence and the artwork in its entirety are those of the original authors. The star-ratings also have been preserved, except where changes to the rock have dictated differently, and these should been seen in the context of the crag only and not of that of the book as a whole.

It is thought that Castle Rock, unlike many of the neighbouring outcrops, is a

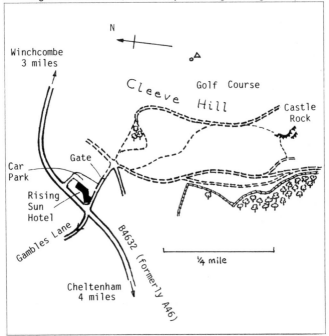

product of natural forces, weathering, and erosion. It is unusual in this respect, not having been quarried. This may explain its hardness compared to the other local loose and friable cliffs. The rock is well worn and many routes have polished holds from over use.

Grades are given for leads, often more protectable than one would think. The rock is a little perverse and the climbing quite strenuous. On the harder routes, abseiling to find the whereabouts of gear might be justified by the hidden nature of the protection on *Corner* and *Piton Direct* and the friable rock. Care must be taken at the top as loose material is frequently knocked down.

Cars should be parked down near the *Rising Sun Hotel*. However, many people who regularly use the crag park below the rock off the track. This is actually illegal, but a blind eye is generally turned if the cars do not number too many or obstruct the access.

This small crag consists of a slight bay, a compact wall with an inverted V of thin cracks (one taken by *Dislocated*), and a longer wall which overlooks Cheltenham. The most has been made of this very limited resource; the climbs are packed tighter than in most other areas covered by this guide. Most or all of the routes have probably been soloed. The rock dries quickly here but the cliff is exposed to the wind.

The short crack in the left-most buttress is Hard Severe 4b.

The Easy   25 feet   Hard Severe   4b/c
The bay is best climbed on its right-hand side. The left-hand line is a couple of grades harder.

Corner 1   27 feet   Hard Very Severe   5b
The blunt arête is an awkward problem with a leaning start and a technical upper half.

Dislocation   30 feet   E1   5c
An enjoyable route just to the right of the arête.

Dislocated   30 feet   E2   6a
Follow the right-to-left-trending crack.

★Eliminate 1   32 feet   E2   6a
A good technical climb which starts as for *Dislocated* before continuing straight up the wall on small holds.

★Piton Direct   33 feet   E3   6a
May be harder since rockfall from the base of the smooth wall. Climb the vertical crack above the start of *Dislocated*. Layback off the continuation edge of the crack to reach the base of the smooth wall above. Climb the

wall direct. Protection is difficult to arrange here without prior knowledge of where the little pockets are. If the flake on the left is used to finish, the climb is the slightly easier **Piton Route**.

★★★**Corner Direct** 35 feet E4 6a
A brilliant set of long reaches and technical moves but with no protection. Start from an inverted triangle of rock and make a hard move to a two-finger pocket at about 12 feet. Climb the left side of the arête via a large pocket and continue up the right side of the *Piton Direct* wall to the small prow.

★**Corner 2** 35 feet E3 6a
A poorly-protected first half. [Photo p.288.] Start as for *Corner Direct* but stay on the actual arête. Move over the nose and exit direct (awkward).

★**The Overhang** 33 feet E1 5b
Start a few feet right of the arête and make a hard pull onto more broken rock. Climb strenuously to the crack above and follow this.

★★**Cave** 33 feet E2 5c
Start below a tiny roof right of *The Overhang*. Climb past the niche via a hard and technical pull (crux) to the pocketed wall above.

Eliminate 2 (E2 5c) provides a hard but contrived finish between *Cave* and *Niche*.

Niche 33 feet E2 6a
Start at the deepest niche hereabouts. An awkward start, and not much easier above.

Eliminate 3 33 feet E2 5c
Climb the wall between *Niche* and the large crack direct. Not really worthwhile and completely unprotected for the hard bits.

1	The Easy	HS	9	Niche	E2
2	Corner 1	HVS	10	Eliminate 3	E2
3	Dislocation	E1	11	The Hand Jam	S
3a	Dislocated	E2	12	In Between	HVS
4	Eliminate 1	E2	13	Middle Crack	S
5	Piton Direct	E3	14	Eliminate 4	VS
6	Corner Direct	E4	15	Right Crack	VD
6a	Corner 2	E3	16	Black Wall	E1
7	The Overhang	E1	17	End Route	HVS
8	Cave	E2	18	The Girdle	HVS
8a	Eliminate 2	E2	19	The Traverse	6a

★The Hand Jam   33 feet   Severe 4a
Follow the left-hand wide crack for its entirety. Quite strenuous.

In Between   32 feet   Hard Very Severe 5b
Climb the wall between the two main cracks. The start is difficult but the rest of the climb can be varied as desired.

Middle Crack   33 feet   Severe 4a
Follow the obvious wide crack.

Eliminate 4   33 feet   Very Severe 4c
Climb the wall between *Middle Crack* and *Right Crack*.

★Right Crack   33 feet   Very Difficult
Near the right-hand side of the wall are a pair of cracks. Climb to the top mainly using the left crack. A pleasant route and the easiest on Castle Rock.

★Black Wall   35 feet   E1 5c
Start below the dark bulge at three-quarters height. Make technical moves to a broken ledge; then layback up a rib to good holds and a thread placement. Gaining the bulge above is the crux – the moves are thin but well protected. Climb the bulge direct and finish either side of the large block above.

End Route   33 feet   Hard Very Severe 5a/b
Climb the right-hand end of the wall – scrappy and loose. Not really worthwhile.

★The Girdle   70 feet   Hard Very Severe 5b
Start up *Black Wall* and climb to the thread. Traverse left along the break until just before the arête; then step up to a huge but hidden thread and belay. For the second pitch, step down left and down again below the prominent nose on the arête. Traverse below the smooth wall of *Piton Direct* (crux) and continue at the same level. Step around the next arête and belay in the groove. To finish, either move up to the top of *The Easy* wall or continue left around the final short buttress.

★★The Traverse   70 feet   6a
A brilliant low-level traverse of the crag, good for exploding forearms. Start up *Black Wall* until a prominent spike is reached on the right. Traverse left at this level until *The Hand Jam* crack is reached. Now move down and left and continue at this level. Passing *Niche* and *Cave* is hard. Go around the arête to the *Dislocation* wall:even harder! Move up, passing the start to *Piton Direct*, and continue at this level around onto *The Easy* wall. It is best to carry on all the way around the broken rocks to the left, and then go back! Try doing this more than four times.

Corner 2 (E3) Castle Rock, Cleeve Hill
Climber: James Collier   Photo: Roland Helps

The Russian (VS) Hollow Rock Area, Symonds Yat.
Climber: Chris Craggs · Photo: Craggs col.

A Climbers' Club Guide to

Symonds Yat

and

Huntsham Crags

by

Roger Lanchbury

will be published Summer 1997

Ethics – Style – The Record

If Ed Drummond's classic assessment of the Avon Gorge's never having been 'ship-shape Bristol fashion' was then true of that crag, how much more so it is of the Wye Valley, or at least of its premier and traditional cliff. The reasons for this are many, and not hard to understand.

Wintour's Leap, though possessing many positive attributes, does combine several of the more notorious characteristics of some limestone cliffs: in particular those of quarrying, vegetation, and unreliability. Before the development of thorough cleaning tactics and the improvement of protection gear, it was regarded as too steep and serious to be suitable for tiros, too loose and vegetated to be of importance to tigers, and too short of the varied rock features found on traditional grit and igneous cliffs (and to a certain extent even the unquarried Wyndcliffe over the river) to interest 'Mr Average'. It was 'The Heap'.

Although, as can be seen from the *History*, it did attract the attention of some notable climbers, even to them it was something of a sideline and they had few protective feelings for it. So the general contempt, or ignorance, in which the cliff was held together with the lack of a guidebook tradition tended to result in the absence of a proper record of good deeds and bad alike, and thus of the establishment of an ethical tradition. Further, the remoteness of the cliff from public gaze and climbers' scrutiny meant that things could be done here that would not be got away with elsewhere.

Several of those earlier pioneers used pegs for aid (other than on explicitly artificial routes) quite freely: this must be viewed in the context of on-sight leads when available holds might be covered with earth, grass, or looseness. And if a detailed record of the aid never appeared, that was not necessarily their fault; in any case, such aid points were often eliminated, not by a superior effort on the part of another climber, but merely by the removal of hold obstruction during the course of one or two repeats.

Such was the situation I faced in compiling the 1977 guide, and I chose (actually, lack of information meant there was little choice) not to record the use of occasional aid points on first ascents except where later elimination resulted in a genuine increase in standard rather than from an improvement in the condition of the climb.

Of greater concern to me then was the indiscriminate use of pegs on both new and established routes, less from the abstractly ethical point of view than because of the damage that repeat insertions and extractions were causing to the rock, and because of the regular 'theft' of *bona fide* fixtures. I like to think that my carefully assessed recommendations in that guide, together with the campaign of cementing, improved matters. And Pat Littlejohn's hammerless first ascent of *The Jackal* proved a milestone.

Alas! in the scramble for new routes that followed, too many of us allowed the arguably defensible laxity of the past to set precedents for the future.

A parallel charge could legitimately be levied against my 1987 guide, where I paid more attention to the detailed attribution of the first ascent of every five feet of rock, however insignificant, than to comment upon the manner and validity of the ascent. Paradoxically, this not only allowed bad practice to go unremarked (and therefore, inevitably, to continue) but also resulted in ill-founded accusations and poorly-argued criticism of its alleged perpetrators. Too much has passed for it to be possible to rectify the situation fully, but it seems necessary to *attempt* a balanced summary of the facts, fables, and fallacies. A future writer may be able to integrate the salient details into the *History*, but this time I felt that the circumstances dictated a separate treatment. The *History* must, of course, be read against the background of this essay.

I have dared to be overtly critical in one or two places; elsewhere *no covert criticism* should be inferred. It is for the most part inappropriate for a guidebook writer or editor to try to lay down the law on ethical matters (and, anyway, aspects of my own record do not allow me the moral high ground from which to do this). The best he can do, in addition to presenting the available facts, is to try to define the arguments and to urge people to consider their actions in the light of them.

CLIMBS AND CLAIMS
This must be got out of the way first. There have been one or two joke entries in the log-book that are easily discounted. But allegations that Gary Gibson did not climb certain of the routes he claimed, or at least that he used undeclared aid, have surfaced here as they used to elsewhere. Most of these are easily dismissed. From the first, in 1980, Gibson wrote up and sent me promptly all his new routes at Wintour's Leap. Climbing prolifically at high standards in all conditions, he would fail or fall on the odd move. He duly noted these occasions in his reports, and, where appropriate, followed them up with confirmations of unflawed ascents in the weeks that followed. *Vapona* and *Fond Adieu* were typical examples. The former has been much sited as a 'frigged' route, but Gibson openly acknowledged that his fall onto the peg on the crux was a rest point and I wrote this into *The Rising Sun* log-book. Shortly after, he reclimbed it clean by a slightly varied line and registered it as such. He also declared repeated falls on *Feline*, and siege tactics on *Hell: Just for Leather* (for which he did not sustain a first ascent claim). How these ascents should be categorized is discussed in a later paragraph, but any shortcomings in the guidebook recording is a fault of mine rather than his. A charge of dishonesty in relation to any of the above-mentioned routes cannot stand.

There was, however, a regrettable lapse on two routes on Kaiser Wall climbed around the turn of the year 85/86, when a couple of wet, though actually not technically difficult, sections were avoided. Gibson subsequently climbed these sections separately, but the full facts were not revealed until his second spilled the beans some months later. The furore that followed inevitably led to wild speculation from people who had not, as I had, witnessed the long weekends he would spend cleaning a dozen or more lines and then making impeccable ascents of them.

It is possible that Gibson once or twice (*Meninjectomy?*) used claiming a route *before* its ascent as a tactic to deter the 'theft' of a line in which he had already invested effort and cash in preparation (this had, of course, happened to him elsewhere). Such a tactic cannot be condoned, but it does not *necessarily* invalidate the ascent made later, though, of course, the recorded date will be inaccurate. Whether he did use this tactic, and more importantly whether he did later complete the ascents (and before someone else), probably only he can tell us. If suspicion remains about the former, I, for one, have absolutely no evidence upon which to doubt the latter.

THE ENVIRONMENTAL IMPACT

All the remaining topics must be considered to a greater or lesser extent in relation to their environmental impact. To some climbers the *sporting* ethic (whatever form this takes) is paramount; to others, it is the unrestricted availability of rock (kept) in ideal climbing condition. Neither of these is now sustainable as an exclusive objective, and attempts to ignore this fact will lead to disappointment far more surely and quickly than coming to terms with it.

A justification of this proposition is set out by Martin Crocker in the paragraph entitled 'The Forgotten Battlefield' on page 15 of his 1992 *Avon and Cheddar* guide. Although the arguments are manifest common-sense, they are there expressed in lucid and compelling terms that could not be bettered. It should be compulsory reading for *all* climbers.

CLEANING AND CHIPPING

This is the most contentious subject, and it is one that those not familiar with this type of cliff find incomprehensible. What to one person is thorough cleaning, to another is blatant hold-creation. But a clear distinction needs to be made between, on the one hand, the indiscriminately enthusiastic or careless removal of large quantities of vegetation and loose rock which may or may not *incidentally* create, improve, or even destroy holds; and, on the other, the *deliberate* creation of one or more specific holds crucial to the planned ascent (or even the *removal* of an unwanted hold!) by a *carefully directed* use of a chisel, drill, or hammer.

The latter is, of course, unequivocal cheating which no-one attempts to defend, though to what extent it is *environmentally* offensive any more than the drilling of a bolt or even the placing of a peg is an open question.

Holds artificially created in blank rock are easy enough to recognize. There are very few, if any, of these at Wintour's Leap or, to my knowledge, elsewhere in the Wye Valley. 'Smashed' holds are much more problematic. The ubiquitous seaming and jointing of the rock frequently allows loose sections to be removed by hand or with minimum force by a nut- or hammer-pick. The result often *looks* indistinguishable from a carelessly or deliberately smashed hold. Of the latter there are certainly some, though equally certainly not as many as might appear. The only sure judge can be someone who had intimate knowledge of the state of the rock prior to the event. Needless to say, positive avoidance of carelessness when cleaning in the proximity of existing routes is even more imperative, and Gibson laid himself open to fair criticsm for injudicious damage inflicted on *Flypast* and *Flying Fortress*.

There are, of course, more grey areas. In the peg-rationing climate of 1978, Arnis Strapcans (not noted for loose morals!) told me that he found inserting and extracting a peg a good way of creating nut placements (and cheaper than leaving the peg!).

As well as the jointing and seaming, there are patches of pastey mixtures of earth, sand, and very soft rock, which one can scrape to order with a nut-pick and no effort. I anticipated criticism for shaping the holds on *Swansong Prelude* in this fashion, but strangely never received it.

Other than in the more extreme cases, the extent to which cleaning becomes over-cleaning and this in turn becomes cheating and/or environmentally offensive can be extremely hard to determine, as everyone's dividing-lines are drawn differently; and any attempt at assessment can be made only by balancing intent, results, and context against *clearly thought-out parameters*. Ultimately, it is up to each individual to square his actions *both* with his own conscience *and* with the weight of collective opinion.

FIXED PROTECTION
The peg problem very soon stabilized in the late 70s, and it is worth noting the self-discipline exercised by first ascensionists between 1978 and 1985 at Wintour's Leap. It had never been a problem at Wyndcliffe and did not become one in the Shorn Cliff development. *Friends* and better-designed nuts had much to do with this, but several bold routes which could well have swallowed many more pegs date from this period.

In July 1982, Gibson placed two bolts on The Angel's Tower, the first protection bolts used in the Wye Valley (though eight aid bolts remained from earlier days), and a year before he tested the water on Peak limestone with *Clarion Call*. The response was muted, but only one more bolt appeared during the next three years. At this juncture, Tony Penning and John Harwood decided to register their opposition. Penning led past the bolt on *Strange Little Girl*, and Harwood, following, chopped it. In retrospect this can be seen as a tactical error. Had they announced that the bolt was chopped 'because it was there' and that any more placed would receive similar treatment, the tide might have been stemmed. As it was, their chosen justification was flawed in that Penning's lead was not on-sight – he had climbed the route at least once before, clipping the bolt. An unprintable comment, for once supportive of Gibson, appeared in the log-book, and the bolt was replaced. The battle was decided with barely a skirmish and the way was open for the drilling to continue unopposed. It has to be recognized that although Gibson started the bolting he continued, at Wintour's Leap, to observe the minimalist ethic very closely, just as he had exercised peg restraint in the preceding years: it was rare for even the longest pitches to have more than one bolt, and none was used to protect moves less than 6a. (The tat and jammed wires that were used more freely are another matter – not only are they often unsightly but their propensity to deteriorate rapidly can soon leave the routes in a virtually useless state.)

Matt Ward had fewer inhibitions. His 1986-7 routes, often at more amenable grades and in more accessible situations, attracted both criticism for 'hold creation' and indiscriminate drilling, and praise for thorough cleaning and decent protection. Again, it was the praise that predominated, and the clip-up routes (the sport-climbing concept had not yet fully evolved) became highly popular.

This set the pattern for the next years at Ban-y-gor, where traditionally-pro- tected routes, clip-ups, and those with the genuinely-minimalist occasional bolt appeared, seemingly happily, side by side. A year or two after Gibson had got to grips with the Main Cliff, sport climbing was established, and the use of the *Hilti* meant that a route could be fully drilled without expenditure of excessive time and effort.

The current drilled-gear policy for the Wye Valley, approved by the BMC Area Committee, is set out on page 17. Whether this is sustainable in the long term remains to be seen. Those who feel it needs change, in any direction, are free to come to Area Meetings and argue their case. Pending such change, I would urge everyone to operate within it.

ROUTES AND OTHERS
The old-fashioned definition of a route was one that started at the bottom of the cliff and finished at the top; occasionally, rock features might dictate that routes would have to join below the top. Now, with sophisticated abseiling devices and techniques, and easy routes to scramble up, climbers can decide exactly where they want their routes to start and finish; in other words, they can to a much greater extent control the limits of difficulty and quality. Such selectivity has many advantages in terms of satisfaction, safety, avoidance of unnecessary disturbance of vegetated areas, and circumventing access prob- lems; but its artificiality must be recognized and not abused.

Wintour's Leap has over the last ten years gained notoriety for its absurd crowding of routes, variants, and eliminates. It is instructive to note that in 1968 Tony Willmott described his *The Pulsating Rainbow* as an eliminate, a route which though starting and finishing in *Kangaroo Wall*, otherwise spent well over half its 300-foot length at least 20 feet (of overhanging rock) from either of its neighbours! Where that leaves the modern eliminate…

This crowding has taken a number of different forms. First, the genuine but squeezed route, the proximity and sometimes fixed gear of which compromises a worthy neighbour. Second, the alternative starts, finishes, and middles which leave the guidebook writer and reader utterly bemused. Third, the stepped diagonal, linking alternatively bits of traverse with bits of vertical routes and only occasional (if any) bits of independent climbing. Worst of all, the constant meandering between and across adjacent vertical routes. Once again, Gibson may have to accept responsibility for starting the rot (but others of us did not *have* to imitate) and Rob Kingston, with his passion for ensuring that every hold was explored in every possible way, for taking it to its ultimate. Just occasionally the new will be a real improvement upon the old, or peacefully co-exist with it, but the assessment is very subjective and not always best made by the first ascensionist!

It seems likely that this crowding will be solved by a combination of revegetation and gear degeneration on the routes that no-one wants! Meanwhile, dealing with this situation is not easy for a writer whose charge is to produce a comprehensive and definitive guide. I have addressed the situation in the Wintour's Leap script, but will not always have got the balance right; in general I would expect my successors to have to be more ruthless!

TACTICS AND STYLE

The record here prior to the early 90s is non-existent. Some first ascensionists will have taken pride in achieving as pure ascents as possible. Others have openly regarded ascents involving full top-rope practice (usually declared), handling and assessing holds during cleaning, custom racking, and varying degrees of resting and yo-yoing as legitimate, which by the 'official' ethic of the day many of them were not. Now, most of these tactics are acceptable in a declared context.

Since 1990, many areas have adopted a code with categories for different styles of ascent, which is, of course, as appropriate for repeats as for first ascents. The best, or best available in the circumstances, is aimed for, but a lesser style is still valid and is a challenge to be bettered by others. Thus, there is:

The **on-sight flash**, which is self-explanatory.

The **beta flash**, which has inevitably become somewhat down-graded – originally, though it allowed some information to be obtained, it was supposed to involve no close-up visual knowledge of the route. But if routes are to be prepared or have to be abseiled into this becomes unrealistic; the 'beta' becomes indistinguishable from a first-attempt redpoint.

The **redpoint** itself allows knowledge, practice, and previous attempts – its requirement is a single-push ascent without weighting any gear, and placing all gear (other than fixtures) on lead.

The **pinkpoint** (generally frowned upon, at least for first ascents, but still practised) allows quickdraws preplaced on fixtures.

The **yo-yo** is when gear or the rope is weighted by falling or resting – one then lowers to the ground, or at least to a no-hands resting-place, before continuing, but the ropes may be left in place.

To work, such a code depends upon the honesty of the climber, but a cynic might suggest that this is more likely to be forthcoming when only the category of the ascent is at stake rather than recognition of the ascent itself! By and large, its application is more satisfactory to repeats than to first ascents, where the type of rock and environment may dictate different tactics. Its adoption is nevertheless worth careful consideration, not least as a good self-discipline! Martin Crocker, true to his exhortations in the *Avon and Cheddar* guide, has recorded his own ascents in this way for the last few years. This information is now in the files and will be available to future Wye Valley authors, but it seemed incongruous to isolate these few entries in the first-ascent list this time.

SUGGESTIONS FOR FUTURE GOOD PRACTICE

1. Before preparing or climbing a new route, consider whether any effect it may have upon the cliff environment or neighbouring climbs is justifiable by the likelihood of its being (or becoming) and remaining of real interest to other climbers.
2. Although cleaning needs to be thorough if it is to be done at all, assess carefully the minimum that is of necessity. (Remember that cutting back brambles just makes them grow faster!) This applies equally to recleaning existing routes where necessary.
3. Remember that trees are protected by law. Possibly the worst thing that has been done by climbers in the Wye Valley was the cutting of trees at Ban-y-gor in 1988.
4. Keep preparation tactics appropriate to the situation; for example, large-scale trundling and heavy bolting of E2 rock may be OK at Tintern Quarry but are not acceptable on the South Bay at Wintour's. Take full account of the ownership and conservation status of the crag. This applies to new areas as well as existing ones.
5. Record the style of your first ascents in accordance with the above-described code.
6. Recording the style and date of early repeats is also very worthwhile and helpful to future guide authors.
7. Some regearing of the better routes will have to be addressed soon if they are to survive. Climbers are invited to consider whether they can contribute to this in any way.
8. Since drilled gear alters the rock irrevocably, please ensure that, as well as being consistent with the policy (laid out on page 17), it is of an appropriate standard and specification.

First Ascent List

WYNDCLIFFE
There appear to be no records of the first ascent details of: **Green Symphony**, **The Crack** (originally climbed in a number of pitches), **The Gully**. These were climbed around 1970 or earlier.

1970 Feb 14	**Cadillac** F Cannings, P Littlejohn (A)	
	Originally climbed in two pitches.	
1970 Feb 14	**Questor** F Cannngs, P Littlejohn, C Morton	
1970 Feb 15	**Phoenix** F Cannngs, P Littlejohn (A)	
	Originally climbed in two pitches.	
1970 Feb 28	**The Firebird** P Littlejohn, F Cannings	
1970 Feb 28	**Sinew, Suncrush** F Cannings, P Littlejohn	
	Sinew *originally climbed in two pitches.*	
1970 Mar 1	**Fibre** P Littlejohn, F Cannings	
	Originally climbed in two pitches.	
1970 Mar 1	**Sundowner** R Teal, N Jago (A)	
	Originally climbed in three pitches.	
1970 Mar 1	**The Don** F Cannings, P Littlejohn	
1970 Mar 15	**Starfinder** R Teal, N Jago	
	Originally climbed in two pitches.	
1970 Mar 22	**Centinon** N Jago, R Teal	
	Originally climbed in two pitches.	
1970 Apr 4	**Expo** N Jago, R Teal	
	Originally climbed in two pitches. Variation called Expo 89 climbed in April 1989 by R Harper and G Cole.	
1970 Apr 11	**Decoy** F Cannings, G Skerratt	
1970 Apr 18	**Purple Haze** F Cannings, I Duckworth	
	Variation (as described) by A Tallant (date unknown).	
1970 Apr 18	**Vanguard** I Duckworth, F Cannings (A)	
	Originally climbed in two pitches. Direct start M Ward (solo) 1986.	
1970 May 2	**Mustang** F Cannings, P Littlejohn (A)	
	Originally climbed in three pitches.	
1970 May 9	**Apricot** F Cannings, P Lewer	
1970 July 5	**Trial** F Cannings, C Horsfield, P Watkin, G Skerrat	
1970 Aug 30	**Andrea** F Cannings, T Doe	
	Originally climbed in two pitches.	
1970 Aug 31	**Cardiac** F Cannings, R Carr, T Doe	
1970 Sept 13	**Monsoon** P Watkin, R Barratt	
	Originally climbed in two pitches.	
1970 Sept 19	**Syrphus** C Horsfield, P Watkin	
1970 Sept 26	**Pinnacle Grooves** C Horsfield, P Watkin	
1970 Sept 26	**Pinnacle Route** P Watkin, C Horsfield	
1970 Sept 30	**Skyjack** C Horsfield	
1970 Oct 3	**Hostage** C Horsfield, P Watkin	
1970 Oct 3	**Strike** P Watkin, C Horsfield	
1971 June 30	**Left Wing Girdle** D Owen, G Reed, M Putnam	
1971	**Sting** I Jenkins, M Plant	
1972 Jan 9	**Q.E.1** T Doe, R Carr (A)	
1972 April 10	**Klute** C Milford, M Putnam	
1972 April 13	**Shaft** C Milford, M Putnam	
1972 April 13	**Zulu** C Milford, M Putnam	
1972 May 29	**Umbo D'Jingo** R Thomas, D Partridge	

1972	**Papillon** F Cannings, P Hicks
1974 May 5	**Wyvern** C Horsfield, C Elliot, P Lewis
1976 Jan 3	**Close to the Edge** A Sharp, T Mathews
1976 Jan 16	**Tizer Grooves** J Mathews, A Sharp
1976 Sept 8	**Pilgrimage** A Sharp, J Harwood, C Horsfield
1976 Sept 15	**Mecca** A Sharp, J Harwood, C Horsfield, P Thomas

The second on-sight attempt proved successful after some minor gardening by others.

1976 Sept 17	**Lyon** C Horsfield, J Harwood
1976 Sept 17	**Piercefield Grooves** P Thomas, J Harwood, C Horsfield

An on-sight lead after gardening by others and a lunchtime drinking session. A block treated with caution was still there in 1996.

1976 Oct 26	**Violater** A Sharp, A N Other
1976	**Christian, Elan** P Thomas, T Oliver
1977 March 16	**Aeriel Combat** J Harwood, W Gray (3 pts aid)

First free ascent: A Sharp, P Lewis on 7 October 1979. Initially considered HVS/A3; the original ascent removed much loose rock.

1979	**Blood Bank** M O'Brien, M Hunt
1979	**The Day of the Trifids** G Lewis, M Price
1981 Oct 13	**Collapse Point** T Penning, J Harwood (1 pt aid)

The overhang was considered unstable even then, necessitating the aid-point – it has now disappeared rendering the route obsolete! First free ascent: T Penning, P Cresswell, A Sharp 1981. Variation as described by P Donnithorne and J Harwood on 26 November 1995.

1983 Oct 29	**President Raygun** J Chapman, M Ward

Direct Start by M J Crocker 1991/2.

1984 Feb 12	**Press the Panic Button** M Ward, P Williams
1984 April 3	**Old Smokey** T Penning, J Harwood
1984 April 17	**Edge of Insanity** T Penning, J Harwood
1984 Sept 18	**Mercury** T Penning, J Harwood, C Court, M Ward
1986	**Don't Ask Me, I Don't Know**

Unknown climbers were off-limits.

1987 Sept 9	**Every Trick in the Book** M Ward, R Kingston

Preplaced gear.

1988 Jan 24	**Transfusion** M J Crocker, M Ward
1988 Jan 24	**What's Gone Is Gone** M J Crocker, M Ward
1990 Aug 7	**Jezebel** R Kingston, G A Jenkin, C Begley
1990 Sept 23	**Canine Crack** N A Coe, G A Jenkin
1990 Sept 23	**Shin Gi Tai** G A Jenkin, N A Coe
1990 Sept 25	**Bogger Bob** R Kingston, P Begley (2 pts aid)

First free ascent: G A Jenkin, A Tallant 30 September 1990

1990 Oct 14	**Still Stuck on You, And the Crowd Went Wild**
	G A Jenkin, A Tallant
1990 Oct 14	**Sweet FA** A Tallant, G A Jenkin
1991 May 19	**Diminishing Returns, Miss Whiplash** G A Jenkin,
	M Ward, A Tallant
1991 May 19	**The Corrective Party** A Tallant, G A Jenkin, M Ward
1991 May 19	**Shadows Run Black** G A Jenkin, M Ward
1991 Aug 6	**Finishing Touch** G A Jenkin, K Marsden, A Tallant
1991 Aug 6	**Mr Whippy** A Tallant, K Marsden, G A Jenkin
1991 Nov 23	**Hong Kong Garden** M J Crocker, E Jones
1993 April 15	**Empire and Revolution** J Hartley

WINTOUR'S LEAP

There is no record of the first ascents of: **Right-Hand Route, Original Route, Corner Buttress I, II, & III, Bottle Buttress, Central Rib Route I & III, The Beginner's Route**. They and their names were in existence by the early 60s, and it is probable that Gloucestershire Mountaineering Club parties were responsible.

The following were defined and named by the author for the 1977 guide, but they had almost certainly all been climbed before: **Cement Groove, Direct Route, Black Wall & Black Wall Left, Grey Wall, Ridge Route & Ridge By-Pass, Wye Knot?**

The Problems, This, Butterfly, Moth were named for the 1977 guide. The earliest *known* ascents were in the early 70s by E Fivelsdal and/or J Willson, but it is likely they had been climbed before.

1958 June 29	**Left Hand Route** G J Frazer, J Peacock
1958 July 13	**Central Route** E D G Langmuir, G J Frazer (A)
1958 July 13	**Symplex** E D G Langmuir, G J Frazer
1961 May	**Zelda** J Grieve, C Boulton *The fine second pitch was added on the second ascent by J Davidson.*
1961 Aug	**Centre Route, Terry's Left-Hand Finish** M Shannon, D T Dove, T Broomsgrove (V)
1961 Aug	**Terry's Right-Hand Finish** M Shannon, D T Dove, T Broomsgrove
1962 Sept	**The Willies** J Grieve, C Prowse
1963 April	**Prang** J Grieve, C Bolton *This ascent may have included further pitches of or similar to Bottle Buttress Direct.*
1963 April	**The Tap** J Grieve, C Prowse
1963 Dec	**Gryke** J Grieve, B Burlton
1964 May	**Compost Wall** J Grieve, D Smith
1965 March	**Greta** D T Dove, T Broomsgrove
1965 March	**Narcotic** C F Tanner, B Burlton
1965 June	**King Kong** T Taylor, C F Tanner
1965 Sept	**The Angel's Eye** T Broomsgrove, D T Dove *This route and the preceding one put Wintour's on the map and prompted Dove to start work on a Wye Valley guide.*
c.1965	**The Wrong Tap** possibly J Grieve *This route was never recorded, and may well have been climbed by an unknown party in mistake for The Tap, which was poorly described in the 1970 guide; the name was assigned by the author in the 1977 guide. The finishing-pitch was added by D Green and J Willson on 25 February 1984.*
1966 May	**Kangaroo Wall** F Bennett, P Lennard *This must rank among the most auspicious crag debuts! A number of aid points were used, and a rope hung down the top ivy-covered wall for some years. The aid was whittled away gradually until C King made the first recorded fully free ascent in 1978. The alternative finishes were added by G Gibson and A Hudson in May 1983 and by G Gibson (roped solo) on 12 December 1985.*
1966 June	**Bacchanalian** J Grieve, D Smith
1966 Aug	**Guytha** J Grieve, B Burlton

Pitch 2 only. The belay was approached by a short diagonal traverse from the original first stance (half-way up the first pitch) of Zelda. The first pitch was climbed by F Bennett et al. in 1967.

1966 Aug   **Technician**   F Bennett, P Lennard
The first of the big artificial routes. Later absorbed by The Jackal and Feline.

1966 Aug   **The Early Morning Traverse**   J Grieve, C F Tanner
1966 Dec   **Kama Sutra**   T Taylor, R Walker, J Charlesworthy
c. 1966   **Bottle Buttress Direct**   D Roberts
Pitch 1. Pitches 2 and 3 were climbed by J Willson in 1976 after top-rope inspection during research for the 1977 guide, but either or both may well have been climbed in 1963 as part of Prang.

c.1966   **Urizen, Aharia**   D T Dove
1967 Jan   **That**   T Broomsgrove, D T Dove
1967 June 4   **The Burning Giraffe**   A C Willmott, F Heppenstall
Willmott joins the fray with what was his only free route at Wintour's. Extension across to King Kong climbed by D Edwards in 1971.

1967 July 13   **The Deceiver**   E Fry, G Coley
1967 Aug 17   **Firefly**   Miss G Pemberton, G Farnsworth, C McDonald (V)
Like Caesar, they came, they saw, they conquered. Unfortunately, no more was seen of this redoubtable trio. Fly Wall, like GO Wall, was opened up with what is still one of its very finest routes. Pitch 2 was climbed at A2 with a finish in the easy corner just left. It was climbed free by R Hazell and J Willson on 9 June 1978. The 15-year-old Hazell was particularly delighted with this as he had been told by Arnis Strapcans that 'it wouldn't go free'. The direct finish was added by G Gibson in 1981.

1967 Aug 19   **Dragonfly**   Miss G Pemberton, G Farnsworth, C McDonald
1967 Aug 20   **Big Fly**   G Farnsworth, Miss G Pemberton, C McDonald
1967 Sept 2   **Flyover**   G Farnsworth, Miss G Pemberton, C McDonald
Pitch 2 at A2, climbed free in 1979 by R A Harrison and G Forward. The original pitch 1 has now been assigned to Flypast and the current pitch 1 was climbed by A Strapcans and C King in 1978.

1967 Sept 10   **Flyte**   P Lennard, D Target
1967 Sept   **Parasol**   F Bennett, P Lennard
A2. The 'impossible' was achieved on 14 December 1991 when the lower roof was free-climbed by M J Crocker and P Oxley. A solution to the upper roof had been found by A Strapcans and H Clarke on 10 June 1978 in the form of Joe the Lion.

1967 Oct 3   **Phoenix**   S Eskel, M Battle
1967 Oct 23   **Peasant**   D T Dove
1967 Oct   **The Umbrella Girdle**   F Bennett, P Lennard
Pitch 2 at A2. Climbed free by C King and S Gough on 14 July 1976.

1967 Dec 3   **Swallow's Nest**   I Ballard, G Jarvis
1967 Dec 12   **Freedom**   I Ballard, G Jarvis, P Henessy
The direct finish was climbed by A Hudson and G Gibson on 12 March 1983.

1967 Dec   **The Split**   P Trinder, N Waghorne
c.1967   **Broken Bottle**   F Bennett
Pitch 1 at A1, free-climbed by A Sharp and P Lewis in 1978.

c.1967   **Cobra, Puma, The Ragged Edge, Kaiser Wall**
F Bennett, P Lennard, R Walker, R Bennett

These routes were not properly recorded. It is quite possible that the first two included some sections of what later became Themeninblack, Hunky Doré, or others.

Kaiser Wall was A2 on pitches 1 and 3. This aid was reduced to one point by A Strapcans and C King in January 1978, and the route was climbed completely free by P Gibson and G Gibson on 5 March 1978. Pitch 4 was added by J Willson and M Ward on 9 April 1986.

1968 Jan	**Interstellar Overdrive**	A C Willmott, J Brown

Pitch 1 had been climbed earlier, on Christmas Day 1967 by Willmott with A Baker. Pitch 2 was A2. Most of the route was finally swallowed by Howling at the Moon.

1968 Feb 3	**Exit**	P Henessy, G Stone
1968 June	**Surrealist**	B Wintringham, W O'Connor
1968 Sept 22	**Ecliptic**	M Battle, D King
1968 Dec 15	**The Pulsating Rainbow**	A C Willmott, M J Spring

Pitch 2 was A3. The route was later absorbed by Hyena Cage and Dog Eat Dog.

1969 Oct 12	**Big Brother**	F Cannings, P Littlejohn (A)

The first 5c pitch (led by Littlejohn) and the first fully free 'XS' in the Wye Valley.

1970 May	**Roger's Route**	R Sampford, J Willson
1972 Feb	**It's a Beautiful Day**	A C Willmott, D Hermalin

Sadly, Willmott's last offering at Wintour's. A2. Mostly absorbed by Big Bad Wolf and Zebra Crossing and other bits and pieces.

1973 Nov	**Joe's Route**	E Fivelsdal (roped solo)
1973	**Central Rib Route II**	E Fivelsdal

Pitch 1. Pitches 2 and 3 were climbed by J Willson in 1976 after top-rope inspection during research for the 1977 guide, but either or both may have been climbed before.

1974 April 21	**Jos'e and the Fly**	T Penning, P Cresswell
1974 July 9	**Zebrazone**	A Strapcans, M Putnam
1974 Sept 22	**John's Route**	J Willson, P Curtis Hayward, A Ashmore

Markers from Penning, Strapcans, and Willson.

1974 Oct 20	**Flypast**	E Fivelsdal, K Lyne

Pitch 2 at A2, climbed free in June 1980 by A Hall and J P de Rohan. Pitch 1 was the original pitch 1 of Flyover.

1975 March 15	**The Angel's Girdle**	J Willson, S Smith, N Smith

Led on-sight until brambles barred the way just before the final section of Joe's Route was reached; the last pitch was reclimbed complete the week after. A peg for aid was used on pitch 3, later rendered unnecessary when it was moved from the pocket to free up a hold. The additional pitch across The North Buttress was climbed by Willson with A Simmins on 11 April 1981.

1975 Oct 10	**Lord of the Flies**	A Strapcans, C King
1977 July 1	**Senta**	J Willson, P Curtis Hayward
1977 Nov 25	**The Jackal**	P Littlejohn, P Boardman

Just a week after the 1977 guide was published, Littlejohn set Wintour's alight with this route and the next, both a good two grades harder than anything that had been done here before. Also noteworthy as probably the first first ascent of any significance at the crag done without carrying hammer and pegs (though, of course, aid relics were fairly plentiful).

1977 Nov 29	**Hyena Cage**	P Littlejohn, C King
1978 Jan	**Vulture Squadron**	A Strapcans, C King

1978 Feb 18   **Flyhole** J Willson, R Hazell
The start of the second blitz on Fly Wall after ten years with only a couple of additions. It also marked the point at which route-cleaning prior to first ascents became the norm at Wintour's Leap. The route was first named Greenfly, but Strapcans, who was eyeing the ready-cleaned line as Willson and Hazell arrived to climb it, had a better suggestion!

1978 April 22   **Bulging Flies** A Strapcans, G A Jenkin, S Marriott
A persistently wet early spring had held up Strapcans for some weeks, but now he and the Bristol 'Clean Hand Gang' got going with a vengeance.

1978 April 22   **Flew** K Wilkinson, S Monks

1978 April 22   **Stone Spider Reaction** A Strapcans, S Marriott
The direct variation was climbed by P Oxley and C Waddy in 1988.

1978 April 22   **Swatter** N Beggs, S K Berry

1978 April 23   **Dazed and Confused** G A Jenkin, F E R Cannings
From a combination of flu medication and lunchtime in The Rising Sun!

1978 April 23   **Wurlitzer** A Strapcans, S Marriott
Pitch 2, with a finish up the easy corner on the left. Pitch 1 was added by G A Jenkin and J Willson on 7 April 1982; and the direct finish by M Ward, R Kingston, and M J Crocker on 29 May 1986.

1978 May 17   **African Killer Bee** M J Peacock, S K Berry

1978 May 21   **Balls Out** A Strapcans, F E R Cannings, G A Jenkin

1978 May 21   **Chameleon** A Strapcans, S K Berry, G A Jenkin

1978 May 21   **Fly or Die** G A Jenkin, S K Berry
Originally a highly-rated E1; after a large flake had fallen off, G Gibson climbed a harder but less satisfying version on 13 February 1983.

1978 May 24   **Bzzz Splat** G A Jenkin, C Coghill, E Moseley

1978 June 1   **Empire State Experience** A Strapcans, S Monks

1978 June 3   **Gemmell's Groove** J Willson, R Hazell
The alternative first pitch by M Ward and M Bellian on 8 April 1984

1978 June 10   **Joe the Lion** A Strapcans, H Clarke
This free-climbed the start of It's a Beautiful Day and the upper roof of Parasol.

1978 June 14   **Loads' Lids, Sowerbutts' Sortie** R Hazell, J Willson
Direct finish to the former by S Rosser and M Rosser on 9 June 1981.

1978 June 21   **Flies Rise** J Willson, R Hazell

1978 July 16   Unnamed pitch on North Wall Top Tier P Gibson, S Smith

1978 Aug   **The Other** R Teed, L Collins

1978 Oct 21   **The Adulterer** M Morrison, M Hunt

1978 Nov 8   **Psychotic** J Willson, R Hazell

1978 Nov 15   **Poet** R Hazell, J Willson

1978 Nov 15   **Something Else** R Hazell, J Willson

1978   **Strawberry Dust** A Sharp, P Lewis

1979 Feb 3   **Nibelheim** J Willson, R Hazell
Pitch 3 was straightened and the poor upper pitch added later by J Willson with Rendcomb College climbing parties.

1979 Feb 24   **Notung** R Hazell, J Willson

1979 Feb 24   **Rheinfahrt** J Willson, R Hazell

1979 April 28	**Tarnhelm** J Willson, R Hazell
1979 June 16	**Split Flies** R Hazell, J Willson
	The alternative first pitch by D Viggers and D Carroll in 1983.
1979 July 1	**The Rising Sun** R Gookey, M Hunt (A)
1979 July 7	**The Perfumed Garden** R Hazell, J Willson
1979 Sept 29	**Nice and Sleazy** G A Jenkin, R Cope
	The first recorded route in The Woodcroft Quarry.
1979 Sept 30	**Clank Honk Tweet** G A Jenkin, D Viggers (A)
1979 Oct 14	**Alluvium** M Morrison, M Quantrell
	One peg for aid. Second ascent free by D Hall and G Hall using a hold which soon broke off. Aid peg restored and finally dispensed with by G A Jenkin on 1 May 1981. The route has subsequently been cannibalized.
1979 Oct 14	**Zipper** J Willson, S R Smith
	The lower half of the second pitch had been climbed, with a traverse left into the Jet Stream groove, by A Strapcans and C King on 15 May 1978.
1979 Oct 24	**Cheetah** J Willson, S R Smith
1979 Dec 19	**Crumble Corner** L Collins, R Teed
1980 Jan 13	**Captain Beaky** R A Harrison, J Edwards
	Pitch 2 had been climbed by J Willson and R Hazell on 7 July 1979 as a second pitch for The Perfumed Garden.
1980 Feb 10	**Gadfly** D Viggers, M Taylor
1980 April 11	**Cryptic** J Willson, S Smith
1980 April 11	**Erda** J Willson, S Smith
	The top pitches were added by D Green and J Willson on 10 December 1983.
1980 June 29	**Suspect Device** J Willson, R Hazell
1980 June 29	**Uptight** M Morrison, M Quantrell
	One point of aid. Climbed free on 12 May 1982 by K Marsden.
1980 July 9	**Antediluvian** J Willson, R Hazell
	Now made redundant by Achilles.
1980 Aug 17	**Themeninblack** G Gibson, D Beetlestone
	Gibson 'arrives' – things would never be the same again!
1980 Oct 12	**Waiting for Themeninblack** G Gibson, P Gibson, S Horridge
	The top pitch was added by G Gibson and A Hudson on 14 March 1983.
1980 Oct 19	**Arabesque** D A B Jones, D Williams
	Jones went off-route from Greta and has never forgiven Wintour's since.
1980 Dec 10	**Barber's Stool** J James, S Thompson
1981 Jan 7	**Camp Freddie's Boil** S Thompson, J James
1981 Feb 7	**Llama** J Willson, J French
1981 Feb 11	**Flyaway** J Willson
1981 March 29	**Meningitis** G Gibson, P Gibson, R Cope
1981 April 11	**Andromeda** J Willson, A Simmins
1981 April 15	**Death of a Salesman** B Barnett, D Viggers
1981 May 18	**Hic Hoc Altera et** J James, S Thompson
1981 June 7	**The Height Below** G A Jenkin, F E R Cannings
1981 June 8	**Paul's Wall** S Thompson, J James, G Howlett
1981 June 28	**Fly Major** T Penning, P Cresswell
1981 June 30	**Spirit of St Louis** T Penning, J Harwood
1981 July 19	**Rape of the Fair Country** M Rosser, S Thompson, S Rosser, J James
1981 Sept 6	**Meninjection** G Gibson, P Gibson

1981 Sept 13	**Vapona** G Gibson, P Gibson
1981 Sept 20	**Hoof Hearted** S Meredith, J James, S Thompson (V)
1981 Sept 27	**Northerners Can't Climb, Tiswas** S Meredith, J James, S Thompson
1981 Oct 11	**Meninboredom** J James, S Thompson

It would take more than a couple of route-names to keep Gibson away.

| 1981 Oct 27 | **Towering Angels, Digitus Extractus** T Penning, J Harwood |
| 1982 Feb 21 | **Big Dong** J Taylor, C Dring |

Pitch 2 only. Pitches 1 and 3 were climbed by J Shaw and J Willson on 15 January 1986, and pitch 4 by the same pair and S Green on 14 December 1985.

| 1982 Feb 23 | **Jannock** T Penning, M Learoyd (A), J Harwood |

Using The Ragged Edge to reach the long corner. Reclimbed by Penning and Harwood using the described start on 4 September 1984. Direct start by G Gibson and M Ward on 19 January 1986.

| 1982 April 15 | **The One that Nearly Got Away** S Meredith, J James, S Thompson |
| 1982 April 18 | **Meninpunkunderwear** M Ward, M Lance-Watkins |

Named, needless to say, some time before Ward met Gibson!

| 1982 April 20 | **Galtieri's Gonads** M Lance-Watkins, M Ward (V) |
| 1982 May 9 | **Zebra Crossing** T Penning, P Cresswell |

Pitches 1 and 2 as far as Parasol and then called Colonel Claw. The final 40 feet were the original A1 second pitch of It's a Beautiful Day, climbed free by G A Jenkin in 1980. This missing link was supplied and the route climbed complete by G Gibson and A Hudson in March 1983.

| 1982 May 18 | **Menincontinent** S Thompson, J James |

The campaign was worth a try, Nifl-Heim; a pity you gave up after this, because success would have left a lot more for the rest of us over the next few years!

| 1982 May 22 | **Jet Stream** G A Jenkin, J Willson |

A first pitch climbed by the same pair a week earlier has since been cannibalized.

| 1982 June 12 | **La Folie** G Gibson, N Harvey |

The first pitch had been climbed by G Gibson and P Gibson in December 1981.

| 1982 June 12 | **Themeninblack: the Soundtrack** G Gibson (solo) |
| 1982 June 12 | **Whip Lash** G Gibson, N Harvey |

Pitch 3 was unseconded. Pitch 1 was climbed by J Shaw and J Willson on 19 February 1986.

1982 June 13	**Flies Aloft** G Gibson, N Harvey, B Miller
1982 June 13	**Time Flies** G Gibson, B Miller
1982 June 19	**Galloping Diabonkers** S Thompson, K Treble
1982 June 26	**Swansong** G A Jenkin, J Willson

Willson suggested the superb blank wall as a worthy final objective for Jenkin before the latter embarked upon a year-long round-the-world tour, though only the upper section was then climbed. On receipt of a postcard from Jenkin a year later announcing his imminent return, Willson set to and cleaned the lower section, which was duly climbed by the pair on 22 June 1983.

| 1982 July 2 | **Strange Little Girl, Sweetheart Contract** G Gibson, M Brown |

The first protection bolts in the Wye Valley are placed. One complete route was climbed that day, but later its lower pitch was assigned to Strange Little Girl and its upper to Sweetheart Contract. The former was extended by Gibson as far as The Angel's Eye thread on 4 July 1982, and to the top by him with M Ward and P Harrison on 2 May 1986. He climbed a first pitch for Sweetheart Contract with P Gibson on 3 October 1982.

1982 July 3   **Claire**   G Gibson, M Brown
Apparently, the 'Strange Little Girl' that Gibson knew. Pitches 2 and 3 only. Pitch 1 was extended from Strawberry Dust by D Green and J Willson on 18 February 1984.

1982 July 3   **Aqualung, Fly Logic**   G Gibson

1982 July 4   **Mosquito Bite**   G Gibson, M Brown

1982 July 5   **The Ring**   J Willson, C Carroll
Pitches 1 and 2. Pitch 3 had been climbed by R Hazell and J Willson on 3 February 1979. Willson and Carroll climbed the route complete on 9 July 1982.

1982 July 19   **Duncan's Dilemma**   S Meredith, J James (A),
Pitch 1. Pitches 2 and 3 were added on 24 July and 28 November 1982, with S Thompson, M Rosser, J Beckwith, K Treble, and G Needs all joining the fun at one stage or another. It was then called Men of Gwent (appropriately you might think, but this is also the name of well-known Newport pub). Early the next year, James and Thompson conceived a novel plan for expedition fund-raising and invited Peter Duncan of BBC Blue Peter to take part in a filmed ascent. This he did, on 12 April 1983, obviously not with unalloyed enjoyment, and he was invited to rename the climb. (Pete's Feat was apparently the initial front-runner!)

1982 Sept 12   **Gendarmerie**   G Gibson, P Gibson

1982 Sept 18   **Joe Direct**   J Willson, D Green, C Carroll

1983 Jan 23   **A Fly in the Eye?**   G Gibson, I Cheshire

1983 Jan 23   **Never Say Goodbye**   G Gibson

1983 Feb 13   **Idealist**   G Gibson

1983 Feb 15   **Liquid Leather**   T Penning, P Cresswell

1983 Feb 28   **May Fly?**   G Gibson, Miss H Carnes
For some time, Gibson had been putting it about that his fiancé was a better climber than himself!

1983 March 1   **Blue Max**   G Gibson, T Penning (A)

1983 March 1   **Pigs Might**   G Gibson, T Penning

1983 March 12   **Flight Barrier**   G Gibson, A Hudson

1983 March 12   **Hunky Doré**   D Green, J Willson

1983 March 12   **Strangled Fly**   G Gibson, A Hudson

1983 March 14   **Papillon**   G Gibson, A Hudson

1983 March 19   **Child's Play**   G Gibson, A Hudson

1983 March 19   **Feline**   G Gibson, A Hudson

1983 April 19   **Mutchos Butchos**   T Penning, A Sharp, J Harwood, M Ward

1983 May 14   **In Quarantine**   G Gibson, A Hudson
Pitch 1 added by R Kingston in 1986.

1983 May 15   **Cat Gut**   G Gibson, A Hudson
They abseiled in to the first stance (100 feet up Kangaroo Wall). As Hudson released the abseil rope and allowed it to swing away to the right well out of reach, he realized that he had forgotten to bring the climbing ropes! While Hudson gibbered on the stance, Gibson calmly soloed up through the Kangaroo Wall overhangs to the top.

1983 May 17	**The Bionic Walnut**	A Sharp, J Harwood
1983 May 24	**Big Bad Wolf**	P Littlejohn, T Penning

For the third time in a fourteen-year period, Littlejohn claims the hardest route in the Wye Valley.

1983 July 1	**Acid Test**	G A Jenkin, J Willson

The main pitch (2). Pitch 1 was added on 17 September 1983 by Jenkin; Willson was denied the opportunity to follow this by the need to drive Jenkin to his favourite hospital (the BRI) with a broken neck.

1983 July 6	**Exodus**	D Green, J Willson

Pitches 4 and 5. The same pair added pitch 1 on 4 December and 2 and 3 on 10 December 1983.

1983 July 8	**Special Offer**	G A Jenkin, J Willson
1983 Sept 17	**Entrance Exam**	G A Jenkin, D Green, J Willson
1983 Sept 24	**Powers of Persuasion**	J Chapman, M Ward
1983 Oct 2	**Gotta Lotta Bottle**	M Ward, M Bellian
1983 Dec 4	**Notung Forged**	D Green, J Willson

Pitch 2. Pitch 1 had been climbed by the same pair on 18 June 1983.

c.1983	**Toad in the Hole, Men without Hats, Ideas for Walls, Gorilla Thriller**	D Carroll, D Viggers
c.1983	**Are We Not Men?**	D Carroll, D Viggers, R Burrows
c.1983	**Safety Dance, Industrial Disease**	D Viggers, D Carroll
1984 Feb 11	**Swansong Prelude**	D Green, J Willson
1984 Feb 18	**Swansong Postlude, Under a Blood Red Sky**	D Green, J Willson

Including Finishing under… As the pair topped out at the end of a remarkably productive February Saturday afternoon's climbing, a magnificent sunset across the river set the sky ablaze. Willson had been waiting for a suitable 'Götterdämmerung' and arrogantly pronounced that this had to be it. Green preferred to stick with U2 and exercised his right to overrule – a double snub to his piano teacher!

1984 March 2	**Power Games**	G Gibson
1984 March 3	**Final Reduction**	G Gibson, G A Jenkin
1984 March 18	**Analysis**	G Gibson
1984 March 18	**Gospel: According to Themeninblack**	G Gibson, M Ward

The start of a highly productive partnership.

1984 March 18	**Pig Iron**	M Ward, M Bellian
1984 March 18	**We've Got the Honeymoon Blues Too**	G Gibson, M Ward, Mrs H Gibson

Make of this what you will!

1984 April 16	**Blossom and Blood**	J Bassingdale, M Ward
1984 May 5	**Mystic**	R Kingston, D Vousden, M Ward
1984 May 6	**Quixotic**	J Chapman, M Ward
1984 May 18	**Analytic**	R Kingston et al.
1984 May 27	**Sid, Vicious**	J Chapman, M Ward
1984 June 7	**Frantic**	R Kingston, B Stadden, M Ward
1984 June 9	**Scarotic**	R Kingston, B Stadden
1984 June 13	**Black Jack**	R Kingston, Miss J Keeble-White
1984 June 16	**Flying Fortress**	M J Crocker, J Robertson, T Farrelly

The direct variant by G Gibson on 26 January 1986.

1984 June 19	**Abacus**	R Kingston, B Stadden

Pitch 1. Pitch 2 was climbed one week later by Kingston with P Begley.

1984 June 19	**Amoeba, Meiosis**	R Kingston, B Stadden
1984 June 19	**Eureka**	R Kingston, M Ward
1984 June 22	**Yr Herwehla**	J James, S Thompson
1984 June 26	**Jugged Hare**	R Kingston, P Begley
1984 June	**Meningectomy**	G Gibson
1984 July 4	**Lurking Fear**	R A Harrison, G A Jenkin (A)

Jenkin is back in business; though, in the circumstances, one might have expected him to avoid routes threatened by loose pillars for a while. The minor top pitch was added by J Willson and M Ward on 9 April 1986.

1984 July 24	**Crazy Horse**	R Kingston, B Stadden
1984 Sept 9	**The Paladin**	T Penning, A Sharp

Pitch 1. The hair-raising upper pitch had been climbed by Penning with C Court on 2 October 1983.

1984 Sept 11	**Lionheart**	T Penning, J Harwood, C Court

Pitch 1. Penning added most of pitch 2 with P Cresswell one week later. This was completed and the top pitch climbed by J Shaw, J Willson, and C Adshead on 8 November 1986.

1984 Dec 21	**Guatemala City**	M Ward, J Willson
1985 March 9	**Pavlov's Dog**	M Ward, R Kingston
1985 March 31	**Valley Forge**	M Ward, J Willson
1985 April 20	**Fade to Pink**	M Ward, J Willson

The second pitch was replaced by R Kingston, I Freeman, and D Vousden on 11 April 1987.

1985 May 6	**Death on a Dinner-Plate**	A Fairbairn, A Payne
1985 June 19	**Chase Darkness Away**	M Ward, R Kingston
1985 Aug 26	**Gordon Bennett**	G A Jenkin, G Gibson, M J Crocker, M Ward

Jenkin identified this groove as one of two climbs recorded but not described by F Bennett in 1967 but which had later fallen down. He reclimbed and subtly renamed it. It promptly fell down again!

1985 Aug 26	**It's Your Life...**	M J Crocker, G Gibson, M Ward, G A Jenkin
1985 Aug 26	**Out-a-Sight**	G Gibson, M Ward, G A Jenkin, M J Crocker
1985 Oct 5	**Agent Orange**	G A Jenkin, N A Coe
1985 Oct 16	**John Bennett**	J Shaw, J Willson

Probably the other 'Bennett groove' (see note on Gordon Bennett just above). It has so far shown a little greater staying power.

1985 Nov 20	**Stairway to Heaven**	J Shaw, J Willson

The main (second) pitch. The first and third were added on 21 December 1985.

1985 Dec 15	**Heil Hitler!**	G Gibson, M Ward
1985 Dec 21	**One Cockatoo**	G Gibson, M Ward
1985 Dec 29	**Crocodile Tears**	G Gibson, M Ward

Pitch 1. Gibson added pitch 2 (and a poor pitch 3 now discontinued) on 2 February 1986. The third and fourth pitches described have been transferred from Cat Gut.

1985 Dec 29	**Howling at the Moon**	G Gibson, M Ward
1986 Jan 4	**Surreal Thing**	G Gibson
1986 Jan 11	**The Isle of Dogs**	G Gibson
1986 Jan 12	**The Flight of the Phoenix**	G Gibson, M Ward
1986 Jan 18	**Fly Havoc**	G Gibson, J Shaw, J Willson
1986 Jan 18	**Fond Adieu**	G Gibson, J Codling, J Lockett
1986 Jan 18	**Slinkin' Leopard**	G Gibson
1986 Jan 19	**Arms Like a Fly**	G Gibson, M Ward
1986 Jan 25	**Mein Kampf**	G Gibson

Pitch 2. The first groove of this had been climbed by G A Jenkin and K Marsden on 26 July 1983 as an alternative to Kaiser Wall pitch 2. Pitches 1 and 3 were climbed by G Gibson and M Ward on 1 February 1986 and 29 December 1985 respectively.

1986 Jan 25	**Fly the Flag, Overcooked Fly** G Gibson

A Fly too far. Not even Gibson could maintain a straight face in claiming the latter.

1986 Jan 26	**Lioness** G Gibson
1986 Feb 1	**The Lurking Smear** G Gibson, M Ward
1986 Feb 8	**Dog Eat Dog** G Gibson

Gibson got the eliminate right here. The poor optional first pitch was added by M Ward and R Kingston on 24 June 1986.

1986 Feb 9	**Queen Bee, The Sweeney** G Gibson, A Richardson

But with these he succeeded only in fouling up two of his own best earlier routes.

1986 Feb 26	**Big Fly Direct** J Shaw, J Willson
1986 March 1	**Endgame** J Willson, J Shaw (A)
1986 March 2	**Animal Magic, Enter the Dragon, Apology** G Gibson, P Harrison

The latter was for utterly wrecking the guidebook publication schedule with his three-month blitz. Fortunately, he then went off to France for an extended holiday.

1986 March 15	**Bottle Out** J Shaw, J Willson, M Stitt

Pitch 1. Pitch 2 had been climbed by Shaw and Willson on 16 October 1985.

1986 March 19	**Little Fly** J Shaw, J Willson
1986 March 25	**Rheingold** J Shaw, J Willson
1986 April 5	**Cast a Shadow** M Ward, G Hughes

Pitch 1. Pitch 2 was added by Ward with J Willson on 18 April 1986.

1986 April 5	**Under a Raging Moon** M Ward, G Hughes
1986 April 6	**Primeval** M J Crocker, M Ward

Straight to the top of the graded list. Crocker takes a serious interest in first ascents at Wintour's at last – he had already repeated most of Gibson's (and most other) routes, and here he beat Gibson to it.

1986 April 12	**Vampire Strikes Back** M Ward, M J Crocker (A)

A straightening out and extension of a line climbed two months earlier by G Gibson and called Catch the Vampire. Crocker was 'punishing' Gibson for making a direct variant on his own Flying Fortress.

1986 April 18	**Xenophobia** M Ward, J Willson
1986 April 25	**Mind over Matter** G Gibson, G Hughes, M Ward
1986 April 27	**Wicked, Let Us Prey** M J Crocker, M Ward

The latter name was a three-way riddle. Crocker had to hurry home early to hear his banns called! And Willson, of whose route Cheetah this was a variant, had held Gibson's ropes on the Flying Fortress variant. Only the section from the tree was climbed. Three days later, J Shaw and J Willson added the connection from the belay, and also worthless top and bottom pitches, which along with their revised name of Let Us All Prey, have now been binned.

1986 May 2	**Sold Out** G Gibson, M Ward, P Harrison

In turn, Ward is castigated for having partnered Crocker on Primeval and Vampire Strikes Back. It turned out to be Gibson's swansong at Wintour's.

1986 May 8	**Never Say Die** J Willson, J Shaw (V)
	Pitches 2 and 3. Pitches 1 and 4 were added on 6 June 1986 by
	the same pair.
1986 May 15	**Anticipation** M Ward, B Stadden, R Kingston
1986 May 18	**I Fly** M J Crocker, M Ward
	Pitch 2. Pitch 1 was climbed on 17 October 1986 by M Ward and
	J Willson.
1986 May 29	**All Wound Up** M J Crocker, M Ward
	Crocker's riposte to 'Sold Out' (see above).
1986 June 10	**Surprise, Surprise** G A Jenkin, T Robbins
1986 July 3	**Sleight of Hand** M Ward, R Kingston
	Based on an A1 pitch climbed roped solo by E Fivelsdal on
	11 May 1975.
1986 July 8	**Sweeter than Sugar** M Ward, R Kingston
1986 July 22	**Hell: Just for Leather** M J Crocker
	Geared and sieged with some aid by G Gibson six months earlier.
1986 Aug 5	**Stay Mellow** M Ward, M J Crocker
1986 Aug 27	**Beside Myself** M Ward, M J Crocker
1986 Aug 27	**Can't Fly Any Higher** M Ward, M J Crocker
	Willson was anxious to have the first and last lines in the book,
	but Ward managed to trump his Endgame.
1986 Sept 10	**Fly Major General** M J Crocker, M Ward (V)
1986 Sept 23	**Natural Selection** R Kingston, M Ward
1986 Sept 24	**Turn a Blind Eye** M Ward, R Kingston
1986 Sept 28	**Endangered Species** R Kingston, M Adams
1986 Oct 2	**Scaremonger** M Ward, R Kingston
1986 Oct 15	**Fugazi** J Shaw, J Willson
1986 Oct 17	**Silence** M Ward, J Willson
1986 Oct 19	**Misplaced Childhood** J Shaw, J Willson
	The direct version climbed by M J Crocker in 1991.
1986 Oct 22	**Real to Reel** J Shaw, J Willson
1986 Nov 1	**First Degree** M J Crocker, M Ward
1986 Nov 1	**Highway to the Dangerzone** M Ward, M J Crocker
1986 Nov 9	**"Yeeaaghhh!"** M J Crocker, M Ward
1986 Nov 9	**Cross-Examination** M Ward, M J Crocker
1986 Nov 26	**Never Never Land** J Shaw, J Willson
1986 Nov 27	**Turmoil of a White Ocean** M Ward, J Willson, J Shaw
1986 Dec 3	**Frustration, Brief Encounter** J Shaw, J Willson
1986 Dec 21	**Childhood's End** J Shaw, J Willson, D Green
1986 Dec 21	**Incubus** J Shaw, D Green, J Willson
1986 Dec 21	**Script for a Jester's Tear** J Shaw, J Willson, D Green
1987 Jan 28	**Age of Enlightenment** J Willson, J Shaw
	Willson had been saving this name for his 50th birthday, but as
	the press reports of his accident five months earlier had already
	accused him of having reached it, he did not bother to wait.
1987 Jan 31	**Yesterday's Dreams** J Willson, J Shaw
	The lower section had been climbed by M Ward and Willson on 6
	January 1987 as a direct start to Antediluvian.
1987 Feb 20	**The Angel's Arête** M Ward, J Willson
1987 Feb 25	**Save Me from Tomorrow** M Ward (solo)
	After top-roping.
1987 March 4	**White Feather, Verdict** J Shaw, J Willson
1987 March 5	**Spinal Tap** M Ward (solo)
	After top-roping.
1987 March 12	**Crystal Tips** M Ward (solo)

1987 March 19	**Come and Get It** M Ward (roped solo)
1987 April 11	**Event Horizon** R Kingston, M Ward
1987 April 11	**Too Clever by Half, On the Outside, Looking In** M Ward, M J Crocker, R Kingston
	On the latter, also: I Freeman, D Vousden, G A Jenkin, D Viggers, A N Other, Spit the Dog, Uncle Tom Cobbley and all… (Kingston)
1987 April 22	**The Bubble Bursts, Iron Lung** M Ward, R Kingston
1987 April 28	**Eva Brawn** M Ward, B Stadden, R Kingston
1987 April 30	**I Used to Be a Werewolf…** R Kingston, M Ward
1987 May	**Clutching at Straws** J Shaw, J Willson
1987 July 10	**The Lurking Sear** M Ward
	Eventually, after repeated and protracted efforts. Others were permitted a try while Ward rested between attempts, but only as far as his previous high-point!
1987 Sept 13	**Wild Cat** R Kingston, I Freeman
1987 Sept 18	**Blitzkrieg** J Shaw, J Willson
1987 Sept 26	**Der Fuhrer** J Shaw, J Willson
1987 Oct 1	**Easier Said than Done** M Ward, J Shaw
1987 Oct 1	**Last of the Wine** J Shaw, J Willson, M Ward
1987 Oct 8	**The Small Time** R Kingston, M Ward
1987 Oct 17	**When the Wind Blows** J Shaw, J Willson
1987 Oct 23	**Better Late than Never** M Ward, J Willson
1987 Nov 7	**Punch and Judy** J Shaw, J Willson
1987 Nov 8	**Flanders Field** R Kingston, G A Jenkin (V)
1987 Nov 21	**End of the Affair** G A Jenkin, T Robbins
	Pitch 2 had been climbed by G A Jenkin and J Phillips on 25 February 1981 as part of a route called Winter's Day. *This climbed the upper part of what is now* Death on a Dinner-Plate.
1987 Dec 2	**Agamemnon** M Ward, J Willson, J Shaw
1987 Dec 2	**Cantassium** M Ward, J Willson
1987 Dec 4	**A Calm Sea and a Prosperous Voyage** J Shaw, J Willson, M Ward
	Pitch 2 climbed on 9 December 1987 by the same team.
1987 Dec 4	**Achilles** J Willson, J Shaw, M Ward
1987 Dec 9	**Electra** M Ward, J Willson, J Shaw
	Superseded Ward's earlier Auntie Perspirant *of 22 May 1986 with R Kingston.*
1987 Dec 11	**Sweetest Victory** J Shaw, J Willson, M Ward
1988 March 31	**Proper Limestone** B Hobbs, L Tetler
1988 May 19	**Lifeblood** R Kingston, M Ward
1988 May 24	**The Valley Road** R Kingston, M Ward (A)
1988 June 3	**Never Say Never Again** R Kingston, G A Jenkin
1988 June 7	**The Song Remains the Same** R Kingston, G A Jenkin, M Ward
1989 April 25	**A Nightmare of Brown Sugar** T Penning, J Harwood
1989 June 16	**Doctor Hay Fever** R Kingston, M Ward
1990 April 8	**An Android's Dream** G A Jenkin, N A Coe
	The latest instalment of Gordon Bennett. Watch this space…
1990 May 10	**Terry's Twin, Terry's Gone Crackers** P Bain, M Peckham
1990 July 5	**Fear Is the Key** R Kingston, I Freeman, M Ward
	The direct version by Kingston (solo) on the same day.
1990 July 7	**One Night One Time** R Kingston, G A Jenkin, J Shaw
1990 July 8	**Avant Garde, The Secret Garden** R Kingston, G A Jenkin
1990 July 8	**Priory Road** G A Jenkin
1990 July 10	**Prestidigitator** R Kingston, B Stadden

1990 Aug 1	**LowGO** R Kingston, G A Jenkin (A)
1990 Sept 4	**King Louie** R Kingston, B Stadden, C Begley
1991 Oct 27	**Dinosaur Heaven** M J Crocker
1991 Nov 5/9	**Monosculpture** M J Crocker
	The two roofs were climbed at different sessions.
1991 Dec 29	**Tony, John** M J Crocker, T Penning, J Harwood
1992 Jan 4	**Angelic Inferno** M J Crocker
1992 Jan 26	**In the Hands of the Deceiver** M J Crocker
1992 Feb 8	**Do What You Want, 9½ Lives** M J Crocker, R Thomas
	Crocker was having a rough time. The evening before, he had narrowly avoided an 80mph head-on collision, and during the cleaning of the latter route a large section under the Agent Orange roof collapsed on and around him.
1993 Oct 17	**That Nice Route** C Heard, M Morris
	The ascent (A) also included Surprise, Surprise as its third pitch and minor variations of pitches 2 and 4 of Jos'e and the Fly.
1996 May 10	**Feline Frolics** M Cattermole, J Hutchings
1996 May 11	**Therapy** M Cattermole, J Hutchings

BAN-Y-GOR

The first four routes (along with perhaps six or eight more) were climbed during the early phase of exploration. It has not been possible to identify the lines they took.

1969 Dec 5	**Amnesia** J C Horsfield, R Thomas
	The lower two pitches only and with a point of aid. A free ascent including a top pitch was made by J C Horsfield and P J Thomas on 6 February 1970.
1970 April 19	**Wait until You See the Whites** F E R Cannings, I F Duckworth (AL)
1970 May 2	**The New Neighbour** F E R Cannings, P R Littlejohn (AL)
1971 June 27	**Impatience** J F Kerry, J C Horsfield (AL)
1988 June 21	**East of Sweden** M Ward, R Kingston
1988 June 25	**Duhkha** R Kingston, M Ward
1988 June 25	**Nelson Mandela** M Ward
	'…a hard route to free.'
1988 June 25	**The Disillusioned Bronto Machine** M Ward, R Kingston
1988 June 26	**Avatamsaka** R Kingston, M Ward
1988 June 26	**Violation of Trust** M Ward, R Kingston
1988 July 2	**Bad Man from Bodie, Felt, Batten, and Smile, Self-Destruction** M J Crocker, M Ward
1988 July 2	**Self-Preservation** M J Crocker (solo)
1988 July 2	**Stars and Stripes** M Ward, M J Crocker
1988 July 3	**Just Too Hot** M J Crocker, M Ward
1988 July 3	**Let's Hear It for Lorenzo** G A Jenkin, R Kingston, M J Crocker, M Ward
	A badly-positioned bolt botches the job.
1988 July 5	**The Tao** R Kingston, M Ward
1988 July 6	**Up a Gum Tree** M Ward, R Kingston
1988 July 9	**Habit of a Lifetime** M Ward, M J Crocker, G A Jenkin, R Kingston
1988 July 9	**Latest Craze** M J Crocker
1988 July 9	**Nation of Shopkeepers** M Ward, R Kingston, G A Jenkin, M J Crocker
1988 July 9	**SoFB Country** G A Jenkin, R Kingston (VL)
	Not what you might think! – Society of Fat Bastards – the name is a cavers' joke.

1988 July 9	**Summertime Blues** R Kingston, G A Jenkin	
1988 July 9	**Too Hot to Touch** M J Crocker, M Ward	
1988 July 16	**Alienation** M Ward, M J Crocker, G A Jenkin	
1988 July 16	**Damn Snaffelhounds, Snaffel Attack** M J Crocker, M Ward, G A Jenkin	
1988 July 16	**Good Jab'** M J Crocker	
1988 July 16	**Lip Service, So Gross, Who Is This Man Dukakis?** G A Jenkin, M Ward, M J Crocker	
1988 July 16	**Ugooloo** G A Jenkin, M Ward	
1988 July 16	**Victimization** M Ward, G A Jenkin, M J Crocker	
1988 July 17	**Craters of Mono, Really Big Sur** M J Crocker, M Ward	
1988 July 20	**Always the Rain** R Kingston, G A Jenkin	

The summer deluge continued and continued.

1988 July 20   **Avidya** R Kingston, G A Jenkin, M Ward

Kingston continued his Buddhist theme on the crag, but nobody knew why!

1988 July 20   **Breaking for Spares** G A Jenkin, R Kingston

The Jenkin crowbar comes to Ban-y-gor.

1988 July 20   **High and Dry** G A Jenkin, M Ward (AL), R Kingston
1988 Aug 14   **Gonna Write a Classic, Mondays Never Rain** M J Crocker (solo)

Crocker is convinced!

1988 Aug 14	**Sperm Wales** M Ward, M J Crocker
1988 Aug 14	**Trans-African Drum Battle** M J Crocker, M Ward
1988 Aug 17	**Gordon, Matt, Peter** T Penning, P Cresswell, G A Jenkin, M Ward
1988 Aug 20	**Ninety-Nine Rabid Feminists, Tinaderm** M Ward, G A Jenkin
1988 Aug 23	**Gobbo Wuz Yer, Private Life, Roof of Gore, Viva Ramirez** M J Crocker
1988 Sept 2	**The Sac Gang** M Ward, G A Jenkin
1988 Sept 4	**Breast Stroke in a D Cup, The Gnarliest** M Ward, G A Jenkin, J Shaw
1988 Sept 4	**Lotus Wing, Slug Control** M Ward, G A Jenkin, J Willson, J Shaw
1988 Sept 4	**Lounge Lizard Leisure Suit, Squelch** G A Jenkin, M Ward, J Willson, J Shaw
1988 Sept 6	**Trishna** R Kingston, I Freeman, M Ward
1988 Sept 7	**B'stard** J Shaw, J Willson

Shaw succeeds after a protracted effort.

1988 Sept 11	**The Parallax Vision** M Ward, G A Jenkin (VL)
1988 Sept 13	**Citadel, Dinosaur, Mammoth** T Penning, J Harwood
1988 Sept 17	**Genetic Engineering, Genetically Engineered Super Mutant** M Ward, G A Jenkin, T Penning
1988 Sept 17	**Josie Swoonpence** G A Jenkin, M Ward

Direct start by G Gibson 1989.

1988 Sept 17	**Kalamazoo** M Ward, G A Jenkin
1988 Sept 17	**Take the Wave, The Microwave Man** G A Jenkin, M Ward, T Penning
1988 Sept 18	**Mushroom Boys** R Lanchbury, T Penning, P Creswell
1988 Sept 18	**Nine Lives Gone, The Gates** T Penning, P Creswell, R Lanchbury
1988 Sept 18	**The Corner** T Penning (solo)
1988 Sept 25	**Jurisprudence** M Ward, G A Jenkin, T Penning

1988 Sept 25	**Stinging on a Star** T Penning, P Creswell, R Lanchbury, M Ward, G A Jenkin
1988 Sept 25	**The Fat Controller** G A Jenkin, M Ward, T Penning
1988 Oct 2	**Free Masonry** R Lanchbury, T Penning, P Creswell
1988 Oct 2	**High Treason, High Society** T Penning, P Creswell, R Lanchbury
1988 Oct 2	**Stone Mason** P Creswell, R Lanchbury, T Penning
1988 Oct 4	**Merthyr Bob** T Penning, J Harwood *Named in memory of Bob Powles.*
1988 Oct 8	**Amnesty** T Penning, J Harwood, P Creswell
1988 Oct 8	**Top Cat, No Big Cigar** T Penning, P Creswell, J Harwood *'Beware the ash!'*
1988 Oct 8	**Standard Deviation** T Penning, P Creswell, J Harwood
1988 Oct 23	**A Little Stiff'ner** G A Jenkin, M Ward, G Gibson
1988 Oct 23	**Dry Day** G Gibson, M Ward, G A Jenkin *The Hilti TE 10A makes its debut at the crag with Gibson at the handle.*
1988 Oct 23	**The Unpure** G Gibson, M Ward
1988 Oct 30	**Darkside** G A Jenkin, M Ward, R Lanchbury
1988 Oct 30	**Crack around the World** M Ward, G A Jenkin
1988 Oct 30	**Morel** R Lanchbury, G A Jenkin, H Wilson
1988 Oct 30	**Shaggy Ink Cap** R Lanchbury, H Wilson
1988 Oct 30	**The Chubby Brown Syndrome** M Ward, G A Jenkin, R Lanchbury, H Wilson
1988 Oct 30	**There's a Lot of It About** G A Jenkin, M Ward, H Wilson, R Lanchbury
1988 Nov 7	**Fly Agaric** T Penning, P Creswell, R Lanchbury
1988 Nov 7	**Mycology** R Lanchbury, T Penning, P Creswell
1989 Feb 10	**Officer Dibble** G Gibson
1989 Feb 10	**The Boss** G Gibson, R Thomas
1989 Feb 16	**Gimmee Back My Head** G Gibson *Appropriately named and the begining of the 'Head' theme. Gibson was almost terminally injured whilst cleaning an adjacent route and the somewhat macabre fascination with the route names hereabouts has continued.*
1989 Feb 16	**Sea-King Me** G Gibson *The second phase of development gets under way.*
1989 May 13	**Left Wall** G Gibson (on-sight solo)
1989 May 28	**Head Tennis** G Gibson *The name says it all; the route that catapulted Gibson into Emergency Ward 10 with serious head injuries. A 'stuck-on' hold provided revenge.*
1989 May 28	**Hummin' Bird, Stitch That!** G Gibson *An impressive day with three choice routes in the bag.*
1989 Nov 12	**On the Game** D Kerr, R Lanchbury, G Gibson
1989 Nov 19	**Gunsel, Kiss of Death** D Kerr, J Russell *Both routes originally led without a bolt runner.*
1989 Nov 26	**Kawrona, Ought'n Be** D Kerr, C Etchell *These routes 'climbed by mistake with nothing better to do!'*
1989 Nov 26	**Perfect Kiss** D Kerr, C Etchell, G Gibson
1989 Nov 26	**Wye Not** G Gibson, D Kerr
1989 Nov 29	**After Midnight** D Kerr, G Gibson *Originally led without a bolt runner.*
1989 Nov 29	**The Beauty of It All, Tier-Gas** G Gibson, D Kerr *A broken hold gave Gibson some unexpected air-time.*

1989 Dec 9	**Baggy Trousers** G Gibson
1989 Dec 9	**Chin Hooks** G Gibson, Mrs H Gibson
1989 Dec 9	**Nod if You Understand** R Lanchbury, G Gibson
1989 Dec 10	**Fresh Fish, In Apedex, It's a Sin, Let's Celebrate, The Correct Use of Soap** G Gibson

Gibson, still recovering from major head operations, took time off to get to grips with as many routes as possible in one go. This batch had been cleaned and worked the previous day.

1990 March 3	**Aerial Combat, Faithful Couple, If So, Wye, Wye Me** G Gibson
1990 March 3	**Helter Skelter** D Kerr

So named owing to the large trundles during cleaning.

1990 March 3	**Wye Should I!** G Gibson, R Thomas
1990 March 10	**Maestro's Wall** G Gibson, D Kerr
1990 March 10	**96 Tiers** G Gibson
1990 March 10	**Yellow Taxi** R Lanchbury, D Kerr, P Lanchbury, G Gibson
1990 April	**Home Is Where the Heart Is** R Lanchbury (solo)
1990 May	**Barbaracue** T Penning, A Tierne

Two pegs were used on the first ascent and removed afterwards.

1990 May	**Heady Days** R Thomas, G Royale
1990 July 7	**In My Hour of Need, Wye're Less** G Gibson, R Thomas
1990 July 8	**All Ten Mill** G Gibson, R Thomas
1990 July 8	**To Bee Or Not to Bee** R Thomas, G Gibson
1990 July 14	**The Drilling Fields** G Gibson
1990 July 15	**Almost Me** G Gibson
1990 Sept 2	**Goodbye Kiss** G Gibson, D Kerr
1990 Sept 2	**His Master's Voice** G Gibson
1990 Sept 2	**Save Your Kisses for Me** G Gibson, R Hilditch, D Kerr

Named because Kerr, sporting a tendon injury, passed the lead to Gibson only to follow with ease – he was not a happy man!

1990 Sept 8	**No Head for Heights** G Gibson

Led and reversed all pitches.

1990 Sept 16	**Up the Garden Path** G Gibson, Mrs H Gibson, R Thomas

Lower half climbed on 16 February 1992 by G Gibson and D Kerr.

1990 Sept 16	**Cocotte, Pet Cemetery, What Presence?** G Gibson, R Thomas

Crocker lands heavily on yet another route clutching yet another detached handhold. Doing second ascents was proving to be a risky business!

1990 Sept 16	**Sausage Dog** G Gibson, Mrs H Gibson
1990 Oct 13	**Free the Radicals, Pocket Tarantula, Slave to the Cave** G Gibson
1990 Oct 13	**Goebbels, Moseley, God, and Ingrams, Mouchette, Snake Flake, Some Chance , There You Go Again** G Gibson R Thomas
1990 Oct 13	**Which Poison?** G Gibson, Mrs H Gibson
1990 Oct 13	**No Chance** R Thomas, G Gibson
1990 Dec 28	**The Motley Crew, You're My Comic Strip Hero** G Gibson
1991 June 28	**Laccaria Laccata** W Gladwin, S Thompson
1991 June 28	**Phallus Impudicus** W Gladwin, J Gladwin, S Thompson
1991 June 28	**We Are the Champignons** S Thompson, W Gladwin
1991 Aug 10	**Blabba Mouth** G Gibson, G A Jenkin

1991 Aug 10	**One Step Ahead of the Blues, That Historic Reach**	

G A Jenkin, G Gibson

A visiting climber on meeting Gary: 'Oh you're the man with the historic reach!'

1991 Aug 11	**Crocker's Ash, Utilizing Eucalyptus, Flat Baps**

G Gibson, G A Jenkin

The line described for Flat Baps was claimed by C Shepherd, R Mitchell, C Jones on 17 November 1990 and graded E3 6a. A determined effort and the addition of two bolt runners were required for the 'second' ascent of this powerful little E6!

1991 Nov 24	**High Fidelity** G Gibson, R Thomas, D Kerr
1991 Nov 24	**James Mason** D Kerr, G Gibson
1991 Nov 24	**The Mason's Arms** G Gibson, D Kerr
1991 Dec 25	**Rockin' Robin, Rudolph's Roof Route** G Gibson

Several attempts saw Gary's belayer, the lightweight Hazel, being dragged skyward.

1992 Feb 1	**Object, Accuracy, Another Day, Boys Don't Cry, No Way Out** D Kerr, R Lanchbury
1992 Feb 16	**Muddy Waters, Slow Boat to Chepstow** G Gibson, D Kerr
1992 Feb 16	**Lux** D Kerr, G Gibson
1992 March 8	**A Gathering of Old Men** G Gibson
1992 May 10	**Gordonzola** G Gibson, R Thomas
1992 May 10	**Les Miserables** R Thomas, G Gibson
1992 June 27	**Polatization, The Forest, Frisco Disco** G Gibson, R Thomas
1992 July 23	**A Date with David Mellor** A Tallant, R Forsyth, G A Jenkin
1992 July 23	**A Liberal Smear** G A Jenkin, R Forsyth, A Tallant
1992 July 23	**Get Them Out by Xmas** G A Jenkin, A Tallant, R Forsyth
1993 May 23	**Costner's Last Stand, Old Smokie, Open Head Surgery** G Gibson, P Harrison
1994 July 14	**Raining Stones** C Heard, G Atkins, J Jones
1994 Aug 15	**Herbsman Hustling** G Atkins, C Heard, J Jones
1994 Aug 15	**Block and Crackle** G Atkins (solo)

Probably done before.

1994 Aug 15	**Gravitational Dyslexia** J Jones, C Heard
1994 Sept 18	**It's a Fluke, Pooh Corner** G Gibson

The latter route solo.

1994 Oct 19	**Indian Summer** M Morris, A Bevan, C Heard
1995 July 16	**Discharge, Doyouthinkhesawus, Spunk Trumpets, Join the Union, Jack** G Gibson, R Thomas
1995 July 16	**The Chimney Crusade** G Gibson

On-sight solo to place a rope!

1996 Aug 3	**Jah Wobble** N Coe, G A Jenkin, C Jones, C Shepherd
1996 Aug 3	**Ivy Sep'** N Coe (solo)
1996	**Totally Manning** G Gibson

TINTERN QUARRY

1993 June 19	**Footloose** G Hughes, M Cattermole, J Clayton, G Ashton
1993 June 23	**Dust Buster** M Cattermole, G Hughes
1993 June 24	**Shake 'n' Vac** J Clayton, G Ashton
1993 June 29	**Broken Glass** G Hughes, G Ashton
1993 June 30	**Fragrance Abuse** G A Jenkin, J Clayton
1993 June	**Dust Devil** M Cattermole, G Hughes

1993 July 7	**Boltisaurus, Dinosaurs Don't Dyno** M Cattermole, G Hughes
1993 July 10	**Chaos Crack** G Ashton, G Hughes
1993 July 22	**Ammonite, Pocketful of Kryptonite** M Cattermole, A Hooley
1993 July 23	**Dispossessed** A Tallant, G A Jenkin
1993 July 27	**Fractal** G Ashton, M Cattermole
1993 July 31	**Sauropods** M Cattermole, G Hughes
1993 Aug 7	**Diamonds and Dust** T Bird, M Cattermole
1993 Aug 16	**Top Cat, Terrific Triassics** M Cattermole, G Hughes
1993 Aug 31	**Raptor** G Hughes, M Cattermole
1993 Sept 4	**Fate of Nations** G Hughes, M Cattermole
1993 Sept 5	**Full Stretch, Classic Jurassic** M Cattermole, G Hughes
1993 Sept 5	**Ashes to Ashes** G A Jenkin, J Clayton
1993 Sept 7	**Dinofever, Dinomania** M Cattermole, G Hughes
1993 Sept 19	**Supersaurus I, Supersaurus II, Supersaurus III** M Cattermole, G Hughes
1994 May 16	**Chossticks, Megabyte, Bad News for Druids** M Cattermole, M Brown
1994 June 8	**An Unkind Cut** G A Jenkin, M Cattermole
1994 July 31	**The Stange Attractor** G A Jenkin, F Haden
1994 Aug 28	**Man in Tears** F Haden, L Creamer
1996 June 15	**Leaping Libidos, Pussyfoot, Quip U for Leisure** M Cattermole, M Puddy
1996 June 16	**Just a Mo** M Brown, M Cattermole
1996 June 16	**Déja Vu** M Cattermole, M Brown
1996 June 20	**Back from Beyond** M Cattermole, J Hutchings *The first two-thirds of this pitch had been climbed by M Cattermole, G Hughes on 19 September 1993 as an approach pitch to Supersaurus.*
1996 June 20	**True Love** M Cattermole, J Makinsky

SHORN CLIFF

Unknown	**The Little White Tower**
c.1975	**...Think of England, Fallacy, The White Tower** S Moss, R Thomas
c.1975	**Beeline, Wet Dreams, Colour Dreams/Dream Topping Finish, Damsel in Distress** R Thomas, S Moss
1984 May 31	**Dirty Harry** M Ward (solo)
1984 June 3	**All for One...** Mrs H Gibson, G Gibson, M Ward
1984 June 3	**Ironside's Men, The Bitter Battle Tears, The Laughing Cavaliers** G Gibson, M Ward
1984 June 3	**The Spanish Inquisition** G Gibson, Mrs H Gibson, M Ward
1984 June 9	**No Musketeers** G Gibson, M Ward *They also climbed the direct finish on the same day.*
1984 June 9	**Peace in Our Time** M Ward, G Gibson
1984 June 30	**...Think of England Direct, Streaker** R Kingston, M Ward
1984 June 30	**Bubble Memory** M Ward, R Kingston
1984 July 1	**Emotional Dyslexia** M Ward, M Bellian
1984 July 10	**The New Republic, War Is Declared** M Ward, R Kingston, P Begley
1984 July 15	**Tigers Don't Cry, The Bone** M Ward, P Begley
1984 July 17	**Night Rider** R Kingston, M Ward

1984 July 17	**One Less White Nigger** M Ward, R Kingston
1984 July 20	**Lundy Calling, Pooh Sticks** G Gibson, M Ward
1984 July 18	**Rebellion** G Gibson (solo)
1984 July 28	**Seven Chinese Brothers** A Hudson
1984 July 31	**Pump It Up... Again** R Kingston, M Ward, P Begley
1984 July 31	**State of Independence, The Phoney War** M Ward, R Kingston, P Begley
1984 Aug 13	**Renaissance** R Kingston, P Begley, Miss J Keeble-White
1984 Aug 14	**Stand and Deliver** R Kingston, Miss J Keeble-White
1984 Aug 14	**Yer Money or Yer Life** R Kingston, P Begley, Miss J Keeble-White
1984 Aug 15	**Another Brick in the Wall** R Kingston, M Ward, P Begley
1984 Aug 15	**Defection, The Iron Curtain** M Ward, R Kingston, P Begley
1984 Aug 17	**Alone in a Crowd, Heavy Plant Crossing** M Ward, P Begley, R Kingston
1984 Aug 20	**Ché Guevara** M Ward, R Kingston
	The route was completed on 22 September 1984.
1984 Aug 21	**Armistice** M Ward, P Begley, R Kingston
1984 Aug 21	**Organ Grinder** R Kingston, P Begley, M Ward
1984 Aug 29	**Breech Birth** M Ward
1984 Aug 29	**Secret Identity** R Kingston, P Begley, M Ward
1984 Sept 1	**Last Call** P Begley, M Ward
1984 Sept 1	**Motion Pictures** M Ward, P Begley
1984 Sept 3	**Self Defence** M Ward, R Kingston
1984 Sept 5	**Probing in the Dark, The Long Reach** R Kingston, P Begley, M Ward
1984 Sept 7	**Social Criticsm** M Ward, P Begley, R Kingston
1984 Sept 8	**...One for All** M Ward, R Kingston, P Begley, C Begley
1984 Sept 8	**Acoustic** P Begley, R Kingston, M Bellian, M Ward
1984 Sept 8	**East to West, The Orphan** P Begley, M Ward, R Kingston, C Begley
1984 Sept 8	**Hydraulic Jump** R Kingston, C Begley, P Begley, M Ward
1984 Sept 8	**One Step Down** C Begley, P Begley, M Ward, R Kingston
1984 Sept 9	**Dictator** R Kingston, M Ward
1984 Sept 9	**No Surrender** C Begley, P Begley, R Kingston
1984 Sept 9	**Side Effects** M Ward, M Bellian, R Kingston, P Begley
1984 Sept 13	**Wolf Whistle** M Ward (solo)
1984 Sept 14	**Complex Variable** R Kingston, P Begley, M Ward
1984 Sept 14	**Touch the Fire** M Ward, R Kingston, P Begley
1984 Sept 15	**Cool Heat, Temporary Truce** R Kingston, M Ward, P Begley
1984 Sept 15	**Traitor** R Kingston, C Begley, P Begley, M Bellian, M Ward
1984 Sept 15	**War of the Worlds** P Begley, R Kingston, M Ward
1984 Sept 16	**Cry Wolf, Intermission** P Begley, M Ward, R Kingston
1984 Sept 16	**Easy Rider** R Kingston, P Begley, M Ward
1984 Sept 16	**Intravenous Feeding** M Ward, R Kingston, P Begley
1984 Sept 22	**Artificial Insemination** M Ward, R Kingston, P Begley
1984 Sept 22	**Indecisive Victory** P Begley, M Ward, R Kingston
1984 Sept 22	**Pretty Baby, Gargoyle, Squirrel** R Kingston, P Begley, M Ward
1984 Oct 19	**Hit and Run** T Penning, J Harwood
1985 April 27	**A Stitch in Time** R Kingston, M Ward
1985 April 27	**Fat Man in Ethiopia** M Ward, R Kingston
1985 April 27	**Higher Flyer** R Kingston, M Ward
1985 May 11	**Insurrection** M Ward, R Kingston
1985 May 11	**Run for Home** R Kingston, M Ward

1985 May 12	**Femme Fatalé, Smart Arse** M Ward, R Kingston
1985 June 14	**Paroxysm, The Pinnacle of Success, White Water** R Kingston, M Ward
1985 June 23	**Edge Game** R Kingston
1985 June 23	**Wet Sunday** R Kingston, D Everly
1985 June 24	**Poka Dot, This Space Reserved** R Kingston, M Ward
1985 June 30	**A Claim to Fame, The First Crusade** Miss J Keeble-White, R Kingston
1985 June 30	**A King's Ransom, Incredible Voyage** R Kingston, Miss J Keeble-White
1985 June 30	**Angry Young Men** R Kingston
1985 June 30	**Party Piece, Rumble in the Jungle** M Learoyd, R Thomas
1985 July 5	**Birth Canal** M Ward, R Kingston
1985 July 5	**Much Ado about Nothing** R Kingston, M Ward
1985 July 11	**Loss of Innocence** M Ward, P Begley, R Kingston
1985 July 13	**Name in the Book** R Harris, R Crewe-Gee
1985 July 27	**Cruisin' for a Bruisin', Jug? What Jug?!** R Kingston, M Hopkins
1985 July 27	**Thread Security** M Hopkins, R Kingston
1985 Aug 2	**Five Pints** M Learoyd, R Thomas
1985 Aug 5	**Rule the Roost** R Kingston, M Ward
1985 Aug 5	**The Green Meanie** M Ward, R Kingston *Most of this had been done by R Kingston and P Begley on 16 June 1985 as a variation start and finish to Motion Pictures.*
1985 Sept 3	**Trouble Brewing** M Ward, R Kingston *Too Close…*
1985 Sept 5	**Brain Washed** M Ward, R Kingston
1985 Sept 8	**A Bolt from the Blue, Second Wind** M Learoyd, R Thomas
1985 Sept 8	**Relics** R Thomas, M Learoyd
1985 Sept 8	**Running on Empty** M Learoyd, R Thomas, L Foulkes
1985 Sept 15	**Freak Brother Convention** R Kingston, M Ward
1985 Sept 28	**Cat Be Nimble, Cat Be Quick, Touché Pussycat** R Kingston, M Ward
1985 Sept 29	**Nosey Bleeder** R Thomas, T Jordan, M Learoyd
1985 Sept 29	**The Hit** M Learoyd, T Jordan, R Thomas
1985 Oct 20	**One-Way Glass, Three Score Years and Ten** M J Crocker, M Ward
1985 Nov 2	**A Is for Apple** J Delamere, N Hillman, N Richardson, R Birkenhead
1985 Nov 2	**Character Assassination, Pink Ticket, Lazy L, Turn to Stone, Walk Don't Run** R Kingston, D Miatt
1986 May 10	**Blanc Wall, Jungle Rock, Running Hot, Symbiosis** R Kingston, Miss J Keeble-White
1986 July 12	**At the Hop, Doing the Bop, Stuck on You** R Kingston, I Freeman
1986 Aug 21	**Blind Rage, Mister Angry, Synapse Collapse** R Kingston *One rest point on the latter. Free-climbed by G A Jenkin and D Viggers on 9 August 1987.*
1986 Aug 23	**Treason** M Ward (solo)
1987 April	**Petit Mort** A Harris, A Statham
1987 July 5	**Lucky Star** D Kerr, P Moulam
1987 Aug 9	**Aquatic Cyclist** G Sutton, G Bennett
1987 Oct 11	**Llamas in the Loft** G Sutton, R Sissmon
1988 May 2	**Oogmuts** G A Jenkin, M Ward, B Stadden, M J Crocker
1988 May 7	**All in a Day's Work** R Kingston, M Ward

1988 May 7	**The Land of Nod** M Ward, R Kingston
1988 May 22	**B is for Bag, Protoplasm, The Numbers Game** M J Crocker, M Ward, G A Jenkin
1988 May 22	**The English Opium Eaters** M Ward, M J Crocker, G A Jenkin
1990 March 25	**On Reflection** D Kerr (solo)
1991 Sept 3	**Expectant Chimp** B Maybank, M Williams
1992 Feb 23	**Chappell of Rest, Colin's Apprentice, Ramraider** M J Crocker, J Harwood, T Penning
1995 Aug 30	**A Great Day for Gravity** C Heard, J Jason (AL)
1995 Aug 30	**Nobby's Piles** J Jones, C Heard
1996 May 11	**Flatlander** M Cattermole
1996 May 11	**Santorini** M Cattermole, C Wyatt
1996 May 25	**Alta Vista** M Cattermole, J Hutchings
1996 May 25	**Bursting the Renaissance Bubble, Gorillas in the Garden** J Hutchings, M Cattermole
1996 May 27	**Blood Brothers** M Cattermole, J Hutchings
1996 May 27	**Heart of Stone** J Hutchings, M Cattermole

THE FOREST OF DEAN QUARRIES

1978 April 23	**Jive'n'Bop** D E Hope, D Harvey
1978 April 23	**Mantrap** D E Hope, V Thomas
1978 April 23	**Spyin' Cop** D E Hope, V Thomas, D Harvey
1978 May 14	**Adrenalin Factor** V Thomas, R W Lanchbury, D E Hope
1978 May 14	**Because It's Theirs** D E Hope, A Mills, I Atkin
1981 Feb 2	**Gravelingas** D E Hope, R W Lanchbury
1981 Feb 8	**Athletes Effete** R W Lanchbury, D E Hope
1981 Feb 8	**Revelstone** D E Hope, R W Lanchbury
1981 July 19	**Crusaders** D E Hope, R W Lanchbury
1981 July 19	**Stonedown** D E Hope, R W Lanchbury
1982 Aug 3	**The Mad Russian** D E Hope, R W Lanchbury
1983 Aug 21	**Forbidden Fruit** D E Hope, R W Lanchbury
1986 March 27	**Thar He Blows** D E Hope, R W Lanchbury
1986 June 27	**The Miller's Tale** D E Hope, R W Lanchbury
1986 June 30	**Love Story** T Penning, D E Hope
1986 Aug 15	**Crack a Doodle Doo** T Penning, D E Hope, R W Lanchbury
1986 Aug 15	**Landwaster** D E Hope, R W Lanchbury
1986 Aug 24	**Fingermouse** D E Hope, P Cresswell, T Penning
1986 Aug 24	**Hey Diddle Diddle** T Penning, P Cresswell
1986 Sept 2	**The Arch of Time** D E Hope, T Penning
1986 Sept 2	**The Power of Love** T Penning, D E Hope
1986 Sept 28	**Pensioner's Puzzle** T Penning, P Cresswell, D E Hope
1987 Aug 28	**Labour of Love** M Ward, M J Crocker
1987 Sept 15	**All the Tea in China** M Ward, R Kingston
1987 Sept 28	**Chinatown** M Ward, R Kingston
1987 Sept 28	**Slow Boat to China** M Ward, R Kingston
1987 Oct 6	**Big Rock Candy** M J Crocker (solo)
1987 Oct 6	**Firedamp** M Ward, M J Crocker
1987 Oct 6	**Swamp Fever** M Ward (solo)
1987 Oct 6	**Twist of Fate** R Kingston, M Ward, M J Crocker
1987 Oct 18	**Honeydew** M Ward, M J Crocker
1987 Oct 24	**Heartbreaker** M J Crocker, M Ward
1987 Oct 24	**Kerb Crawler** M Ward, M J Crocker (V)
1987 Oct 24	**Universal Bond** M J Crocker, M Ward
1987 Nov 15	**The Outlaws of Physics** M J Crocker, M Ward
1987 Nov 15	**Woody Ward Pecker** M J Crocker, M Ward

1987 Nov 18	**Triumph of the Bourgeoisie** M Ward, R Kingston
1987 Nov 28	**The Dividing Line** M J Crocker, G A Jenkin, R Kingston, M Ward
1987 Nov 28	**The Snails of Justice, A Snail of Two Cities, Snails of the Unexpected** M Ward, R Kingston, G A Jenkin, M J Crocker
1987 Dec 15	**China in Your Hands** M J Crocker, J Willson
1988 April 23	**Acid Rain, The Rain in Spain Falls Mainly on the Plain..., Rain Shadow** M Ward, M J Crocker, R Kingston
1988 April 23	**Eczema, Phlebitis** M J Crocker, R Kingston, M Ward
1988 April 23	**Rain Maker, Rain Dance** R Kingston, M J Crocker, M Ward
1988 April 23	**Trash, Garbage Grinder** M J Crocker (solo)
1988 May 1	**Round the Horn, Del Fuego** M J Crocker (solo)
1988 May 7	**Dust Devils** R Kingston, M Ward
1988 May 7	**Dustin Hoffman** M Ward, R Kingston
1988 May 7	**Rain Drops Keep Falling on My Head** R Kingston, M Ward
1990 Aug 9	**Dust Storm** S Thompson, W Gladwin
1991 May 27	**Ruth Is Stranger than Friction** N Hellyer, C Goodchild
1991 Aug 12	**Dusty Springfield, Sandy Gall, Little Treasure, Dirt Bogart, Dirty Harry** A Moore, D Moore
1991 Dec 4	**Going for Gorse** A Moore, D Moore
1992 Feb 2	**Day Tripper** J Hartley
1992 May 4	**Thin Air, It's So Loose, Sign of the Times, Rain Machine** J Hartley
1993 April 15	**Get on Your Zimmer Frame, Flat Landers** T Hartley, J Hartley
1994 April 17	**Donald, Digital, Crash Dummies' Day Out** J Hartley
1996 May 15	**Nice Noddy Holder, Get Down and Get With It, Desert Planet Kidz** M J Crocker
1996 May 27	**Grit Reflections** M J Crocker (solo)
1996 June 30	**Get On Up, Mutant, Chimes of Nausea** M J Crocker
1996 Nov 25	**Follix** D Moore (solo)
1996 Dec 4	**Heart of Glass** A Moore, D Moore

Index

SOME USEFUL ADDRESSES:

Dave Viggers   (CC co-ordinator for new route information)
3 Henleaze Road
Henleaze
BRISTOL BS9 4EX

John Willson (Current CC SW Editor and BMC Wye Valley Access Rep)
2 Sunnyside Cottages
Woodcroft
CHEPSTOW (Tel:01291 625433)
Monmouthshire NP6 7JA

Nigel Coe (CC SW Editor-designate)
3 Oxford Street
CHELTENHAM
Glos GL52 6DT

British Mountaineering Council
177-179 Burton Road
West Didsbury
MANCHESTER M20 2BB (Tel: 0161 4454747)

Ian Parnell (BMC SW Development Officer)
BMC SW Office
St Werburgh's Church
Mina Road
BRISTOL BS2 9YH (Tel:0117 9542425)

Jim Hewitt (Chairman Severn Area Rescue Association)
1 Highfield
Gloucester Road
Tutshill
CHEPSTOW (Tel: 01291 624740)
Monmouthshire NP6 7DF

Accident Procedure

FIRST AID
If spinal or head injuries are suspected, do not move the patient without skilled help, except to maintain breathing or if this is essential for further protection. If breathing has stopped, clear the airways and start artificial respiration. Do not stop until expert opinion has diagnosed death.
Summon help as quickly as is compatible with safety. Do not hesitate or delay.

RESCUE
In the event of an accident where further assistance is required, dial 999. For Wyndcliffe, ask for the Gwent Police. For all other cliffs, stress that you require the Gloucestershire Police. Since all the phones (except in the Forest of Dean Quarries Area) have Chepstow codes, if you do not do this you may be connected to the Gwent Police, which can cause delay.
State that you require cliff rescue, and report the correct location and details of the accident. Be prepared to give your own details and location, and to arrange for someone to meet the rescue services and guide them to the spot.

NEAREST PHONE POINTS
It is always advisable to locate these before climbing.

Wyndcliffe Drive south to the village of St Arvans or north to Tintern.

Wintour's Leap and **Ban-y-gor** There is a public phone in Woodcroft opposite The Rising Sun.

Tintern Quarry and **Shorn Cliff** There is a public phone outside Tidenham Chase Church, half a mile to the north on the B4228. It may be quicker from Shorn Cliff to run down to Tintern. Bear in mind, however, that the emergency services can reach the cliff only from the B4228, and so this should not normally be done unless there is someone else available to meet to meet the rescuers on the Forestry track.

In the event of a pressing emergency or of a public phone being unavailable, most private house-dwellers willingly allow the use of their phones. In particular, approaching one of the following in Woodcroft may help to facilitate the optimum response:
1. *Quarry Gates*: the square-fronted house, next door but one to The Rising Sun and immediately opposite Woodcroft Close.
2. *2 Broadrock Cottages*: the cottage immediately adjacent to the parking pull-off at the top of the Wintour's Leap Easy Way Down.
3. *2 Sunnyside Cottages*: half-way between the two; the right-hand half of the isolated stone cottages on the west (cliff) side of the road opposite the centre of the large field.

CASUALTY EVACUATION

Depending upon the prevailing conditions, state of tide, availability of resources, and nature of a casualty's injuries, evacuation may be by winch to the cliff-top, a stretcher carry-out, inshore rescue-boat, or helicopter. All climbers in the vicinity are asked to heed promptly any requests or directions from the rescue team leaders.

HELICOPTER

In the event of a helicopter evacuation, **all** climbers on or off the cliff should take heed. A helicopter flying close to the cliff will make verbal communication very difficult, and small stones and other matter will be dislodged by the rotor downdraught. All loose equipment should be secured, and climbers in precarious positions should try to make themselves safe.

CASUALTY

Those able to reach hospital under their own steam will find a list of casualty departments on page 14.

FOLLOW-UP

After an accident a written report should be sent to the Severn Area Rescue Association (see page 333, giving details of: date; extent of injuries; and name, age, and address of the casualty. Normally this information is collated at the scene by the police or rescue team, who will require also the names and addresses of those climbing with the injured party. The information is then passed to the Mountain Rescue Council Statistics Officer.

If unreasonable equipment failure is suspected, then the British Mountaineering Council's technical committee may wish to investigate; the address will be found on page 333. However, in the event of death or serious injury, any equipment used by the casualty is usually impounded.

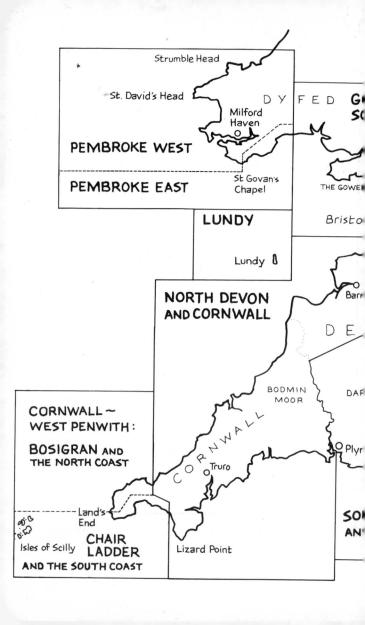